Governing Least

T0346701

OXFORD POLITICAL PHILOSOPHY

GENERAL EDITOR: SAMUEL FREEMAN, UNIVERSITY OF PENNSYLVANIA

Oxford Political Philosophy publishes books on theoretical and applied political philosophy within the Anglo-American tradition. The series welcomes submissions on social, political, and global justice, individual rights, democracy, liberalism, socialism, and constitutionalism.

Governing Least

A New England Libertarianism

Dan Moller

OXFORD
UNIVERSITY PRESS

OXFORD
UNIVERSITY PRESS

Oxford University Press is a department of the University of Oxford. It furthers
the University's objective of excellence in research, scholarship, and education
by publishing worldwide. Oxford is a registered trade mark of Oxford University
Press in the UK and certain other countries.

Published in the United States of America by Oxford University Press
198 Madison Avenue, New York, NY 10016, United States of America.

Library of Congress Cataloging-in-Publication Data
Names: Moller, Dan, 1975– author.
Title: Governing least : a New England libertarianism / Dan Moller.
Description: New York, NY, United States of America : Oxford University Press, [2019]
Identifiers: LCCN 2018033647 (print) | LCCN 2018010446 (ebook) |
ISBN 9780190863241 (hardcover) | ISBN 9780197697511 (paperback) |
ISBN 9780190863258 (updf) | ISBN 9780190863265 (ebook) |
ISBN 9780190863272 (online component)
Subjects: LCSH: Libertarianism. Classification: LCC JC585 .M795 2019 (ebook) |
LCC JC585 (print) | DDC 320.51/2—dc23
LC record available at https://lccn.loc.gov/2018033647

Paperback printed by Marquis Book Printing, Canada

◼ CONTENTS

PART FOUR ■ Theory and Practice

1 Introduction

Toward a New England Libertarianism

Libertarianism is the widely reviled idea that we should use reason and persuasion to accomplish our distributive aims. *Only* reason and persuasion. According to the libertarian, it is wrong to utilize threats or violence in the form of state-sponsored coercion, however sublimated by bureaucratic routine, in order to redistribute property that we have an antecedent claim to. Aiding the worse off or promoting economic equality may be worthy aims, but these are endeavors we should persuade our fellow citizens to join, not mandates to be enforced by the state. Promoting these goals at the end of a pitchfork, whether ours or our representatives', is a moral mistake according to the libertarian.

Talk of threats and violence may seem overblown. What is at issue is generally redistribution through taxation, and what's so bad about voters democratically deciding on laws that require us to fill in certain tax forms once a year? The forms are boring but hardly violent. But threats and violence are in play whenever the state issues its demands. When the state mails us the forms requesting our money, it is not asking nicely; the demands of the state are backed by force. And when voters decide on laws that culminate in demands from the state, they are deciding to compel those around them to do their bidding, again with the implicit threat of force. In fact, the reason that threats and violence seem so far removed from the process of peacefully debating laws and filling in forms is in part that these threats are so successful: it is only when threats are *un*persuasive that one must employ violence. Of course, many people agree with the state's demands and are happy to cooperate—I don't wish to exaggerate the coercive element. But the bureaucratic routine shouldn't blind us to the fact that the state and, by extension, democratic majorities aren't asking nicely.

Libertarians of all stripes are skeptical of encroachments by the state, but the "New England" version I propose to defend is distinctive in two respects. First, libertarianism is often grounded in an uncompromising approach to individual rights, which others absolutely must not infringe. By contrast, in my account libertarianism emerges from everyday moral beliefs we have about when we are permitted to shift our burdens onto others. In fact, my account intentionally downplays the role of rights, and is motivated by doubts about what we may demand of others, rather than outrage about what others demand of us. As I will argue, if we recognize even modest strictures on making others worse off to improve our lot, if we acknowledge even defeasible claims to ownership, we quickly run into a form of libertarianism. This is because it turns out to be very hard to justify permanently transferring our misfortunes to others in the way an expansive welfare state requires. One goal of this book, then, is to defend a version of libertarianism that rests on modest premises about burden-shifting. Because this view is inspired by the spirit of self-reliance in figures like Thoreau, Emerson, and Melville, I think of it as having a New England cast.

A second distinctive feature of this book is that it ranges widely across history, economics, and politics, as well as philosophy. I have cast my net widely in order to take up such questions as the transmission of wealth across generations, reparations for slavery, and the politics of political correctness. The reasons for this are partly substantive and partly methodological. Substantively, our responses to complex philosophical arguments move both forwards and backwards—from accepted premises to accepted conclusions, as well as from rejected conclusions to rejected premises. Even if the moral arguments I make about burden-shifting were initially persuasive, we would reject them if they seemed to have absurd implications when projected onto the world at large. If libertarians seem to ignore the fact that many who are poor are so through no fault of their own, or that rich countries got rich in the course of an incredibly violent history, they will hardly be persuasive on the basis of tidy syllogisms alone. Political theories are inevitably assessed in light of a much broader picture of the world and how it works, and philosophers ignore such pictures at their peril.

Another reason for casting the net wide is methodological. Anglophone political philosophy has—with some notable exceptions—become an increasingly arid and insular field, disconnected from economics, history, and politics. (Of course, in part this just reflects a broader trend toward parochial specialization.) Academic Marxists write books that ignore the triumphs of the market economies; libertarians write books that ignore the vast injustices that accompanied the era of economic growth. It is noteworthy, for instance, that works discussing the Marxist theory of *history* rarely mention *the past*—in contrast to Marx's own practice.[1] I want to resist this narrow approach. Quite apart from the substantive conclusions I reach, I hope to reconnect with an earlier tradition of philosophers practicing political economy who wallowed in the murk of history and weren't afraid of the occasional fact or figure. (Imagine John Stuart Mill or Karl Marx without a little murk!) Accordingly, the later parts of the book don't directly defend libertarianism, narrowly construed as resistance to the welfare state, but champion a more broadly classical liberal perspective that emphasizes limited government, free markets, and the system of private property, in the tradition of John Locke and Adam Smith.[2] My hope is that this broader perspective both creates a more hospitable environment for assessing libertarianism, and helps us reconnect with the earlier approach to political economy.

At the end of this introduction I offer a more detailed preview, but first let me try to motivate what I am calling the New England approach a bit more.

▪ THE SPEECH

Imagine calling a town hall meeting and delivering the following speech:

> My dear assembled citizens: I know most of us are strangers, but of late I have fallen on hard times through no fault of my own, by sheer bad luck. My savings are low, and I don't have friends or family to help. Now as you know, I've previously asked for help from you as private citizens, as a matter of charity. But unfortunately that hasn't been sufficient. Thus, I'm here now to insist that you (yes you, Emma, and you, John) *owe* me assistance as a matter of *justice*. It is a deep violation if you don't work additional hours, take fewer vacations if need be, live in a smaller house, or send your kids to a worse school, in order to help me. Failing to do so is no less an injustice than failing to pay your debts.
>
> Moreover, calling this an injustice means that it's not enough that you comply with your obligations by working on my behalf. No, I insist that you help me to *force* your fellow citizens to assist me. It doesn't matter if these others say to you that they need the money for their own purposes, that they prefer worthier causes, or if they're just hard-hearted and don't care. To the extent you care about justice, you must help me to force these others to assist me whether they wish to or not, since that is what is owed me in light of my recent bad luck.

Could you bring yourself to make this speech? The essence of the dispute between moral libertarians and anti-libertarians is that libertarians think that they could not in good conscience make this speech, and neither would they be persuaded by others making it. And in their view, a redistributive welfare state is simply the speech put into action and writ large through taxes and transfers. Later on we will consider some of the complexities of global capitalism and modern property regimes, but I believe that the important disputes about economic justice largely boil down to this speech.

I don't want to wade too deeply into the philosophical issues the speech raises yet, but we can at least anticipate a few immediate reactions. Inevitably it will be said that to the extent the speech bothers us it is because of its rhetorical flourishes, various pragmatic features, its name-calling and first-personal gusto, or because the speaker seems presumptuous, or otherwise annoys us. Compare, then, a similar speech advancing a different substantive claim:

> My dear assembled citizens: of late, some of you have been stealing my money. I'm here now to insist that you (yes you, Emma, and you, John) give it back. This means that you *owe* me thousands of dollars which you stole. It's a deep violation if you don't work additional hours, take fewer vacations if need be, live in a smaller house, or send your kids to a worse school, in order to pay me back what you stole. Failing to do so is no less an injustice than failing to pay your debts.
>
> Moreover, calling this an injustice means that it's not enough that you comply with your obligations by working on my behalf to repay me what you've stolen. No, I insist

that you help me to *force* the thieves among you to pay restitution. It doesn't matter if these thieves say to you that they need the money for their own purposes, that they prefer worthier causes, or that they're just hard-hearted and don't care. To the extent you care about justice, you must help me to force these others to repay me what they stole.

No one is likely to be embarrassed by this variant. Even if we are shy and uncomfortable about confronting others in public speeches, there is nothing strange about the *idea* of giving such a speech, or about *someone* giving it. To the extent there is a problem with the first speech it lies not in its manner but its substance.

Another reaction is to dismiss the relevance of the speech. Just because that speech isn't the way to make the speaker's case doesn't mean that there isn't a case to be made. We can envision a range of speeches marshaling various considerations that vary in their effectiveness, and picking out just one of them and knocking it down doesn't prove anything. Moreover, the speech focuses our attention on face-to-face moral arguments with other individuals, whereas what is at issue with redistribution nowadays is the design of social institutions intended to benefit and coordinate the lives of millions; we may be skeptical about how much light the former can shed on the latter. But any speech making the same substantive point will share the same core features. All of them will announce that it is an injustice not to remedy the speaker's bad luck—not just a kindness to be sought by persuasion—and all of them will suggest that the speaker may use threats and violence to make sure this happens. Any speech incorporating these elements is likely to bother us to the extent that we are bothered by the original, unless it introduces quite powerful assumptions that will need to be defended in their own right. And while it's true that the design of social institutions produces some unique complications, it should at the very least give us pause if we are advocating social institutions that enshrine a moral logic we reject in face-to-face encounters.

Even if we do feel uncomfortable making the speech, it is a further question why we should resist other people making such appeals. But before coming to that, I want to insist that, perhaps contrary to other presentations of classical liberal ideas, the core impulse isn't outrage about being asked to *give*; it is in the first instance a bewilderment at the suggestion that we are entitled to *demand*. The impulse moves through the table of conjugation: *I* couldn't issue such a demand; on reflection it would be outrageous of *you* to make such a demand of them; and so it becomes clear that *they* shouldn't make such a demand of us. Libertarianism is in this respect connected to the old New England tradition of Emerson and Thoreau (and more broadly to writers like Hawthorne and Melville), who didn't stress classical liberal political views, but who were preoccupied with self-reliance and with the moral—even spiritual—importance of the separateness of persons and the way our burdens are our own to bear. The inspiration here is *Walden*, not *Atlas Shrugged*. The independence these New Englanders advocated tended to be intellectual ("envy is ignorance . . . imitation is suicide"), but Thoreau's hut by the pond was material enough, as were the enterprise and ingenuity of the traders he so admired, and he did of course insist that "that government governs best which governs least."[3] It would be a farcical self-reliance that urged fierce originality and remonstrated with us to preserve our "vital heat" as dearly as possible to preserve independence of thought—and then made the speech above, or advocated a cradle-to-grave welfare state. Neither seems compatible with a certain humility about our relationship to those around us. According to the New Englanders, those to whom we would issue the relevant demands possess an awesome authority (and responsibility) over themselves.

This kind of talk is always liable to suspicion—easy for the rich and privileged to talk of self-reliance. But Thoreau was not rich. He lived under subsistence conditions much of the time, and there is no suggestion that he expected others to enable him to achieve even those.[4] And many of the most able expositors of New Englander attitudes have been precisely those fighting various forms of exclusion, notably Thoreau the abolitionist once more, and feminists like Elizabeth Cady Stanton:

> [T]here is a solitude which each and every one of us has always carried with him, more inaccessible than the ice-cold mountains, more profound than the midnight sea; the solitude of self. Our inner being which we call ourself, no eye nor touch of man or angel has ever pierced. . . . Such is individual life. Who, I ask you, can take, dare take on himself the rights, the duties, the responsibilities of another human soul?[5]

Neither Stanton nor Thoreau is defending libertarian ideals per se, but both put their finger on the sense in which an appreciation of the independent moral personality of others should fill us with fear and trembling when it comes to asserting control over them, as in our imagined speech. And both register the ways in which this point of view can be liberating. Expansive assertions of state or social authority will go badly wrong from time to time, and circumscribing it will often prove prophylactic. In fact, it is striking that a number of *non*–New Englanders fighting for recognition have emphasized personal and moral independence—the gap between us, so to speak—notably Virginia Woolf in books like *The Waves*. This will only strike us as paradoxical if we neglect Stanton's point that refusing to see each other as fully separate personalities is ultimately a threat, especially to those whose independence it has historically proven convenient to neglect.

There is admittedly a romantic streak in some of these writers that is partly a matter of temperament, and Thoreau's survivalist program for economic independence is ill-suited to our times. We can perhaps all discover "whole new continents and worlds within" us; we cannot all live in a hut by a lake like Thoreau.[6] But reflecting on why we might feel uncomfortable about making the speech to our townsfolk reveals an *argument* that goes beyond temperament or romantic yearnings for solitude. For in issuing the demands in the speech, we are insisting that those around us are required to take up our burdens, and in insisting that they use force to compel one another to remedy our misfortunes, *we are attempting to shift our burdens onto others by force*. This, I believe, is the fundamental source of the misgivings some of us will have about the speech. Insisting on the right to improve our position at the cost of other people, by threats or violence if need be, is the moral mistake that animates this version of libertarianism. And this mistake is ultimately the same in the first and the third person; unfair burden-shifting is wrong whether I do it to others or they do it to me. Making sense of this claim is the central task of the first part of this book.

This New England approach doesn't particularly emphasize freedom, it is worth noting. In some formulations, libertarianism is supposed to be the outlook engendered by a deep reverence for liberty—as the name might suggest—as if those who cared more deeply about some other value would have grounds to demur. On this picture, different people attach different weights to various political values or ideals, and those who recognize how important liberty is are drawn to libertarianism, while those attracted to equality or fraternity (etc.) head elsewhere. But this picture is confused. The disagreement between libertarians and their antagonists is not over how much values like freedom or equality matter, but over whether it is permissible for the state to use *force* to promote these values in various ways. To see this, notice that libertarians and their opponents may in fact agree that equality or fraternity is of great importance; they could join forces and work tirelessly on behalf of some such value, provided these contributions were voluntary. As long as anti-libertarians focus merely on how much they care about equality, or how terrible poverty is, or on their vision of a better world, they have made no progress at all in identifying a point of disagreement. The disagreement only arises once the value in question is placed within the ambit of the state and its coercive apparatus. As long as equality and fraternity are the outcome of voluntary appeals, of reason and persuasion, there is no need for dispute. Nor is there any need to settle whether happy "communitarian" values should triumph over the base "atomism" of the libertarians. The question isn't whether to view ourselves as lonely islands or amiable communities, but whether the state should create the relevant community by compulsory means; we can all agree that marriage is a blessed state while insisting that it emerge voluntarily. We would avoid a world of confusion, in other words, if only those arguing for the state promoting some value would add the rider, ". . . and I favor the use of threats and violence to promote this value if need be." The focus on burden-shifting captures this crucial point. What matters isn't the relative importance of negative liberties as against other political values, but whether it is permissible for the state to compel the transfer of burdens in the manner of an expansive welfare state.

A legal analogy may help here. In the American judicial system, the Supreme Court may rule on whether laws conform to the Constitution, and this determination is independent of the substantive merits of the law in question. However, issue-partisans find this fact almost impossible to keep in mind. Thus, one finds impassioned praise or else denunciation for decisions based on whether those decisions favor the substantive positions of the partisans, without even a pretense of concern for what the Constitution in fact says (according to their favored method of interpretation—I'm not trying to make a point about hermeneutics). In theory, there ought to be a gap between one's substantive position on abortion, or capital punishment, or gun control, or flag burning, or campaign spending, and what the Constitution says about these things, which would create the possibility of painful tensions—"I support abortion, but must concede that the Constitution contains no right to abortion"; "I support unlimited campaign spending by corporations, but deny that the Constitution carves out such a right." The fact that one so rarely encounters partisans of issues tormented by constitutional barriers to their side prevailing indicates that in practice we are reluctant to acknowledge the distinction between substantive values and legal process—a depressing sign of how powerful motivated reasoning is. (A good test of our intellectual honesty is how often we experience this kind of torment.)

Just so, when it comes to political philosophy and what the state should be doing, the issue shouldn't be our substantive concerns, but rather what kinds of things we should be using threats and violence to compel those around us to do. People can agree about the morality of abortion or campaign finance while disagreeing about the higher-order question of their constitutional status, and so too people should be able to agree about the moral significance of equality or poverty while disagreeing about the kinds of threats or coercion that may be employed to address them, which is to say, whether the state should be involved. And just as conflating substantive moral opinions with distinctively juridical questions tends to eat away at the rule of law, as respect for the impartial legal order comes to be replaced with outrage at losing the substantive battle, so conflating social values with the proper objects of state enforcement eventually undermines respect for the state, and ultimately for politics as an organizing principle.

■ PREVIEW

My case for the classical liberal view unfolds in four parts.

The first, on property, offers a reassessment of the libertarian argument against the redistributive welfare state and in favor of respecting private property. Because that argument draws on moral premises, I begin by considering the relationship between morality and the state. Collectives like the state may not treat us in ways that individuals never could, and yet, says the libertarian, the welfare state proposes to do just that through its redistributive policies. I then argue that resistance to redistribution need not be rooted in an obsession with individual rights, as has been often supposed, but can rather appeal to humdrum beliefs most of us share—particularly beliefs about burden-shifting.

But arguments against redistribution don't amount to much if we don't take private property seriously in the first place. Accordingly, I develop a theory of property, again grounded in our everyday moral beliefs, in this case concerning when we get to claim control over some asset. My theory takes as its inspiration John Locke's account of property, but also tries to update it. And whereas Locke focused on "mixing our labor," I show that this is just a special case of the many things we can do to strengthen a moral claim to control over an asset. On this view, property is a *moral* phenomenon, not just a legal or political category, and constrains the state just as moral claims against harm or arbitrary detention do. I also examine the extent to which treatments of property by philosophers have tended to remain rooted in Locke's 17th-century agrarian paradigm, which is now obsolete. Economic activity in developed countries largely revolves around services, and many redistributive arguments that made sense in an agrarian context make little sense in a service economy.

Finally, I consider the objection that redistribution is just morally required aid in disguise. Against this, I point out several reasons why we might have soft-hearted attitudes toward aid, while rejecting the state as its facilitator. Helping the needy is a noble cause, but one we should pursue with reason and persuasion, not state-sanctioned coercion.

Part II takes up a series of interrelated questions about markets that the discussion of property raises. These include what kinds of market exchanges we should promote or forbid, and the role that luck plays in the transmission of wealth in a free market system. These questions are important because the classical liberal view tends to leave more outcomes to the market. For this reason, I emphasize the ways in which markets enable people to improve their positions, even and especially when poorly positioned to begin with. I also try to draw some sober conclusions about which opportunities luck cuts off and leaves open to us. The picture I offer is a complex one, in which some evidence indicates that luck plays a far from trivial role in social outcomes—for instance, by the persistence of status across generations—but in which choice still opens the way to a decent life for almost everyone in developed countries. I also argue that considerations of luck don't lend themselves to egalitarian views without powerful background assumptions.

From another point of view, skepticism about markets can center on doubts about whether they and the economic growth they foster make us happy. Some research suggests that economic growth doesn't do much for average happiness, even if out-earning our neighbors gives us a boost. Reflection makes clear that this will inevitably be true in the future and may be true at present, raising the question of why we should care so much about growth and commercial life. I try to answer this question by comparing it to a parallel question about disability, which produces a similar disconnect between how observers rate our objective welfare and how happy we feel. In both cases the lesson I draw is that there is more to life—even the parts that concern only us—than happiness. I round out Part II by pointing out that markets don't just matter for normative reasons, but have an epistemic significance as well. In fact, the signals that markets send us, especially about popularity and incentives, constitute valuable evidence that should inform our choices, but which is generally overlooked.

As I described earlier, the point in taking up these issues is not so much to incrementally advance a narrow libertarian argument, but to consider the broader intellectual framework we bring to bear in thinking about such an argument. The classical liberal perspective that champions free markets and limited government no longer comes naturally to most people, and so it's worth stepping back a bit for a wider view, in order to give libertarian doubts about redistribution a fair hearing. Additionally, working through these questions gives us an opportunity to reconnect with political economy as a method, and lets us forge connections with other disciplines working on problems political philosophers care about.

Part III turns to history. Philosophers have generally neglected important themes like the "Great Divergence" between countries with high and low growth trajectories over the past few centuries, as well as research into how various capitalist and socialist forms of economic organization have fared. I argue that over the long haul, things have worked out pretty well under capitalism, especially for the worse off. Economic growth has done more good for the world than all of the acts of beneficence ever performed. And the vast disparities we see between the global rich and poor mostly reflect inevitable differences in the onset of economic growth, not injustices. Exponential economic growth was never going to occur simultaneously everywhere, and what we observe mostly just reflects that fact. But libertarians for their part have tended to neglect *correctives* to the past which might be warranted by the theory of reparations. I agree that reparations are warranted, but I also try to show their natural limits, and to explain why such claims fade over time, and not just due to apathy or status quo bias. More generally, I try in Part III to show that thinking about economic justice in terms that are informed by history can pay dividends. Theories of reparations, for example, are often developed with little discussion of the actual past, but sometimes the details of history make a difference to how we react to such theories.

Finally, Part IV develops two themes at the intersection of political theory and practice. One concerns the concept of political correctness and its bearing on public discourse of the sort this book participates in; the other relates to the utopian character of classical liberal ideas, which may now seem a bit out of their time. The first theme is relevant because there is often a certain politically *in*correct quality to libertarian discussions of topics like poverty, work, and reparations. However, my goal is not to dismiss politically correct norms and taboos. In fact, I try to explain the good reasons we have to introduce barriers in our public discourse against ideas that might threaten some people's public status. My goal is rather to show that these norms come with real *costs* and consequently set up dilemmas we should acknowledge. The point about utopianism is important in turn because the welfare state isn't going anywhere, making resistance to it seem quixotic. I thus conclude the book by trying to show how libertarians can object to the present regime as unjust while advocating slow, conservative reform rather than radical change. If I could press a button and bring about the libertarian revolution tomorrow, I would not press it. Instead, I would try to slowly persuade people to see things my way.

All this is plenty—perhaps too much—to discuss in one book, and yet I should also concede how much is being left out of this reassessment of classical liberal ideas.[7] For one, I generally ignore challenges to libertarianism emanating from those who want even *less* of a state than libertarians do—philosophical anarchists. (Thoreau hopes for a government one day that governs "not at all"—once men are prepared for it.) Their views are important too, but explaining why a state is permissible at all will occupy us only incidentally (I do sketch a proposal in chapter 5). I also ignore the many non-economic causes that libertarians have sometimes taken up, like free speech, gay marriage, and drug legalization. This is the *fun* part of libertarianism and requires little heroism to defend. Many disagree with such policies, but few think their sponsors cruel or ungenerous, while resistance to the welfare state and programs intended to foster economic equality evoke precisely that response. (Telling your students or colleagues you favor drug-sentencing reform evokes murmuring approval; telling them you oppose wealth transfers—for broadly similar reasons—evokes stunned silence.) Misunderstandings of libertarian views about the welfare state strike me as far more acute than misunderstandings of libertarian views about drug legalization. For this reason I will be concentrating on the no-fun-at-all controversies surrounding distributive justice.

PART ONE

Property

2   Morality and the State

Morality constrains the state, or at least it should. This is true of how the state treats outsiders, but even more true of how it treats its own. It was a central insight of what Karl Jaspers called the "Axial Age," in which philosophers like Plato and Confucius first advanced ideas about the relationship between the state and broadly moral concepts like *justice* or *the mandate of heaven*.[1] Small wonder: the states they observed were increasingly strong, to the point that their exercise of power could transform an entire region like the Mediterranean or East Asia, and attempts to bind state-sanctioned force by moral means had become a topic of public discussion, as in historians like Thucydides and a little later Sima Qian.[2] Later epochs have continually rediscovered the Axial insight, as Aquinas, Locke, and the American framers testify in their diverse ways. Indeed, one suspects that the Axial thinkers were themselves systematizing ideas that far preceded them— ideas glimpsed, perhaps, in codes like those of Hammurabi and Ur-Nammu. (Even Sumerian potentates evidently felt the need to advertise the moral quality of their rule, that they "established justice in the land.")[3] The idea that morality constrains the state can seem naive from a certain postmodernist perspective—a prelude in B-flat major in the age of Cage. But the morality involved need not be parochial, and it can, I believe, draw on widely shared beliefs. And in the end there is no real alternative for explaining why we resist imperialism or arbitrary detention. The exercise of collective power inevitably elicits moral demands for its restraint.

▪ WHICH MORALITY?

Since morality constrains the state, what we believe about morality affects what we think the state may and may not do. For this reason, it is customary to begin discussions of justice by considering the seemingly fundamental divide among moralities, between utilitarian theories and those called deontic, after the Greek term for duty, *deon*. Utilitarian theories tell us to do whatever will produce the best (net) consequences. Deontic theories tell us that there is a fundamental duty to respect certain rights people are endowed with, for example not to be exploited for the sake of the greater good, or those featuring in the Ten Commandments. In the stereotyped disputes that follow, utilitarians are supposed to allow for such things as executing the innocent to appease a mob if that brings about the greater good, while rule-worshipping deontologists supposedly won't lie even to save a life. This deep-sounding distinction tends to wobble, however, as soon as we enter into details. What turns out to be important for political philosophy aren't the theoretical differences among moral theories, but the practical differences for how we may treat one another, which often turn out to be surprisingly few.

There are several reasons utilitarians may end up recognizing rights or something pretty close as a matter of practice. Writers like John Stuart Mill take rules, not individual acts, as the target for promoting good outcomes, which means they will often end up agreeing with their deontic rivals. Executing the innocent won't make for a good general rule, however tempting in carefully cooked-up thought experiments. Other utilitarians openly mimic deontic features of our folk morality by co-opting them into the class of consequences that get counted. It's easy to make utilitarianism have crazy implications if all we attend to is whether an act maximizes human happiness; it's harder if we announce that *not getting what you deserve* and *being exploited* are bad consequences that matter in their own right.[4] And some utilitarians have given elaborate arguments for why even simple forms of utilitarianism often turn out to be self-effacing, like the Cheshire cat. This can be because they just think that, surprisingly, utilitarianism ends up validating the folk wisdom of their age, as when Jeremy Bentham offered elaborate arguments in the 18th century to show that men should have the final say in marriage. Alternatively, in the 19th century Henry Sidgwick argued more systematically that departing from folk morality will tend to threaten moral observance in a society, so that even those who know better should generally stick to the conventions of the times—Victorian sexual mores and all.[5]

Conversely, deontic theories emphasizing the need to respect people's rights initially sound as if they have an absolutist, anti-utilitarian cast. And sometimes they do—Kant famously thought it better not to lie to a murderer asking you about his target's whereabouts. (At least your hands stay clean.) But here, too, things are less clear than they seem. In fact, on the modest theory of rights that I advance in the next chapter, rights aren't insuperable; when enough is at stake, and the right is weak enough, sometimes people get to harm us for the greater good. What's important on this view is acknowledging that there is a *threshold* that must be reached before such infringements become acceptable. This sounds a lot like some versions of rule utilitarianism. Of course, philosophers will still care about what the deeper basis for superficially similar moral views is, and it would be a mistake to dismiss such further probing as idle. (Cynics might think of William James's exasperated pragmatism on hearing disputes about whether a man chasing a squirrel around a tree circles the squirrel.)[6] Different moralities can still disagree about the *reasons* they offer for their prescriptions, and these reasons matter. In my view it would be a deep mistake, for instance, to respect someone's right against being raped just because such a rule generally tends to make people happier—this would disastrously mistake the nature of the moral relationship we bear to others.

Moreover, there may remain structurally unbridgeable chasms between utilitarians and their enemies. Part of the charm (or horror) of thinking in deontic terms is that we specifically embrace the worse of two possible outcomes, if doing so is the only way for us to avoid *doing* certain things we have a duty to abstain from. If two innocents will be tortured unless I torture just one innocent (perhaps by torturing a terrorist's little girl—his only weak point), I may demur because the girl has a right I may not infringe. It has often been pointed out that this demurral will be difficult to mimic within a utilitarian theory, since the whole point is to promote the overall good.[7] Since utilitarianism doesn't care about what *I* do, but only about the end result, it is hard to see how it can accommodate any reluctance we may have to harm some for the sake of preventing others from suffering even more. In fact, the strength of utilitarianism is that it can capture the other side of our conflicted feelings in such cases—the sense that it's crazy to follow a morality that tells us to allow more of the very bad stuff it tells us to abstain from, seemingly just so that we can avoid doing it ourselves. That is *its* charm. Perhaps some complicated form of rule utilitarianism can bridge even this gap without collapsing in on itself. (Torturing one to prevent two more torturings may itself produce terrible side effects as a general rule.) Or perhaps not. What is important for our purposes is just that many divergent moral theories converge on similar results in practice, on many occasions.

Since our interest is in political theory here, not the nature of morality, we can take an ecumenical approach. We can just ignore the deep question about the nature of morality and make assumptions only at the superficial level of practical prescriptions. In that spirit, I propose simply to assume that the common-sense picture of morality's structure is on target, for the most part, including its various deontic features.[8] I will assume, in other words, that sometimes we can't do things to people that would promote the overall good because doing so would exploit them or infringe their rights. I will assume that people deserve certain things in virtue of what they have done in the past and that we do wrong in ignoring desert. I will assume that we have a right to favor those we love, so that we do right lavishing our rotten kids with Christmas presents that could go to the needy instead, and that we may own televisions and cars rather than giving it all away. Just because your money would do the neighbors a bit more good than it would do you doesn't mean that I may steal it and give it to them. At the very least, some very high bar would need to be met to justify such an act. Just because you would generate more happiness by giving money away than spending it on your kids or on yourself doesn't mean that you have to. These beliefs seem to be widely shared, making them useful assumptions. But although I will borrow the deontic trappings of folk morality and talk of "rights" and "desert," I don't intend to rule out some utilitarian (or any other) basis for these notions, and readers are welcome to replace them with their preferred equivalents—whether utilitarian, religious, or otherwise. What matters, again, is only that we can agree that in *practice* morality bars such things as harming or stealing from people for the sake of some marginally better outcome. This means recognizing that people have something structurally equivalent to individual rights, and that morality has a superficially deontic cast, but only in a very weak form, and with complete agnosticism about the underlying basis of this practical stance. Since many utilitarians have spent their lives trying to demonstrate the utilitarian basis of common-sense morality, presumably they at least would accept this ecumenical proposal.

But some will reject it. In particular, some utilitarians deny that there exist anything like individual rights, even construed in weak, non-absolute form, even as a matter of practice. They likewise deny that it is okay to favor our kids or to own frivolous luxury goods like televisions. They insist, rather, that each act we perform really should be judged on whether it promotes the best overall consequences, and they think that *in practice* this will have counterintuitive implications out of step with common-sense or folk morality. We can call this *revisionist utilitarianism* to distinguish it from ecumenical varieties that in practice have implications similar to our everyday beliefs. Peter Singer appears to be a representative of this camp.[9] We were able to take an irenic approach toward ecumenical views since our interest lies only in the practical upshot for questions about distributive justice. But revisionist utilitarianism would have very strong and distinctive implications for distributive justice (and everything else). This is because of two ways in which revisionist utilitarianism diverges from folk morality and the rights and duties the latter seems to recognize.[10] In the one direction, revisionist utilitarianism rejects any constraints on our actions apart from maximizing the good. Revisionist utilitarianism doesn't even recognize a threshold that we must pass before pressing on toward the better outcome. As long as it's true that the world would be a better place if I steal your money and give to others, I may steal your money. So revisionist utilitarianism doesn't recognize any constraints on my actions following from duties to observe people's rights.

On the other hand, folk morality suggests that we aren't subject to a requirement to relentlessly pursue the good at our own expense. We should be reasonably generous in emergencies, but aren't obligated to sell all we own to help distant strangers. We have the *option* to sell, but we don't have to. To put it another way, most people think there is such a thing as going above and beyond the call of duty. This category—"the supererogatory" in the philosopher's argot—would just cease to exist if we took revisionist utilitarianism seriously. For if it was always wrong to do anything that failed to make the world a better place overall, then we would never have the option to buy subwoofers instead of giving to charity, or lie in bed on Sunday instead of working at the soup kitchen, and so doing the reverse wouldn't mean going above and beyond. So revisionist utilitarianism is both too permissive by the standards of common-sense morality, and too demanding. Too permissive since it lets us steal our neighbors' stuff, at least in theory, and too demanding since it makes us sacrifice ourselves at every turn.

"But I have an ingenious way of reconciling utilitarianism to common sense!" someone will say. Then we're back to the ecumenical proposal.

■ IGNORING UTILITARIANISM

Having delineated an important moral theory that would completely upend our thinking about distributive justice, I now want to argue for aggressively ignoring it. Instead of trying to refute utilitarianism, as many political philosophers have undertaken, I will simply make clear my (unproven) assumption that the revisionist variety is mistaken, and that the ecumenical varieties can be taken on board. If I am wrong about this and it turns out that we should be executing the innocent to appease the mob, or selling our children's Christmas presents, then much of what I have to say will be mistaken. But then, if such things turn out to be true, being wrong about distributive justice will be the least of our worries.

There are two main reasons for this cowardly approach. Ironically, one is that utilitarianism really is a profound and important thesis, one that deserves its own book or books. It amounts to the project of seeing people from a detached, impartial point of view, and of rejecting any attempt to hedge for the fact that *I* will be the one *doing* this thing to someone èlse, or that it is *my* life that will go worse if I engage in self-sacrifice. This project would mean seeing ourselves less as agents with a personal perspective, and more as conduits for bringing about optimal states of affairs. That idea is too profound to dismiss casually in a few pages, as political philosophers are wont to do, in the rush to get to questions of justice. It would be as if we tackled a controversial theory of the French Revolution by first refuting skepticism about the external world. John Rawls, for instance, emphasizes that classical utilitarianism may, in theory, ignore the unequal distribution of goods for the sake of generating a greater overall quantity.[11] But it's a simple enough variation to announce that radical inequalities in distribution are undesirable consequences in their own right, or that under anything like real-world conditions the opposite is more likely. (That is, exacerbating inequalities is likely to produce less overall happiness or other good consequences, not more.) Only those already unsympathetic to utilitarianism are likely to be swayed by Rawls's brief observations. Those who begin their political philosophy by defending the morality of rights don't so much preach to the choir as exorcize the elect.

This doesn't yet explain helping ourselves to a deontic version of morality. Granting that assumptions must be made, why choose one way or the other? The deeper reason for ignoring revisionist utilitarianism is that I don't think most of us could live with it. This may seem surprising: there are actual utilitarians out there, walking about, so how hard can it really be to live with their views? But it's telling that few utilitarians exhibit much utilitarianism. By this I don't intend the childish ad hominem often raised against those calling for more aid to the poor and the like. Peter Singer, for instance, modestly concedes, "I don't think my indulgences can be justified. I know that I'm very far from being a saint. I should spend less on myself and give away more of what I earn."[12] This amounts to successfully living with utilitarianism in the sense that we should care about.

Living with a view doesn't require fully implementing it. The significant question of whether we can live with an ideal like secular humanism or Marxism or Christianity isn't whether we fall short of the ideal; it's whether we can bring ourselves fully to *accept* the ideal in the first place, I submit. The real question for the aspiring Christian isn't, "Can you be sure you'll avoid sinning?" It is rather, "Can you bring yourself to accept that there is such a thing as sin and a need for redemption from it?" And in this sense, I doubt that we can bring ourselves fully to accept the utilitarian ideal. The problem isn't superficial weakness; the problem is a profound incompatibility between utilitarianism and what we are. If there were a button that said, "Implement utilitarianism!" that would (somehow) set in motion steps that would compel us to comply with its dictates, thus removing the difficulty of constant choice, I don't think many of us, on reflection, could bring ourselves to push it.

Challenges to living with utilitarianism tend to focus on what I called options—the option we think we normally have to flout the overall good when we rather sleep in, or buy a subwoofer instead of donating to charity. But what really cuts ice are constraints on our actions. Singer and others emphasize that they can accept that they do not, as utilitarians, have the option to loaf about when they could help others, however much they fall short. But what is really hard about living with utilitarianism isn't *self*-sacrifice but *other*-sacrifice, paradoxically enough. This wouldn't be so if we were purely self-interested, but we aren't, and the prospect of exploiting others for the greater good thus terrifies us. Of course, it's rare that harming innocents will produce much good, but it's easy enough to come up with cases:

> *Grandma*: Grandma is a kindly soul who has saved up tens of thousands of dollars in cash over the years. One fine day you see her stashing it away under her mattress, and come to think that with just a little nudge you could cause her to fall and most probably die. You could then take her money, which others don't know about, and redistribute it to those more worthy, saving many lives in the process. No one will ever know. Left to her own devices, Grandma would probably live a few more years, and her money would be discovered by her unworthy heirs who would blow it on fancy cars and vacations. Liberated from primitive deontic impulses by a recent college philosophy course, you silently say your goodbyes and prepare to send Grandma into the beyond.

If this seems too outré to take seriously, we can try this instead:

> *Child*: Your son earns a good living as a doctor but is careless with some of his finances. You sometimes help him out by organizing his receipts and invoices. One day you have the opportunity to divert $1,000 from his funds to a charity where the money will do more good; neither he nor anyone else will ever notice the difference, besides the beneficiaries. You decide to steal your child's money and promote the overall good.

Recall that we've already set aside ecumenical views that side with deontic morality in practice. So it's no use to protest that the true utilitarian theory has some esoteric feature that lets us ignore the case, say because we should only follow rules with good consequences, and killing those around us to reduce hunger would have terrible consequences overall. The only views left on the table at this point are precisely those that *are* willing to contemplate that, at least in some circumstances, rubbing out Grandma and stealing from our children is the right thing to do. The problem, then, is that most people don't seem able to accept even that they ought to *aspire* to such behavior, let alone engage in it. Exploiting those we love isn't an ideal we fail to attain, it's the very antipode of the ideals themselves. Just consider contexts in which we are specifically seeking to articulate them, as when we instruct our children. Do revisionist utilitarians sit down their sons and daughters and implore them to steal from their friends when it is possible to do so undetected and to divert the money to famine relief? There are many books by revisionist utilitarians telling us that we ought to do more to live up to the demands of morality through self-sacrifice; the fact that there are so few urging us to engage in more *other*-sacrifice would be surprising if revisionists really could take their philosophy seriously in practice.

It may seem as if I am trying to argue from the fact that you cannot kill your grandmother to the falsehood of utilitarianism. But that would be the kind of lame attack that I was lamenting earlier; my point is not that these histrionic vignettes in any way refute or even count against utilitarianism. All they really do is dramatize the nature of the utilitarian commitments, and emphasizing commitments isn't much of a counterargument. The point is rather that it doesn't make sense to initiate a debate about social organization on the basis of assumptions few if any of us can live with. Being unable to live with a view, even aspirationally, doesn't mean that it's false, but given that we aren't going to get to the bottom of the matter here and now, it's a reason to assume the opposite for purposes of the discussion. Again, it would be folly to open a book about the French Revolution by first refuting skepticism about the external world. This is so even if the interest of the former depends on the falsehood of the latter. (If I'm a brain in a vat being fed delusory sensory impulses, then who cares about Robespierre?) But if we persuade ourselves that we could not even take skepticism seriously as something to aspire to, then it is best assumed false for purposes of such a book. The underlying rationale for this is that the goal of inquiry is either practice, or belief, or both, and that goal will be frustrated if our inquiry rests on assumptions we cannot take seriously as the basis for action or a premise for further reasoning and belief. (In appendix A I argue that we can reconcile the existence of utilitarians with their doctrine being unlivable by appealing to common cases of self-deception.)

Stalwarts may scoff at my faint-heartedness: why on earth shouldn't we face up to whatever the truth is and find a way to live with it? If an infallible angel announces revisionist utilitarianism to be true, what else could we do but add it to all the other "unthinkables" that have turned out to be true—Darwinism, the Milgram experiment, and the like? Some will indeed see things this way, and so it cannot be said that *no one* is capable of living with utilitarianism in the sense specified. Of course, it is difficult to imagine revisionist utilitarianism being confirmed in this way—as a revelation from on high, or an argument so irrefragable that its crazy-sounding implications wouldn't allow us to reject it. But in any case, no one is insisting that we write off utilitarianism come what may; we are only making an assumption for present purposes, in light of how we see things at present. If the trumpet sounds and radical utilitarianism is proven true, we can still make our stand at that time.

My claims in the next few chapters amount to saying that we can't both accept anything resembling common-sense morality and the anti-libertarian welfare-state structures that admittedly characterize most advanced states at present. The idea is to argue for exciting conclusions from boring premises about common-sense morality. (It's easy to establish a radical political philosophy if you get to assume that all our moral beliefs are wrong, and that we ought to have the attitudes of a eusocial ant colony.) And in fact, this structure provides yet another opportunity for slinking back to revisionist utilitarianism. If we face up to the choice between common-sense views of morality and a redistributive welfare state, and decide in favor of abandoning homely notions of individual rights in favor of revisionist utilitarianism, that would be a valuable realization. I would welcome this as progress in understanding what the nature of the disagreement really was. Of course, anyone so tempted will want to consider carefully how willing he is to interact with his friends and neighbors on a basis that dispenses with the concept of desert and something functionally equivalent to rights, but as a point of logic this move will remain open.[13]

■ DOES THE STATE HAVE EMERGENT MORAL POWERS?

Acknowledging features like individual rights and desert in morality (or their equivalents) doesn't yet settle what role they have to play in arguments about the state. For on some views, our day-to-day thinking about interpersonal morality has little to tell us about what the government may do. *I* may not *rob* you (as we say) to pay for someone's surgery, but it doesn't follow that the *state* may not *tax* you (as we say) to fund the procedure. Or so it is claimed. Essentially, the issue is whether there are emergent moral powers of the state—permissions that the state enjoys that mere individuals do not. It is an important assumption in some of my arguments that we can compare the actions of the state to the actions of individuals, and that objections to what individuals or groups of individuals do to us by way of infringing our rights can be objections to what the state does, assuming the circumstances and grounds of infringement are similar. I will assume, that is, that it makes sense to ask such questions as, "Could I and my friends break down your door and compel you to give us your money for reason X under circumstances Y?" and to draw conclusions about what the state may do. We can call this the *non-emergence assumption*.

We should get a few trivial points out of the way. No one disagrees that what individuals may do in the presence of a legitimate state authority is different from what they may do otherwise. Citizens may not take justice into their own hands or, with rare exceptions, perform the functions of law enforcement or the military. This means, of course, that there is a trivial sense in which we cannot infer anything from the impermissibility of breaking down our neighbors' doors to appropriate money for surgery. If we're going to invoke interpersonal morality against the state, we must first assume that there isn't a *superseding authority* present. The usual way of doing this is by presenting a scenario in which the state is absent or nonfunctional. Since such scenarios are inevitably unusual and removed from everyday life, they may inspire some skepticism. But they needn't be more exotic than emergencies in which state authorities are unable to respond in time, or Hurricane Katrina–like situations in which the state is temporarily nonfunctional in some region, or even just special communities (say the Amish, or among remote hiking trails) where the state exercises little effective control. In any case, we should distinguish methodological doubts about thought experiments from the more basic point that the reason I cannot personally "tax" you for my needs is initially because there is a superseding authority. (I ignore here the question of how such superseding works, of how some people get to announce that they are the government and that they have a monopoly on various exercises of authority.) It is after the issue of superseding authority has been defused that we get to the question of what it means when the state claims authority to do things that we don't think individuals or groups could do (*absent* a functioning state).

We should also set aside powers residing in groups to make decisions that no one has a special claim to influence. If five of us are on a life raft and we need to decide who gets the last water ration, no individual has the moral authority to claim it for himself, or to decide on a decision-procedure unilaterally. But the group or its representatives may award it to someone. A vote or lottery or other fair procedure can invest the collective with this right that no individual possesses. However, these kinds of cases aren't what we're interested in either. It's not as if the collective is overcoming what would otherwise be moral barriers in virtue of its collective status. In fact, it's the opposite: were I to unilaterally claim the last ration, I would be violating the others, who are entitled to a fair procedure whose selection they should be able to influence. What really matters is if individuals can't harm or steal or otherwise violate someone under conditions CDE, but the collective—in virtue of having more people and perhaps various forms of interaction between them—can. That is the type of emergent power we are interested in.

In considering this, we should be mindful of two contrary dangers. To the one side lies the fallacy of composition, whereby we mistakenly infer something about the whole from something about the part, as when we reason that the brain cannot produce consciousness because individual neurons don't.[14] It may look as if the non-emergence assumption involves a version of this fallacy, since it tries to infer something about the moral powers of the whole of the collective from those of the individuals composing it. On the other side lies reification, treating a set of individuals as if they compose some distinct entity in its own right, with values and powers that don't derive straightforwardly from the individuals composing it. Some forms of extreme nationalism involve this error—what ultimately matters isn't the abstract entity *the nation-state*, but the people who compose one. Our attitude toward the non-emergence assumption will depend on how we approach the arguments associated with these respective dangers.

■ INSTITUTIONS AND COOPERATION

One reason for insisting on emergent moral powers is that when we are assessing what the state does we are assessing institutions and the justice of those institutions. And we might worry that there is no simple relationship between the interpersonal morality of individuals and the justice of macro-level institutions. The functioning of the judiciary or of the tax system may seem too different from our everyday interactions with our neighbors to apply the same kinds of norms. Rawls makes a related point about the "basic structure" of a society, its fundamental social, political, and economic institutions:

> There is no reason to suppose ahead of time that the principles satisfactory for the basic structure hold for all cases. These principles may not work for the rules and practices of private associations or for those of less comprehensive social groups. They may be irrelevant for the various informal conventions and customs of everyday life . . . [or] the fairness of voluntary cooperative arrangements.[15]

There is an innocuous reading of this passage according to which we're making the mundane point that entering into a grand social contract might not be the best way of determining who should do the dishes tonight. If nothing else, there may be gross structural mismatches between collective decision-making and the assignment of interpersonal duties among couples. But a more aggressive interpretation is to deny that we should assess rules of justice according to their implications for everyday life. On this interpretation, objecting to a social rule as unfair because it implies something that we would reject as immoral in everyday life would be improper.[16] The mundane view concerns moving top-down from institutional justice to interpersonal morality; the aggressive view resists movement in the other direction, from interpersonal morality to views about the (in) justice of institutions.

Notice that the mundane view does not imply the more aggressive view. The mundane view is only that we can't infer from the nature of just social institutions what justice in non-institutional situations might look like. We can accept this modest caution without accepting the far more aggressive proposal that everyday moral principles can't constrain reasoning about justice. There is no logical connection between these two thoughts. In fact, I suspect that whatever temptation there is toward the aggressive view is rooted in confusing it with the mundane view. It is possible to pursue the aggressive view in its own right, moved perhaps by the observation that there are many things the state may do that individuals may not, as we have already noted. It would indeed be silly to object to the state trying a forger because I can't try a forger in my living room. But this still would not motivate the non-trivial cases we're interested in, where the state wishes to kill someone, or lock someone up, or take someone's possessions, on grounds and under circumstances that would be wrong for any individual, even when appropriately situated. And the mere fact that the activity of the state is often embodied in abstract entities called "institutions" doesn't seem to help much either. The fact that it isn't just John Smith but *Judge* Smith, an arm of the judiciary apparatus, doesn't make it less objectionable for Smith to take your property without adequate moral justification, or to lock you in a dungeon without very good moral reasons. (If anything, the fearful powers wielded by institutions like the police makes them *more* susceptible to such objections, one would think.) It is obviously true that the principles for drawing up institutions are different in nature from those for working out interpersonal moral principles. We can't sit down armed only with the Ten Commandments or Kant's moral philosophy and derive the structure of representative government or intellectual property rights. But that doesn't show that we cannot legitimately object to such institutions if they turn out to permit grossly immoral actions, like executing the innocent or stealing property someone has a firm claim to.

Another tack is to claim that the institutions of the state are constitutive of right and wrong, at least in certain domains. If so, then posing fundamental moral objections will be misguided, since there is no right and wrong independent of the institutions themselves. Put differently, the institutions can be just or unjust, but this won't be a function of how they mesh with independent moral norms, but of institution-specific criteria, like whether they were chosen fairly by following some acceptable procedure. This is probably a reasonable suggestion in domains that are fairly remote from homely moral norms, developed over eons of face-to-face encounters. Take, again, intellectual property. There are some connections to common-sense morality, which suggests that some are better positioned than others to make claims on various assets. But these connections are relatively weak, and so it's hard to see how to raise a forceful objection to international treaties on copyright that are rooted in basic moral convictions, except perhaps for some very gross cases. But we still might reject the institutions involved as unjust, say if they were devised by some unfair procedure that favored multinational corporations at the expense of the public good.

This point is fine as far as it goes, but it is perfectly compatible with the nonemergence assumption. The exercise of state powers to conclude treaties isn't a power not enjoyed by individuals, except in the trivial sense of superseding authority. (We conclude "treaties" of cat-watching with our neighbors all the time.) What would matter would be if the content of the institutions and their outputs that couldn't be derived from fundamental moral principles were capable of *contradicting* those principles, but that does not follow from anything we've seen. Arcane conventions and treaties fill in a space that is mostly left void by basic moral convictions, but they don't trample over those convictions in virtue of an institutional trump card. And when there is such a conflict, our reaction is generally just the opposite. When trade agreements, say, turn out to permit animal cruelty or worker mistreatment, or when they allow for unfair and inscrutable arbitration procedures, we *do* have basic moral reactions, and whatever we make of the specifics, no one dreams of announcing that our moral convictions just don't count or are trumped.

Alternatively, we might worry that allowing morality to constrain the state leads to absurdity. The purpose of the state is in part to facilitate cooperation on a larger and larger scale, and introducing such micro-level constraints may seem destined to frustrate such cooperation.[17] We can illustrate the problem in the domain of war. Some writers claim that the justification of state-organized warfare is just the same as that of individuals fighting one another: we may defend ourselves and our families against aggressors, and just wars are simply lots of individuals banding together to defend themselves or other innocents.[18] But one might worry about whether the moral principles governing my defensive actions against surly street-thugs really scale to international conflict. Individuals, for instance, may not attack those whom they should know to be innocent, and can be punished if they do. This is true even of those posing a threat to me, if they do so for good reasons. I may not harm those defending their home against my own aggression; if I am burgling and am (reasonably) threatened by the homeowner, I must leave or surrender rather than harming him. But according to traditional just war theory, soldiers acting on lawful orders may kill other soldiers who have done nothing wrong and are simply defending themselves. Although these other soldiers are combatants, since they are merely defending themselves against my unjust attack, they are in the relevant sense innocent, just as is the homeowner defending himself against my invasion. Thus, if we allowed interpersonal morality to constrain the state, it would appear we should tell all soldiers that they are liable for killing enemies they have been ordered to attack, unless their cause is just and their attack warranted, whatever their orders. We would then prosecute soldiers engaged in what they should have known to be an unjustified war for *murder*, even if they committed no war crimes, allowing for various mitigating excuses. (Even Nazi soldiers weren't so prosecuted, only their leadership and those committing specific war crimes.) And this suggestion may seem absurd. State-organized violence isn't the same as individual violence, and confusing the two as in this line of reasoning makes war impossible—even just war—since telling individual soldiers to rely on their own moral reasoning will inevitably lead to chaos. And even if it didn't, it would imply that individual soldiers are on the hook for working out, from the trenches somewhere, whether they may shoot back at uniformed enemies firing on them, or whether some arcane treaty violation means they must rather surrender.

Extending the thought, we might think something similar applies in the economic sphere. Insisting that every tax dollar be justified in interpersonal moral terms (or at least not conflict with interpersonal moral norms) may make it much harder to justify some taxes. This will in turn make many essential operations of the state, and of large-scale cooperation more generally, impossible. If we insist on holding all movement toward large-scale cooperation hostage to moral impulses developed in face-to-face encounters—often tribal and parochial impulses—we cut ourselves off from the modern institutions that make for successful states, goes the worry.

It is impossible to answer this sort of charge in the abstract, and so for the most part we will simply have to face questions of cooperation and scale as we go along. But notice that on closer inspection the doubt expressed here isn't about cooperation at all, but about forcing *non*-cooperators to do our bidding. The worry about the soldiers isn't that people banding together in defense of a cause they accept to be just will prove impossible, it's that we won't be able to coerce those who *don't* wish so to cooperate into fighting when we tell them to; the worry about taxation isn't that those who want to run a school system or insurance scheme won't be able to manage, it's that we won't be able to force those who *don't* wish to participate to pitch in. This may still be a problem, but we shouldn't frame it in terms of cooperation, as if what were at issue were the logistics of willing volunteers coordinating their efforts. And the general solution to the problem is that there are plenty of occasions on which we may indeed force others to do our bidding. But even when we do, this isn't in virtue of emergent moral powers. The justification for war sketched above may be wrong, but not because the state gets to order us to kill the innocent. Taxation is often warranted, but not because the state, unlike us, gets to steal. As a rough sketch of how this might work, a plausible principle (defended later on) holds that we can compel others to join in efforts like self-defense or funding certain public works that they benefit from, and whose benefits we can't easily decline or let them opt out of. This sort of principle seeks to explain why coercion might then be defensible. But the defense will be akin to the defense we might offer to our neighbors in situations where the state is ineffective or absent.

Sometimes, however, there will be no principle that lets the state force people to do what it wants, and sometimes it will be difficult to acknowledge this. Accepting this will sometimes means big losses to some or all of us. Of course, this is part of the status quo. Not punishing the innocent comes with all kinds of costs. It may well be that we'd be better off lowering our standards of conviction on a consequential basis, since we're unlikely to be falsely accused and producing fewer false negatives in the judicial system would produce a lot of good. But we just accept that, even were this so, not all social gains are accessible from within a moral framework we can bring ourselves to live with.

▪ REIFYING THE STATE

It is notable that many who wish to block rights-based objections to state action are nevertheless eager to enter their own moral objections to what the state does. Many of those unsympathetic to attacks on taxation rooted in individual rights also portray the absence of welfare provisions or various immigration policies as "unconscionable." There is nothing inconsistent about this; the one set of moral claims may be right and the other confused. But the objection then cannot be based on the emergent moral powers of the state. We cannot both reject appeals to individuals rights on the general grounds that morality has nothing to tell us about what may emerge from government institutions, and then do just that, substituting our own preferred brand of interpersonal morality. Once we notice this, support for emergence should shrink drastically, since it will only come from those who think there are *no* policies of the state that can be rejected on fundamental moral grounds. The non-emergence assumption per se has no particular ideological leanings.

There are also more principled doubts about emergence to consider, the chief of which involves a certain kind of reification. Of course, there really is such a thing as the state, with its own distinctive legal norms, institutions, and capacities. The mistake in reifying the state (or the family, or the corporation) isn't one of abstruse metaphysics, of recognizing the existence of such things. The mistake lies in reifying them in a normative sense, in pretending that they have underived, sui generis normative status apart from whatever legal or other conventional standing we endow them with. We can gesture toward the mistake with calls to do things for "the good of the country" or family, or to promote the interests of the firm at the expense of the welfare of the stakeholders. Sometimes these expressions refer harmlessly to the good of various people—"the good of the country" may just mean "the good of all citizens." But other times we go astray by endowing the whole with a normative authority it lacks. Consider calls to promote the "glory of Rome" through one more conquest, or insisting that a son or daughter become a doctor to preserve the family tradition, or keeping an ancient firm going when shutting it down would be better for employees and owners. With the right details, these will reflect a misguided sense of the importance of the whole, when what matters are the people who are its parts. Making the country great at the expense of its citizens, or burnishing the family name while making the people comprising it miserable, is just confused.

It is a similar kind of mistake that is involved in thinking that the state has the moral authority to violate people in ways that relevantly situated individuals could not. They may be accorded that authority by law or convention, or we might insist that designated agents of the state and not just anyone perform certain kinds of acts. But nations are just groups of individuals standing in certain relations and interacting in various ways, and it's puzzling why adding a few more people to the mix should suddenly switch the valence of an act from wrong to right. There are features of people that generate moral constraints on their treatment, such as their capacity for feeling, wanting, planning, and reasoning. And there is nothing in the nature of a big collection of people interacting in various ways (swaddled in a flag, chanting the national anthem, if we like) that would confer on it special rights to set aside or neglect those features and the moral constraints they produce. If that were possible, I should be able to accomplish my otherwise nefarious goals simply by assembling a large enough group and performing whatever the required forms of interaction are. (Provided, that is, my nefarious purposes were of the right sort; the emergentist needn't assert that the state can do just anything.) This may seem unfair; perhaps those interactions are more impressive in concrete form. They may include, for instance, solemn agreements, majority vote, declaration of law, or judicial review. But these are all easy enough to accomplish, and it remains unclear how, when I stand outside your home and wish to perform what would otherwise be a horrible violation, simply calling enough neighbors and signing some documents could transmute my violation into a permissible act.

There is a simple diagnosis of why this may not seem obvious at the outset. The state inures us to its activities by custom, history, and routinization. If all our lives long everyone around us fills in some dull-looking forms that divert money from an electronic account in a manner sanctioned by law and by decent people everywhere, it's no wonder that calling this process into question will seem bizarre. And this produces a latent emergentism, since we say to ourselves that this unremarkable process doesn't look like any great violation, and yet as we will see shortly, it is difficult to defend structurally similar behavior by individuals. We stop applying the everyday morality we apply to our friends and neighbors because doing so would produce an objection that we find difficult to take seriously in light of custom, history, and the bureaucratic routine. Positing emergent powers of the state lets us paper over the inconsistency between our moral convictions and the government activities we have become inured to.

To avoid confusion, let me stress that no one is claiming that we cannot do all kinds of horrible things to our neighbors, like blowing up their homes. It's just that what would justify blowing up someone's home isn't adding lots of people and holding a vote; what would do the justifying would be such moral facts as that the person posed a threat that made him or her liable to violence. Such a justification would be available (in principle) to just me or you, provided we were appropriately positioned, that there wasn't a superseding authority, and so on. The Axial idea of moral constraints on the state ultimately rests on the claim that people have an underived moral significance that cannot be diminished by others' say-so. What is important isn't whether we act individually, or in concert, or through abstract institutional intermediaries; what matters is that we must answer for violating the moral authority of individuals, whatever form this violation takes.

3   Libertarianism

A Classic Argument Revisited

Libertarians are generally opposed to redistributive social systems. In practice, the main target of this opposition is the welfare state, which attempts to bring about goals like income equality or poverty reduction by taxation and either transfers or in-kind benefits. Libertarians need not resist these goals in themselves. No one is against reducing abject poverty. What libertarians oppose is the state bringing about such goals by compulsory means. Doing so means utilizing threats or violence, if only implicitly, and these are the wrong way to bring about goals that must rather be achieved by reason and persuasion.

In fact, libertarians oppose all forms of appropriating people's property outside of a small number of narrowly defined circumstances (to be considered in due course). In theory, then, libertarian attacks could be focused on public funding for the arts and many other programs besides the welfare state. But what makes the welfare state special is that it is both expensive to the point that it sometimes imperils public finances, and dedicated to programs that are often seen as morally urgent. Neither of these is true of public programs supporting the arts. The welfare state's goals make it seem imperative to its proponents, and yet its costs make it a target to its enemies—that is why it is central to the debate about limited government.

What leads libertarians to their unpopular resistance to the welfare state (and similar programs)? The answer is a simple, classic argument. There are many other arguments that have been offered for libertarian views, but in chess terms most of these are variations on what deserves to be considered the main line:

Premise 1:   Appropriating property we have a right to is wrong.
Premise 2:   The welfare state appropriates property we have a right to.
Conclusion: The welfare state does and is wrong.

The second premise obviously raises the question of how we come to our property and what rights we have to it. According to various anti-libertarian views, we have no prior claim to most of the income or wealth we enjoy, and thus the welfare state does no wrong in appropriating a significant fraction of it. Just to illustrate, this will be so if private property is theft, or if all property is jointly owned, or most private property has not been legitimately acquired in the first place. In another vein, we may owe the poor part of our property as a matter of morality, and thus not be entitled to the fraction of our property that the state appropriates. Or perhaps wealth and income ultimately derive from natural resources that no one has a special claim to, except under conditions that have not typically been met.[1] For now, though, let us set aside questions of property and focus on the first premise.

Here the point of contention is whether the welfare state does something wrong in appropriating property we have a right to. It may just seem obvious that it does—isn't that what violating someone's rights means? But in fact, this does not follow unless we make strong assumptions about the nature of those rights. It may be that we have such rights but that the state is warranted in *overriding* them for the sake of promoting equality or promoting other worthy ends. After all, the state sets aside many rights without much controversy, as when it invokes emergency powers to compel us to stay at home during an epidemic. This can be resisted by insisting that the relevant rights are *absolute* and can never be overridden, and indeed it is often supposed by critics that libertarianism rests precisely on an exaggerated conception of individual rights.[2] As these critics point out, that assumption is difficult to sustain. Most of our ethical thinking does not suggest that rights are absolute in the sense that nothing can ever justify violating them. A crucial question, then, is whether the libertarian premise can be defended without appealing to an implausibly stringent conception of individual rights.[3] I believe that a moderate version of libertarianism can be so defended. Indeed, as I will show, we can eschew rights-talk altogether, if we wish. The classical liberal outlook, at least its moral core, does not rest on strong assumptions about individual rights. A quick glance at the argument above will also reveal that it doesn't rest on fetishizing individual liberty. Freedom from state intrusion matters, but it isn't the deep basis for resisting the welfare state. As we will see, the argument for libertarianism rests on modest, New Englander assumptions about the reasons we have for not transferring our burdens onto others unfairly.

■ REASONS AND RIGHTS

Robert Nozick, the modern standard-bearer of philosophical libertarianism, famously relegates discussion of whether individual rights are absolute to a single footnote. And in that footnote he simply announces that he hopes to avoid the subject. Since this subject is at the core of the main argument for libertarianism, this is not the right approach.[4]

In considering this problem, it is tempting to focus on cases of the sky falling: if we need to violate someone's rights to prevent the End of the World, we might grow faint-hearted about those rights. The usual scenarios revolve around needing to lie to prevent a murder, or to steal a loaf of bread to feed a starving child. But the problem is much more mundane than these cases suggest. The problem is simply that *rights come in degrees of strength*.[5] The problem is not just that some catastrophes are so great that we have trouble imagining rights so strong as to compel us to accept them, it's that many rights are just feeble to begin with. Thus, my right against you tickling me without permission, or deceiving me in very trivial ways, is extremely weak and so easily overridden even sans catastrophe. There is reason for you not to tickle me, but if doing so would avert even modest harm, you may tickle away. Talk of "rights" tends to obscure this, since traditionally rights-talk has been applied to highly important political rights asserted against the depredations of the state. And those particular rights—against unjust imprisonment or execution—have in turn been connected to absolute-sounding features of people like their human dignity or rational agency.

Rather than attempting a heroic defense of absolute individual rights, then, let us concede the point and assume that rights can be overridden. What does a moral theory look like that recognizes deontic features of morality but avoids exaggerating their significance? Recall the revisionist brand of utilitarianism that I proposed to rule out in the previous chapter. Unlike its moderate cousins, which find some way of mimicking our ordinary moral views, revisionist utilitarianism says that we really must promote the best outcome at every turn, perhaps by always maximizing overall welfare, and it doesn't recognize special duties that constrain our pursuit of those ends, not even as a matter of practice. Now consider what we may call the *threshold view*. The threshold view is intermediate between revisionist utilitarianism and the claim that individuals are absolutely inviolable, and thus enjoy absolute immunity against unauthorized tickling, come what may.[6] Revisionist utilitarianism errs, on this conception, in supposing that any transfer of goods that is net welfare-enhancing (say) is mandatory. Since the only moral reasons revisionist utilitarianism recognizes are those that arise from promoting welfare, what we ought to do is simply a function of how those reasons balance. With the right details, this implies that I can walk into your living room, point toward your TV, demonstrate that I would get more out of it than you, and then sternly reprimand you if you try to interfere as I walk off with your TV. After all, with the right details the transfer will be net welfare-enhancing and therefore mandatory, and the mere fact that I am *taking your stuff* counts for nothing.

Against this, the threshold view says that there are reasons over and above those arising from welfare, and in particular special deontic (i.e., duty-related) reasons to avoid such acts as lying, stealing, and killing. Since these additional reasons are often powerful ones, they can create a threshold that the prospective liar, thief, or killer must overcome in order to be permitted to act. For there will be moral reason for him to abstain from his act unless his reasons overcome both those generated by the victim's losses *and* those agent-relative reasons generated by the fact that he is taking my stuff. But this threshold is not infinitely high. It varies with the relevant welfare gains and losses and with the strength of the deontic reasons. The threshold thus creates a buffer zone against other agents. It blocks your neighbors from wandering into your home and collecting your belongings whenever such transfers would be welfare-enhancing. But thresholds can be breached, and so this view is also opposed to absolutist conceptions of rights, according to which your neighbor could *never* break into your home and take your belongings, even to save a life. On this view, if your neighbor sees a child going into anaphylactic shock and runs into your house to grab the medication he knows is on your desk, he may act permissibly, even if you specifically deny him permission.

Where, we might wonder, do these special deontic reasons come from? What do lying, stealing, murdering, and the rest even have in common? What underlying feature of such acts generates these deontic reasons? And isn't it suspicious that these acts tend to be welfare-destroying, and thus isn't there a risk of double-counting in giving them independent weight? All these and many more questions represent deep problems for anti-utilitarians, but this is not the place to take them up. Suffice it to say that there's nothing in the threshold view that particularly aggravates these problems. They just mean that threshold theorists are left struggling with their tattered and tear-stained copy of Kant's *Grundlegung* (or the Ten Commandments, etc.) like everyone else.

■ THRESHOLDS

Let us zoom in on the kinds of cases that will prove critical. These are those where a third party is deciding about harms or losses to be imposed on a victim in order to aid a needy beneficiary, and other things are equal (no promises have been made, desert and responsibility are not at stake, etc.). We can then represent a crude sketch of the threshold view as in figure 3.1, where points above

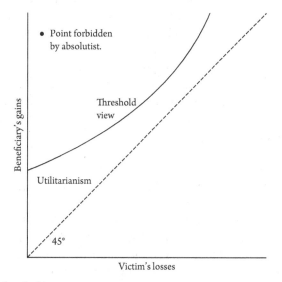

Figure 3.1 The threshold

the solid curve represent permissible interventions on behalf of the beneficiary. Revisionist utilitarianism would make interventions permissible, and in fact mandatory, anywhere above the 45-degree line, since those points represent cases of net welfare gains. Against this, the threshold view pictures permissible points as ones where the gains to the beneficiary exceed by some large margin the losses to the victim. There is a standing reason not to harm the victim by default, even when doing so would promote the overall good. Justifying harm requires overcoming the barrier set by the threshold, however high that may be. However, it is likely that the relationship is not linear. Rather, as the losses to the victim go up, the gains to the beneficiary must go up by an ever higher margin in order to justify the transfer, leading to an ever steeper slope. The idea is that it's permissible to knock someone down to get a child to the hospital for a serious emergency, but that much more would be required to justify seriously injuring the victim, and if what is required is torture or killing, perhaps only some supreme emergency could render this permissible. The curve is thus represented as getting steeper, but not quite asymptotic. Finally, the absolute rights theorist, of course, imposes a hard line against harms, even if the losses would be trivial and the gains enormous, as illustrated by the northwest point in figure 3.1.

There are several complications that aren't easy to visualize. One is that talk of "gains" suggest that what matters is only the size of the gains, not the baseline against which they arise, but this isn't so. The moral importance of improving a hungry, destitute person's welfare is greater than that of improving the life of someone who is already rich and well fed. The moral importance of benefiting, in other words, flattens out with the welfare of the recipient. Superficially, this sounds like a point about diminishing marginal utility, but in fact the points are distinct. For suppose that utility fails to diminish and in fact greatly increases across some interval for some rich person, perhaps because of kindling effects whereby the millionaire comes to appreciate the finer things and hence develop a craving for them—the first 10 bottles of fancy wine train the palate, the 11th brings the huge payoff. We nevertheless think that the moral significance of feeding the hungry is greater than aiding the millionaire, simply because our reasons for aiding diminish as the beneficiary's position improves. (Denying this would sometimes mean letting children go hungry in order to aid bibulous millionaires.)

The second complication involves the number of beneficiaries. Figure 3.1 refers to a simple two-party case. But when there are many potential beneficiaries, there arise difficult questions about how the benefits must be structured to justify imposing costs on the victim. We might wonder, for instance, about whether the benefits can be small but distributed across many, or whether they must accrue to individuals who each meet the threshold requirement. It strikes me that the spirit of the threshold view is to insist that benefits need to meet the threshold for particular individuals, so that we cannot impose huge costs on the victim merely in order distribute candy to a large number of children. Part of the rationale for a threshold as against utilitarianism is to insist that people can be exploited for the greater good only for grave and pressing reasons; collapsing increased benefits to individuals into increased benefits for the many would undermine that rationale, insofar as there really isn't much of a reason to make sure lots of people get some candy. Since this is a notorious and difficult problem, however, I will simply observe that figure 3.1 (which is for two parties) isn't meant to settle that issue.[7]

Third, I have been writing in terms of what it is *permissible* to do to another person, not what we are required to do. When thinking about cases in which we have the option of harming someone else in order to benefit ourselves, there can be no question of requirements, since we are never *required* to harm others to benefit ourselves—at most, we are permitted to. (Self-sacrifice is always an option.) Indeed, it is one of the puzzling features of utilitarianism that it seems to ignore this, since from a detached, impartial point of view it will often make the world a better place to promote our own interests, which would mean we *are* required to favor ourselves.[8] It's hard to believe that I am obligated to watch TV and drink beer rather than take my daughter to piano lessons if it turns out she gets very little out of these and I get a great deal out of TV and beer. But in third-party cases things are murkier, since we sometimes think that third parties have an *obligation* to harm someone in order to benefit another. A simple case involves knocking someone out of the way in order to help a child about to get run over—required, not just permitted. I suspect that moving from its being permissible to harm to its being obligatory to harm involves yet another threshold to breach. Intuitively, more needs to be at stake in order for us to endorse claims that a person was morally *required* to harm someone. In order to avoid tedious complications, however, I will generally refer to a single threshold and will just assume that it may need to be higher depending on whether a third-party obligation is at stake or not.

This, then, is the picture of threshold deontology I will take for granted in what follows. In some respects it should trouble us, even though I think it represents reasonably well the structure of what most of us believe. On the threshold view we are not inviolable. In theory at least, we are subject to all manner of harms if the price is right. We can adjust the slope of the threshold-curve in figure 3.1 in ways that reassure us, but the very fact that we are in principle violable may bother us. Certainly it is inconsistent with talk of our "inviolable dignity" that one hears from politicians and reads in highfalutin charters and treaties. Here, though, it is important to bear in mind the dialectic. If it turns out that the threshold view errs in the direction of *under*estimating the strength of individual rights, then all the better for arguments for libertarianism. Relative to absolutism, the threshold view is generous to opponents of libertarianism, not its defenders. To the extent that thresholds are controversial, they're controversial in the right direction for our purposes.

■ RESIDUAL OBLIGATIONS

It is crucial to be clear about the nature of the moral reasons envisioned under the threshold view, and the way in which they fail to generate absolute rights. Often this is explained in terms of exceptions or qualifications:

> Some assaults are very minor inconveniences, and some assaults do an enormous amount of good, so a blanket *exceptionless* prohibition is unreasonably rigid . . . [Any] remotely plausible statement of a set of rights intended to form a set of fundamental moral principles would have to include *qualifications* to the individual rights.[9]

There are different ways in which reasons that normally have force can fail to get a grip on us on a given occasion. One is epistemic: the reasons were merely prima facie, and a closer look shows us they aren't in effect just now. There is prima facie reason to arrest a gunman at the airport, but the reason disappears when it turns out he is an undercover officer on the job. Then there is the more complicated case where certain reasons are said to be "silenced" and have no force at all, as when the rapist's pleasure fails to count as a reason in favor of rape that must be contingently outweighed. (It's not that there's a great deal to be said in favor of rape, except that generally those considerations get outweighed by the harm to the victim.) Particularly in this last kind of case, talk of exceptions might be in order: "Normally pleasure counts in favor of an act, but this isn't so without qualification, and in some cases it has no force at all," we might say.[10]

But the reasons relevant to the threshold view are not like either of these. When we harm some for the sake of benefiting others, the reasons against harming the victim are not merely epistemic, nor are they disabled altogether, as in the rape case. The reason to avoid harm remains in force, even as we respond to the still stronger reason to benefit someone. The threshold view thus envisions cases of permissible harm as simply *overriding* the still active reasons to avoid such harm. They are akin to straightforward prudential cases like tolerating pain at the dentist for the sake of some greater good, where the reasons to discontinue the painful treatment remain powerful despite the greater good. There isn't really an exception here at all, except possibly in the sense of statistical irregularity. All of the reasons against harming people still stand (without exception or qualification), and the expected outcome in light of the still stronger reasons to benefit others likewise emerges without exception or qualification. Sometimes these kinds of reasons are called *pro tanto* reasons.

This means that there are two crucial questions that will always arise when appealing to the threshold view in order to impose harms for our own or someone else's benefit: (1) Has the threshold in fact been breached? Obviously we need to know this, since we are supposed to be imposing a gap over and above the utilitarian 45-degree line in figure 3.1. And (2), more subtly, what additional moral obligations are triggered by the fact that the reason to avoid harm is still engaged?

This second question can be illustrated in a simple example.[11]

Emergency: A robber jumps me as I am walking near your house while you are away and demands $1,000, threatening to break my arm if I don't deliver. Deeply worried about my health, I call you at work and ask permission to break into your house to access the emergency funds I know you keep on hand. You, however, refuse: you need the money for your own purposes, you say, and urge me to take my chances. I conclude the threat to my health warrants ignoring your non-consent, break into your house, and deliver the $1,000 I find under your mattress to the robber, who runs off.

Let us stipulate that the threshold is met in this case: it is permissible all things considered to break into your house and take your $1,000 to avoid serious bodily harm. (Readers who disagree are invited to adjust the ratio of threat level to dollar amount until this seems true; readers who feel this will *never* be true are likely absolutists who a fortiori should have no quarrel with the libertarian premise.) Despite the threat to your arm (and conceivably more than that), I still had a powerful moral reason not to take your $1,000. The question is, what obligations does that overridden reason trigger? I propose the following non-exhaustive list of *residual obligations* for cases like *Emergency*:

Restitution: although I didn't do wrong, I must repay the $1,000 if possible, perhaps in reasonable installments.

Compensation: to the extent you are otherwise harmed by my actions, I should attempt to compensate you. For instance, if I smashed your windows getting in or forced you to incur some loss because you had to come home at short notice, I must compensate you at some reasonable rate.

Sympathy: it is incumbent on me to convey, if not an apology for my (permissible) actions, at least sympathy for the harm I have caused you. ("I'm very sorry I had to do that" would be the natural if slightly misleading phrase.) I cannot offer a Gallic shrug at your distress and announce, "I did nothing wrong—it's your problem" as you survey the wreckage of your home. To do so would exhibit a serious character flaw.

Responsibility: my obligations are not just backward looking, but forward looking. If I can reasonably foresee that some action of mine will put me in the position of facing an emergency that will then render it permissible to harm you, I must take responsibility to avoid such actions if possible. I should *not* think that I have less reason to take responsibility because I can avoid harms by transferring them to you instead. And failing to take responsibility weakens my claim to impose costs on others when the time comes.

A related principle is worth mentioning as well:

Need: my warrant for harming you depends on how bad my situation is. I cannot harm you if I am doing fine already merely in order to improve my position still further. I may be permitted to take your $1,000 to avert a physical threat, but not in order to make a lucrative investment in order to get even richer.

The general thought is that the overridden reason to avoid harming you produces these residual obligations for me despite my not having wronged you. They represent a kind of moral remainder that is left over. This contrasts sharply with other kinds of deactivated reasons, like those that are silenced. There is usually reason not to practice deceit, but sometimes it is fine, for instance faking a jump shot in basketball. Here, no compensation, sympathy, or the rest is owed.[12]

Why believe in these residual obligations in cases of overriding? We might be skeptical in light of the maxim, *Someone who does no wrong can't owe anyone anything.* ("Compensation for *what*?") The reasoning behind these residual obligations is that when we suffer a misfortune, there is a powerful moral reason to avoid shifting the attendant burdens onto the innocent if at all possible. When my car breaks down, I may not commandeer yours with the justification that my bad luck is your bad luck. (Generously allowing that we should split the costs by compelling you to lend me your car on alternate days is still wrong—I may ask nicely, but no more.) The converse policy would amount to *Misery loves company* with a vengeance. And when retrospective restitution or compensation or prospective avoidance is possible in a case like *Emergency*, we are then faced with the question of whether to transfer our misfortunes onto innocent bystanders. The overriding emergency confers on me permission to smash your windows and temporarily appropriate your money, perhaps, but it is another matter entirely whether I may make this shift in burdens *permanently* yours, the innocent bystander's. It may be replied that if you, the homeowner, are innocent, so am I, the emergency beneficiary. But this only goes to underscore the extent to which I am myself the victim of someone else benefiting himself at my expense; this does nothing to justify my doing the same. The answer to the question, then, of how I can owe you anything when I haven't done wrong is that fundamentally I am *not* compensating you for a wrong; I am rather observing my duty not to shift my misfortunes onto you without your consent. Since the two superficially resemble one another, they are easily confused, but the distinction is real for all that. Failing to pay you back the $1,000 isn't an attempt to repair a moral harm in the past; it's simply doing my duty not to make you suffer for my misfortune in the future.

■ A LEGAL PARALLEL

It is useful to compare legal reasoning in the law of torts. In the oft-cited case *Vincent v. Lake Erie Transportation* a ship was tied up to a dock in order to avoid sailing into a dangerous storm, despite the non-consent of the dock owner. The storm then caused the ship to damage the dock, the dock owner sued, and an appeals court ultimately upheld a judgment of damages in favor of the plaintiff.[13] (Note that consistent with the threshold theory, there was no talk of having committed a *crime* such as trespass because of some inviolable right being infringed.) And since then, the common law has generally held that compensation is owed in cases of damage inflicted out of "private necessity." Here, too, there has occasionally been suspicion about whether the innocent could really owe anyone anything; in fact, a dissenting opinion in *Vincent* itself held that since the captain had exercised all due care, he hadn't been negligent or at fault and consequently couldn't be held liable. But this reasoning involves the same mistake we noted earlier, at least as far as morality is concerned. The shipowner doesn't owe damages for acting wrongly in the past, but so as to prevent unfair burden-shifting to the dock owner in the future. Saying that the captain did no wrong in the past is beside the point; the claim is that he *will* be doing wrong if he doesn't pay up now. Fundamentally, the misfortune befell Lake Erie Transportation, and the company isn't entitled to force Vincent to subsidize its costs.

Interestingly, the court's own opinion raises a different kind of problem in observing that the shipowner would *not* have been liable in a case of unintentional damage (if the ship, say, had been non-negligently at sea and had been tossed against the docks by a sudden squall). We can model this in terms of *Emergency* by considering the difference between *Emergency* and another scenario in which my car is picked up by an unforecast tornado and causes your house a $1,000 worth of damage after striking it. It might look as if there isn't a relevant difference between the former and latter case in each pair, and we might then wonder why, if the absence of fault cancels compensation in the latter cases, it doesn't do so in the former. But of course there is a difference: I didn't *do* anything when my car was picked up and deposited on your house, whereas I clearly did cause you to lose the $1,000 in *Emergency*. It is tempting simply to say that liability requires an intentional action of some sort. But on reflection this can't be the whole story, since it leaves unexplained *why* causation matters in cases like *Emergency* or *Vincent* where causation is unaccompanied by fault. I believe that the stricture on burden-shifting is once again crucial. When a robber attacks me and demands money, the misfortune is clearly mine. You the homeowner in *Emergency* aren't even on the scene; to the extent you are involved it is only because I involve you. If the hand of fate tosses my car into your house, on the other hand, the misfortune is as much yours as it is mine. I did not do anything to introduce you into the scene. This is what makes it true that in the one case I am burden-shifting and in the other I am not, since in the latter it is not purely *my* misfortune to shift—it is properly *our* misfortune.

Talk of whose misfortune something is may sound nebulous or subjective. But consider the malfunctioning car again. I knock on your door and announce that because my car isn't working you must give me yours, at least on alternate days. It isn't at all nebulous that this demand is outrageous, and the fact that it is *my* misfortune and not *yours* is what explains why. Alternatively, suppose that after a tornado my car is lodged in your house, and that I suggest I pay to repair my car and you pay to repair your home. This is not at all outrageous. You cannot angrily reply that I have somehow transferred my costs onto you. The point about burden-shifting, once again, makes sense of this. This isn't to say there aren't tricky gray areas. Ducking harm comes to mind. If I duck so as to let an oncoming fastball hit your face instead of mine, it's a little unclear whether I am transferring my misfortune to you, or merely avoiding a misfortune at your expense.[14] But my claim was that there's a clear moral difference between clearly shifting burdens and not doing so, not that it's always obvious whether something constitutes burden-shifting in the first place.

All of this emphasis on avoiding shifting of burdens raises the question of whether the threshold view doesn't involve a kind of bad faith: it promises to avoid exaggerating individual rights by cognizing overriding reasons, while sneaking absolute rights back in by insisting on restitution, compensation, and avoidance. It may not seem like much of a concession to announce, "You can ignore individuals' rights to their property, but only if you pay them back the market value." But two clarifications are in order. The first is that nothing I have said rules out permanently transferring misfortunes under some circumstances. This will be permissible when the overriding reasons are sufficiently strong as to allow for harming the innocent and yet no avoidance or compensation or restitution and the rest is possible. Perhaps it is permissible to kill the innocent who thus go uncompensated in some extreme circumstances, or to harm people in lesser ways even when it is logistically infeasible to compensate them. (But does the threshold for harm shift with the victim's degree of compensability?)

The second thing to consider is that forcing people to aid you or a third party against their will even *with* compensation is a serious concession. Forcing people to give up large amounts of money as they strenuously object would hardly be considered a light matter even if you could guarantee making them whole, simply because of the violation of autonomy involved. Avoiding preventable permanent transfers of burdens is the minimum we owe to others. If we *were* generally entitled to shift burdens onto others whenever we suffer a misfortune, then much of the morality of duty would be wiped out. For anyone who is worse off than he might be is in some sense suffering a misfortune, and anyone who is better off is someone onto whom such a misfortune might be shifted, for example by stealing his property or otherwise harming him.

At this point it is worth restating the classic libertarian argument in light of the considerations that have now emerged. We can do so without referring to rights at all, if we like, though this is mostly a matter of taste:

> Premise 1: Appropriating property we are entitled to without meeting the threshold and satisfying the residual obligations to property owners is wrong.
>
> Premise 2: The welfare state appropriates property we are entitled to without meeting the threshold and satisfying the residual obligations.
>
> Conclusion: The welfare state does and is wrong.

Thus far we have been focusing on the first premise, but now we can turn to the second, though I will continue to hold the question of what property we are entitled to in abeyance.

■ THRESHOLDS AND THE WELFARE STATE

It is natural to suppose that once we lower the bar against appropriating people's property to a threshold, we can then caper over it on our way to the welfare state. But this is only the beginning of the conversation; we now have to face the two questions we have flagged, concerning the threshold and the moral remainder we just identified. The more important of these are the residual obligations, but by way of softening up, let's start with the threshold. What standard needs to be met before we can harm people for the greater good?

Consider the threshold we assign to taking people's money without their consent in everyday life. How high a bar must we meet before we can take ("steal" we would normally say) $1,000 from someone over his urgent protests? *Emergency* was pulled out of a hat, so it does not establish anything about the lower bound at which the reasons against such transfers can be set aside, but I propose that, as it happens, *Emergency*-type cases in which life or limb is in imminent danger constitute roughly what the lower bound is in everyday moral thinking. This is very vague, of course, but that isn't important. What would be important would be if the lower bound were much lower—if we could take the $1,000 in an emergency, but could similarly do so if the beneficiary just really needed a car, or hadn't had a nice vacation in years, or desperately wanted to send her kids to a better school, or needed to pay for exploratory surgery for her niece. But our verdict seems to be against the moral permissibility of such acts. My evidence for this claim is simply that there seems to be widespread condemnation of people who break into other people's homes or otherwise take large amounts of people's money without their consent in the absence of imminent danger to life or limb, and that reactions aren't sensitive to sub-emergency rationales. Pleading that one wanted to get exploratory surgery for a niece would go over well with a jury and would stir public sympathy in a way that mere greed would not, but wouldn't, I claim, elicit nodding heads or murmurs of, "Well then it was all right." Third-person cases look just the same: there is little support for the overall permissibility of Robin Hood robberies. It is, in fact, crucial to the moral appeal of the actual Robin Hood narrative that the victims' wealth is seen as independently illegitimate and those Robin Hood redistributes to are seen as unfairly exploited; it is telling that we don't get popular Robin Hood stories in which those expropriated are hard-working middle-class types. A good Robin Hood narrative must begin, so to speak, by denying the second premise in the classic argument.

All of this suggests a rather high threshold. It isn't important to my purposes to get clear on exactly how high, only to insist that in turning away from absolute rights to a threshold view we aren't unduly cheapening what it means to be entitled to something. And anti-libertarians should embrace this view in general, since they are just as eager as libertarians to protect individuals from exploitation, with a difference perhaps in the class of victims they tend to worry about most. This brings us to our first problem for the welfare state as justified by overriding entitlements to property: it looks as if there will be trouble getting over the bar for many of the typical services provided by the welfare state. A partial list of services modern welfare states provide is as follows:

- Public safety
- Emergency healthcare
- Non-emergency healthcare
- Education
- Pensions
- Unemployment insurance
- Poverty assistance

The problem is that only the first two are likely to satisfy a high bar in an obvious way, and those aren't the ones that distinguish the welfare state from its minimalist rivals. If I see a house on fire, perhaps I may commandeer your possessions to rescue those still inside, and perhaps that explains why we may tax some in order to fund public safety services for the poor. But it is much less clear what the overriding reason is for taxing some to pay for other people's education or poverty abatement or retirement or even non-emergency healthcare. These services are morally comparable to a third-party imposing a $1,000 loss on you (or someone else who didn't consent) for the sake of improving someone else's position when life or limb is not at stake—just what we said earlier was generally impermissible.

There are two replies open to the anti-libertarian. One is methodological and focuses on my use of stories about breaking into people's houses to steal their stuff for redistributive purposes. We may deny that interpersonal moral norms apply to state institutions, or insist more broadly that we cannot infer from the impermissibility of a private act that the state is similarly constrained. These, of course, were the target of the earlier discussion of morality as a constraint on the state. As I argued there, it is implausible to announce that the state gets to violate us in ways individuals may not, merely because it is the expression of a collective acting through institutional intermediaries. I did acknowledge the phenomenon of superseding authority, however. I cannot make arrests and hold trials·in my living room when there are authorized institutions that already perform such functions. Bald appeals to breaking-and-entering may seem to fall into that category. There are in turn two responses to this. One is that in the kinds of cases at issue, it isn't credible that we are responding to that feature. For if we just vary the good that is accomplished by violating you for the sake of someone else's benefit while keeping the superseding element constant, we move from permitted to forbidden acts. Breaking into your car to drive myself to the hospital to save my life is perhaps all right; breaking into your car because mine broke down and I need to get to work is not. What we are responding to is the fact that the former scenario gets us over the threshold while the latter does not.

The more basic response, though, is to go back to first principles and consider cases where the state is more obviously absent. (In a sense, local emergencies are already such cases, since the government isn't able to respond in time.) We can consider remote mountain communities in which the sheriff drifts by once a week, or post-disaster scenarios in which the state is disabled. Extreme Hobbesians and other conventionalists about morality may deny there are any facts about what we may do in such scenarios. But consistent with the goal of pursuing exciting political conclusions from boring moral premises, I will assume that this is false. It is not the case that you can torture people for fun when social conventions break down and the state is absent. If you are in a war zone where all order has disintegrated, it is not the case that you get to pillage, however difficult it may prove to enforce such norms. It's the other way around: your moral duties require you to take whatever steps you can to impose a social order that reflects the antecedent impermissibility of murder and theft. Suppose, then, that I am considering breaking into your home in a remote frontier village or in a city after a devastating series of natural disasters, either to save my life or to hire a tutor to improve the education of my children. I claim that even with these elaborate steps taken to rule out concerns about a superseding authority, there are differences in justifiability. In such circumstances, I can morally justify breaking down your door to save my life (fulfilling my residual obligations later on), but not to tutor my kids, or to buy a car, or to hire a doctor to check out the limp I've developed. For these reasons, I am skeptical of a methodological response to thresholds.

Alternatively, friends of the welfare state might reply to doubts about making it over the threshold by insisting that all or nearly all of the welfare state services *do* fit into the life-or-limb category. For non-emergency healthcare, it's easy to see the outlines of this thought. Heart attack patients are in imminent danger, but diabetes patients are in an acute health crisis of their own, albeit one that works more slowly. Since the effects of slow-working or chronic diseases and other health conditions are ultimately threats to life or limb, we might try to pole-vault healthcare over the bar, and then try something similar for the others as well. Retirees without access to pension funds presumably face threats to life or limb eventually, so too for the poor, and those insufficiently educated to support themselves.

We can acknowledge that the life-or-limb principle is vague and cannot be sharply drawn. However, there are grounds for skepticism here as well. Part of the problem is empirical. The proposed link between routine healthcare and imminent physical danger is less obvious than one might suppose; what research there is seems mixed at best. In the few randomized controlled trials or natural experiments available, the connection between expensive subsidized healthcare and dangers to life or limb doesn't look especially strong, though we shouldn't put much weight on the sparse data.[15] What appears to happen is that those with serious illnesses are motivated to pay for treatment, while subsidizing healthcare often causes people to spend money on treatment, including large increases in emergency care, that doesn't do a great deal to improve objective health outcomes.

One study of a Medicaid lottery "didn't find any evidence that patients' physical health improved over the two years." Many Amish communities in the United States opt out of most of the healthcare system altogether and seem to be the healthier for it.[16] They also live quite differently, of course, but it is helpful to think of such cases to set some upper bounds on marginal effects. Some will find the absence of a strong connection between health and subsidized healthcare incredible, and perhaps further study will change our views. Students of incentive effects (or Molière) will be less surprised. And the other links are even thinner gruel. There is even less evidence that unemployment insurance or pensions respond to a life-or-limb emergency that would warrant breaking down a neighbor's door rather than seeking the next best option, be it seeking family support, or private charity, or improved planning prior to the need arising.

We can once again connect the abstract point with vivid moral illustration. Imagine I appear on your doorstep (in a remote location, if we like) demanding $1,000 to see a doctor about my limp, or to tide me over after being laid off, or to help in my retirement. You demur, saying you'd love to help, but that you have your own expenses just then—perhaps another time. I then threaten to harm you or imprison you if you do not contribute. The reply to the threshold-based objection that we are considering requires you just to accept this; you are required to fork over the $1,000, and I am warranted in making threats against you if you don't. But this is not easy to believe. Unless we doubt that there are serious reasons to respect what you claim as your property, or revert to a revisionist form of utilitarianism, it is hard to believe that I may threaten to imprison you or use force against you just because you prefer to spend your $1,000 sending your kids to college, say, instead of helping me out. This is the core of what I've been dubbing the New England basis of libertarianism: for me to make such demands of my neighbors seems to me outrageous, and we can feel this way without a lack of sympathy for those worse off, or indulging Randian visions of a society of parasites.

Since this is all just by way of softening up, I don't want to try to settle the matter—perhaps some of the traditional welfare-state services will eke their way past the threshold. But many, it appears, will not, and perhaps few or none. This represents a serious problem for those who think the welfare state is grounded in a rejection of the libertarian's inflated conception of individual rights.

■ RESIDUAL OBLIGATIONS AND THE WELFARE STATE

Next let us turn to the residual obligations of *restitution, compensation, sympathy, responsibility*, and *need*, the moral remainder. This is the crux of the matter. A welfare state justified in virtue of overriding reasons to promote the good of the beneficiaries incurs these residual obligations. Flouting them amounts to unfair burden-shifting. What would it look like actually to satisfy them? For starters, if I were the beneficiary of some emergency medical procedure that a third party compelled others to contribute to—say a state agency—I would be obligated to repay those charged for my benefit, possibly with some compensatory surcharge. If unable to pay, I would be required to pay in installments, with the agency keeping track of my income and tax records to ensure that my repayment were in line with my means. (To keep things simple, we can suppose that the agency doesn't actually repay anyone, but uses the incoming "repayment" funds to offset outgoing expenses; the net effect would be a lower tax bill for those paying.)

Moreover, in repaying, my attitude toward my fellow citizens ought to be one of gratitude for coming to my assistance, as opposed to viewing these services as entitlements due to me as a matter of citizenship. This may seem curious: by hypothesis, the services I received made it past the threshold, meaning that the wealth transfers involved were permissible, and since I am repaying, they won't even be net transfers in the long run, barring misfortune. Depending on how badly I needed aid, aiding may even have been obligatory on a third party. Why should I express gratitude for others fulfilling their duties? Consider the *Gallic shrug*—that supreme expression of indifference at someone else's misfortunes, while disclaiming all responsibility for rectifying them, frequently encountered in Parisian cafés. Why shouldn't I shrug my Gallic shrug at the rich complaining about their tax bill, and point out I merely got what I was entitled to, as would they in a similar situation?

This complaint would be apt if appropriate moral responses were a function solely of whether our acts are required or permissible. But there are all kinds of inappropriate moral responses even when what we have done is permissible or when what the other has done was required. If we are to meet for lunch and an urgent business affair obtrudes itself, I may be permitted to skip our lunch, but I shouldn't treat putting you out lightly. What makes a Gallic shrug a vice here is that beneath the outer layer of permissibility there remains an inner structure whereby you have been harmed for my sake, which ought to be a source of concern, leading to some appropriate expression of regret if I am a decent person. And the same is true in the case of welfare services. This is easy to ignore because of the opaque veils of state bureaucracy. But behind the faceless agency lie people who are harmed for the sake of benefiting me. Viewing these benefits as something I'm entitled to would be like viewing my putting you out at lunch as something I was entitled to. In one sense this is true, since by construction the act is permissible. But in another sense it misses the fundamental point that other people's interests have been thwarted for no other reason than to assist me. Parenting presents another kind of example. Parents are obligated to care for their children, but that doesn't make it less of a character flaw for children to take their parents' sacrifices for granted (as in the distinctive teenage shrug). The contrast here is with other services of the state that really are due to me merely as a citizen, for instance procedural justice in the administration of the law. A judge who points out to a defendant that being impartial and thorough in administering a complex case would be tedious for him *does* deserve a Gallic shrug.

Prospectively, there is a duty to take responsibility so as to avoid occasioning welfare services to begin with, and for the agency to impose a requirement of need. In everyday life we all have a duty to avoid doing things that result in imposing costly aid on our friends and relatives, say by not seeking employment and then becoming a liability to our children or friends. These duties aren't strict, of course. If dropping out of the labor force is due to illness or because of a dangerous work environment or after futile and protracted efforts, then our children may get stuck with the bill, but this should be our last resort, and again not something we view as an entitlement. And if we pursue welfare services as the product of overridden reasons against harm, then the same will be all the more true of the strangers whom we will be harming if we fail to do our best to avoid such services. (Our thought as we approach the dole should be, "I am prepared to compel others to support me since I have no reasonable alternative, and I would accept their using force to compel me to support them if our positions were reversed.") Failing to take responsibility in this way weakens my claim to impose costs on others; the state agency ought, within reason, to attempt to assess whether someone's claim to aid is due to negligence and perhaps prorate assistance to that extent.

Further, the agency administering the services must ensure that a genuine need is being satisfied. It is doubtful that mere inequality, for example, would get any weight. A third party can break into your house, perhaps, and take your $1,000 to give a beneficiary, but not in order to make a well-off beneficiary even better off, so as to close some inequality he suffers compared to his even richer neighbors. How "need" is defined will inevitably be hazy, but in any case it must be defined relative to our moral judgments about imposing large costs on the unwilling. And those judgments suggest that something like imminent danger to life or limb is the appropriate standard. Thinking otherwise is to conclude that it would be permissible for me to enter your house and take your $1,000 in order to benefit a perfectly healthy, well-fed individual over your strident objections. There may be other justifications for this—perhaps you weren't entitled to the money to begin with—but mere improvement to an already decent condition or mere redress of inequality doesn't appear equal to the task.

This, then, is roughly what welfare services would look like under a regime attempting to satisfy the residual obligations, and even this is available only in those cases that make it past the threshold.

There are two options at this point. One path would be to accept all of this, and to urge radical restructuring of the welfare state. This would let us deny premise 2, which says that the welfare state doesn't make it over the threshold, and observe the residual obligations when it taxes us for its services. Moderate libertarians who reject absolute rights should accept that such a restructuring may be possible and keep an open mind as to what the final outcome would be.

This would depend in part on complex normative questions I haven't tried to settle, concerning where exactly we fix the threshold against harm, but also on empirical questions like what kinds of services are required to save life or limb. It's easy to see that the result would be radically different from the status quo, but difficult to say exactly where things would end up.

The problem with this approach, though, is that the final result still doesn't sound much like a welfare state. The worry, in other words, is that premise 2 is close to a conceptual truth, since anything that observes both the threshold and the residual obligations won't resemble anything like what we commonly mean by "welfare state." The result of the relevant restructuring, while hard to predict in detail, would be a comparatively minimal state, and could probably be best described as a moderate libertarian state. For it wouldn't provide any welfare transfers except for dangers to life or limb, and even these would generally be treated as a kind of emergency loan rather than a grant. This result might sadden the very hardiest of libertarians, but to anyone else I suspect it would sound fairly close to the libertarian end of the spectrum.

But my suspicion is that friends of the welfare state will instead pursue the other option, and conclude that, supposing the arguments above to be right, there must be something else wrong with libertarianism. And here I think there can be common ground. The lesson is simply that the welfare state isn't based on overriding the threshold-rights of individuals, or equivalently, the problem with libertarianism is *not* that it involves an exaggeration of individual rights. Whatever else we might say about minimalist visions of the state, the issue is not one of exalting the moral powers of individuals in ways unfamiliar from day-to-day moral reasoning. Any robust view of the respect we owe individuals and their property has libertarian implications if it is combined with the assumption that people are by and large entitled to the wealth they have. As I stated at the outset, if it turns out that people by and large have little or no claim to what they have, then it will be much easier to explain why the state may coercively redistribute it.

■ INTUITIONS

We have already confronted one set of doubts about methods, involving the appeal to interpersonal morality in the context of the state. But we can conclude with another set of worries, this time about the more general use of intuitions in appealing to cases, such as the recurring $1,000 vignettes. Many philosophers have raised doubts about appeals to case-intuitions, sometimes because people disagree in their intuitive reactions, or because they are parochial (culture- or gender-specific, say), or because they reflect cognitive biases and so are unreliable.[17] For example, if we reflect on commandeering a neighbor's car when our own breaks down and then attempt to infer something about morality as a constraint from our reaction to such a case, we might worry that our thinking about emergencies is colored by all kinds of distorting influences shaped both by how we've evolved to respond to short-term crises and by a culture of sedentary mass-society permitting the accumulation of personal property. We might wonder whether we can rely on such intuitive reactions to cases.

However, this way of putting things seems to me misconceived. The situation is this: we are trying to determine how to organize the state in regard to distributive justice, and we wish to do so in a way that respects our fundamental moral convictions. In making an argument for a particular approach to distribution, then, naturally we must explore what those moral convictions are and how they bear on distributive questions. The purpose of the vignettes is not to demonstrate by appeal to intuition what the moral facts are—I have made no such appeal.[18] The idea is rather to stimulate reflection on what we believe and to express clearly my own assumptions in these matters. It's of course easy to envision a culture in which it is considered respectable to use violence to commandeer one's neighbor's car to get to work; for that matter, we all know how Genghis Khan felt about raping and pillaging. (It's diverting to imagine Genghis in a psychology lab responding to delicate probings of his moral intuitions in order to deliver the shocking result that people's moral codes vary, resulting in many highly cited research papers.) But that doesn't show anything about what *we* are prepared to accept as a premise for reasoning and action. My ambition in thinking about such cases is to bring out what we must accept in running our polity in a certain way, and to show what implications my and hopefully many readers' moral convictions have. Genghis Khan and readers with other (nicer!) moral persuasions will differ from time to time, and I don't pretend that they should be swayed by my or anyone else's opinion about one-off cases, as long as we're all clear on the ramifications.

"All the worse for the argument," it may be said. "Then things just come down to differences in opinion about cases." This isn't right either, though. The cases are meant to illustrate broader attitudes about morality, and how we may treat others, and what kind of treatment we are prepared to accept. In order to reject the argument as I have presented it thus far, one needs to do more than just have different views of some cases. One needs to accept, more broadly, that it's fine for people to exploit you for their benefit without meeting a high bar, or that the state is unconstrained by interpersonal moral norms, or something similarly general. Nor is it the case that these kinds of principles in turn rest on nothing but blank intuitions for which there is no further argument. On the contrary, we've seen that there are all kinds of arguments that may be given against some of them. It is certainly true that the appeals made above won't seem persuasive to utilitarians or others fundamentally out of sympathy with the picture of moral thresholds against harm, but not because of some standoff of intuitions. In order not to seem disingenuous, let me concede that it may well be that some moral differences are beyond argument. If anthropophagic space-aliens beam down to eat us, perhaps arguments won't persuade them, even if they turn out to be supremely rational. It would be bizarre if it were otherwise, since there are propositions beyond argument in all domains—maybe we're brains in vats connected to a computer simulation, perhaps the world was created five minutes ago with false impressions of antiquity, and Sextus Empiricus questioned logical inference itself. But none of this shows that the disagreements between libertarians and others need come down to a standoff of intuitions.

A variation on these doubts is subtler. I've been banging my fist on the table with appeals to our everyday moral beliefs in order to attack what might be characterized as our everyday political beliefs. We have some firm convictions about when you can lay hold of your neighbor's TV, but don't we also have convictions about the welfare state? In particular, most people think it is pretty reasonable to win elections and then to exercise majority control to build up a welfare state that combats poverty and inequality through wealth transfers. So why should we be more impressed by the moral convictions I emphasize than the political convictions pointing the other way? Well, perhaps we shouldn't be. The point the libertarian is making is ultimately just that there is a *conflict* between our ordinary moral beliefs and the welfarism that people take for granted now. The libertarian is not denying that we could resolve this conflict in favor of the welfare state, for instance by embracing revisionist utilitarianism. Compare a vegetarian argument against eating factory-farmed meat. Why can't we rebut this by invoking our antecedent conviction that eating cheeseburgers is no great crime? The answer is that we can. It's just that we must then give up some other belief about factory farms, or the moral significance of animals, or the like. What we can't do is pretend there is no conflict, supposing the vegetarian's logic is valid. One way of putting the libertarian point, then, is that we face a choice between our moral beliefs about the appropriate use of threats and violence against our neighbors on the one hand, and beliefs about how to address problems like inequality on the other. Libertarians find it easier to believe that in the end we need to address those problems by reason and persuasion than that we should abandon moral norms about when it's permissible to use force against our neighbors. And we should remember that libertarians can *agree* that we should help the worse off, that poverty is a scandal, and so on. None of that is in dispute. What is in dispute is whether the right *way* of addressing such problems is by using force against our neighbors.

4 Property as a Moral Phenomenon

If libertarianism doesn't rest on absurd views of individual rights, it might equally be suspected to rest on a dubious theory of property. The classic libertarian argument assumes that we are generally entitled to our possessions, but the philosophical theory of property is a notorious quagmire. On the one hand, apart from the most radical among us, we feel broadly entitled to most of the goods we have. "Property is theft!" declares Proudhon, but most of us don't believe him; Rousseau declares that property is founded on the "simplicity" of those duped into acknowledging its existence, but this too seems overwrought.[1] We accept that we may owe part or even much of our property to various other parties, but our monthly paycheck does not for the most part look like the ill-gotten gains of a thief who has no claim to the money in the first place. You and I are not on the same footing when it comes to your bank account, your laptop, your steak knives. But on the other hand, accounts that attempt to specify in detail how we come to have a distinctively *moral* claim to private property tend to inspire incredulity. The most prominent family of such accounts is broadly Lockean, and the incredulity they inspire is legendary.[2] Three problems are especially acute.

First, Lockeans attempt to provide a theory of the initial acquisition of property, which can seem to involve bewildering metaphysics. Lockeans often speak of "mixing" their labor with objects, almost as if in so doing the objects became a part of us, but these mereological stories look quite opaque. In fact, even their improved surrogates, drawing on self-ownership and the thought that ownership of self passes on to objects through labor look not a little dusky. Second, if we're to rest moral weight on initial acquisition, we need to believe that such acquisitions were fair, that they didn't amount to an underhanded land-grab. But the scene of initial acquisition is typically the hazy past (setting aside contemporary Mars colonies), and a sober view of history doesn't suggest that initial acquisition involved much fair play. And third, after the initial acquisition there must follow an account of the legitimate transfer of what is initially acquired, and the history of the world once again fails to inspire much confidence in the moral purity of such transfers. If the "transfer" of property has largely consisted of plunder and pillage, what could such an account contribute to the justification of our claim to our monthly paychecks?

I will sketch a resolution to these problems over the next few chapters by appealing to two important truths, one normative, one partly empirical. The normative truth is that property rests on claims to control certain physical or intangible assets, claims that aren't metaphysical but moral in nature. Contrary to views on both the left and the right, property is not a social convention or function of laws we can adjust willy-nilly so as to promote the social good. There are actions that agents can perform that endow them with moral claims to exercise control over goods, and that is what constitutes ownership. Moreover, the famous mixing of labor Lockeans talk about has been widely misunderstood by Lockeans themselves. Labor, it turns out, is just one among many morally relevant factors; Locke himself focused on a special case that has tended to artificially narrow the scope of discussion ever since. The claims to property arise from any one of several lower-level facts that can strengthen or weaken our claims in concert with one another. These moral claims to our property are not absolute, but they are often strong enough to constrain the state up to some high threshold. The empirical truth that I map out is that modern economic value is overwhelmingly grounded in services people have recently provided for others, not in physical goods or even in the transformation of those physical goods through manufacturing. For this reason, the actual history of acquisition and transfer of property in the distant past is largely irrelevant. We cannot reject the libertarian view because of complaints about the past. The upshot, eventually, is that the libertarian assumption that we are generally entitled to our property is sustained.

It is important to keep this thumbnail sketch in mind in this chapter, since the broad moral theory of property that I offer lays out criteria for the just acquisition and transfer of property, which may give the impression that I am following the standard Lockean suggestion that all current property claims are genetically rooted in past property claims along with appropriate transfers. But although this is true in some cases, I will be stressing a different approach. Although I do believe a vaguely Lockean account of acquisition and transfer is right and sometimes applies, I offer that account mostly for the sake of illumination and completeness, not because I believe that our claim to our weekly paychecks or our homes rests on optimistic assumptions about the initial acquisition in the Garden of Eden. In most cases, one's claim to the paycheck rests on a contractual exchange of services, not anything to do with the distribution of land or other natural resources.

▪ **LABOR AND ENTITLEMENT**

Claiming something as our private property means asserting control over it in various ways. The extent of that control is murky to be sure. It generally includes claiming a title to locate something, use it, modify it, transfer it, and destroy it, but the full list of the "incidents" of property is elusive, as is what if anything unites the list, especially when we look to the law.[3] In fact, it could be that the *legal* concept of property disintegrates into a multitude of disparate notions tracking various social concerns of ours (a heterogeneous "bundle"), but that doesn't show there isn't a core *moral* notion of property hinging on control. Children shout and fight over *who gets to decide what happens* to some disputed toy, and it is this kind of ordinary, everyday case we should focus on, rather than the undoubtedly labyrinthine distinctions encoded in property and contract law. The philosophical problem of property concerns the moral basis of this claim to control, in its various manifestations. For in asserting control over some asset, we are denying the correlative claims of others. In asserting the right to locate my car in my garage, I am denying your right to locate it in yours; in asserting the right to use my car how and when I please today, I am denying your right to do so. Making something my property means making it subject to my will in certain ways. The deep problem thus isn't to explain what all I am permitted to do with some possession, but to explain how I am able to *exclude you* from exercising your will in equivalent ways. As Allan Gibbard puts it, "The issue is not the moral permissibility of a physical act, called appropriation: in the case of land, for instance, the issue is not whether it is morally permissible to clear land, but the moral status of cleared land," i.e., what makes it the case that others are subsequently excluded from exercising control over that land.[4]

The problem here is not the general one of explaining how we could possibly alter the rights of others to their disadvantage without their consent, as has been suggested.[5] There are all kinds of things we do that alter people's permissions without their consent. I may occupy a certain volume of space in a public park other things equal, but not if you get there first and I cannot displace you without wrongdoing. Your legitimate actions canceled my right to occupy those particular coordinates at that particular time. (You didn't have to seek my permission to walk your dog in the park and sit down for a moment.) We can, if we wish, insist that my right to occupy that space was always circumscribed and contained implicit exceptions, but we can say that in the case of property as well. The important thing is that other people can sometimes change what we are allowed to do without our having a say-so. The problem we face is rather the more specific one of explaining how exactly it is that *property* claims manage to alter what others can do so as to exclude them from various forms of control.

In dealing with this fundamental issue, Locke himself stressed that it was the mixture of labor that made something yours and only yours:

> Though the earth and all inferior creatures be common to all men, yet every man has a property in his own person. . . . Whatsoever then he removes out of the state that nature hath provided and left it in, he hath mixed his labor with and joined to it something that is his own, and thereby makes it his property.[6]

On first hearing, this can sound almost metaphysical, as if the point were that, as transplanted bone marrow becomes yours in virtue of becoming a part of you, so land becomes yours by becoming an extension of you. But of course this is nonsense; your wallet isn't literally a part of you. Property is a moral and legal category, not a metaphysical category—mereology is the wrong place to look to make sense of ownership. An account in the spirit of Locke should stress that labor has a distinctive *moral* significance. On one view, the key is self-ownership, a theme Locke himself stresses in the passage above. The story might run: we own ourselves; we own our labor derivatively; and when that labor is mixed with external objects we win a moral claim to them. The trouble with this, however, is that it does nothing at all to explain the crucial connection between labor and a moral claim to an object. "Why," as Nozick once asked, "isn't mixing what I own with what I don't a way of losing what I own rather than a way of gaining what I don't?"[7] The chain starting with self-ownership terminates in the metaphor of *mixing*, which either takes us back to wrongheaded metaphysics or else needs to appeal to some other moral notion.

One obvious candidate for explaining the moral connection between labor and object is *desert*. When you work all season long planting and harvesting, you seem deserving of your harvest in a way that I, who lazed about watching, do not. However, desert is too strong of a moral concept to employ; the related but weaker concept of *entitlement* is better.[8] The difference is that desert implies that it is morally better for you to have something because of the moral character of what you have done and the choices you have made. You deserve the harvest because you are the one who worked so hard to get it. This makes desert vulnerable to luck, since luck destroys the claim to have gotten something in virtue of your own actions and choices. This is why we laugh at the trust-fund heir who claims to deserve what he has. But often we *do* have a claim to something in virtue of our labor, despite luck having played a prominent role. Add to our story a third character who also worked hard but was unlucky with her crops and got nothing. Since the difference in outcome for her and the harvester is a function of luck, it cannot be a matter of desert. And yet we may well judge that you are nevertheless *entitled* to the crop; you may be permitted to resist the unlucky farmer's attempts to take your food. And of course the market is full of such desert-destroying luck. I slave over my clothing line for years, while you make yours as an afterthought and with little effort, but yours makes you rich because of a random celebrity endorsement while I go broke. This doesn't mean I can take your money. Entitlement expresses the fact that some act or a certain status can confer on us a moral claim to something even if the universe as a whole doesn't become a better place as a result of us exercising such a claim (as when we are undeserving). Consider, then, the suggestion that certain kinds of labor entitle you to unowned goods you create or modify, no doubt with many other conditions needing to be met.

It's worth noting that on anything like this view we can ignore self-ownership or even deny it. Suppose for argument's sake that self-ownership is conceptually incoherent because we lack full ownership over our selves (argument: we can't sell ourselves into slavery). There is nothing about the claim that working all day collecting seashells entitles you to those seashells that depends on self-ownership. The idea behind the entitlement theory isn't to transmit the ownership in self down through one's fingertips into the external objects; it's to press the independent moral truth that (under the right conditions) a certain thing we do or a status we have gives us a moral claim, and this could be so even if the concept of self-ownership were incoherent. It might be wondered how things like collecting seashells could generate such a claim if *not* in virtue of transmitting some more primitive ownership of self. But this is to conceive of ownership as a kind of occult substance, to revert one again to a metaphysical conception of property. Keeping in view its moral character, there is simply no reason to doubt that various actions of mine might generate a moral claim to something, any more than my bad deeds might (non-derivatively) make it true that I deserve a certain kind of treatment. So entitlement doesn't require self-ownership, but on the other hand, as we noted earlier, the self-ownership story *does* require something like entitlement or desert if it's to avoid implicit appeal to the metaphysics of parthood. This makes appeals to self-ownership for purposes of justifying private property otiose. Lockeans defending private property should ignore self-ownership, and attacks on Lockean or libertarian claims resting on attacking self-ownership are shooting in the wrong direction.[9]

■ THE BROAD MORAL THEORY OF PROPERTY

Moral theories of property have tended to focus narrowly on labor for the simple reason that this is what Locke emphasized. This kind of *narrow* moral theory of property is an improvement on metaphysical theories, but we should reject any such narrow theory all the same. The initial problem isn't with the substance of such accounts but with their unmotivated narrowness. In explaining this, it is useful to compare Locke's theory of personal identity, according to which what makes it true that Emily and Lisa are the same person at different times is that Lisa carries Emily's memories.[10] Here, too, there are substantive doubts—perhaps the memory criterion is circular since something won't count as Lisa's memories of what Emily did unless they are the same person. But supposing we are in the market for a psychological theory of personal identity, the real objection is that the memory criterion is implausibly narrow. Why shouldn't intentions, beliefs, and other mental states count toward establishing personal identity as well?[11] It's unclear why Emily should think she will continue as Lisa if her memories will survive but every other item in her mental inventory will change radically. If she acquires a completely different personality (one unrecognizable to anyone around her), ceases to love her children, finds a new spouse, switches careers, and forms new plans, insisting on her continuity looks strained, at least from within a psychological framework. And in the other direction, it may seem overblown to call those who lose their memories but retain everything else new people, as opposed to the same people suffering from a terrible injury. The analogy, then, is that just as memory may seem too narrow to be a viable criterion of personal identity, so we should worry that labor is too narrow to perform its role in establishing ownership.[12]

Once we fully grasp that property is a moral category rooted in having a legitimate claim to controlling some asset, it should strike us both that there are many other routes to such a claim besides labor, and that such claims are a matter of degree, meaning that there are many ways to strengthen or weaken such a claim even within a category like labor. To start with, consider *discovery, creation, priority*, and *adding value* as phenomena strengthening moral claims to control. It's important to stress that the idea here is not that these are supposed to be individually sufficient conditions for absolute control under any and all circumstances. Discovering a planet through your telescope doesn't make it yours. The idea is rather that these kinds of factors can, under the right circumstances, *strengthen* your moral claim to an asset, and that sometimes such claims will be strong enough to exclude others in various ways. Obviously a great deal would need to be said in particular cases to conclusively settle the disposition of some contested object.

Some simple illustrations bring out the moral force of these factors, starting with discovery. Little Emily finds a pretty seashell in a place where there are thousands of shells free to the public, and little Mark wants it; he doesn't see any others quite the same lying around. Emily doesn't exercise any non-trivial labor in picking it up, but her claim is a bit stronger in virtue of being the one to discover it. (Imagine seeing this, and then seeing Mark attempting to take the shell from Emily and being asked to arbitrate who gets to keep it.) Less trivially, a researcher on vacation on the high seas dips her beaker in the water and fortuitously discovers a scientifically fascinating specimen. Her envious rival demands she hand it over or at least flip a coin for rights to the first examination and publication; she demurs. In cases like this, discovery carries some moral weight toward excluding others in certain ways, though of course more would need to be said to establish exactly how far-reaching such control was in the particular case.[13] Creation, too, has a moral significance apart from labor, as when Mark uses his remote control vehicle via laborless thumb-movements to construct a sandcastle Emily wishes to rearrange while Mark resists. Or again, without any effort at all a grownup Emily creates a gorgeous impressionistic sketch with her pen that others offer to pay her lots of money for, and Mark suggests they flip a coin for ownership of the drawing she just created. Emphasizing the labor involved seems once again misplaced. Priority, in turn, directs our attention to the simple fact of prior control, which can sometimes matter. Denying this would imply that the aboriginal island natives who have inhabited their land for a thousand generations have no more claim to their land (which we can imagine uncleared but supporting a simple hunter-gatherer system) than the would-be settlers who show up off the coast one day, proposing a coin flip for control of their land. This seems deeply unfair. The prior inhabitants have built up reasonable expectations about their continued livelihoods there is at least some reason to respect.

And within the category of labor, factors such as how much value we add can amplify or attenuate our claim. Laboring on some land on a deserted island by uselessly pounding the dirt doesn't obviously confer much of a claim against anyone else who washes up and wishes to plant some vegetables, even if pounding the dirt is exhausting.[14] By contrast, constructing an elaborate system of irrigation that produces food might well support a moral claim against someone else who wished to appropriate this now-valuable land, at least under the right conditions. (Picture another castaway showing up and announcing that there should be a coin toss for the laboriously devised irrigation system, since he would rather avoid doing the work himself.) We might even wonder whether labor in itself has *any* moral weight—certainly working ten times harder to produce something doesn't give you ten times more of a claim to it than those who happen to be more efficient and thus use less labor. This would be pushing the point too far, however, since the fact that someone worked incredibly hard at creating or discovering something might engage our sense of merit or entitlement and at least intensify claims to control.

Still other moral factors are ones that Locke himself pointed out, but seems to have conceived of as minor codicils. One is that ownership is limited by the ability to make use of something, a *no waste* factor we must consider. Clearing land and erecting a fence around it doesn't produce a very strong claim if you can't make use of it, so that the produce you grow on the land just ends up rotting and others could eat it, Locke suggests. (Later, though, he notes that money tends to circumscribe the application of this condition rather dramatically.) More famously, Locke adds "the proviso"—the claim that what we appropriate must leave others with *enough and as good* left over, so that they are not harmed by our ownership, which we might think of as another fairness-related factor to consider.[15] But it is a mistake to see these as mere codicils or background conditions. Instead, they are simply yet more factors that strengthen or weaken our moral claim to control, every bit on par with the others we've considered.

There is no reason to elevate labor to some special status not enjoyed by these various other moral considerations. After all, reflection shows that these other factors will often dominate labor, as when hard work doesn't turn out to create or add value to anything, or when the hard work was applied under unfair conditions (say, when others didn't have the chance they should have to benefit from applying their own labor). And once labor is knocked off its pedestal, I believe, many morally relevant factors will suggest themselves. So far I've suggested as candidates *discovery, creation, priority, adding value, labor, no waste,* and the *proviso,* but no doubt many others could be added to this list. A useful heuristic is to imagine parties before a neutral arbitration panel being asked to submit non-question-begging considerations favoring moral claims to control. ("But it's *mine!*" would be the tempting but question-begging response we need to avoid.)

It can seem puzzling that Locke would have focused so much on labor if there are all these other categories that matter, but this is easily explained. First, as I've pointed out, Locke didn't really ignore (all) the other factors so much as he exaggerated the importance of labor and treated the proviso as a proviso instead of a symmetric, independent consideration. But there's also the simple historical point that at the time Locke wrote, economic value was overwhelmingly agricultural, and agricultural value was largely a function of labor—a point that will occupy us in a later chapter. Which kinds of moral considerations will be most important is highly context dependent; in our own society creation and discovery have much greater relative importance. Locke focused on labor because he happened to live in a time and place when labor dominated value, and Lockeans and their critics have simply followed him. Yet in doing so they have overlooked a central resource for explaining private property as a moral phenomenon, which *is* a bit puzzling. Few writers show any interest in the basic moral "data" provided by the ubiquitous, everyday-life cases I have stressed, in which people press moralized claims to control and exclude. This, too, is a testament to the influence of Locke, and more generally to the path-dependent nature of intellectual history. (Aristotle mumbled something about friendship, and so philosophers have discussed friendship but until recently ignored marriage.)

The broad moral theory of property conceives of property as defined by there being a morally justified claim to control once the full gamut of factors is considered and worked through. I won't attempt either to offer an exhaustive list of such factors or to detail how such considerations interact and net-out, except to caution against a simplistic balance-of-reasons approach. Some of these considerations undermine the force of the others—priority, for instance, may undermine later claims issuing from creation or value-added, a contractual relationship may undermine claims to goods a worker creates. This blocks any simple monotonic approach whereby some positive weight is assigned to each item on the list and the outcome is determined just by summing up. I also won't try to say what all the items on the list have in common; it wouldn't surprise me if there were simply a wide range of independent factors that can support someone's claim to control. Instead of entering into such intricacies, we must turn to fundamental problems with the very idea of property as a moral phenomenon.

∎ FACTORS THAT COUNT TOWARD PROPERTY

Exactly which kinds of moral considerations count toward determining who has a claim to controlling an asset? In terms of our arbitration-panel heuristic, which kinds of considerations should be ruled in or out of bounds? One proposal is to allow just any morally significant consideration to play a role. This would have dramatic implications. Suppose that *utility* or *need* or *promoting objective value* or *equality* or other consequential factors were to factor in determining moral control over objects.[16] This would eliminate many claims to private property since people's needs or possible improvements in utility or objective value would often seem to dominate other kinds of claims, at least if naively ranked by impersonal importance. (Creating something seems morally significant, but someone else's going hungry often seems much more so in the grand scheme of things.) Of course, this will strike many as an attractive and indeed intuitive result, especially if we are suspicious that factoring in labor but excluding need looks like a ploy to advance the interests of certain groups against those of others. People who care about the worst off might find such an arrangement especially perverse and correspondingly welcome a theory of property that gives something like need a role.

This "all-in" approach to property can be bolstered by pointing out that the alternative may look a little pyrrhic. If we rule out considerations like utility or need, we will be forced to recognize them later anyway once it comes to determining what one ought to *do* with one's property. To illustrate, Thomas Aquinas claimed that in extreme emergencies property reverts to the common pool, and so we may sometimes "steal" the grain we need to eat. Nozick seems to say something similar about our ownership of the only waterhole in a desert if everyone else's hole dries up.[17] These are examples of letting something like utility or need entering into determination of property, in Nozick's case even retroactively. But if we rule out these considerations, we presumably will still believe that those who have precious grain during a civil war are obligated to help those starving, and that the water-owner can't let everyone else die of thirst. So the same moral considerations get a grip on us one way or another. Property plus moral reasons to act in certain ways with our property sounds like a complicated way of denying ownership or at least absolute ownership, which is what the effect would be of including all relevant moral considerations in the determination of property in the first place. So why does it matter whether we grant someone ownership and proceed to insist that there are moral reasons to exercise ownership in certain ways, rather than denying ownership in the first place by allowing the relevant moral considerations to enter in straightaway?

There are two reasons, one superficial, one deep. The superficial reason for narrowing the scope of moral considerations determining ownership is that otherwise we get very strange implications for what we own and how ownership changes. On the all-in view, the television in your living room or the art that you've created may become *mine* just because I need it more, or would feel happier having it, or would create a better world possessing it, or because I gambled away my money and became unequal to you. This would be so if the latter considerations turned out to be morally important enough. Of course, some deny such things *are* morally important, but the point is that the all-in view makes what we own contingent on what seem to us facts that are quite irrelevant to property. The money in your bank account doesn't turn out to be mine just because I was recently fired and so I need it slightly more. The threat here isn't just that Lockeans and especially libertarians would frown on such a result; it's that this would completely destroy the intuitive notion of private property. Ownership that vanishes with the fluctuating needs or preferences of those around you isn't ownership in anything like the normal sense at all. Perhaps private property deserves to disappear, but this should be accomplished by a successful revolution, not by the philosopher's wand.

Another way of making the superficial point is to say that we normally maintain a firm grip on the distinction between private property and reasons for *using* that property in certain ways. Perhaps you should give your bagel to a homeless person, but that doesn't make the bagel in your hand *his* bagel. Suppose that you're considering eating it yourself, giving it to your brother, or giving it to the homeless man, that the moral reasons favor giving it to the homeless man, and that you give it to your brother. It would be absurd to claim that the bagel is now stolen property or ill-gotten gains, to call the police, or demand compensation. Or again, if Nietzsche is right about what makes the world a better place, perhaps you ought to give Wagner lots of money to finance his grandiose operas (except for *Parsifal*), but even granting Nietzsche a great deal, that doesn't make your money Wagner's. Failing to distinguish properly between which kinds of moral considerations should and shouldn't feature in determining control, in other words, would collapse the reasons for *doing* certain things with property into the moral fact of property itself.

The deeper point to notice is that *property* is a deontic concept, like *liability* or *desert*, and that unlike concepts like *utility* or *equality*, these are focused on the past. Suppose we announce that whether Emily *deserves* a raise should reflect whether the world would be a better place in the future if we give her a raise. ("After all, what does it matter whether we factor in those future-directed moral factors into *desert* rather than confronting them afterward?") This produces the result that whether or not Emily deserves a raise for her work will depend on other people's wants and needs, which distorts the basic idea of *desert*, just as in the examples involving *property*, and for the same reason: deontic concepts like *property* or *desert* are shaped so as to reflect the morally relevant history of the world, not just the general desirability of outcomes. The fundamental idea, I believe, is that certain things that we have done confer on us a presumption or entitlement to be treated in certain ways, and against various forms of interference by others. That is why working hard confers desert on Emily which other people's needs don't cancel, and similarly for *property*. The historical nature of deontic concepts reflects the moral conviction that what we have done, achieved, or become matters morally and needs to be registered in a special way.

A skeptic might push harder. What's curious isn't just the backward-looking nature of concepts like *property* and *desert*, it's the combination of historicity and the entitlements that these concepts are associated with. At the very least, there's a presumption in favor of getting what you deserve or what is just, or controlling what you own. And this combination represents a decision to let past actions exercise a peculiar moral power over present and future outcomes. We might wonder whether it represents more than a conservative tendency to bias our actions toward the past and against radical change in the future. Why else do actions in the past get us various rights and entitlements, while the needs of the present or welfare of the future get relegated to a lesser status, forced to overcome the presumptions of desert, justice, property, and the rest? Here, though, we push up against questions beyond the scope of a discussion of property, important though they are. In the end, these are questions about the nature of morality itself and of whether the deontic structure of common-sense morality is just a mistake. Notice, though, that critics of property pursuing this line commit themselves to very far-reaching views about morality. Such a political philosophy would be based on radical rather than boring moral assumptions.

■ ACQUISITION BY TRANSFER

The vast majority of our property is not initially acquired but transferred to us, usually by commercial or contractual exchange, or by gift or bequest. My home, my paintings, my subwoofer, and the contents of my bank account were all transferred to me by others. Property cannot be a moral phenomenon unless property transfer can have a moral basis. For most people in the modern era, initial acquisition is trivial compared to transfer in accounting for their property. Suppose, then, that I am entitled to my banana and you to your bread and that we wish to trade. On the moral theory of property, what must be true after the trade is that we are entitled to exclude third parties from control over the goods we have acquired. But after the trade I cannot exclude third parties by claiming that I made the bread or contributed anything of value to the production process. Moral accounts of property thus face the problem of explaining the source of moral reasons for respecting property after transfers have destroyed the moral grounds for respecting initial acquisition.

The obvious solution is that initial acquisition confers on owners rights of transfer, and that after the exchange the new owner simply inherits the rights to control from the initial owner. But while this is straightforward enough for a legal account of property, it's much less clear what the analogous moral reasoning would be. With appropriate social institutions, legal rights can be transferred at the stroke of a pen or by uttering some phrases. But moral entitlements generally cannot be transferred by fiat. There is nothing in the world I can do to make my child deserve what I deserve without my child doing deserving things. If you promise to meet me for dinner I cannot transfer the obligation to someone else who wants to have dinner with you. So how can I transfer moral entitlement to control over an asset to someone else? Equivalently, how does the third party wrong me, what duty does he violate, if he insists on flipping a coin for the bread?

The answer, I believe, lies in abandoning the model of property transfer as a transfer of entitlements.[18] Although goods may literally be transferred, what entitles the recipient to the asset isn't some sort of moral transference, but rather the claim he has against others to respect his liberty of exchange. Third parties have moral reasons to respect legitimate exchanges (including gifts and bequests as limit cases) that people enter into of their own accord. The sources of these moral reasons map onto the roles the parties play in the exchange. On the one hand, we have reason to respect the right of the parties qua givers to control what happens to their assets, and interfering with a legitimate exchange (even after the fact) flouts that reason. Rights to control may not be unlimited, but in general the moral title to control an asset gives us reason to recognize a permission to pass it on to someone else. Denying this right while affirming other mundane forms of control like permission to let other people make use of the asset would be extremely puzzling; giving something to someone else is just the same as "keeping" it but irrevocably promising to let someone else do whatever the person wants with it. The right to give is a logical consequence of other rights to control, setting aside the empty metaphysics of who "really" owns the good.

And on the other hand, we have reason to respect the traders' acts qua recipients, since they have exercised their liberty in what are generally permissible ways. Third parties don't have any claim of their own on the asset received in exchange since it isn't in the common pool anymore, once the giver has exercised his legitimate powers to permit the recipient to assume control. Other things equal, attempting to usurp that control would simply harm the recipient without justification. Moreover, denying these moral reasons to control after the exchange (say, by insisting we flip a coin for the transferred asset) would imply that swapping goods destroys both parties' claims to them. Obviously this would be unfortunate as a matter of institutional incentive structures since all exchange would immediately cease if people took such principles seriously, but the real point is that this is implausible morally speaking. Swapping my banana for your bread isn't a way of both of us losing our claim to either. The existence of reasons to recognize legitimate exchange explains why. Of course, sometimes there are other reasons at play as well; often the recipient has earned and therefore *deserves* the asset, as when someone works hard for a paycheck. But desert is by no means necessary; plenty of exchanges produce gains for traders who don't particularly merit or deserve those gains, but that doesn't mean their assets revert to the common pool.

Property can be transferred, then, even if moral rights cannot, since the parties to an exchange have moral claims to control over property they can assert against third parties. But nothing said so far suggests these claims are absolute. In fact, contrary to the usual Lockean way of thinking about property, I don't think there is any reason to draw a sharp distinction between transfer and the reasons favoring rights of control we considered above. Legitimate transfer should be viewed as just another item on the list of things that *strengthen* a claim to control, alongside creation and the rest. We could then abandon the model of justifying initial acquisition by the special activity of labor, and saying that all subsequent transfers simply inherit moral status from the Garden of Eden. If nothing else, this would counteract the tendency to think that what really justifies a property claim nowadays for a Lockean must be some primordial event at the dawn of time, as if the moral claim I have on my house depends on what happened 10,000 years ago. This would also force us to acknowledge that these various grounds of control can conflict in interesting and hard-to-resolve ways, as when it is discovered belatedly that some piece of land was transferred to someone, but long ago, and in the meantime others have improved it.[19]

Against this, it might be objected that transfer doesn't deserve independent moral weight, that it always inherits whatever moral force it has from prior acquisition. Transferring stolen goods a few times doesn't improve someone's claim to them just in virtue of their having been transferred. That is true, but what's under discussion is *legitimate* transfer, so the initial transfer of stolen goods won't count toward justifying anyone's claim. This in turn might sound like conceding the point since the same will be true for all future transfers, but that needn't be so. Legitimacy in this context is complicated. Suppose that after 500 transfers, those entitled to the stolen goods have died and all their heirs are either extinct or unknown, and that the current possessors have no knowledge of the initial theft and wouldn't have engaged in the transfer if they had believed it to be illegitimate. (I take something like this to be the position that nearly all homeowners in fact are in.) It's unclear why such a transfer should count as illegitimate, and doing so would render almost all land transfers on earth illegitimate forever, which is absurd. A principled solution would be this: a legitimate transfer requires that the giver has moral claim to control an asset, which entails that the asset isn't owed to anyone else as restitution or compensation. In the scenario described, there will at the very least be a priority-claim to the property, and by construction nothing is owed anyone else. In such a case it seems perfectly reasonable to claim that the transfer (from the previous owner of your home, say) was legitimate and to put that transfer forward as a reason toward strengthening your moral claim to control, without denying that the initial acquisition was unjust and that early transfers were impermissible.

Perhaps this approach to transfer need not validate all of its manifestations. There is reason to respect your liberty to transfer money you have earned to your heirs by bequest. However, this is the first link in a chain that may eventually fail to command much respect. After 50 generations, perhaps we arrive at the idle trust fund heir with no more than a tenuous moral connection to the person who initiated the chain. Just now I argued that transfers that started out illegitimate can become legitimate, as when there is no longer anyone to compensate for wrongdoing in the remote past—is the reverse possible as well? Do we reach a point when this wealth passing through history comes to resemble a natural resource that certain people just happen to get their hands on through the luck of the family tree, with no deep claim on it? Can the rest of us demand our cut? I confess I am uncertain. Even if we accept the natural resource analogy, I'm not sure what my claim would be on the valuable meteorite that randomly lands in my neighbor's yard. And inheritance forks at every branch in the family tree, gets spent, periodically resets to zero in calamities, and the like, so that it is unclear to what extent the diminution in moral authority of inheritance over time isn't more or less reflected in the state of nature. Nor is it clear why inheritance should differ much from gifts, and if we imagine a (strange!) series of 50 giftings among strangers over the course of a year, each passing along what remains of the initial fortune, it is not obvious to me that I have a claim on the money that remains. In any case, I don't propose to resolve all of these complexities here, and leaving some of these questions open shouldn't bother us. What is it important is that transfer can be given a respectable position in a Lockean account of property and need not presuppose that we can transfer moral rights by fiat.

▪ PROPERTY IS NOT A SOCIAL CONVENTION

Thus far I have been pursuing the internal features of the Lockean account. However, the most important claim made by Lockeans doesn't concern these details, but rather the moral basis of ownership. Contrary to Hobbes, Hume, Bentham, and many modern-day writers, Lockeans assert that there exist natural rights in the state of nature and that among them are property rights. Quite apart from the doubts about the internal coherence of Lockean accounts of appropriation and transfer, one might doubt the larger point about natural rights, which sounds ambitiously metaphysical.

To get a flavor of the differences, consider Hume's view that respecting ownership is nothing more than an "artifice" or "convention" instituted in view of the advantages of such a system.

> Our property is nothing but those goods whose constant possession is established by the laws of society; that is, by the laws of justice . . . a man's property is some object related to him. This relation is not natural but moral, and founded on justice. . . . The origin of justice explains that of property. The same artifice gives rise to both.[20]

Contemporary writers whom we'll encounter later on speak, similarly, of the "myth of ownership," and economists and writers in the law and economics tradition routinely write as if property arrangements need only take into account considerations of utility.[21] Hume's idea is that what we own is just a matter of whatever laws we happen to pass, of the conventions in our society. We can't reject property laws as unjust for failing to conform to the underlying moral facts of ownership since what the laws are *constitutes* ownership. He does mention laws of *justice*, but it's clear that this isn't an appeal to natural rights, but rather to the artificial nature of justice itself. Hume doesn't mean that we must decide what property is by some actual vote or primordial agreement; he is subtler than that, pointing to language or simple cases like oarsmen rowing as examples of implicit conventions coordinating behavior without necessitating an explicit pact.[22] Nor does he mean that property is arbitrary. Red traffic lights rather than blue ones are conventional without being arbitrary, and regimes of private property are tremendously advantageous, making them very far from random. However, they are ultimately conventional in that there is no external moral check on our passing laws radically revising or abrogating private property regimes, should these be deemed disadvantageous. Hume rejects the classical liberal move of insisting that the state and society at large are constrained in what they do by underlying natural rights. For example, should it emerge that large inequalities were a drag on the economy or social cohesion, Hume would reject arguments against a corrective redistribution founded on appeals to natural rights.[23]

In resisting Humean conventionalism, modern Lockeans should adopt a deflationary conception of natural rights, consistent with our restatement of the classic argument for libertarianism. "Natural" here need not mean that the rights are created by God. We can stipulate that it simply means "state-independent."[24] And we can once again dispense with talk of rights, if we like, and put things in terms of reasons. That is, our claim can be simply that there are moral reasons to respect our control over various goods independent of the laws or other conventions of society and the state. The Lockean claim is that even in a pre- or post-legal state of nature there exist moral facts about who is entitled to control various assets, and that among the factors strengthening or weakening such entitlements are discovery, creation, priority, adding value, labor, waste, the proviso, and transfer. The laws of the state must take these facts into account. If they are to be ignored, only very weighty considerations can justify doing so, and residual obligations apply.

Arguments for Lockean natural rights to property correspond to the various circumstances in which we can make property claims independent of social conventions. Instead of stating them in the abstract, I will illustrate several such circumstances with an example or two and discuss what makes these persuasive cases for recognizing a moral claim to controlling some asset.

Extra-legal: suppose that we're roommates, that we routinely use each other's things, and that I break your blender while being a little careless. Because of the minor nature of the incident you know there is no point in summoning the police—the costs to you of doing so in time and energy would exceed the value of the blender. Ought I to buy you a new blender all the same, or otherwise make things up to you? Or if I run off without replacing your blender and bump into you again months later, ought I to apologize for having wronged you? Should I feel guilty if I ran off leaving you with the broken blender? Would you be inclined to feel moralized resentment if I didn't pay up, and would your friends be right to feel indignant? The Lockean view explains why the answer to all of these questions is yes.

The point is that even in small-bore cases that don't implicate social institutions, property is heavily moralized, contrary to the conventionalist claim that ownership is "established by the laws." It might be said that our moralized responses are secondary to the underlying social institutions; we wouldn't normally call the police over a blender, but the fact that we *could* do so, that the laws recognize your blender as property, is what underlies these responses, in line with Hume's suggestion. This is partly right; no doubt having laws against

X tends to reinforce whatever extra-legal responses we have already. But social convention doesn't produce moral convictions out of nothing; no one has moral responses to the mere fact that the state requires certain forms to be filled in or proscribes mail-ordering more than one case of wine per month. At best, we have derivative responses rooted in a vague, general desire that people "follow the rules" and uphold the social order. But reactions in the blender case seem anything but derivative. Robbed roommates seem to feel deep, seething moral emotions in a way that just doesn't fit a non-moral account of property. And if push came to shove and some loophole allowed me to get off without paying, this wouldn't be an argument in favor of your changing your reactions, it would likely seem to you an argument in favor of changing the law or social convention. The "direction of fit" seems to go from moralized reactions to social institutions in these cases, not the other way around. It's not just that we have social conventions between roommates about property, it's that those conventions are rooted in pro-found moral responses that *fix* those "conventions."

Cross-conventional conflict: suppose that our clan has peacefully occupied some territory on the Atlantic coast for many generations, and that European colonizers turn up insisting that they have an equal claim to the land. Since we don't share a set of social conventions, these can't settle the matter for us. But de-spite the absence of a legal system of property governing both groups, we seem capable of rendering basic moral judgments on the case. These seem to track the contents of moral property judgments indicated earlier, especially the pri-ority factor, but that isn't of the essence here. What matters is just that the mere fact that there isn't some convention or "artifice" governing both groups doesn't seem to affect our ability to make sense of the moral situation, consistent with a Lockean view.

Pre-/post-legal: more exotically, suppose that in part of a developing country, legal and social norms have widely broken down following a massive earthquake. Looting is widespread, police and other law enforcement are overwhelmed and have largely joined the looters, and there is no prospect for a return of control for several years. Outside analysts predict a rise of warlords and fiefdoms à la Somalia. It's easy to see why there would be pressure to change from this state of nature into a regime of stability; as Hume points out, we shouldn't expect a state of nature to last for long.[25] But many such regions exist today and have persisted for long periods. Suppose, then, that we inhabit such a region and that you ac-quire a loaf of bread by trading the carrots you grow in some unclaimed fields. If we reject the Lockean view of property as a moral phenomenon, then apparently you don't have a claim to your bread, and when local gangs come to take if from you, you have no moral title to resist. But this is false. You *do* have grounds to re-sist highway men trying to steal—as you would think of it—your bread. If locals showed up hearing the commotion, the moral claims you would make might be widely recognized: you got the bread fair and square, the trade was legitimate, you had some carrots that you worked to grow yourself. None of this need be regarded as unintelligible (as it ought to be, according to conventional views of property), despite the absence of a functioning legal regime or (statistical) property norms. On the contrary, the pressure toward law and order would in part result *from* the desire for upholding the moral order.

Wrong property norms: suppose the legally supported social convention in our country is that everything in the end belongs to the Dear Leader, who is widely esteemed as a fusion of religious and political authority, like the pharaoh. You grow your carrots on some unused patch of land and use them to feed your family. One day the Dear Leader's officials come to claim your carrots in order to enhance the Dear Leader's already bountiful table. It may well be a widely shared assumption that this is permissible, but that doesn't make it so. There might be sufficient reasons to confiscate your carrots on occasion—some kind of public health crisis, for instance—but the spiritual priority of the Dear Leader isn't one of them. We should reject such confiscation, and the Lockean appeal to natural rights—or their deflationary surrogates—explains why. There may be reasonable variations in what an appropriate property regime looks like, but the key is that there are underlying truths that fix the limits of such variation.

The general point is that conventionalist views have the implication that what we are really entitled to can change willy-nilly with changes in conventions or shared understandings, which precludes the possibility of a society *getting it wrong*. Rejecting the Lockean view commits us to a kind of relativism most of us reject when it comes to other harms. Some of the shared understandings people once had about various groups' moral status in the 1800s were just wrong; similarly, it's possible for there to be consensus about property regimes that are simply mistaken because they overlook the underlying facts that give rise to moral claims to control assets as described above.

These cases and the considerations they give rise to constitute evidence that we have natural moral rights to property, in the deflationary sense of "natural." There are basic moral facts about who is entitled to what, and changes in convention are incapable of changing those facts. Property rights aren't absolute, and the reasons strengthening some property claim are only pro tanto; but often enough, as in some of the cases just canvassed, those reasons rise to the level of an overall entitlement it is wrong to violate. There is nothing mysterious about this, at least not if we already accept nonconventional norms against rape, murder, and unfair treatment.

Despite these arguments, it is worth noting what is right about a conventional view of property. One diagnosis of that theory is that conventionalists have confused *legally enforceable private property* with *private property* simpliciter. There is a great deal of non-overlap between these categories. As the blender case or countless family tiffs over personal effects show, there are many moral instances of property we don't want cluttering the legal system, if only on grounds of expediency. And conversely, there are myriad legal rules about copyright law or stock trading, say, that have at best a tenuous connection to morality and that must be teased out by thinking about arcane implications for incentive structures or corporate governance. It is fine to press on the latter kinds of cases to insist that not every instance of legal property is grounded in the bedrock of moral conviction, and we rightly tsk-tsk legal entities trying to convince us otherwise, as when corporate conglomerates compare copyright violation to stealing a handbag. But it's mistaken to extend this thought to the general category of private property. For comparison, notice that the state frequently extends other categories of wrongdoing beyond moral bedrock as well. In some jurisdictions, participating in a felony can result in murder charges if someone is killed in the process, even if the death is accidental, even if the one charged did not do the killing, and indeed even if the person killed was one of the criminals, shot by someone defending himself.[26] Such a felony murder rule might reasonably be deemed a pragmatic convention rather than a reflection of underlying moral truth. But that doesn't show that, in general, strictures on killing aren't fundamentally responding to a moral phenomenon.

5 Property as a Constraint on the State

The case for property as a moral phenomenon is simple and powerful. There is a coherent theory of its contents, and there are many circumstances in which our moral responses can't be explained but by appealing to a moralized conception of property. Why, then, do many deny that moral claims to property constrain the state in any meaningful way? It is worth examining three sources of resistance. First, some philosophers have held that principles of justice emerge from an idealized social contract and have left moral claims to property out of their contracting story. But, second, confronting such claims forces us to acknowledge that libertarians themselves favor some forms of compulsory taxation. After all, they aren't anarchists. Naturally, they will want to say that they manage to do so while respecting private property, but explaining how that is supposed to work without embracing the social contact tradition they reject isn't trivial. Friends of the welfare state may seize on libertarian taxation as the thin end of the wedge in order to make room for a more expansionist vision of the state. And finally, some have emphasized the original state in which property is said to be held in common. If we think of property as originally belonging to a common pool that no one has a prior claim on, we might be skeptical that anything I have referred to thus far would be capable of so drastically altering the initial situation as to exclude people from those resources.

■ CONTRACTUALISM

Contractualists hold that property rights, like the rest of the basic structure of a society, should be determined by some idealized hypothetical decision-procedure. It is this idealized, hypothetical element that sets the modern contractualists like John Rawls apart from a traditional contract theorist like Locke, who (confusingly) was a stout defender of private property. The key difference is that Locke thought that a social contract must respect the basic moral facts of property rights, whereas those favoring an idealized, hypothetical decision-procedure to determine principles of justice typically do not. Rawls explains his basic idea so:

> [S]ince everyone's well being depends upon a scheme of cooperation without which no one could have a satisfactory life, the division of advantages should be such as to draw forth the willing cooperation of everyone taking part in it, including those less well situated. Yet this can be expected only if reasonable terms are proposed.[1]

Reasonable terms are those that would emerge from the privileged contract-procedure Rawls describes, in which we consider (roughly) what sorts of social principles a reasonable person would pick if he didn't know what his place in society would be. In other words, we're to ask which principles it would be reasonable to live under if we faced some unknown risk of turning out to be among the worst-off members of our society. Although the implementation details of these principles are left vague, Rawls ultimately decides that when it comes to economic justice, "reasonable terms" are those that would give everyone an equal share of income and wealth, except when inequalities would benefit the worst off. This doesn't preclude private property, but the important point is that there is no attempt significantly to *constrain* the state in classical liberal fashion by appealing to underlying moral facts about property. If it should turn out that a socialist state that placed the means of production in the state's hands was best for the worst off, then we ought to pursue such a course, and in any case we should pursue massive wealth transfers unless doing would somehow be bad for those *benefiting* from the transfers.[2] Whatever emerges from the hypothetical contract goes, since justice is "constructed" from the rules governing that contract.

This view isn't conventionalist the way Hume's is, since it doesn't make property a function of whatever our social norms actually are. But it bears a deep similarity insofar as it denies that there are non-trivial moral facts about property the state must respond to, and subsumes these under a generalized concern for a just society. A similar view is advanced in Murphy and Nagel's *Myth of Ownership*. They suggest that we cannot have a general claim to control our pretax income because we cannot evaluate what we are entitled to before we have settled what a just society would look like:

> In the absence of a legal system supported by taxes, there couldn't be money, banks, corporations, stock exchanges, patents, or a modest market economy—none of the institutions that make possible the existence of almost all contemporary forms of income and wealth. It is therefore logically impossible that people should have any kind of entitlement to all their pretax income. All they can be entitled to is what they would be left with after taxes under a legitimate system, supported by legitimate taxation—and this shows that we cannot evaluate the legitimacy of taxes by reference to their pretax income. Instead, we have to evaluate the legitimacy of after-tax income by reference to the legitimacy of the political and economic system that generates it, including the taxes which are an essential part of that system.[3]

Here, again, the suggestion is that what we must evaluate is the justice of the overall social system without introducing prior constraints in the form of basic moral judgments about private property (or income). The difference is that in Rawls this point emerges from the contractualist method of privileging a decision procedure that leaves open what kinds of property arrangements prevail, whereas in Murphy and Nagel it emerges more straightforwardly from a point about the relationship between income and the state's infrastructure that allows for such income.

Hypothetical contract theories are only as plausible as the rules they provide for the privileged decision-procedure that yields the contract. If a given procedure yields some absurd principle, for instance one that licenses slavery, that itself constitutes grounds for rejecting it. In such a case, there is no need to address the general theory of hypothetical decision-procedures; it is perfectly sufficient to point out that the output of the procedure is wrong in licensing slavery, and therefore something has gone wrong in the specification of the procedure. Contractualists can then respond by refining their procedure, for instance by adjusting the choice situation so as to steer the parties to the contract in one or another direction, though this tends to leave critics wondering what the point of the exercise is. If we already have independent knowledge of what the right output would and wouldn't be, and if we're reduced to tuning the decision procedure "by hand" to ensure such outputs, it's unclear what the *independent* force of the decision procedure is supposed to be. In any case, the important thing to see is that a failure to reflect underlying moral realities is a fair objection to any given contractualist theory, even granting the legitimacy of the overall approach.

Should a contract theory—or any other theory for that matter—be constrained by the underlying morality of private property? I believe that it should, and that it is an objection to any such theory that it gives undue latitude to the contracting parties to select principles that don't reflect the moral basis of property. As I have argued, there are independent reasons to think that there are moral truths about ownership, and principles of justice that fail to reflect these adequately cannot be right. This doesn't mean that there isn't *any* such latitude. Since property rights aren't absolute, and since a wide variety of ownership norms might be devised to reflect the underlying moral claims, principles of justice might manifest a range of attitudes toward property. Nothing I have said suggests that the state couldn't adopt a more or less expansive system of eminent domain, for instance, for various sufficiently important purposes. But the same is true of other rights. Principles of justice must recognize a right against state coercion and for freedom of speech, but there are a range of ways of doing so and a range of exceptions that might be permitted. (A philosophical theory of justice needn't specify the correct form of libel laws.) What is crucial is that the state recognize that there are moral reasons against any violations, and that in general some high threshold must be met for allowing any. Similarly, what matters in the case of property is that the state recognize that there are moral grounds for claiming control over various assets and that only weighty considerations can overcome such claims. Not doing so is inconsistent with recognizing that property is a moral phenomenon and that it expresses fundamental moral claims.[4]

It might be objected that Rawls's theory *does* meet all of these conditions. After all, "the right to hold (private) property" is mentioned as a core liberty right, whose satisfaction is strictly prior to the distributive aims of the state.[5]

Allowing parties to fix the exact extent of such a right might then seem to fall within the penumbra of an adequate theory of justice. But while initial mention of this core liberty right is encouraging, it evidently isn't to be interpreted as very extensive, since it turns out to be compatible with insisting on an equal distribution of income and wealth, subject to exceptions only when inequalities would benefit the worst off, and with state ownership of most businesses. This still might sound all right, as long as such aims were strictly limited by the prior satisfaction of the right to private property, but it's clear that this isn't so to any non-trivial extent; Rawls plainly envisions the possibility of extensive redistribution in order to produce equality, without constraints introduced by private property (which are never mentioned again, except in the context of approving socialism as a possible outcome of social choice). Nor is this surprising; the intention, it's worth bearing in mind, is to view the "distribution of natural talents as a common asset,"[6] which is difficult to reconcile to a serious regard for property as a constraint. If our talents are a common asset, presumably there isn't much hope for our bank accounts.

Let us assume, then, that we are dealing with a contractualist theory that does allow the parties to engage in large-scale expropriation to secure desirable social outcomes, and to produce a socialist economy of largely state-run enterprises. (If a given proposal turns out to be tailored to forbid such an outcome, the issue is moot.) The objection in that case is that the moral claims of owners are simply not being given the weight they deserve. And there is nothing unique about Rawlsian contractualism in this context; any theory of justice with similar implications is susceptible to this objection. To focus ideas, let us consider a standard case. You sign up for a job and your employer pays you $50,000 by the end of the year. Other things equal, it is natural to suppose that you are now entitled to your income, though in a moment we will consider objections even to this. Suppose that the contracting parties agree to principles of justice permitting the state to take 40% of your income to promote socially desirable goals like equality or social mobility or to neutralize the effects of bad luck on life-fortunes. Libertarians can agree that these are worthwhile goals—that a world with more of such things should be ranked as a world superior to worlds with fewer such things from a normative point of view. But recognizing moral entitlements to property means that there exists a high threshold against depriving people of that property. Otherwise they aren't really entitlements. And like other moral thresholds against lying, killing, and otherwise harming people, we normally assume these thresholds are rather high. Your neighbors cannot take $1,000 of your money without *very* strong reasons. Any acceptable theory of justice must introduce these thresholds into its principles, and any contractualist decision-procedure must be tailored to reflect them no less than basic moral thresholds against physical harm. Denying this is just to deny that property is a genuine moral phenomenon that generates anything like deontic constraints. When Emily creates an elaborate piece of art and Mark announces he wants it, an arbitrator can't consistently recognize Emily's moral claim and then proceed to announce rules for who gets what that neglect those claims.

This may just look like a standoff. Libertarians and others think that property is a moral phenomenon and must be reflected in hypothetical-contract procedures; contractualists evidently do not, or else think that it poses no significant obstacle to large-scale redistribution. But it's not as if Rawls or other contractualists somehow refute the case for property as a moral phenomenon. They neither confront it nor explain why, if they do accept that phenomenon, it turns out to pose no obstacle to egalitarian redistribution. It is as if someone were to argue that justice is determined by a hypothetical-choice situation and then were to show no awareness of political equality as a constraining norm on the nature of that choice, and were to write as if political equality posed no significant obstacle to institutions that violated it. This wouldn't be a standoff but an objection.

■ THE MYTH OF OWNERSHIP

Murphy and Nagel raise the more concrete worry that it doesn't make sense to view the $50,000 you earn at your job as entirely yours, even when it is legitimately transferred, since this exchange relies on a background of state activities and more generally a "legitimate system" supported by "legitimate taxation," implying we can only determine what you have a claim to *after* determining what you owe as your contribution toward that system. Taking the $50,000 as some sort of moral baseline against which we can protest the encroachments of the government gets things backward, from this point of view. Since this theme has been a deep one in democratic politics right through Greek and Roman class conflict, it is worth rehearsing the politically charged version of this point as well. Here is Senator Elizabeth Warren, in an informal campaign speech:

> There is nobody in this country who got rich on their own. Nobody. You built a factory out there—good for you. But I want to be clear. You moved your goods to market on roads the rest of us paid for. You hired workers the rest of us paid to educate. You were safe in your factory because of police forces and fire forces that the rest of us paid for. You didn't have to worry that marauding bands would come and seize everything at your factory. . . . Now look. You built a factory and it turned into something terrific or a great idea—God bless! Keep a hunk of it. But part of the underlying social contract is you take a hunk of that and pay forward for the next kid who comes along.[7]

Let us distinguish various strands in these related claims of Murphy, Nagel, and Warren: (i) exchanges generating income are only possible because of government services (enabling roads, law enforcement, etc.) that must be paid for through the tax system and to which we must contribute a share of our income; (ii) exchanges require a background of social cooperation, and others can only be expected to cooperate if they are included in a legitimate system that recognizes them and their interests in a fair way, including through taxation and redistribution; and more specifically, (iii) third parties may threaten to interfere with private exchange without side-payments that must be paid for through the tax system and which we therefore owe. (I set aside Warren's concluding appeal to intergenerational justice for the sake of simplicity.) Each of these poses a somewhat different problem.

It is true just as (i) says that if we currently owe someone else money, we aren't entitled to all of what we have, and libertarians (as distinct from anarchists) acknowledge that we owe money to the state for various minimal services, such as law enforcement. This shows that we can't resist taxation by claiming that we have a right to income that we owe to others, including the state. But of course it's unlikely anyone was confused about that. Presumably even right-wingers didn't imagine that they could resist ordinary creditors just by announcing they had a right to their income, and the point about the state is just the same. What is under dispute is whether moral claims to property play a constraining role in determining what *is* owed to the state. As we have seen, in contractualists like Rawls, it looks like the answer is substantially No. By contrast, libertarians hold that moral claims to exercise control over various goods raise very serious impediments to taxes for things like wealth transfers to benefit others. Denying these impediments is to deny that property is a moral phenomenon that produces strong reasons we must respect, which I have argued it does. And once we acknowledge that property *does* constrain the state, (i) merely tells us that we aren't entitled to the amount required of us for the suitably constrained, minimal state that doesn't ignore our moral claims. Thus, for (i) to make any headway in justifying anything beyond a minimalist libertarian state, it would need to explain how and why the non-minimal services of the welfare state overcome the moral barriers thrown up by moral claims to property. And there is nothing in (i) to do this. At best, (i) explains why taxation for the *minimal libertarian* state is warranted.

Another way of making the point is this. It is true that, absent some of the services of the state, you would not be making your $50,000. (In the state of nature, it would be hard to earn this figure.) But this counterfactual truth does not cancel the moral facts concerning you and that money—the fact that you entered into a contract, say, with someone else and worked for it, which others did not do, and so on. Libertarians accept that you have reason to respect the minimal claims of the state, and thus owe the state a fraction of that money. But *that* fraction isn't under dispute. What's under dispute are the *non*-minimal claims the state makes. And those cannot be grounded in the mere fact that we wouldn't earn the full amount in a state of nature. By way of rough analogy, this is like supposing that I have a claim to your entire salary because I gave you the subway token you had forgotten and needed to get to your job interview, in the absence of which you would have earned nothing.

It is only (ii) and (iii) that make any real progress toward justifying the taking of our property for a welfare state. They tell us that we require a much broader system of social cooperation to produce income-generating exchanges than the minimal services of the welfare state. What is involved is partly "nice" cooperation in the form of an educated, healthy workforce, and generally a stable and well-ordered society. But at least in Warren there is a hint of "nasty" cooperation as well, where we need to worry about "marauding bands" tearing down our factory. Perhaps these are mentioned just to reinforce the importance of law enforcement, but we can note the possibility anyway of disgruntled third parties who won't accept inequalities generated by exchanges they don't participate in, or a poor quality of life overall, necessitating the side-payments mentioned in (iii). The latter suggestion, however, sounds more like a protection racket than a moral justification for the welfare state. It may well be that third parties won't be content to allow us engage in income-generating exchanges or production without "wetting their beak" or keeping up with our level of affluence, which may inspire their envy. But this doesn't yield a moral rationale for anything; it merely describes a threat we find ourselves facing, and perhaps a reason to expand our budget for law enforcement. It is good to be aware of threats, but they cannot contribute to an account of what we *owe* to others.

This leaves us with the social cooperation that figures in (ii). To be relevant, the claim has to be that we owe money to the state because of the broad social cooperation necessary to our private endeavors. And for reasons just stated, the type of cooperation involved cannot amount to mere non-interference like the protection racket, or the minimal services of the libertarian state. The question is what such cooperation could look like, such that citizens owe the state for it so as to defeat the claims to control over our assets. Run-of-the-mill social cooperation doesn't generally produce such debts. Suppose that a group of us are enmeshed in a complex economic web, wherein some of us deliver raw materials, some of us process it, others refine it further while giving feedback to the suppliers, and still others bundle and sell it, while buying up recycled product and returning it to the suppliers for reprocessing. Moreover, we require still others to supply us with the conditions necessary to conduct our affairs, for instance by supplying food, shelter, and various forms of training. Where in this social microcosm does the debt get generated? Obviously I owe those who supply me raw materials whatever we agreed to, and the same for the third parties who render income-generating activities possible, e.g., the person who makes my lunch. But these debts are merely private obligations that have nothing to do with what we owe the state, which must emerge from something over and above our private interactions, whose costs and obligations are settled privately in the market. But what could the source of those debts be? As we remove mere non-interference, minimal services, and private market cooperation from the scene, the answer becomes more and more obscure. In fact, I suggest that there is no satisfactory answer. Generalized social cooperation will involve many costs borne by individuals that they can be expected to be compensated for at a better or worse rate in the market, but no emergent debt that must be separately taken care of in the form of taxation.

The legitimacy of a system might be thought to have emergent properties. Even if our social microcosm involves no injustices—I pay for my raw materials fair and square—radical inequalities that evolve over time may seem wrong in a way hard to trace back to individual malfeasance. There may be some independent argument for thinking that large inequalities are in their very nature wrong, and in that case perhaps we couldn't object to taxes used to fund a "legitimate" system that addresses such unfairness. In thinking about this, remember that the point we are considering is not whether the state can, in general, force us to contribute to a sufficiently important cause. We have already acknowledged that this is true once we meet some very high life-or-limb threshold, and accompanied by re-sidual obligations. The idea is rather supposed to be that we aren't entitled to some fraction of our property because we *owe* it to others, similar to the way we might owe money to our creditors. But how could an emergent ill like inequality make it true that we owe others something when we did no wrong? Emergent social ills would then have a status similar to other bads no one is personally responsible for, like the decay of the Acropolis. It would be reasonable to ask for a contribution to preserve the Acropolis, but it's much harder to see how its decay could make it the case that we *owe* money to the preservation society, so that some of the money in our bank accounts isn't even rightfully ours anymore. Victims of an emergent ill might point out that something terrible was hap-pening to them, but not that they were being wronged, which makes it difficult to make sense of talk of our owing them. To conclude with yet another comparison, it would be as if the neighboring town were suddenly struck by an earthquake. It would be reasonable to ask for help, and perhaps now one could claim that life-or-limb principles warranted compulsory expropriation. But supposing your net worth to be embodied in a house, your house wouldn't suddenly cease to be all yours because of your debts to the earthquake victims, as if they were creditors you had failed pay.

■ THE ANTI-FREE-RIDER PRINCIPLE

Perhaps the real challenge lies a level deeper. Libertarians may seem to exhibit an inconsistency. Why does ownership pose a barrier to taxation for the sake of transfers to the worse off, but *not* to coercive taxation on behalf of the minimal state? If rights to property are so powerful, how come they don't reduce us to stateless anarchy, since even building roads, enforcing contracts, and the other activities of a minimal state will be rejected by some, meaning coercion will be required, often in cases that *don't* meet any life-or-limb test. What some of the worries canvassed above may really reflect is an unease over the use of property rights to reject welfare-enhancing projects of the state on grounds that don't seem consistently applied to the minimal state the libertarian envisions. To pose it as a dilemma that Nozick first outlined, libertarians seem stuck either with rights to ownership so powerful they wipe out the state altogether, resulting in anarchism, or else weak enough to permit the welfare state.

We can begin our response by noting the concept of a *public good*. Public goods like clean air or national security are difficult to provide to some while excluding others, and their cost doesn't increase much with an increase in utilization (they're "non-excludable" and "non-rival"). Classical liberals since Adam Smith have advanced something like public goods as part of the raison d'être of the state and a scheme of justified taxation:

> According to the system of natural liberty, the sovereign has only three duties to attend to . . . first, the duty of protecting the society from the violence and invasion of other independent societies; secondly, the duty of protecting . . . every member of the society from the injustice or oppression of every other member of it . . . and thirdly the duty of erecting and maintaining certain public works and certain public institutions, which it can never be for the interest of any individual, or small number of individuals, to erect and maintain.[8]

Smith's third category resembles public goods, since it will usually not be in anyone's interest to provide goods that cannot be excluded from non-payers who will nevertheless enjoy the benefits of the good. And although Smith writes as if the third category were separate from the first two, we might plausibly collapse all three into the public goods category, since national and domestic security are generally public goods. (Smith may have felt that there were additional reasons the state had to provide security over and above the incentive-based argument.)

However, the mere fact that something is a public good does not justify forcing people to pay for it. A piece of public art like a statue that anyone can see is non-excludable and non-rival, but it isn't obvious why that means everyone should be compelled to subsidize it. Many won't care about art or about this statue in particular. Public goods aren't public needs. We cannot claim that those who aren't interested in our statue are *free-riders*—those who unfairly enjoy public benefits while trying to shirk paying their fair share. And even if we do benefit from the statue, it's obviously false that we can force people to pay for anything that benefits them; the roving guitarist who serenades us in the park unbidden may ask nicely for a donation, but he may not issue a moral demand for payment for services we did not ask for or consent to, even if we do benefit.[9] Nevertheless, the concept of a public good along with our fear of free-riders can form the basis of an adequate account, I believe. The key is to identify the circumstances under which we may compel others to pay for services because *not* doing so would be unfair to *us* in virtue of what we stand to lose if we cannot provide the goods in question or else leave ourselves open to free-riders taking advantage of us.

Here is a proposal:

Anti-free-rider principle—it is permissible to compel payment for unrequested, unconsented services when:

The providers cannot avoid providing the service without undue costs to themselves; cannot provide service in a way that excludes those who don't pay; offer reasonable terms; and have grounds for taking themselves to be the appropriate people or organization to provide service; and

The beneficiaries could otherwise free-ride, or be reasonably suspected of doing so; and are given an exit option at least as good as getting no service or fees, to the extent that doing so isn't an unfair burden on others.

As an additional consideration amplifying the moral force of charging for unconsented services we can add:

The beneficiaries *need* the service or something like it and would have recourse to some provider or other left to their own devices.

To anticipate, the strategy will be to claim that we can compel payment for things like law enforcement on anti-free-rider grounds, while wealth redistribution fails this test.

To see that something like the anti-free-rider principle must be true, consider a small-scale case:

The barbarians have finished burning down the neighboring village and are headed our way. Accordingly, many of us villagers start to build up our defenses since the alternative is death. In doing so, it is impossible to provide for the defense of some but not others, since the village will stand or fall as a unit. In asking that everyone contribute to the defense of the entire village, we don't make absurd demands or misappropriate the resources we collect. And without these measures of self-defense everyone will die, the evidence suggests, meaning people generally need them. The only alternative is to flee the city and take one's chances against the barbarians in the wild, and that option is left open. Our duly authorized leaders demand that anyone who remains contribute toward the defense of the city they have arranged.

This vignette illustrates the moral logic of the principle. The point is not that in staying in the village the denizens have implicitly or hypothetically consented to be charged for its defense. The principle is not an implicit or hypothetical consent principle. The option to exit should be preserved if possible on simple liberty grounds, but that isn't supposed to imply any kind of meaningful consent. The idea is rather that it is wrong to avoid contributing to a service *when others cannot at reasonable cost to themselves give me the option to avoid service short of my exiting,* at least without letting me free-ride.[10] This is all the more true when I require the service in any case. To put it another way, others aren't required to die or suffer serious harms simply to ensure that I have the option to avoid service without exiting, and it's wrong of me then to free-ride on those who are paying. A complaint would only arise if there were reasons to contest the service providers' claim that *they* (and not I or others) make decisions about the service. Of course, in the vast majority of everyday situations, it is perfectly easy to avoid providing service in the first place, which is why the guitar serenader is pulling a scam when he claims that I owe him money. There is no sense in which the serenader is compelled to offer me his services without my consent. Similarly for the public statue. But in those special cases in which it isn't possible to avoid providing me service (especially when I require it in any case), I must contribute on reasonable terms. Not doing so would be exploitative on my part.

Next, suppose that I refuse payment for a service like self-defense or law enforcement because I don't require those services. This means dropping the final clause about my needing the service whether someone else provides it or not. In the village story, perhaps I'm friends with the barbarians and stand to benefit from their attack, or perhaps I just look forward to the afterlife. Here I am not benefiting from the service or utilizing it in any sense at all, meaning that I'm not in any intelligible sense free-riding. (The service is, so to speak, just washing over me unbidden.) In this case, the reasonable suspicion and exit clauses are crucial. Others may be entitled to *ensure* that I don't free-ride by requiring me to exit if I don't contribute. Theater owners, for instance, can ask me to leave if I don't pay for a movie, even if I don't really want to see it and snuck in because I made a bet, and despite not incurring any incremental cost due to my presence. And the owners need not accept individual attempts to prove that the apparent free-rider isn't trying to shirk, if doing so would come at an unreasonable cost, or produce disastrous incentive effects for other would-be free-riders. (The theater owner isn't required to perform elaborate investigations into someone's claims about having lost a bet.) In the village case, authorities may insist that non-contributors exit without holding detailed investigations into each claim of nonbenefit, if having a straightforward policy about the matter—"Contribute or leave!"—is the only feasible way to avoid the costs of investigating each case, or else either not providing for their self-defense at all or succumbing to free-riders.

The reasonable suspicion clause cuts the other way as well, however. Suspicion of free-riding cannot be willy-nilly or the product of mere paranoia. If you need to practice piano tonight for a concert you're obligated to perform, I may enjoy it from my neighboring apartment. Unlike the roving guitarist in the park, you aren't shaking me down, and you cannot at reasonable cost forgo conferring on me the benefit. But you still may not charge me on the grounds that you suspect me of free-riding. There is no case at all to be made that I am free-riding on your private performance. Nothing in the circumstances supports a reasonable suspicion that I am attempting to derive benefits I have reason to pay for while shirking my contribution. Moreover, you couldn't claim that you were the appropriate authority to provide the services in question and enforce payment or declare a mandatory policy. You weren't elected to do so, nor are you operating a business that is authorized to impose terms for the benefits it provides, as is the case with a theater built on private property where the proprietor may restrict entry.

The exit option referenced in the principle may be very bad. Perhaps it would involve grave risk of harm, or leaving work and family behind, and I may protest I shouldn't have to choose between the many drawbacks of exit and fees for some unwanted service. But according to the principle, the exit option is generally to be no worse than not getting service—no fair introducing coercive penalties. And if the service forgone is something as serious as security or law enforcement, it isn't unreasonable to offer only an option that risks serious likelihood of death or extreme hardship, since those are the hardships security services are intended to ameliorate. And the exit option must not introduce unfair burdens on the service provider. Providers aren't responsible for idiosyncratic costs of exit that aren't connected to the very fact of not obtaining service. If my enemies from the past have threatened to kill me if I ever leave the village, that doesn't mean you are required to let me stay without contributing or else provide me with a private security detail at your own expense. If someone sneaks into a theater on a bet and stands to lose $1,000 if the owner throws him out, that doesn't mean the owner must let him watch for free or else pay him $1,000. In fact, there may be rare occasions in which no exit option need be offered at all. If the barbarians are likely to capture all those who leave the village and torture them to discover the nature of our defenses, permitting exit would impose unfair burdens on the villagers, and the exit option may be canceled. (Whether the absence of a reasonable exit option should affect how fees are applied and exemptions offered is an interesting question I will ignore.)

The principle may seem excessively generous to providers, who get to charge us fees, make up policies, and threaten us with exit. What happened to the glorious moral authority of property? But the range of circumstances in which we can be compelled to pay or exit is very narrow. It is quite unusual that some group of people cannot reasonably forgo providing a service in a way that benefits us, since usually the costs of not providing the service at all is low (serenading guitarist), or else non-payers can be excluded (most commodities sold). And even then, there has to be justification for a particular entity to provide the service rather than others; it isn't as if the principle licenses random individuals to announce policies and compel fees. How such a justification should go is hard to describe in the abstract, but obviously we will need to explain why we are better positioned, morally speaking, than others offering rival proposals for similar services, and why we are well-enough positioned in absolute terms to announce policies of compliance and the like. When there are legitimate political structures, these will naturally feed into such justifications, but there isn't any bar to people in a non-state situation (in a remote locale, or following a natural disaster, or washed up on an island) making such claims, if they respect the moral authority of others. Property rights aren't absolute on the picture I have offered, and we cannot use them to insist that others tolerate grave harms to themselves in order to avoid succumbing to free-riders.

▪ APPLYING THE PRINCIPLE

Leaving the village and other toy cases behind, the suggestion is that the anti-free-rider principle applies to those minimal services the libertarian endorses, and that it doesn't apply to more expansive services of the welfare state. This is why it isn't inconsistent of the libertarian to say that claims to property constrain the state in the latter cases but not the former. As the classic argument says, the welfare state (but not the minimal state) appropriates property we are entitled to since it isn't owed to anyone for the purposes the welfare state uses it for. Which services, exactly, are "minimal" and which are those falling under the heading of "welfare statist"? I can't answer that question in detail. The important thing is that discussions about funding roads, education, food stamps, and the rest should be conducted on the principle that what is owed to the state is a function of what services people cannot without grave harm to themselves avoid providing to all, and therefore may charge citizens for without their consent in order to bar free-riding. Identifying the precise boundary established by the principle is not as important for our purposes as establishing that there *is* a principled distinction.

Some of the broad outlines of the resulting picture are tolerably clear, none-theless. Public goods like national security, law enforcement, and basic infra-structure are relatively straightforward to derive from the principle. Just as in the village case, it would impose an enormous burden on most citizens to avoid deploying roads in a way accessible to all, excepting the occasional toll highway, or a future high-tech system. Not doing so would cripple most people's prospects for earning a living and so deprive them of something they need, and it would be very difficult to exclude the few who don't want or need them. And being entitled to build the roads, citizens aren't required to tolerate massive free-riding. People should be left with an exit option at least as good as living without roads, and the possibility of moving into remote forests or emigrating meets that standard. Such places will be poor and unpleasant, but that is precisely what life without roads is like, and those who opt out presumably want something like a survivalist existence. I believe something similar applies to public safety and adjudication services, though I won't argue for that in detail here.

On the other hand, goods like universal healthcare care or a guaranteed min-imum income do *not* pass muster. It is easy enough to provide healthcare to those who pay for it while excluding others from both services and fees—ordinary healthcare isn't anything like a public good. (Epidemics might be another story.) Nor is it clear why there would need to be a monopoly on healthcare instead of many different companies offering similar services we could then choose from without being charged by the state for its preferred service. The same holds for guaranteed minimum income, where once again there is no difficulty in excluding people from both service and fees. In these kinds of cases, there is little to be said for thinking that we owe something to our fellow citizens because we are otherwise free-riding on services they cannot reasonably forgo providing and that people generally require in any case. All that is happening is that people around us are appropriating our property through threats or violence in order to benefit themselves or others.

Sometimes welfare programs are justified as a form of social insurance. State-run healthcare and safety-net programs might be viewed as justified by the desire many citizens will have to reduce risks to themselves by insuring against misfortune, and at a high enough level of abstraction they might be said to benefit all who participate in them, in the same sense that home insurance benefits owners who pay out large sums through the years without receiving tangible benefits in return. "Look," we can imagine the villagers saying, "unless we organize a village-wide system to provide for those down on their luck, it will be an enormous burden to those struck by illness or unemployment, and all those covered will benefit, if only by mitigating risk. We have determined that a village-run monopoly is the only viable system under the circumstances, and also that letting some people opt out would lead to adverse selection and doom the system. For these reasons we must insist that everyone receive the benefits of the social insurance system and contribute in turn." This, it strikes me, is one of the better strategies for making a case for why we owe the state for welfare programs without violating people. At least, this strategy avoids naked appeals to utilitarianism that are more common in the public sphere, e.g., "If we just tax the top 1% more we can make the lives of the 99% much better," which appear to be simple exhortations to exploit the few for the sake of the many.[11]

The difficulty with insurance arguments emerges when we reflect on the reasons given for not excluding those who don't want insurance. We can imagine a very small-scale example: four poor and sickly individuals find themselves in a hamlet with one rich and healthy individual. The four propose a social safety insurance system; the one isn't interested. "Look," say the four, "it will be an intolerable burden on us if you don't join the system, since otherwise there won't be anyone there to put into the system what we the sick and poor are taking out." But it isn't really true that the four cannot forebear providing service to the one. Unlike cases of public goods like national security or even roads, there is no difficulty at all in excluding the one from service. The core idea behind the anti-free-rider principle is that we don't get to forbid people from caring for themselves when doing so must take the form of providing us services unbidden, and failing to charge us means free-riding. But in our hamlet, no one is preventing the four from pooling their resources and doing anything they like to improve their well-being without making the one worse off by providing him unwanted service. What is "burdensome" to the four is not *excluding* the one, but rather not getting hold of his money. This is burdensome in the same sense that it is burdensome to me if you don't give me your gold or gift me a new car. Since I have no prior claim to such things, it is misleading to call your inaction burdensome at all; it's just that it would be much better for me (and worse for you) if you did. Thus, the insurance argument isn't a genuine appeal to the principle at all. It represents, once again, unfair burden-shifting that we have moral reason to resist. It is no different than announcing that my neighbors must join my new neighborhood-level social insurance system, whereby they, who are rich and healthy, must subsidize me, who am poor and sickly, since it will be a burden to me not to be part of such a system. (Imagine your reaction if I knocked on your door demanding fees to participate in such a plan.) On inspection, involuntary insurance schemes of this sort are just thinly veiled utilitarian schemes to introduce compulsory wealth transfers. Such transfers may be justified if revisionist utilitarianism is correct. But it would be a mistake to confuse a compulsory scheme for utilitarian wealth transfers with a genuine respect for people's moral claims to property.

■ THE ORIGINAL COMMONS

It is worth thinking about one more set of reasons for doubting that moral claims to control assets can do much to constrain the state. According to Christian theorists in the natural law tradition (whom Locke echoed), the assets of the world were originally in a common pool. Divorced from its theological origins, such a view is still plausible if "originally" is taken to mean "independent of morally relevant actions people take to endow themselves with a claim to excluding others." If we both see an oasis in a remote desert, I cannot announce to you that it's mine independent of some morally relevant difference between us. Any oasis we should stumble on would need to be viewed, at least initially, as a commons. Of course, the Lockean story I have given in the last chapter is precisely a sketch of how to go about improving one's claim to excluding others. But in reflecting on the importance of the original common pool we might begin to feel skeptical about using property claims to sharply constrain the state. In particular, we might wonder whether, given that our assets (or their value) originally resided in a common stock, our actions could endow us with *total* as opposed to merely partial or limited control over them. Saying the latter would allow friends of the welfare state to concede the moral phenomenon of property, while insisting that the common origin of the good should be reflected in its disposition as well. The state, it might be said, is ultimately appropriating goods that were originally in the common pool, and (ideally) using them to promote the common good. Doing so would be justified by the fact that all physical goods (or their source materials) are originally part of the common stock, and by the fact that our property-generating claims at best give us *some*, not total, control over an asset. Since our contribution to the value of some good is at best partial, complementing that contributed by the common element of the natural resource itself, our claims to control cannot be total. Perhaps this is a reasonable gloss on what certain critics of private property regimes like Proudhon had in mind all along.

We can consider two ways of making this concern concrete, one partly metaphysical, one tied to consent. G. A. Cohen takes up the Lockean claim that since labor contributes most of the value to things, labor ought to permit us to remove goods from the common pool, such as the fruits of cleared and cultivated land. As I argued above, this focus on labor is misguided, and as I will argue in the next chapter, the focus on natural resources as the source of wealth is also mistaken. But Cohen's criticisms are worth pursuing nonetheless. His complaint runs,

> [I]f J R Ewing, or Donna Krebs, produces a well yielding one thousand barrels of oil per day after five minutes' excavation, then we cannot infer, on the Lockean ground that no oil comes without digging, that his or her labor, *as opposed to the land*, is responsible for all of that oil. That conclusion is unavailable, not only because it is absurd so to praise so mere a whiff of labor, but also because, by the same Lockean token, labor is responsible for *none* of the oil, since a digger on oil-less land produces no oil.[12]

In other words, labor and land are both necessary conditions of the resulting valuable resources, and to exalt one rather than the other in order to promote a strong moral claim to removing the good from the commons is absurd. At best we will have a limited, partial claim to the value of the resource, and the state may reasonably reclaim some fraction of it as reflection of the fact that the value was just as much a function of the resource as anything the agent did. (Cohen expresses doubt that there is any serious principle that would establish precisely how much one or the other factor contributed.)

The other way of pressing this point is to insist that since goods are originally in the common stock, people have a veto on their removal. This would likely lead to anti-libertarian results, as Alan Gibbard points out, since some people might refuse to permit private property unless they were paid off on generous terms, or unless a state working for the common good maintained partial control of the assets or the value they gave rise to. (Why should the infirm or less talented abdicate their natural rights to control over the common stock in exchange for anything less than the best deal they can extract from prospective appropriators?)[13] It's only a short step from this thought to a kind of rationale for the welfare state as compensating those who would otherwise be entitled to vie with owners for the assets they hold. Perhaps redistributive transfers may be thought of as the outcome of a bargain struck between those better able to utilize goods and those less able to but with an equal original claim.

Cohen is clearly right about the necessary contribution of natural resources toward the value of physical goods. And as noted, it is plausible that the oasis we both stumble on in the desert should be viewed as common stock between us, and that exercising control over the asset in a way that would adversely affect your interests must be negotiated as per Gibbard's suggestion. But on some of the likely sequences of events to follow, neither of these points would be relevant to whether property constrains the state. If we agree to divide up the arable land and we each do our best to make a living as we choose, there is no basis for either of us to claim that the original commonness of the stock warrants partial confiscation of the other's goods. Any such warrant is presumably canceled by the agreement we made. Suppose, then, that there is no such agreement, and that we simply go about our business cultivating different parts of the oasis, without interfering with the other. At the end of the week we meet with our products and trade. As it happens, I have accomplished nothing more than sharpening a rock. You, by dint of ingenuity, hard work, and some luck, have managed to construct a device for harvesting coconuts, of which you have collected three. Eager for a coconut, I give you my rock for one of the three. The suggestion we are pursuing in effect says that I can now demand *another* coconut (or perhaps fraction thereof) as a reflection of the original common pool, since you are not entitled to the entirety of the goods you remove from the stock, no matter what your contribution to its value, and no matter that I made no contribution. In one variation I pose this demand ex post by pointing out that the common element supplied by nature was a necessary condition of your current holdings, in the other ex ante by vetoing your plan to get some coconuts unless you promise me a cut over and above anything I could obtain by exchange alone.

Are these reasonable demands? The ex post strategy depends on thinking that whatever an agent does compared to those around him, he can *never* improve his moral claim to control to the point that the other won't have a claim to part of his output because of the original common-pool origins of the physical inputs. This view, however, is difficult to defend, as is most easily demonstrated in cases where the Lockean proviso is obviously satisfied (i.e., where physical inputs are abundant). You take your kids to the beach, and Emily works industriously on her sand castle while Mark swims; he returns and demands equal rights to modifying the sand castle in ways that Emily despises on grounds that the sand was part of the common pool. You suggest he just make his own castle, but he insists on taking over Emily's creation for the rest of the afternoon, which Emily violently protests ("That's not fair!"). It is true that the sand was necessary for the castle and that Mark has as good a claim to the common stock of sand as Emily. But there nevertheless seems to be a simple case for recognizing Emily's control of the castle, at least up to some threshold, and duly noting that sand castles don't matter too much (to desiccated grownups, anyway): Emily contributed all of the scarce, non-trivial inputs to the good, while Mark contributed nothing at all, and even the common stock he has a claim to is unconstrained and therefore trivial.

We can see this counterfactually: without Emily's efforts, there would be no castle, while the reverse does not hold. This is why Emily, and not Mark, has generated value. The common-pool origins of the sand will only seem relevant if we think that our common claim to such goods confers on us a moral claim to anything made up of them. But what could be the basis of such a claim? It's easy to see that we would have a complaint if someone else's use of a common-pool resource deprived us of some opportunity—that is what the proviso captures. The ex post claim we're exploring in effect says that we should be able to collect *rent* from goods toward which we have contributed nothing, and whose use by others deprives us of nothing (otherwise the proviso would be activated). This sounds like depraved rent-seeking at its worst. In thinking about goods like sand castles and fun, we cannot easily quantify the value of Emily's labor. But that shouldn't stop us from seeing that Emily has produced a morally important difference between herself and her brother in virtue of supplying all of the non-trivial inputs to the disputed item.

Next we can take up the ex ante approach of claiming that I should get one more of your coconuts because I can demand a prior agreement that you don't get to have any coconuts unless I get my share, even if I contribute nothing at all. This view depends critically on conceiving of the original common stock as conferring on everyone a veto on anything productive that anyone does with the common stock without everyone's consent. This is what enables the less capable or advantaged to drive a hard bargain. Notice that it is not enough simply to say that consent is required to make others *worse off*, say by removing critical assets from the pool without compensation. That, once again, is already factored into the proviso and what it means to have legitimate access to the goods one works on. No one thinks that you can secure a title to goods that you have labored at, but only after first misappropriating the physical inputs from others; that case can be dismissed as trivial. On closer inspection, though, this claim to a veto turns out to be just another way of formulating a claim to rents on molecules. The difference is only whether we conceive of rents proceeding from the ability to extract resources from you ex post in virtue of my co-ownership of a necessary input for the asset, or ex ante in virtue of my veto power. Either way, this is a standard instance of a resource (co-)owner extracting payments for access to goods above and beyond what he paid to bring them online, i.e., rents. Rent isn't intrinsically wrong, though rent-seeking behavior that exacts a toll on other people's productivity without contributing or motivating any future contributions in its own right isn't something one can view with much enthusiasm. We have rather different attitudes, it's worth noting, toward rentiers who extract payments in virtue of politically obtained monopolies, and toward companies that build housing, motivated in part by profits from renting out the properties, even after they have recouped their investment. But asserting a right to rents simply on the fabric of the universe, while contributing nothing and idly watching others exercise ingenuity, discover new advances, and work hard, is outrageous, and this is ultimately what the principles we have been considering amount to.

6 Property and the Creation of Value

Thus far, we have been taking for granted the usual picture in which the initial acquisition of natural resources is central to the discussion of private property. And certainly any thorough account of property will incorporate a treatment of initial acquisition, just as mine has. But in this chapter I want to challenge the usual picture and argue that this natural resource paradigm is no longer relevant to large swaths of modern, service-oriented economies.

To see the basic thought, we need only consult our own bank account and consider how much of its contents is due to primary sector extraction or agriculture, or even secondary sector manufacturing. Empirically speaking, in modern economies, wealth is overwhelmingly the product of services, not of the initial acquisition of natural resources. For countries like the contemporary United States or Japan, the distribution of natural resources has almost nothing to do with who is rich or poor and why. This might seem unimportant if we imagine wealth from services must ultimately trace back to natural resources, but as I will try to show, that is not the case: for most of us, it is services all the way down. Getting rich by writing code or practicing law is fundamentally different from getting rich by laying claim to arable land. And it turns out to be substantially harder to justify anti-libertarian principles of redistribution once we focus on the moral characteristics of a service-oriented economy. Briefly put, it is harder to drive a wedge between wealth and the value-generating activities of those who come to enjoy it in the context of services, and it is harder to interpose an obviously egalitarian element such as the initial commons of natural resources.

■ THE RESOURCE PARADIGM

It was natural for Locke to focus on natural resources in the 17th century. For him, the discussion of property revolves around appropriating acorns, or water from a fountain, or working farmland. For instance, he writes, "Though the water running in the fountain be every one's, yet who can doubt but that in the pitcher is his only who drew it out? His labor hath taken it out of the hands of nature where it was common." For the central case of farming, he writes, "as much land as a man tills, plants, improves cultivates and can use the product of so much is his property." And addressing the no-waste condition that he favors, he says, "As much as any one can make use of to any advantage of life before it spoils, so much he may by his labor fix a property in."[1]

Locke was aware of the importance of features of the economy besides in-itial acquisition, and he writes at some length about money; however, he does so mostly in order to explain how money renders inequality possible, since it permits limitless accumulation despite the no-waste condition. He is also sensi-tive to the many forms of labor that go into agriculture besides directly working the land, for instance the labor in breaking the oxen that clear the field and the labor in manufacturing metal tools.[2] However, on the whole, Locke presents a simple picture whereby wealth is largely the product of natural resources accessed through agriculture. Given the time and place, this was reasonable, though even then trade was a highly conspicuous and increasingly important generator of value. (Locke's experience of tea and pepper, if nothing else, would have rendered this vivid.)

What is more surprising is that neo-Lockeans writing 300 years later would take a similar approach. Robert Nozick essentially adopts the terms of Locke, even when expressing disagreement with his substantive judgments. Nozick refers to such situations as "a private astronaut [clearing] a place on Mars," shipwrecks and castaways appropriating new territory, and scientists synthesizing new molecules. And although he importantly shifts the emphasis from acquisition through labor to the justification of acquisition through a weakened proviso, the emphasis remains on resource acquisition. E.g., "If the proviso excludes someone's appropriating all the drinkable water in the world, it also excludes his purchasing it all."[3] Moreover, his critics follow him in this emphasis. We saw an example in the last chapter in G. A. Cohen's discussion of oil, which is representative of his approach. Yet again, there is talk of enclosing beaches and appropriating the land. What has changed are only the substantive judgments, not the paradigm as a whole.[4]

Finally, it is worth noting that so-called left-libertarians, who in principle rec-ognize a right to the fruits of our labor, but insist on an egalitarian approach to natural resources, are also invested in the paradigm. Michael Otsuka, for ex-ample, argues for an egalitarian distributive scheme by acknowledging that we may be entitled to the product of our labors, but not to the natural resources we utilize. In response to Nozick's claim that taxation represents forced labor, he writes:

> But when . . . one must make use of the world in order to earn income, Nozick's com-plaint against redistributive taxation is much more difficult to get off the ground. Consider the case of a farmer who is forced . . . to give half of whatever income she earns from farming to hungry orphans. . . . [Nozick must assume that] she possesses a right of ownership over the land that she farms that is as full as her right of ownership over herself.[5]

Otsuka's point is that libertarian views like Nozick's are hard to defend once we accept equal claims to ownership over natural resources like land. He does recognize the possibility of obtaining wealth without natural resources, but his central example of this is someone weaving a piece of clothing out of his own hair, suggesting that these cases strike him as unusual or aberrant. For the most part, we are still in the realm of Locke's laboring farmers.

▪ THE SERVICE SECTOR

What is puzzling about the various opposing views just outlined is not any specific matter of detail, but rather the entire framework of the resource paradigm. About 80% of the value of American economic output (by GDP) derives from services.[6] The United States is toward the high end of the spectrum—modern European economies are closer to 70%—but the trend toward GDP being dominated by service-sector work in advanced economies is unmistakable. "Services" is a somewhat diffuse term in this context, but it corresponds roughly to tertiary sector output, not the result of primary resource extraction, farming, or secondary manufacturing, including construction. It includes fields such as banking, retail, hospitality, dining, entertainment, law, healthcare, education, design, and computer programming.[7] The economic importance of the kinds of agricultural activity that so preoccupied Locke and that feature prominently in philosophical discussion has plummeted until now it is completely trivial, however important to our daily bread.[8]

Contrary to what one might suspect, the weight of services is not skewed by especially remunerative fields like financial services or the law; services dominate the percentage of *workers* per sector in about the same proportion as contribution to GDP.[9] And on the other hand, the value of natural resources is comparatively low. Saudi Arabia commands staggering oil reserves, yet its GDP per capita is less than that of Israel or Japan, which have few natural resources of value. The value of all known oil reserves is equal to only a few years of the Gross World Product, to give a very rough intuition-check.[10] Real estate, likewise, is fairly trivial in the scheme of things, with the value of all real estate in the United States estimated at perhaps a single year's worth of economic output in some sources and a few years' worth in others—a few decades if these estimates are off by orders of magnitude.[11] The value of these resources is enormous in absolute terms (especially when concentrated over small populations), but the point is that just a few years' worth of service-related work would produce their equivalent. There is of course capital which produces hefty returns in relation to overall economic growth,[12] but much of that capital was in turn originally produced by services, not natural resources, which is inevitable when one considers that exponential economic growth ensures that most wealth is recent wealth, meaning that current means of getting rich tend to dominate past means of getting rich.[13] Fortunes from the distant past eventually dilute by the forking of the family tree, and by the ever greater value generated by successive means of wealth creation. J.D. Rockefeller was the richest person in recent times and his richest current heir, David, is still a billionaire, but his fortune doesn't compare with Bill Gates's, whose own great-grandchildren will have little in comparison to the next generation of rich, judging by historical trends (though they will still be rich in absolute terms, and relative to most people). If nothing else, the size of the market is likely to be much bigger, leading to increased opportunities, even as the forking family tree tends to diminish fortunes of the past, meaning "old money" rooted in agriculture or resource extraction is unlikely to figure prominently in an accounting of the sources of contemporary (and future) income and wealth. And then of course there are the periodic shocks from wars or economic cataclysms that occasionally reset the field.

A glance at recent Forbes lists of the richest 400 individuals—another very rough intuition-check—is consistent with all this. Here and there someone's source of wealth is oil or real estate, but the list is dominated by such categories as technology, media, financial services, investments, sales, travel, fashion, casinos, dining, and hospitality. And even when the source of wealth *is* something like oil, this is often misleading. Even in the age of the underhanded robber baron, say a J. D. Rockefeller, it isn't as if his scheme consisted of stealing the people's land and absconding with the oil. The schemes revolved rather around consolidating control of refining plants, buying out rivals in strategic markets, or outmaneuvering competitors by monopolizing transport through secret agreements. These practices may seem dubious, but the source of wealth wasn't fundamentally natural resources, but competitive and logistical acumen, however underhanded. (One gets the feeling that oil just happened to be an opportune field for Rockefeller's shady genius; if it hadn't been oil, his zeal, shrewdness, and rapacity would have found the next available outlet, say in newspapers à la Hearst. Criticizing the robber barons for *resource* appropriation is a superficial mistake.)

The exact explanation of the rise of the service economy is subject to some debate, but one plausible theory is that as incomes rise,

> the increase in the consumption of more skill-intensive wants leads to a rise in the importance of market-services, and an increase in the quantity and price of skills. The higher price amounts to a higher opportunity cost for home production, leading high-skilled workers to purchase an even wider range of services in the market.[14]

In other words there is a kind of service spiral whereby, as people get richer, they want more refined goods that involve services (haute cuisine, physical therapy, financial management). This bids up the wages for those jobs, which in turn lures more people into them, especially as increased specialization means greater productivity in high-skill service fields. And, finally, those now working in service industries require more and more services to fulfill needs it is no longer efficient to fulfill themselves, like fixing their cars or looking after the kids.

Although specialization and comparative advantage play a role in an account like this one, it is interesting to note the fundamental importance of how what people want seems to shift with income. Maslow's hierarchy of needs may not seem all that plausible to anyone who has observed the relative weight placed on things like television and beer in the ordering of expenditures. But there is still a pattern to wants that emerges as incomes rise, ensuring that the return to skills rises with incomes. As we come to want good software, refined foods, and bourgeois consumption goods like yoga sessions, the skill component rises, and the more likely the occupation involved is a service.

Pressing this point may, however, seem fundamentally misguided. In fact, it may look as if I have simply confused the issue of initial acquisition with the issue of transfer. Services don't involve the appropriation of resources, it might be argued, but they do involve transfers, and that just kicks the can back one step (or however many more) until we arrive at the initial acquisition of resources that are the object of transfer. "On any characterization of private property, the question of what constitutes original acquisition of it enjoys a certain priority over the question of what constitutes a rightful subsequent transfer of it, since, unless private property can be formed, it cannot, *a fortiori*, be transferred."[15] It may, then, seem that transfers for services aren't really central to private property despite their pervasiveness in the modern economy, since the normative basis of such exchanges still remains the initial appropriations that end up being exchanged at the end of a long chain of transfers.

However, while it is true that one cannot transfer something that doesn't exist, it is a mistake to infer from this that wealth must ultimately derive from natural resources, or that private property nowadays isn't fundamentally a matter of services and transfers, or that these invite the same normative analysis as that appropriate to initial acquisition. There are two ways of showing this. First, historically, many countries have gotten dramatically richer in the last two hundred years without natural resources playing any significant role. Mexico, Switzerland, and Japan are far richer now than before, but not because of stumbling on extra deposits of gold. Vast amounts of wealth were created without natural resources playing an important role. It is true that some of that wealth involved manufacturing or processing physical assets, but even then the reasons for the sudden wealth-creation weren't discovering some extra trees and rocks to make into houses and airplanes, but technical innovation, specialization, trade, and the other appurtenances of modern capitalism. And conversely, vast amounts of wealth get destroyed independent of natural resources. If people stop showing up to work (because of some crisis of confidence, say), everyone gets poorer even as the natural resources sit there just the same as before. Nor is this just paper money like stocks, whose value rises and falls because of changes in people's attitudes; we are richer now than our ancestors in the very real sense of having vastly higher levels of consumption for reasons largely unrelated to natural resources, and if we stop showing up to work, we will experience a symmetric decline in those levels.

Alternatively, we can consider the fabled island of castaways in order to make painfully clear how wealth gets generated without resources playing a non-trivial role. Say a group of us inhabit a small island with a fixed stock of materials for shelter, a stable supply of fish, and a stream of water. It is easy for us all to become much richer without any change in those physical assets. Simply by becoming more productive through the standard mechanisms of innovation, specialization, trade, or exploiting comparative advantage, we can move to a situation in which our consumption levels are much higher. At the second stage, for example, we may end up with more leisure time, and services like food preparation, hut-mending, song-singing, or tourism. If we keep track of trades with some rare shells as money, our money will now support higher levels of consumption per shell. Thus, we may go from eking out a wretched subsistence existence to a comparatively affluent one without increased appropriation or the discovery of new natural resources. In such circumstances, where the value generated by services (or more generally, by innovation, trade, etc.) dominates value derived from natural resources, it would be a mistake to focus on initial appropriation, since the latter plays no important role in making people wealthy.

This way of getting richer without appropriating anything corresponds to the actual wealth-creation involved in the service economy, for example that associated with the growth in design, software, architecture, teaching, and medicine over the last century. In practical terms, when you receive a paycheck, there is no reason to think that the money must inevitably trace back to appropriating a chunk of gold or plot of land. Suppose your check comes from an architect or software engineer. That person in turn was likely paid by someone in the service economy, and so on. Of course, there is also wealth generated by extracting oil or from land, but as we've seen, that component is relatively trivial.

▪ MONEY FOR NUMBERS

Creating value through services is now the central case of value creation, and barring catastrophe forever will be. To get a clearer sense of private property in a service context, let us consider a specific, stylized example that highlights the differences between getting rich from providing a service, as against digging up potatoes:

> *Money for Numbers*: A software developer needs an algorithm that solves some problem for his code, and you decide to supply him with one. Your work consists in sitting on a park bench and thinking for many hours. You then meet the developer and recite a long number representing the algorithm. After you have recited the long number, he then recites a different number, representing the confirmation code for a hefty bank transfer to go through. Later on, you use your wealth to acquire goods by reciting still other numbers representing still more transfers. Your transactions thus consist of sitting around and reciting numbers, and getting rich meant finding someone willing to hire you to devise and recite a long number.

The vignette is accented for emphasis, but not much, really. Executives earn a living tapping on keyboards and shouting into phones, designers draw pictures, doctors ask questions and dispense advice; their chief contribution is purely informational, and so is software work as in the vignette, even if I've exaggerated its level of abstraction for dramatic purposes. The natural resource contribution to these activities is virtually nil. And looking to the future, it is easy to see that cases like Money for Numbers will come to encompass a greater and greater fraction of value-generating activities. Already, there are a number of people who earn a living entirely in a virtual economy, for instance by designing and coding objects in virtual games that people pay for in order to clothe or arm or decorate their virtual avatars just as they would "In Real Life." Money for Numbers thus illustrates that it is possible to get rich without appropriating anything at all, drawing on transfers that themselves owe little or nothing to appropriating resources. To think otherwise is just to succumb to the fallacy that wealth must take the form of stuff and that wealth creation must take the form of appropriating physical objects.

We might resist making too much of Money for Numbers by emphasizing two points where natural resources and initial acquisition still obtrude themselves. One is that physical objects are still *used* in Money for Numbers, if only in the form of buildings, chairs, and telephones. More broadly, sophisticated software work requires a social framework containing plenty of manufactured goods and energy that trace back to natural resources. The other possible entrée is with the goods ultimately acquired, say the house and land you acquire with your earnings. But neither of these looks like plausible grounds for claiming that initial appropriation is fundamental to wealth in any sense that is relevant to the normative theory of private property. Certainly we should admit that without various bits of matter, we couldn't earn money or translate it into certain forms of wealth, any more than we could earn money without oxygen or own land without gravity. The number of necessary conditions implicated in economic activity is truly vast. But this would only be relevant if these necessary conditions impinged on the moral claims people have to the assets in question, and it's hard to see why they would. We can assume that the telephone you use to earn your living and the land you buy or rent were legitimately acquired, that no one was robbed or defrauded or otherwise holds a claim on them while refusing you permission for their use. (Presumably even under conditions of ideal justice it won't be impossible to find people willing to permit you to use some atoms in the form of a telephone, or buy or rent some property in return for fair compensation that benefits them on net.) If so, then there is no obvious reason to deny that the morally relevant facts about your earnings in Money for Numbers are captured by the vignette; i.e., you simply provide an informational service for someone else at the person's request for an agreed amount, and get rich by providing a service.

Another worry specific to Money for Numbers is whether it doesn't in fact open the door to emphasizing initial acquisition once again, if not of natural resources, then of intellectual property.[16] This would at least derail my attempts to get us to stop emphasizing initial acquisition in thinking about modern-day private property, once we've set aside lunar colonies and a few other oddball cases. And those skeptical of intellectual property would then presumably reject the emphasis on services altogether. But while some enterprises require a background of intellectual property, others do not. If the only viable business model for a software company were charging for programs that it sent to customers who wouldn't pay unless the company could enforce its property claims against copycat rivals, then initial acquisition in intellectual property would obviously be crucial. And occasionally the extent to which corporations seek to make such claims on behalf of abstracta is quite striking, as when a consortium claimed to own the encryption key hex-number for HD DVDs and sued those who publicized it. In a sense, the claim was that the following is an *illegal number*: 09F911029D74 E35BD84156C5635688C0. But nothing in Money for Numbers depends on intellectual property, or believing in illegal or immoral numbers; we can continue to stand up for the virtuous primes and unsullied integers. We could abolish intellectual property altogether, and people could still generate income by providing services like those described, though naturally there might be changes in the business models software companies would want to pursue. (Plenty of software engineers earned money before 1981, when legal protections began to emerge for them in the United States.) So we don't need to conceive of intellectual services as anything like acquiring property, which is even more obvious in fields like primary care or fine dining or fashion, all of which flourish and provide income in the absence of intellectual property.

■ JUSTIFICATIONS FOR REDISTRIBUTION

We need to accept that large numbers of people acquire and hold wealth in a manner similar to Money for Numbers. Acquiring and holding large amounts of property, represented informationally on some hard drive, need not and increasingly does not have anything to do with natural resources. Even when wealth enables people to acquire or rent land, doing so will often be unimpeachable even in an ideal, perfectly just world, since this will frequently *benefit* ideally just landholders. The tendency of writers both on the left and the right to focus on initial appropriation of resources is a mistake. In itself, this would perhaps be merely interesting. But I believe that this fact has some important normative implications as well. And these strike me as more damaging to projects of the Left.

One obvious consequence is that egalitarian strategies that rely on the natural resource paradigm are in trouble. Recall the left-libertarian approach we noted earlier, whereby we concede that there are things we can do in order to give us a strong claim to property (as when we weave a sweater out of our own hair, and are entitled to resist others who would take it from us without our consent), but then go on to insist that natural resources form a commons to which no one has a special claim, unless the claim satisfies some very strict proviso. And since satisfying that proviso would, at least under certain favorable conditions, bring about an egalitarian condition, justice in distribution is said to imply egalitarianism or something near enough. Crudely put, the strategy is to concede the initial point about our ability to exercise claims over assets to the Right, but then rescue egalitarianism by pressing equal claims to natural resources. In one version of this general strategy,

> Lockean initial acquisitions provide a tremendous opportunity for gain to individuals who obtain them and to society in general. . . . Even if [the very indigent] are better off than they would have been if we had remained in the state of nature, they have not obtained their fair share of the gains which result from the system of property rights developed through Lockean initial acquisitions. . . . The contemporary indigent are, therefore, entitled to compensation for the infringement on their rights involved in the initial Lockean acquisitions.[17]

The problem for such views is that, even granting all of the normative claims, it turns out that the money is in services, not in initial acquisition. This strategy is directed, so to speak, at plundering an empty bank vault. In order to bring about non-trivial redistribution, let alone anything very egalitarian, the story needs to be one that latches onto cases like Money for Numbers, and it's hard to see how to forge such a connection with anything that's on the table thus far. When you get rich selling your algorithm, you aren't taking advantage of any Lockean initial acquisitions, and as we have seen, it isn't true that the money transferred to you is particularly likely to have either. As people have exercised their ingenuity in increasingly productive fashion over time, they have generated wealth increasingly independently of natural resources, and you and your algorithm are the latest to benefit. Only a false picture of wealth mined like gold from the earth and spread through society could cause us to think otherwise.

Another way of putting the point is this. Suppose the poor *were* given a fractional share in the natural resources of the country, so that they received either a lump-sum payment representing the cash value of those resources at the time, or else (whichever benefited them more) a veto right on any access to those resources without their consent, seemingly giving them massive leverage. This would be an extremely generous arrangement, of course, since it would benefit even those who wouldn't or couldn't have done anything productive with those resources. But even this arrangement wouldn't do much to help the worse off. The problem is that (a) the vast majority of wealth creation would continue apace as if nothing had happened in the service sector; (b) this means that those holding shares in the natural resources would quickly end up being relatively poor; and (c) their bargaining position, as holders of relatively worthless assets would not end up conferring on them significant leverage; so that (d) they would presumably sell or rent their assets on terms that would continue to leave them poor.

■ REDISTRIBUTING WEALTH FROM SERVICES

This leads us to the central question of whether there is a basis for redistributing the wealth generated by services. I believe that this is much harder than justifying other kinds of redistribution. There is thus a symmetrical contrast with what I am claiming about natural resources. Natural resources are—I would concede—relatively easy to justify redistributing if some reasonable proviso has not been met, but it turns out they just aren't very important in a modern economy. Wealth generated by services, on the other hand, *is* important, but it isn't easy to justify redistributing.

The most obvious, least controversial ways of justifying taking someone's possessions and handing them over to someone else involve three kinds of argument:

- The asset was *never legitimately transferred* to the current possessor in the first place and should therefore be returned to its rightful owner, as when I've taken your book with me by mistake, or by theft, or by accepting stolen goods.
- The possessor *wronged someone* in the *transfer* of the asset, who is therefore owed compensation, as in the case of fraud or coercion.
- The possessor *acted unfairly* or failed to follow applicable rules of competition in coming to *acquire* the asset and therefore doesn't have a claim to it, as when we commandeer resources in violation of the proviso.

Notice that almost no one rejects these principles in practice. Almost no one denies that if a car was stolen it should be returned, that a buyer who is defrauded has a claim against the seller, or that it's wrong for some group of people to grab all of the resources in an area just because they got there a minute before the next group. The problem with justifying the redistribution of the money you earned devising your algorithm is that none of these arguments seems to work. There doesn't seem any reason to suppose that the money transferred to you need be illegitimate (we can imagine it to be money from transfers all the way down, if we like); nothing in the transaction suggests fraud or coercion—on the contrary, you are paid because the software developer benefits from the transaction; and, crucially, there isn't any obvious sense in which your intellectual labor involves misappropriation or unfair dealing with potential rivals in the use of resources.

Occasionally, this kind of point is denied. Cohen, for instance, asserts that, even in service transactions, we can deny that we are dealing with a fully voluntary exchange in light of our frequent ignorance.[18] He rightly notes that we are troubled by someone's selling cheaply what the person doesn't realize is a real diamond to an unscrupulous buyer, which, even if not legally an instance of fraud, seems disturbing in light of the information asymmetry which renders the transaction exploitative. But it's much harder to see how this is to apply to garden-variety transactions like yours when you sell your algorithmic services.

Normally we can surface the exploitative character of a transaction by considering the scenario in which all relevant information is known to both parties (in which case the diamond owner wouldn't sell), but notice that test doesn't condemn Money for Numbers. Unless we are considering incipient Marxists who haven't yet pondered the hideous consequences of enriching certain individuals, there is no reason to suspect that your algorithm transaction won't go through once the buyer is made to reflect on the fact that you will now be richer. Pressing these uncontroversial arguments into service on behalf of confiscating your earnings does not seem promising.

To put it another way, the picture of the rich and powerful grabbing hold of resources before others could get their share gets things wrong. Even the appropriation of natural resources frequently has a non-zero-sum quality that it is a mistake to overlook—appropriators often benefit non-appropriators by developing resources in a way that does not make others worse off even than they would have been had *they* appropriated instead.[19] (I am no worse off for the farmer in California producing some arugula and selling it to me, not even in comparison to the scenario in which *I* have the opportunity to pick up a shovel and try to grow arugula.) But when you create value with your algorithm, it is all the clearer that your gains have not come at others' expense. Creating value in the services is strikingly a non-zero-sum game. To the extent others are worse off after your gains, they are worse off for mere positional reasons—their changes are mere "Cambridge changes." Of course, being positionally worse off can be a serious matter, but it's a far cry from being cheated out of one's fair share.

These issues may call to mind Nozick's famous discussion of Wilt Chamberlain, whom we are to imagine having a special box bearing his name at each game, into which each spectator who wishes to see Wilt play deposits a quarter. At the end of the season Wilt ends up rich, and Nozick emphasizes that the mere exercise of the spectators' liberty will upset any preferred distributive pattern we may cherish—say, that of equality—absent constant interference.[20] However, as critics immediately pointed out, putting the point in terms of liberty and patterns isn't very compelling, since it is rather easy to maintain such patterns via a simple tax system, and so the normative dispute should revolve around whether it is wrong to *uphold* such patterns, not whether liberty upsets them. The real lesson of Wilt's service (nota bene) is simply that it becomes much harder to explain why redistribution is warranted without resorting to an ambitious general theory of justice rather than homely beliefs most people have about such things as lying to others so as to get hold of their stuff. Without such an ambitious theory we will be left wondering why it is permissible to exploit you for the sake of others when we confiscate the money you earned.

▪ CAPITAL AND LAND

A natural strategy for resisting these claims is to emphasize that a significant fraction of people's income and wealth derives from capital broadly speaking, not labor in the form of services or otherwise. Bill Gates isn't rich because of his wages. Some of us may feel uneasy about redistributing income in cases like Money for Numbers, but things may look different when income derives from capital in the form, say, of profits from a business or gains from financial assets like stocks or bonds. Perhaps we picture the sudorous worker and contrast him with the capitalist who watches the profits rolling in from his divan.

However, establishing a morally relevant difference between income from capital and from labor is often difficult in the context of services. It is easy to imagine our purveyor of algorithms incorporating, hiring some assistants, and providing the same services as a business rather than a worker. In the one case, income would come from profits and in the other from wages, but it's hard to see why that technical difference should matter. Bill Gates didn't get rich through wages, but more broadly through his intellectual efforts; surely the exact financial and legal structures involved don't matter. The normative points made earlier would still apply, and there still wouldn't be an obvious land-type commons for egalitarians to invoke. Moreover, capital is often just accumulated wages. To the extent that capital income represents service wages successfully invested, the situation does not differ much from what we have been considering all along. If it is hard to defend transferring someone's income earned in services, it won't get any easier just because that income has been transformed into capital. Or to put things even more fundamentally, wages become capital more or less the moment they are deposited in a bank account, and the alternative to income from capital is generally consumption (or perhaps bundles of cash under the mattress). And what's so bad about deferring consumption?

I suspect that what really encourages discriminating between service wages and capital income is the fact that the latter is often inherited. Thomas Piketty points out that in France, for instance, capital only dominates the composition of annual income among the richest 0.01%, but inheritance nevertheless makes up about a quarter of people's total lifetime resources on average.[21] When we think about houses or investments inherited by the children of the (working) rich, we may naturally view that wealth differently than we do the service wages of the parents. However, the deep point here concerns the role of luck in the distribution of wealth, not anything about natural resources and services. Accordingly, I defer discussing such cases until we take up luck in chapter 9.

Another approach picks up on the role that real estate plays in capital accumulation, without emphasizing inheritance.[22] Suppose that you own a home that is valuable in virtue of its location—you don't add significant value to it yourself, and the same house located elsewhere would be worth little. We may then be tempted to resurrect left-leaning arguments that you are benefiting from a resource others have some claim to. After all, it is the land and its location that make your real estate valuable, and arguably your fellow citizens have at least some claim to that value, since it is generated by a natural resource commons. Just as no one has a prior claim to the value residing in a country's mineral deposits or antiquities, unless and until the person has met whatever standards are set by the social agreement governing these goods, so we might think that those who own valuable land are subject to other people's claims. We can think of the ensemble of physical land plus desirable location as a resource on par with oil; petrochemicals endow the one with its value, social facts the other. We could then argue for a Georgist unimproved-land tax, which in fact remains a popular policy suggestion in some circles.[23]

In considering this proposal, it's important to recognize that, because the value of service-related labor is so high, simply redistributing the value of land once and then starting over won't achieve much. After the redistribution, the resulting egalitarian improvements will be rapidly wiped out by differences in productivity. To really get somewhere, a Georgist tax must be structured as a perpetual assessment of some high percentage of the land value—perhaps all or nearly all of its continually reassessed imputed rental value. Even then, it is unclear that we could achieve much to do away with service-related inequalities. Often capital income is just an epiphenomenon; those who have savings from income want to invest them somewhere, and land may just be an opportune if risky investment strategy—one that is fungible with other strategies having nothing to do with land. If the tax system takes a certain form, millionaires will just invest in other ways, perhaps in securities. Not all millionaires will want to move from seaside vistas to a swamp, but obviously there will be substitution effects, and in general it's important to recognize that most people getting rich with real estate have alternatives. (Recall the superficial mistake about Rockefeller we encountered earlier.) There isn't much use in complaining about how unfair it is for people to get rich from a resource that is viewed as a commons if it turns out that there are myriad similar investment vehicles that will bring about the same result. The fundamental problem from the point of view of inequality isn't that some get rich with land; it's that some people earn so much more than others that they can invest in *something* highly remunerative. And it seems strange to penalize those who transform income into capital via land but not those who prefer other vehicles, or who just prefer to save.

Setting that aside, how plausible is it that I have a claim to the value generated by how badly people want your land? In a way, perhaps this isn't so strange. It is just another way of saying that I have as much of a claim to the rental value of your unimproved property as you do. Consider, though, the case of someone who purchases a home, partly to live in and partly as an investment vehicle. How is this different from someone who buys a diamond necklace or a thoroughbred puppy dog for similar reasons? All three are the fruits of nature, unimproved by the buyer in the relevant sense, even if previously cleared, cut, and domesticated, and we can imagine all three producing economic rent in virtue of high demand and scarcity. (But notice once again that these investments involve risk; referring to "unproductive rent" from natural resources can obscure this important point.) In light of these other kinds of cases, the Georgist proposal should be seen as saying that we have a claim to the value arising from demand for *any* unimproved natural object. And this thought, viewed in its full generality, seems to me wrongheaded. Someone somewhere has a puppy dog that is suddenly valuable because one like it was on TV—so I am owed my cut. Someone's worthless land, legitimately acquired, is worth a fortune now because the dreaded hipsters have descended—so he owes us vast sums. What is peculiar about these inferences is that they seem to presuppose that there is nothing you can do to obtain an entitlement to gain from natural resources without paying me a share, even if I am completely removed from the scene. However, I have already argued that there are all kinds of things we may do that entitle us to exercise control over natural objects and so to make money from them. The reason for this is not that certain actions like labor effect a mysterious metaphysical connection between owner and land; it's that various things we do can confer on us a moral claim to use things (and exclude people) in certain ways. Sometimes that claim is partial or weak, but there's no reason it *cannot* be strong enough to exclude others from the gains. Examples include cases like the following:

The puppy dog: you could have invested $100 in anything, but you choose to purchase a thoroughbred puppy. These puppies are scarce, but there are many similar investment opportunities open to others. (You satisfy a kind of meta-proviso.) No one else has a prior claim to the puppy, and you acquire it by legitimate transfer. I live 3,000 miles away from you, and have nothing to do with you or your puppy. Under these circumstances, you have a moral claim to the value of your puppy, and to exclude me from your gains.

Japanese land: a very limited amount of useful land is available on the island of Japan, a still smaller amount is for sale at any time, and throughout history many injustices have shaped the distribution of that land. However, land is no longer a significant determinant of whether people end up poor or rich, a few intergenerational inheritors and rural farmers aside. For the most part, holdings in expensive land reflect your income, or perhaps in part your parents' income. It is not the case that facts about the distribution of land appreciably deprive many people of the opportunity to earn a decent living or become well off. Many people gain from landholdings, but these are mostly fungible with other forms of investment. Under these circumstances, one Japanese citizen does not have a claim to the proceeds from the land sale of a fellow citizen just in virtue of cocitizenship.

Denying these claims would require some very strong assumptions, it seems to me, perhaps something to the effect that the constituent parts of the universe are inalienably jointly owned, such that there is no possible set of circumstances under which anyone could lay clean claim to the gains from investment in natural resources, i.e., something like the rents in molecules from the previous chapter. Such an assumption strikes me as incompatible with our mundane beliefs about puppy dogs and diamond necklaces, but I won't attempt to probe any further here. Instead, let me offer a possible diagnosis.

The Georgist may be confusing the important truth that there are *some* contexts in which we don't have a moral right to exclude others, at least not fully, with the falsehood that we *never* have such a right. It is easy to slide from one to the other by overemphasizing a narrow range of cases or misdiagnosing them. For example, in a feudal agricultural society it is highly unlikely that the aristocracy is within its rights excluding peasants from the land. We may then feel tempted to explain this by invoking joint-ownership assumptions. Or in contemporary terms, we may want to insist that natural resources like oil off the coast of our country or mineral deposits in Antarctica are subject to collective agreement about their disposition and shouldn't be subject to individual prospecting. Such cases may encourage Georgist reasoning. However, there are far less dramatic routes to the same conclusion, routes that leave room for cases like the puppy dog and Japanese land. Feudal aristocracies violate a whole host of moral norms whose observance makes a feudal society with an oppressed peasant class more or less impossible—e.g., representative government, the absence of legally enforced social status, and rule of law. Natural resources in areas not already privately owned are likely to be the cause of bloodshed without carefully worked-out social coordination, and so we have reason to prevent a free-for-all. And so on. No need for exotic theories of ownership that would render impossible gains from investing in natural objects without payments to strangers thousands of miles away.[24]

■ THE BIG PICTURE

One of the lessons of these reflections is that how easy or hard it is to justify redistribution of assets depends partly on how value actually got generated. At the risk of seeming grandiloquent, let me conclude by placing this observation into the broader context of three economic ages sedentary societies seem to pass through.[25]

Agricultural. Agriculture was the dominant way of generating value in most mass societies until very recently. Under an agricultural regime, there is simply no way to generate substantial value in close proximity to others without accessing scarce resources that, other things equal, people will have claims to. Of course, often other things aren't equal—land can be legitimately acquired, claims can be rebutted. But at least there is an obvious and direct route to pursue redistribution, as Locke and others recognized, and in practice situations of mass inequality in which feudal lords, say, compel landless peasants to work on their behalf would rarely stand up to detailed normative scrutiny. It is technically possible for such a situation to emerge through sheer bad luck, but the odds of it persisting under conditions of just initial acquisition, rule of law, and political equality are vanishing.

Industrial. During a short transition period, the processing and refinement of primary resources managed to capture a large fraction of value generated by leading economies. Here, the key normative questions concern (a) the sources of wealth required to generate income by capital-intensive investments in factories and machinery, and (b) the relations between workers and their employers, who are often in a position to exploit them. Here, too, there are obvious arguments to pursue for redistribution, at least if we can show that buildups of capital proceed from agricultural-era wrongdoing or the exploitation of workers. (It is often overlooked how much Marx stressed such simple, bottom-up arguments as exploitation of workers in addition to the more recherché theory, even in *Das Kapital*. Newspaper clippings play as much of a role as philosophical argument.)

Services. Although services (including information-based services) have existed a long time—medieval bankers traded and speculated with remarkable sophistication— their economic dominance in the developed world is recent. The wealth generated by services is different from the wealth generated in previous eras in that the key factors generating value are more difficult to assess as commons. The theories enabling such claims are far more controversial and have failed to command as much popular support. The problems raised by a service-dominated economy are thus fundamentally different from those in the past. Services can be corrupt and fortunes can be accumulated by unscrupulous means just as in the other eras, but it is easy to make a fortune in the manner of Money for Numbers, and such cases are common enough to raise these problems. It is possible to try to connect the service era to the other two, say by focusing on the transmission of capital, but I have suggested such strategies face formidable obstacles.

Glancing over this admittedly trite summary, it is striking that the norms discussed by philosophers like Locke and Marx were, reasonably enough, keyed to the dominant sources of value they observed. But we need to face up to the shifts that render a focus on those values less useful (though not, of course, completely irrelevant).

7   Aid

We have been considering, somewhat loosely, the main line in the argument for libertarianism:

> Premise 1: Appropriating property we are entitled to without meeting the threshold and satisfying the residual obligations to property owners is wrong.
>
> Premise 2: The welfare state appropriates property we are entitled to without meeting the threshold and satisfying the residual obligations.
>
> Conclusion: The welfare state does and is wrong.

We began by examining why we should believe in the threshold and residual obligations the first premise refers to, and more recently we have considered the claims about property featuring in the second premise. The last point I want to consider is the objection that individuals have duties to aid others, and that the anti-libertarian welfare state is merely enforcing those duties. Enforcement of this sort is coercive, the objector allows, but coercion must be assessed relative to this background of moral obligation, and proper enforcement of those obligations. The objection is then that there isn't any reason to respect our property when morality requires us to transfer that property to others (or alternatively, we often aren't entitled to what is de facto our property), and therefore the welfare state does no wrong in taking it. Complaining about redistribution, on this view, is like complaining about other instances of compelling people to meet their obligations, for instance to feed their children. A similar way of making the point is that we cannot endorse both non-trivial duties of aid *and* political libertarianism. For if there were such duties, these would undermine the basis for libertarianism objections to coercive transfers.

An older, more severe libertarian tradition was out of sympathy with aid as a matter of principle—one thinks of Ayn Rand's ululations over social altruism, and even Thoreau, the New Englander's lodestar, is surprisingly hostile toward aid. He, too, draws invidious comparisons between perfectionist achievement and altruism that in some ways anticipate Nietzsche. ("There is no odor so bad as that which arises from goodness tainted. It is human, it is divine, carrion. If I knew for a certainty that a man was coming to my house with the conscious design of doing me good, I should run for my life.")[1] This tradition simply denies that there is much of an obligation to aid, or perhaps it is better to say that it prioritizes the many and powerful non-moral reasons we have to do things. I propose a more moderate approach. Although I think there is something deeply right about insisting that moral values don't trump all other values—saving X% of the Louvre surely trumps preventing Y toe-stubbings—I don't want to rest too much on this point. The larger strategy so far has been to try and show that moderate libertarianism doesn't depend on exotic moral commitments, and it is hard to believe that decent people won't want to extend significant amounts of aid to those in need sometimes (leaving the Thoreaus out there to run for their lives).

The alternative I pursue here is to argue that there are several reasons why, granting at least some duties to aid, these may not warrant state *enforcement*, and that consequently libertarians can affirm duties to aid while rejecting an expansive welfare state. In other words, we should use reason and persuasion to get others to offer assistance when we think they should, not state-sanctioned threats or violence. For this reason, commonly offered links between the need for assistance and statist policies tend to misfire. Pointing out that people of goodwill should be appalled by the existence of poverty amid wealth, or that permitting massive inequality is not "who we are," fails to identify a consideration that uniquely counts in favor of the welfare state. What is in dispute are not these sentiments, but rather whether to *pursue* them by reason and persuasion or rather by force.

Such, at least, are the outlines of a narrowly tailored response to the question of aid. But it would be superficial to neglect substantive questions about the character of aid itself. Let us then first consider some distinctive elements of a classical liberal approach to aid, before turning to the narrower issue of whether our duty to aid, whatever its contents, is state-enforceable.

▪ LIMITS TO AID

The world is full of enormous suffering, particularly where economic development has been slow to arrive, and that suffering gives us reason to help when we can. (Picture children going blind or in pain from easily preventable diseases.) When what stops us from helping is our inability to empathize with others, to fully engage with what it is like to suffer deprivation, we most likely are not meeting our own standards. And I take this often to be the case. Sometimes we don't help because it is impossible to do so, or because our resources are needed elsewhere, but often enough we don't help for reasons that are indefensible morally or even rationally, given our own convictions. This comes into focus when we think about the gap there often exists between what we are willing to do when other people's needs are vivid to us and when they are not, despite having the same relevant information available to us. If we are only motivated to save for retirement when vividly confronted with the needs of old age, perhaps after visiting our elderly relatives, we are most likely behaving irrationally, not just responding to new information. Similarly, the fact that most people feel compelled to give more to aid in the presence of vivid reminders of the needs of others suggests that we probably ought both morally and rationally to give more.

On the other hand, a confusing wrinkle emerges when we reflect that we could probably do more good by delaying our aid, since the money could appreciate over a lifetime and then be used to do more good later—if invested in a non-depreciating asset like a house and left to charity as a bequest, it could even make doing more good less painful for most people. (Benjamin Franklin's modest bequests to Philadelphia and Boston were worth many millions when the trusts came due after a hundred years.) But let us set this aside as a puzzle case. If we do, then we can agree with some of what even revisionist utilitarians have to say about aid.[2]

There are nonetheless some distinctive qualifications classical liberals will want to enter, not, on the whole, to cancel our duty to help the worse off, but to correct misunderstandings about its application. Some of these pertain to a sober assessment of how people are actually likely to become better off. Most of those who are badly off are not poor people in rich countries but poor (or even average) people in poor countries. What these countries need is what the now-developed countries historically had, which is economic growth—internal economic activity that results in greater output in goods and services. The reason France does not require aid is not because some external group took pity on the French, but that they were able to generate exponential economic growth themselves. This makes it puzzling that philosophers write long books about aid without mentioning economic growth, and generally seem to imply that the path to escaping poverty lies through individual altruism.[3] Why ignore the only mechanism that has ever succeeded in lifting millions of people out of poverty when thinking about poverty?

There may be strategic reasons for this. As long as individuals can save lives by contributing to NGOs, they have a reason to do so, whether or not this is a mechanism likely to solve the problem of global poverty. Moreover, it may seem as if there isn't much individuals can do to foster economic growth—for that matter, it may not seem like there is much that any *group* or organization can do to reliably foster economic growth from the outside. This is, in fact, another theme classical liberals are keen on, the difficulty of helping people externally, and the tendency for trying to do so to produce unintended consequences or simply to fail. As development economist William Easterly points out, Western nations have given over $2 trillion in aid the last few decades without much obvious success; the poorest countries have averaged about 0% growth over that time.[4] To be sure, some of this aid could have been more wisely directed in hindsight, but zero is a fairly low number, even considering. Naive hopes that simply investing capital in impoverished regions—building roads or factories in the hinterlands—would promote growth have been dashed. The United Nations and other organizations continue to pursue these "big push" strategies replete with road maps and five-year plans, but there is considerable debate about whether "this time" will be different.[5] There is a tendency to treat the mistakes that waylaid great projects in the past as easily preventable, as if such mistakes were exogenous to the project itself, whereas one fears that having foreign experts directing large-scale projects in a region they may not understand very well produces such mistakes as a matter of course. (We can compare cost overruns in large construction or defense projects, and the mysterious-seeming inability to correct for these iteratively.)

For these reasons, it might seem sensible to emphasize NGO-mediated aid at the individual level, and I don't wish to contest this line of response as far as it goes. However, we still should not lose sight of the fact that making any significant progress on fighting poverty means generating economic growth, which in turn means a focus on promoting business development, fighting corruption, creating incentive structures likely to foster a positive business climate, and other things philosophers tend to ignore. If nothing else, it is surely worth registering the striking fact that uncoordinated, non-altruistic economic activity has done more to lift the wretched of the earth than all the generous acts of kindness and altruism combined. (I take this to be a straightforward implication of the rise in living standards over the last 200 years.)

Classical liberals will also be sensitive to how limited institutions and agents of the state are in their capacity to address fundamental human needs. To switch to a domestic case, consider homelessness. In a garden-variety instance, a veteran returns from the war, struggles to maintain a healthy home life, falls out with his boss at work, starts to drink, loses his family, misses some mortgage payments, and one day finds himself on the street. State institutions can address some of this person's problems, most obviously by offering a housing voucher or income support. But what is striking is how much gets left out by most political or philosophical treatments of such a predicament, as opposed to the treatment of a novelist or even a cleric. The problems occasioned by such a predicament include *the feeling that nobody loves us, a sense of hopelessness and futility, the loss of pride, dignity, and a sense of self-worth, a diminished capacity for resisting temptation, an inability to foster positive relationships with others, an inability to raise children and support a family effectively, being sapped of motivation*, and many other things that state institutions are poorly equipped to address. The reason they are poorly equipped has nothing to do with a lack of goodwill or funding. There are simply profound limitations to what impersonal institutions or the paid agents of the state are able to do to make us feel loved or make us good parents. These kinds of considerations are difficult even to talk about in academic policy terms; the profound personal or even spiritual barriers that confront those truly kicked to the curb are, again, more readily illuminated by priests and artists. (What would a high-powered white paper on feeling like no one ever really loved you look like?)

It will be tempting simply to reply that state institutions do what they can, and that their limitations are no reason not to do precisely what we can for people by their intermediation. This is once again fine as far as it goes, but it shouldn't obscure the manifold ways in which the state is largely incapable of touching fundamental problems that are often at the root of what eventually metastasize into social ills. It makes an enormous difference to analysis and diagnosis whether we frame the problems with our veteran and perhaps eventually his children as (mainly) insufficient funding for social programs, or as far more profound personal problems the state can't really speak to. This frame will determine such crucial features of our response as whether we concentrate our collective efforts on state institutions rather than on entities like the family, the church, or civic associations, on national or regional levels of organization rather than the interpersonal or local level, whether we push for more money for social programs or not, and ultimately whether the problem is one we should be trying to solve by legislative measures rather than reason and persuasion. Many important threats to well-being seem to fall into the second category; think of "bowling alone"-type problems, or helicopter parenting, or the toll taken by divorce and broken families.

One way of bringing this out it is to note the difference that culture can make to social outcomes, even against an invariant legal and (formal) institutional background. Often it is culture that lies behind norms leading to problems with productivity, childrearing, susceptibility to addiction, or corruption. When it is, it may still be possible to make a difference for the better with institutional aid, but it will be even more obviously an analytic mistake to frame the problem primarily in terms of legislation and funding. At the personal level, there are familiar cases like the dramatic changes in divorce rates and family structure in developed countries in the 20th century. At the municipal level, there are the changes in the attitudes of primary school students and how teachable they are over the decades—how easy it is to maintain discipline in troubled schools or to get parents involved. The public discussion of failing school systems largely takes place in terms of institutional design, class size, tenure, testing, and funding, but we can acknowledge that these might make marginal differences while worrying that focusing on them distracts us from broader cultural issues that are the real drivers. And at the regional and national level, there are contrasts such as between Sicily and Lombardy, the latter of which is twice as rich as the former. It would be possible to analyze Sicily's woes as a function of insufficient aid from the north (even though Sicily is already subsidized at levels that inspire talk of northern secession). But from a cultural perspective, it will seem more salient to wonder why, for example, Sicily employs 26,000 forest guards and has struggled historically with widespread corruption.[6] In such cases, focusing on aid seems misguided, despite the real and very significant disparities, and doing so is likely to distract us from the real problems, which aren't ones that the state can easily ameliorate. The institutional apparatus in such cases is more likely to succumb to a maladaptive culture than vice versa.[7]

A final caveat to enter concerns the ultimate aims of aid, and the role of incentive effects in achieving or frustrating them. A central aim of aid ought to be self-sufficiency. All aid should be structured with this end in mind; the task is the difficult and paradoxical one of introducing certain forms of dependency in order ultimately to make people non-dependent. This will mean thinking carefully about what forms of aid are more likely to produce self-sufficiency and especially about how to avoid perverse incentives, as for example with "subsidy cliffs" that cause individuals to manipulate their income so as to avoid losing a subsidy. Such manipulations may sound far-fetched if we focus on general and abstract questions like whether people *want* to remain poor, and yet empirical evidence seems to confirm their existence, which isn't surprising when we focus instead on concrete, marginal decisions, as when taking a promotion means losing valuable benefits and so seems self-defeating.[8] At the international level, it is notable that philosophical work on international aid rarely if ever mentions the goal of self-sufficiency and how that goal should structure our efforts. The implicit picture seems to be one of open-ended need to be met by open-ended aid, with no prospects or plans for independence, or priority given to fostering self-sufficiency. (Easterly ironically echoes Kipling's phrase "the white man's burden" in this context.) Alternatives to this approach might include, say, sponsoring entrepreneurship programs, or funding MBA scholarships, or at least taking seriously the worry that perverse incentives may pose a barrier to self-sufficiency.

Raising these kinds of issues can seem politically incorrect or insensitive, since they carry the implication that state assistance may encourage dependency ("We shouldn't pay people not to work!"), which may in turn suggest a condescending or uncharitable attitude toward the worst off. Relatedly, Joseph Heath refers to

> the fallacy underlying the "personal responsibility" crusade of the right. Conservatives blame government handouts for undermining the spirit of self-reliance. This is just a moralizing way of describing a generic problem with insurance systems, where indemnity ("handouts") tends to generate moral hazard ("irresponsibility"). What conservatives fail to realize is that the moral hazard effect in question is a generic feature of any type of insurance system . . . [They] chronically make the effort of drawing an invidious comparison between the moral hazard effects of government insurance and the moral hazards effects of *no insurance at all*. It's no surprise that the latter wins.[9]

Heath notes these conservative criticisms seem especially misbegotten when the state is functioning as an insurer of last resort precisely because moral hazard makes private insurance of the relevant type impossible.

This is an apt criticism of some of the hostility that gets directed toward welfare programs. To the extent that these are predicated on identifying something uniquely terrible about government programs, they are indeed misdirected. But surely there is a more substantive concern that remains; in fact, somewhat oddly, Heath puts his finger right on it, for moral hazard *is* an important problem that afflicts many insurance programs. It isn't as if, once identified, this problem goes away or shouldn't be an object of study or source of criticism. Moral hazard can be viewed as a subset of the phenomenon known as *risk compensation*, whereby people compensate for safety features like seatbelts, antilock brakes, condoms, or bicycle helmets by taking greater risks, feeling themselves more protected, thus canceling to some greater or lesser extent the effects of the safety feature.[10] People respond to incentives, as economists are fond of saying, and a safety feature is an incentive to take more risk. To put it another way, if we were willing to take some particular level of risk in our driving habits, say, without the safety feature, it is unclear why we would shift away from that particular risk preference after the safety feature has been added—why not suppose that we will maintain our initial risk profile? It isn't as if we were selecting the minimum risk profile *before* the safety feature became available, so why would the desired safety level rise? In practice, this kind of "risk homeostasis" isn't always or fully observed, and so there is scope for safety features, of course (seatbelts have saved lives), but it's hardly eccentric or willful to point all this out in the context of social programs. At least, it's unclear why it makes sense to consider risk compensation in the context of automotive safety, but not unemployment.

The personal responsibility crusade Heath refers to, in its more plausible manifestation, will then combine several of the points we have discussed. Perhaps it will go something like this: "The ultimate goal of aid is self-sufficiency, and many of the problems that put us in need in the first place can be addressed by the state only poorly or not at all. With that in mind, it's crucial not to undermine the incentive system that pushes us toward self-reliance, especially not systemically. There may be no price to pay for a comprehensive welfare system that shifts the burdens of mishap onto others when the society in question is rich, homogeneous, and suffused with norms that inculcate adaptive social practices independent of the incentive structures set up by the state. (Traditional Japan, say.) But not every place is like that, and elsewhere there is a real danger of fostering social norms that are maladaptive or self-reliance undermining. It's reasonable to argue these costs are outweighed by various other gains, but unreasonable to ignore them altogether, or to ridicule those who worry about them." Worst of all, we might add, is what can be called "reverse hypocrisy," whereby those lucky enough to have been inculcated with highly adaptive, self-reliant social norms (often in high-functioning and relatively affluent families) refuse to uphold those norms publicly, either failing to see the importance those norms have had for themselves, or not wanting to seem preachy or judgmental.[11] (See chapter 15 on political correctness for more on this theme.)

■ CAN LIBERTARIANS BELIEVE MORALITY IS DEMANDING?

With all of these caveats entered, libertarians should nevertheless accept that duties to aid may in principle be demanding. Earthquakes and famines abound; decent people should want to help. But is it coherent to adopt reasonably "generous" moral principles alongside "stingy" principles of political justice?

Judith Lichtenberg articulates the matter in terms of moral as opposed to political libertarianism:

> *Moral libertarianism*: "This is the position that all non relational duties are negative: people have positive duties only to those with whom they stand in certain kinds of relationship. . . . In short, people have no humanitarian duties."
> *Political libertarianism*: "[T]he state may not *force* A (one of its citizens) to aid B (another citizen)."[12]

What political libertarianism says is clear, but we should note that moral libertarianism in effect says that individual moral norms are "stingy": the only way we can acquire moral obligations is by bearing one of a small number of special relationships to others. The most prominent is that we have chosen to undertake some obligation, perhaps in the form of a contract, but there are also involuntary relationships that carry with them special obligations, like being someone's child, or parent, or spouse. Being in one of these special relationships means we have positive duties not just to forebear, but to aid or otherwise promote people's welfare even when we'd rather not. But when it comes to everyone else, according to moral libertarianism, we only have negative duties of avoidance—we mustn't rob or hurt strangers we run into, but we don't have to help them if we prefer not to. The mere fact that someone is a human being in need is not, on this view, a morally compelling factor.

Libertarians like to think that they are committed only to political libertarianism, that they can reject the stingy-sounding moral libertarianism. But Lichtenberg worries that political libertarianism may actually *entail* moral libertarianism. The key question she raises is "why one who conceded that helping is morally required would in principle oppose government enforcement" given that such a person does not oppose enforcing personal obligations not to harm and also obligations to keep one's contractual promises.

> There must be some *principled* difference . . . between moral duties not to harm, which libertarians believe are enforceable, and moral duties to aid, which are not. And only two possible explanations for the difference are available, I believe. One is that, however small the cost to the donor and however large the harm to the recipient, not helping is never as bad as harming. The other is that not helping does not rise to the level of wrongness or moral unacceptability that justifies state coercion.[13]

Lichtenberg goes on to cast doubt on both possibilities, in part because we have humanitarian duties to aid those we *aren't* in any special relationship with, and in part because our special relationships to others are broader than libertarians sometimes appreciate. For instance, we might see ourselves as part of a worldwide cosmopolitan community even with respect to distant strangers, or we might find that we bear complex economic and historical relationships to, say, far-flung workers in China or Indonesia. Those relationships might themselves generate positive duties, connected perhaps to exploitation or historical injustices.

Let us focus on the high-level claim that in order for political libertarians to avoid moral libertarianism, they must insist on some deep asymmetry between aiding and harming, between positive obligations to promote someone's interests and negative obligations to avoid harm. Libertarians should reject this claim and can (and in my view should) concede much of what Lichtenberg says about positive humanitarian obligations to strangers, though of course there's room for disagreement about exactly how strong such obligations are, about the general stringency of duties to help strangers as against harming them, and about particular cases. They can also agree that the distinction between negative and positive duties is a slippery one, and that it would be unwise for libertarians to stake everything on maintaining that this distinction is both sharp and deep. Of course, this is not to accept that letting distant strangers die by failing to sell one's television and donate the receipts is morally equivalent to mailing those same distant strangers poison cookies, or even close. Although the exact lines of what is being conceded here are rather blurry, I hope that in practice matters are clear enough. The overall task is to see whether political libertarianism *depends* on some sort of radical moral view, not whether libertarianism can *accommodate* some radical moral view. The challenge libertarians face is to explain what if not moral libertarianism prompts them to reject importing common-sense humanitarian obligations into the political sphere.

■ IMPERFECT DUTIES AND AN EPISTEMIC OBJECTION

One reason for the libertarian view emerges from considering imperfect duties. As Kant pointed out, some duties are perfect or strict in the sense of applying always and everywhere, for instance our duty not to murder. On each occasion we have to discharge this duty we must do so. But others, he noted, are imperfect insofar as they prescribe a general goal that enjoins action on some but not necessarily all occasions, and whose completion isn't obligatory in individual instances.[14] Thus, we may think we have a general duty to help those in need, but that doesn't mean that we must help *every* stranger in *every* circumstance on *every* occasion. (The distinction here does not align with the act-omission distinction; some perfect duties are acts, like feeding your baby when he or she is hungry.) It is difficult to reject Kant's suggestion. On the one hand, it is hard to believe that we really do have a *perfect* duty to do such things as promote a green planet—on every single occasion for picking up trash or reducing pollution that presents itself. On the other hand, it seems equally implausible to suggest that there is no real obligation at all. We ought to work toward a planet less marred by pollution and garbage, but our own plans and inclinations can play a role in determining how, when, and how often we discharge that duty, whereas we don't enjoy any such latitude in regard to murder.

Suppose, then, that we accept the notion of imperfect duties. This opens up the possibility of the libertarian arguing:

1. The duty to aid needy fellow citizens is an imperfect duty.
2. The state ought not to enforce imperfect duties.
3. Therefore, the state ought not to enforce the duty to aid needy fellow citizens.

Granting the argument would mean granting that political libertarianism does not entail moral libertarianism, that we can be compassionate or morally strict at the personal level but not at the political level. For the truth of the conclusion would show that one could consistently hold that people have individual obligations to be generous, while denying that the state ought to enforce them. The story would go: various facts give rise to imperfect moral obligations attaching to individual citizens, but their imperfection blocks their being transferred into the political sphere where we coerce our fellow citizens.

Is the duty to aid needy fellow citizens perfect or imperfect, as the first premise asserts? The duty "to aid the needy" is obviously vague. If we clarify that the duty refers to rare, face-to-face emergencies in which, say, we come upon a bleeding accident victim or a child drowning in a pond, and in which we can intervene at little cost to ourselves, we could plausibly specify a perfect moral duty. But obviously such a narrow duty would be of little interest in the present context of rebutting the libertarian main line and justifying the welfare state. We already noted that rights against harm aren't absolute and that we can harm or rob others if certain thresholds are met, and yet none of this does much to encourage redistribution by the welfare state, since such harms trigger duties to repay and repair and apply only in emergencies and when various conditions of desert are satisfied. Perhaps such a rationale could justify taxation in support of emergency care, but even then the duties to repay would remove any resemblance to the contemporary welfare state. Similarly, a state proposing to transfer wealth on the rationale of enforcing a perfect but very narrow duty to aid would face the problem that we only have such a duty in cases like those that show up in the emergency room, and even then only the more serious ones. And here, too, there would be duties of repayment, and questions of desert and responsibility. For this reason, appealing to a perfect but therefore inevitably narrow duty—i.e., denying the first premise—is of little use to the anti-libertarian.

What remains to consider, then, is the second premise concerning whether the state should generally avoid enforcing imperfect duties as such. The practical problems are easy to spot. The initial problem is vagueness. China, for instance, has a law that children must be nice to their parents. The law dictates that children visit their parents "often" and "occasionally send them greetings."[15] Here the state explicitly recognizes the features making the moral norm imperfect, but simply passes those features on to the law, at the cost of making the law vague in the extreme. If the problem were only vagueness, though, we would need only to insert a few existential quantifiers to sharpen things up, perhaps to the effect that children must visit at least once a year and send at least three greetings, text messages not included. The numbers obviously look arbitrary and perhaps absurd, but they are no more arbitrary than the dollar amount defining Class C felony theft. In fact, "assault" and "fraud" are hopelessly vague as well, but we expect legislators to craft rules fitted to the needs of a legal system, even if doing so introduces precision that is to some extent artificial.

The real problem with enforcing imperfect duties is that for most people, the latitude in their fulfillment is so great that there is no way for the state to assess whether our duties have been fulfilled, at least not within reasonable limits on the powers and invasiveness of the state. Philosophers, by and large, have not appreciated the magnitude of this problem. Allen Buchanan, for example, offers arguments intended to show that "appropriate institutional arrangements for specifying and distributing duties to aid can eliminate the indeterminacy that is definitive of imperfect duties without altering their status as duties of charity."[16] But nowhere does he offer concrete suggestions for what such arrangements might look like, and how they could possibly produce the information needed without evoking *1984*. As Kant notes, the problem is partly that the discharge of imperfect duties may be influenced by inclination, but they can also be influenced by our other duties. We can put off helping the needy if we would rather go on vacation and do some volunteer work the week after instead, but we can also beg off aiding the needy in order to help our child learn to read or to do our share of the chores around the house. (I assume we have an imperfect duty to promote our child's welfare and to help manage a household with a spouse.) Suppose, now, that we are morally committed to helping the needy, but that we have many other goals and ambitions as well, some deriving from other imperfect duties, some from non-moral concerns. For local color, we can imagine over the course of the past year, our time, money and energy was allocated very roughly and impressionistically as follows:

- Sending our (non-needy) child to a fancy college, and assisting a learning-disabled child with school work: 20%
- Dealing with a (non-needy) spouse's anxiety disorder: 20%
- Helping (non-needy) Uncle Bob with some loans: 5%
- Donations to overseas needy: 4%
- Donations to the domestic needy: 1%
- Family vacation: 10%
- Everything else (housing, food, car, etc.): 40%

Have we fulfilled out obligation to help the domestic needy as most people conceive of it, given our desire to go on vacation (and have "everything else") and meet our other obligations?

We can make a credible case for the affirmative, even granting that helping our family members doesn't count as aiding the needy. The key is that we can reasonably claim to recognize the goal of helping the domestic needy while justifying contributing a relatively small amount (1%) toward promoting that goal. Our reasons would not be ones of indifference or contempt or distraction; they would be ones of prioritizing other ends that are also deeply important, some of them morally important. Given those particular reasons, we could, in my view, make a credible case to have fulfilled our imperfect duty to aid strangers. Some will disagree, but for reasons that aren't relevant here. Utilitarians think that we don't just have some vague imperfect duty to aid the needy, but rather a stringent duty to bring about the greatest good for the greatest number. My point is only that, *as far as the imperfect duty goes*, we can make a plausible case even when contributing relatively little, given the role other obligations and inclinations play in setting the contents of such a duty.

In fact, I'm inclined to think that most of us could meet our duty to help the needy while contributing *nothing* in a given year, even if we're reasonably well off. Imagine Aunt Esther intoning mournfully, "I wish I could give, but I just can't this year—not with the rent, and paying for Kathy's dental work, and helping out Uncle Bob with his loans!" Aunt Esther clearly shares the relevant humanitarian values and recognizes their importance; given that she contributes nothing to it in the present only because of other legitimate priorities, there is no reason to condemn her on the grounds that she fails to help the needy. If we did, she could rightly complain that *had* she materially contributed, she would just have been condemned for neglecting all the other imperfect duties she has. Thus, we can claim that domestic aid to the causes that the welfare state promotes might approach or equal zero in light of our other priorities. And there would be nothing inconsistent in adding that we agree that duties to aid can be quite stringent under some conditions, as when other priorities have been taken care of, we are making a vast fortune, or in the presence of unusual emergency circumstances.

What this shows is that, even granting that there is an imperfect duty to help the needy, and even granting that it is or can be fairly stringent, the state will find it impossible to determine whether we have fulfilled such a duty without very complex consideration of, more or less, our entire lives. Crucial facts will include how we expended time, energy, and money in relation to family members, or foreign rather than the domestic poor, or how we advanced our own projects of various kinds, over the past year and last few years as well. The state could cut through the vagueness of imperfect duties by insisting, say, that we give at least X% to the state-run or some other charity, but the point is that a reasonable figure here will depend on everything else, and the reasonable minimum may be *nothing*. Cutting through the vague judgment that stealing a lot should be punished more harshly than stealing a little is easy: the exact dollar values we throw out defining a Class C felony will be arbitrary, but the underlying moral reasoning won't be distorted. By contrast, ignoring the structure of our deliberations in deciding not to give much or anything to domestic charity *would* grossly distort the moral nature of our actions. And the problem, naturally, is that no reasonably configured state is capable of dealing with this inevitable and morally essential complexity. (Notice we haven't even touched on the complexities pertaining to the *recipient* of aid, who may deserve more or less aid depending on his or her actions.)

For these reasons, there seem to be a serious epistemic objection to at least some cases of enforcing imperfect obligations. I haven't tried to establish that these claims are true of *all* imperfect duties (though I suspect the interaction effects between imperfect duties will render enforcement pretty hopeless), and so perhaps the first premise in the argument envisioned above should be narrowed. But I have argued that the state should not generally enforce the imperfect duty relevant to libertarianism, and so the general strategy of the argument outlined above seems to me vindicated, at least as it applies to most people. We can be political libertarians without being moral libertarians because there are reasonable grounds for insisting that not all moral duties should be reflected by the state.

■ THE RICH AND AN INTRINSIC OBJECTION

I have been emphasizing epistemic doubts, and this naturally suggests focusing on cases that are clearer cut. The state might try to dispel the ambiguities of imperfect obligation by focusing on those who are so rich that no reasonable person could imagine them to have legitimate reasons not to contribute to domestic aid. Perhaps most people could mount such a claim—the median American household is tens of thousands of dollars in debt—but that leaves plenty of rich people who can presumably look after their relatives and fulfill any reasonable personal ambitions while still helping out the odd neighbor. If the argument against enforcing imperfect duties is broadly epistemic, then the rich may look like safe harbor. Perhaps this isn't absolutely clear in every single instance, say, when a Bill Gates chooses to emphasize overseas charity or an Elon Musk invests in interplanetary travel as a hedge against global extinction. But the scenarios to explain how one could have fulfilled one's obligations to aid despite being both rich and giving little or nothing to the domestic poor get more and more baroque. And as they become more rarefied it becomes less plausible to claim the state couldn't fairly easily verify that there were legitimate reasons not to aid. This is why the epistemic objection applies to most people, but doesn't seem as persuasive applied to the rich.

This prompts us to confront the intrinsic moral permissibility of compelling compliance with an imperfect duty to aid. Certainly it is obvious that not all imperfect duties are enforceable. We cannot batter down our neighbor's door to enforce the imperfect duty to be kind to strangers, not even if we're reliably informed that they are flouting that obligation, and if we are in a position to issue a deterring punishment. Even less may we batter down the door in order to compel participation in our favored *method* of satisfying the duty, e.g., a neighborhood program to give away cookies to strangers that we founded and that our neighbor happens to find unappealing. In fact, it seems clear that not all *perfect* duties may be enforced. We don't batter down our neighbor's door to force him to be honest with his friends.

Why are such enforcements wrong?[17] The issue has nothing to do with the act-omission distinction, at least not directly—there are plenty of omissions we might observe through our neighbor's window that we could remedy by force, including battering down his door, as when he watches his spouse slip and slowly bleed to death while doing nothing to help. There appear to be a number of distinct grounds barring enforcement. Superficially, enforcement may sometimes require using a degree or kind of force that would be disproportionate to the end, as when our neighbor leaves us no choice but to attack his fortress-like home with a tank if we are to compel him to return a hammer. More interesting are cases in which enforcement would require an invasion of the private sphere that we tend to zone off from enforcement even in the case of very great harms to welfare, as when lovers lie and betray one another and so shatter lives, or parents make poor work/family trade-offs, or people ignore self-directed duties to develop their talents. It would be easy to write laws penalizing such behavior or for the neighborhood to intervene against guilty parties so as to punish them or exact compensation, but members of liberal societies tend to feel that it's *just not any of our business*. We recognize that the duties in question, though directed toward important ends, are part of an intricate network of considerations that we think it unwise to adjudicate from without, especially given the high costs of promoting a culture of enforcement (in terms of invasions of privacy, likely mistakes, and the like), so that we're better off waiving enforcement even in those cases when we are inclined to issue criticism and chatter disapprovingly amongst ourselves.

Of course, not all domestic affairs are beyond intervention, and none of this aligns in any neat way with traditional distinctions between the domestic and the public sphere; you may certainly break through your neighbor's windows to prevent child abuse. Nevertheless, I take it that there is a high threshold against forcing our neighbors to comply with moral duties. Something very great must be at stake before we would agree our neighbors were in the right to invade our homes and force us to comply with a duty they decided we had neglected, or vice versa. Typically, what is at stake is something that puts us bystanders at risk by undermining the public order. If nothing else, such harms—say theft, or abusing a family member—are likely to invite (permissible) retaliation that may spiral out of control, or else they augur additional violence against the innocent, thereby licensing intervention. The same is not true of private harms, assuming you may not retaliate with violence, say, against your friends or lovers who have betrayed you.

Imperfect duties like domestic aid, even for the rich, seem to me to fall into the morally unenforceable category. Saying this doesn't imply the duty is trivial or lax. (The requirement not to betray your friends and crush their hopes and dreams may not be morally enforceable, but neither is it trivial.) Often the problem will be epistemic, since even when it is obvious someone is rich it won't be obvious what kind of aid and/or other legitimate causes the person has taken up. But even when—as we are now stipulating—we have perfect knowledge of the facts, forcing our neighbors in anything but dire emergencies to comply with an obligation they are ignoring falls well short of the standard we accept in ordinary cases, I submit. I am unsure how to prove this if it were seriously contested, so let me simply bring the claim back to the touchstone of everyday moral judgments. If a wealthy cousin began abusing her children, we would be unsurprised and unoutraged at the thought of a neighbor intervening with force if necessary; not so if Mr. Neighbor declared he had come to take off our cousin's belongings because she wasn't contributing enough to local charity. If nothing else, the former threatens to undermine public order since such violence may bring permissible retaliation from other family members and suggests we are all at risk living beside an agent prone to reckless violence; the latter case does not. The extreme violations of privacy and personal space, and the concomitant dangers of establishing a policy of neighbors invading one another's homes in pursuit of our judgments of unobserved duties, are overcome by imminent danger to life and limb in the former case; not so in the latter. Assuming, then, that the relevant moral standards are those we would apply in thinking about confrontations with our neighbors, even the unrealistically clear case of the uncharitable rich does not lend itself to an argument for enforcing the duty to aid.

■ COLLECTIVE PERFECTION

Focusing in such a granular way on individuals pursuing their legitimate ends may seem to run the risk of losing track of the big picture. We each have our individual obligations, but then we might also suppose that we *collectively* have a duty to the poor. And that collective duty may be perfect: perhaps a rich society like ours isn't permitted just to be randomly generous as individual citizens are, but rather it has an obligation to *guarantee* that the worst off in its midst are taken care of.[18] This may smack of reifying society into something that bears moral obligations, of confusing the individuals who have duties with a fictitious superorganism that cannot. But consider a company of soldiers that has an obligation to hold a position. ("Bravo Company must hold the bridge!") A plausible deflationary interpretation is that we mean that each individual soldier has a duty to *cooperate in a reasonable scheme to help the unit achieve its goal.* We don't blame the soldier who fails singlehandedly to defend the position, but someone unwilling to participate in a reasonable structure for cooperatively arriving at that result merits opprobrium. In particular, when officers devise a reasonable plan and issue orders to facilitate that plan, individuals are required to cooperate. And this duty, I take it, is perfect. There may be contributions soldiers could make that are optional—presumably each has an imperfect duty, for instance, generally to do helpful things for the unit, like helping out fellow soldiers in need of assistance. But the duty to participate in reasonable plans of authorized leaders to achieve the unit's mission is *not* optional; cooperation is compulsory. At least, that seems to me a reasonable sketch of non-reified obligations groups can have, and the anti-libertarian can draw on such a view. Let us assume, then, that the idea is that we as a society have a duty to the poor in the sense that *we each have a perfect duty to cooperate in a reasonable plan for achieving the morally important goal of aiding the needy.* The welfare state and a concomitant funding scheme via taxation represents just such a plan. And the government is merely requiring us to comply with our perfect duty when it sends us a tax bill. Thus, concludes the argument, once we move past focusing on atomistic imperfect duties of assistance, we really do arrive at an enforceable obligation to aid, and so political libertarianism really does depend on denying such obligations, i.e., on moral libertarianism.

To avoid caviling, we should sympathetically assume that the state is confronting us with demands for contributing to a narrowly tailored and efficiently designed program that applies only to those both genuinely needing and morally deserving help, so that there is perfect overlap between the plan of the state and any aid that we might have moral reason to give. It wouldn't be of much interest to exercise the "reasonable plan" clause and then to insist that welfare schemes must inevitably be unreasonably broad or inefficient, despite the prevalence of such complaints in our politics. Even so, there remain serious doubts about both the duty itself and its enforceability. The suggestion is that we are required to cooperate with any reasonable plan to achieve an important moral purpose, but this cannot be right, or at least it is incompatible with standard attitudes toward moral demandingness. (Of course, these attitudes might be wrong, but in keeping with our basic assumptions, I want to examine the prospects for libertarianism given widely shared, common-sense moral views—it's obvious from the start that libertarianism is incompatible with all kinds of radical revisionary moral views like utilitarianism.)

If we took seriously the general principle of a perfect duty toward *any* reasonable plan to address *any* important moral cause, we would be flooded with such duties, supposing that reasonable plans aren't a limiting factor. For clearly there are a great many important ends that are morally worth promoting. Examples besides domestic poverty relief include not only foreign poverty relief, but also preserving the environment, ending global warming, inventing new transport techniques for the disabled, curing genetic diseases, or bringing comfort to the sad and lonely. Many of these are arguably more important than at least some instances of assistance to the domestic poor. Contributing to any reasonable plan for any worthy goal would convert what initially seem like modest demands into a *very* demanding set—far beyond what widespread beliefs about morality suggest. Certainly these would quickly begin to clash with our other legitimate interests, like sending our kids to music camp, or going on vacation now and then. Presumably what can be demanded of us from within the constraints set by anything resembling common-sense morality is at most that we contribute to some *subset* of those plans contributing to the achievement of important moral goals, with a great deal of latitude for our own views of which matter most and comport with our other legitimate interests, and which kinds of plans seem to us good methods of achieving the relevant aims. But this is just another way of saying that the duty is imperfect after all—it isn't the case that anyone failing to contribute to any given plan is eo ipso doing something wrong.

There is also the additional question of whether such a duty would be morally enforceable, but since the considerations are similar to those described above, there is no need to repeat them here. It suffices to point out that the collective responsibility argument requires us to believe that, for any of the countless important moral ends that there exist reasonable plans to address, we may force our neighbors to cooperate, with no discretion yielded for choosing among these, or for epistemic limitations. This, once again, looks inconsistent with our considered moral judgments. For these reasons, then, the collective version of the argument from enforcing private duties seems unpersuasive.

■ FORCING OURSELVES TO DO OUR DUTY

So far we have been focusing on the straightforward suggestion that political libertarianism implies moral libertarianism, i.e., stingy attitudes toward aid, an implication I have sought to cast doubt on by pointing out the various reasons one might have for resisting enforcement of such a duty, and by emphasizing what a reasonable interpretation of that duty might look like. An alternative way of proceeding is to consider the contrapositive claim—that the *falsehood* of moral libertarianism implies the *falsehood* of political libertarianism. Once again, modest libertarians will be chary, since conceding will mean that anyone who admits extensive obligations to help those in need must dismiss political libertarianism. Since this is logically equivalent to the claim we have just discussed, in a sense nothing changes, and arguments against the one are ultimately arguments against the other. But it is worth separately considering the claims more naturally associated with the contrapositive.

Assume, then, that we have significant but imperfect obligations toward others, and consider what this might mean for how we ought to organize the state. On some views, part of what we are accomplishing when we create institutions that enforce duties to aid is to enforce duties on *ourselves*. The goal isn't so much—as libertarians tend to present the matter—to compel others to aid those we feel sympathy for, but to ensure that we ourselves do what we believe we ought to. If this sounds odd, Thomas Nagel offers an explanation:

> It is acceptable to compel people to contribute to the support of the indigent by automatic taxation, but unreasonable to insist that in the absence of such a system they ought to contribute voluntarily. The latter is an excessively demanding moral position because it *requires voluntary decisions that are quite difficult to make*.[19]

Nagel highlights "excessive demands of the will," but he also independently stresses the problem of "assurance"—the worry that without enforcement we can't be confident that others are aiding just as we are. In fact, it is worth distinguishing several distinct rationales for self-enforcement that are in the neighborhood:[20]

> *Self-binding rationale*: recognizing our obligation to aid, but fearing we won't comply with that obligation, we institute a forced payment system via the state.

> *Difficulty-avoidance rationale*: instituting a forced payment system relieves us of the difficulty Nagel references which we would otherwise face, as we struggled to get ourselves to comply with our duty.

> *Assurance rationale*: without a compulsory system, we have no way of knowing that we are not "suckers" contributing aid while others shirk their duty.

The self-binding rationale calls to mind other instances, like signing up for automatic deductions from our paychecks for a pension fund. In addition to the convenience, we may wish to do so to avoid engaging in iterated deliberations about whether to consume now or later. If we were forced to face this difficult choice over and over, we might frequently succumb, either due to weakness of will or else, in Plato's image, because of perspective-shifting that causes the distant good to look small compared to the gigantic dimensions of our present desire. We sign up for automatic deductions like Ulysses tying himself to the mast before the Sirens. And in the moral analogue, too, we may fear succumbing to weakness of will for doing the right thing, or perhaps here Plato's suggestion is still more plausible, since people often seem to lose sight of the respective importance of other people's suffering and their own.

Others have noted, however, that despite the plausibility of the psychology, it is unclear how this generates an argument for the *state* to compel *all* of us to contribute.[21] In fact, it suggests just the opposite, since it makes it clear how to produce a non-coercive alternative via private deduction schemes, such as those connecting our bank accounts to automatic charitable contributions. If the point of compulsory aid is really *self*-directed, there is no reason for the state to compel us to make contributions if we haven't previously opted in. This still leaves us with the one-off occasion on which we must sign up, but it is surely carrying a good point too far to insist that our dilemmas of self-binding ramify into needing to be bound to self-bind.

The difficulty-avoidance rationale focuses on the mental anguish produced by needing to decide to contribute. (It is not, however, focused on worries about the outcome of such deliberations; otherwise we are back to the self-binding argument.) Certainly such decisions can be painful. It can be irksome, annoying, or mentally fatiguing to take up subjects we aren't enthusiastic about and to summon the mental energy to pull through. Certainly this gives us a reason to do something like sign up for the automatic transfer. But here too it is unclear why the state needs to be involved, and if it is involved why it needs to compel both the willing and the unwilling to contribute if the rationale really is just difficulty-avoidance. After all, there is the automated alternative that needn't involve others.

The assurance rationale, by contrast, is more promising, since it contains a clearer link between my own obligation to aid and the state compelling everyone to do so. There are various ways of spelling out the idea. It may seem tempting to say that lack of assurance as to other people's behavior tends to excuse me from fulfilling what would otherwise be my obligations, but I think that would be a mistake. So long as (a) I really do have an obligation to contribute to aiding the needy rooted in facts about the needy and myself, and (b) there is some marginal value to my contribution whatever the others do, it's unclear why other people's behavior should let me off the hook. Some have indeed argued that the content of my obligation to aid is a function of what those around me *should* do. For example, it is sometimes thought that it's unfair to expect me to pick up the slack for others who don't do their bit, and that therefore my obligation only extends to contributing what would be needed to satisfy our collective duty if everyone did their fair share.[22] But of course these two positions are consistent. The first point is that if I ought to do X, the fact that others flout their duty doesn't give me license to flout mine; the second is a theory about what my duty actually is, and doesn't refer to other people's actual behavior in any case. Let us assume, then, that whether or not fairness plays a role in determining our duty, assurance doesn't bear on what we are permitted to do.

This still leaves room for a lack of assurance about others' behavior to have deleterious effects on what we *actually* do. As a psychological matter it seems perfectly realistic to propose that people feel demoralized when they suspect or reasonably fear that they are alone in engaging in self-sacrifice. Even if they aren't contributing enough to be significantly disadvantaged in relative terms, the sense that they might be "suckers" can have a demotivating effect that is considerable. Such is human frailty. But how does such frailty support coercive measures against our neighbors? I have already argued that our *neighbors'* frailty does not permit us to compel them to render aid (the case of the rich man who won't help), in which case *our own* frailty can hardly permit us to do so. To put it another way, faced with human frailty and the haunting suspicion that our neighbors aren't doing their bit, we have two options: try to do better ourselves (i.e., fight the temptation not to aid just because our neighbors might not do so), or institute coercive measures to make sure everyone else behaves in ways we don't find demotivating. The assurance argument focuses on the second option, but it is the first option that is more in line with how we generally think about our moral shortcomings.

To sum up, the general problem we have been encountering is that anti-libertarians want to infer from the fact that we ought to render aid that there cannot be an objection to the state *compelling* us to do it. But this inference is invalid, as I have argued. Libertarians can think morality is demanding while favoring limited government.

PART TWO

Markets

We noted at the outset that political philosophies are judged not just by narrow syllogisms, but by what they tell us about things like economics, history, and politics. This makes it imperative at least to gesture toward classical liberal ideas in these areas. Moreover, there is independent value in pursuing a methodology that ventures beyond conceptual analysis and logic chopping—the analytic philosopher's comfort zone—into the murk of political economy, as practiced by figures like Mill and Marx. Accordingly, I turn to addressing some key classical liberal ideas about markets, history, and politics in the rest of the book. No reasonably sized work could treat these topics systematically, but the hope is that the New England-style libertarianism I have sketched turns out to support a range of reasonable views in each domain.

8 Morality and Markets

Philosophers, on the whole, haven't displayed much enthusiasm for markets, generally making a few perfunctory gestures toward their virtues before rushing in to identify the perils. This might be taken as a reaction to American-style commercial culture which hardly needs encouragement, were it not for the amazing consistency of intellectuals in this regard, Western and Eastern, ancient and modern, across many domains of inquiry. Neither Plato nor Aristotle shows any great enthusiasm for commerce, nor does the tradition of Confucian scholars, and the contemporary scene mostly reprises these sentiments, with some important exceptions.[1] In historical figures one must struggle to find much beyond indictments against greed and "unnatural" usury, or worries that trade will disrupt stability and virtue; and it remains rare to find attention given to the incredible value realized by trade, or even just the role of commerce in promoting the exchange of ideas and innovation. These advantages aren't obscure or recent and should have been obvious to anyone familiar with Phoenician merchants in the Mediterranean or Islamic traders in the South China Sea. It wasn't beyond Plato to recognize that Phoenician commerce brought the Greeks their (semitic-Egyptian) alphabet.[2] Gerard Manley Hopkins sums up the intelligentsia's attitude in "God's Grandeur": "And all is seared with trade; bleared, smeared with toil;/And wears man's smudge and shares man's smell."

Accordingly, discussions of the free market tend to be about how to "tame 'the inexorable dynamic of a money economy,' to make money harmless," or about the "ethical limitations of the market," or "noxious markets," and they come with titles like *What Money Can't Buy*.[3] The surprise in this doesn't lie in arguments for banning certain transactions—everyone agrees that some things really shouldn't be for sale. (Find an economist urging us to sell the Medal of Honor or get-out-of-jail-free cards.) The surprise is rather that these arguments tend to be insensitive to the positive *good* of exchange, and correspondingly blind to the value that is destroyed when impeding it. It is reasonable to suppose that there are virtues and vices of markets, but the pattern among intellectuals has been to ignore the former in the crush to emphasize the latter. A moderate approach will recognize the powerful reasons we have to respect and indeed promote exchange, and will strive to locate the limits to markets in the more general facts about what we may prohibit others from doing as they seek to advance their interests.

■ THE FUNDAMENTAL BENEFIT OF EXCHANGE

There are many goods promoted by markets, some subtle but important, others obvious yet underrated. They include the collection and dissemination of information through the price system, which broadcasts crucial facts about supply and demand it would be impossible to convey explicitly, and the incentive scheme relative prices provide. As a whole, this structure is capable of coordinating the activities of billions of people without explicit oversight, as Friedrich Hayek emphasized.[4] None of us needs to know what is happening at banana plantations around the world, or how good refrigeration technology on ships is, in order to make sensible decisions about bananas; we can just glance at the sticker in the store and we know what to do. Obvious though they may seem in hindsight, these coordinating benefits are of the first importance, as we can see if we think through what would need to happen in order for us to coordinate our activities with respect to just bananas if we took away the price system, or if we render it less meaningful by interfering with the markets that set it (say, with a large distortionary tax or a price ceiling, either of which is like a giant eraser deleting crucial information).[5] And everyone is familiar with other useful features of the market, such as the specialization it permits when sellers can operate at scale, and the resulting diversity of goods and concomitant choice that consumers tend to enjoy.

But the benefits of markets that are important in moral terms and that tend to be neglected by philosophers are much more brute than this. The core feature of a market is that it facilitates exchange, and the logic of exchange under favorable conditions is that the trade will only occur if both parties think they will benefit. And this in turn produces *the fundamental benefit of exchange*: trade can create value for free, from nothing. In a well-behaved market, each trade will generate value for the participants they would not otherwise enjoy, and yet that value will arise from nothing other than and with no other cost than the opportunity to trade itself. This can be described as merely achieving efficiency in distribution, but we shouldn't be blasé about the fact that markets allow a kind of perpetual motion machine that takes the gap between our respective preferences and exploits that desire-gradient to generate value from nothing. Trade is the ultimate non-zero-sum interaction.

The simplest of examples: my son gets a toy he doesn't like; my daughter is given a candy bar she doesn't want. Noting their envious glances, I create a market by announcing they're free to swap. Accordingly, they trade and each is delighted. Both are better off than they were before (in simple hedonic terms), and yet it cost nothing to produce this incremental improvement in their well-being. Mere trade made both better off for free, in the sense that no more goods were needed to produce the benefit. Or in the adult version, I prefer some piano lessons to the goods equivalent to the purchasing power I lose by forking over $500, and my piano teacher feels the reverse, enabling us both to get ahead. Of course, markets can themselves be expensive to set up (e.g., eBay), and transactors face transaction costs in the form of fees, information costs, and risk. "For free" must be interpreted to mean only "without costs external to the transaction itself," but this doesn't alter the fundamental point. In a way, this idea about distributive efficiency is unimpressive at the macro level, since we aren't going to grow collectively rich simply by exploiting differences in what we like; that requires things like comparative advantage, technology, specialization, and bourgeois culture, all enmeshed in trade. But for philosophers interested in the moral prospects and limits of markets, it matters a great deal.

A doubt about this cheery view arises from trades between parties who stand to benefit differentially per dollar, say between poor and rich, where the poor may benefit more per dollar than the rich.[6] The effect may then be that the poor bid down the price of some good, perhaps unpleasant labor, to a rate far below what the rich themselves would accept, and praising the result as mutually beneficial may then ring hollow. The fact that the poor are desperate for another dollar and the rich only very modestly interested in labor (in dollar terms) may not look like a reason to celebrate the successful exchange. But in fact, the logic of exchange and the resulting benefits apply no matter how terrible and wrong the initial distribution of goods is. Suppose you have been given lots of tamales and pears, and I have been unfairly given few of both, so that the distribution is at point A in figure 8.1. (The top and right lines are drawn from the "You" perspective, as if you had turned the page upside down, so that "more" for you is to the top left and bottom right.) Assume that our preferences define indifference curves as indicated, arising from our indifference as between lots of pears but few tamales or vice versa. Our intersecting curves produce a lens-shaped region, and moving into the lens will be advantageous for both of us, since a point like

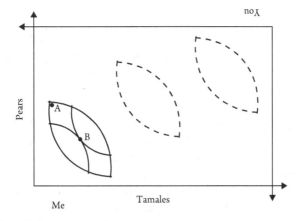

Figure 8.1 Mutually beneficial trade

B will place both of us on a higher indifference curve that we both prefer, since it involves a favorable balance of goods. (This movement may make us worse off along one dimension, of course, since indifference curves tend to be concave in virtue of the diminishing marginal utility of the goods.) As the parties move inward along Pareto-efficient lines (meaning at least one party is better off and neither is worse), they will also stop at a point like B, where their indifference curves "kiss," since further movement will be disadvantageous to one or the other party. But of course we could start anywhere in the box with similar results, and doing so would produce a "contract curve" connecting all of the middle areas in the various lenses thereby defined. So whatever distribution we start with, and whatever its moral qualities, given these garden-variety indifference curves, trading will be to both parties' advantage for structural reasons arising from the logic of exchange.[7]

This doesn't mean that the final results will be just, or even any less unjust, and this creates a temptation to emphasize the limits of Paretian efficiency and to move on. But the fact that initial conditions and final results might be unjust does not show that the worse off don't really *improve* their positions through trade in the manner diagrammed—they do. The fact that Pareto efficiency isn't the end-all of justice doesn't show that exchange doesn't improve the position of the worse off—it does. We might prefer to reset the initial conditions of society in various ways, but this will frequently be impossible or produce an even worse state of affairs, and in those contexts markets might be vital. Philosophers often stress the predicaments that the worse off find themselves in entering the marketplace, but without contesting those specific claims here, the foregoing makes it obvious that trade will often be a vital tool for the worse off to ameliorate their position. If we don't like the initial position of the market, we're free to protest that trade in such a market doesn't reflect our values. But such a protest fails as an indictment of trade itself, which should be expected to improve the situation, not make it worse. Fulminating against the initial distribution of pears and tamales isn't a substitute for piecemeal advancement in our little story, and I am apt to view attempts at blocking the trade as a harm to me, short of wholesale, consequence-free "reset."

Sometimes the social importance of markets is presented in terms of the two fundamental theorems of welfare economics, and sometimes what we have just reviewed is presented as roughly equivalent to one of them, but this is a mistake. The first theorem says (roughly) that markets in a competitive equilibrium will produce Pareto-efficient outcomes, the second that any given Pareto-efficient outcome can be achieved by fixing the initial conditions of the market, i.e., by redistributing in a lump sum and then letting the market run its course.[8] The theorems require assumptions that may hold only rarely, but set that aside. The real problem is that *these* results don't really imbue market outcomes with any impressive moral properties. It's of course interesting that in theory markets can produce outcomes that cannot be improved for some without making others worse off, but we've just seen that that doesn't show anything socially or morally valuable about such outcomes. And likewise, the fact that the market is one way of achieving a given outcome is not particularly remarkable for our purposes (though it might play a small role in discussions about how to accomplish redistributions). What is impressive, I have urged, is rather the humble fact that trade permits both parties, including the worse off, to improve their position, for free. While the first theorem shows that free markets will, under certain conditions, produce that result, what matters is the normative fact that individual exchanges really do allow people to make themselves better off. If the first theorem were refuted tomorrow on technical grounds, nothing of consequence would change in that regard.

■ **MORAL REASONS TO PROMOTE MARKETS**

Interfering with markets causes the preference-gradient machine to break down, producing deadweight losses, which should be a source of sorrow and lamentation. Even when market-impairing interventions are required, we should regret them insofar as we always have a *reason* to favor exchange in a benign marketplace. The object of our regret is simply that traders were unable to improve their positions. To illustrate, consider the deadweight loss resulting from a price floor, perhaps because we have decided that humanely sourced sneakers should cost at least X dollars. In terms of the supply and demand curves in figure 8.2, the floor F moves the price from position $1 to $2,

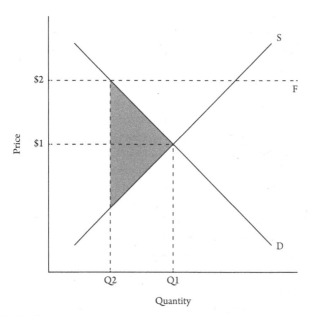

Figure 8.2 A price floor

and moves the quantity sold from Q1 back to Q2, resulting in the lost value designated by the darkened deadweight-loss triangle, representing lost consumer and supplier surplus. This value, it's important to underscore, is lost for no other reason than a reduced willingness of agents to swap some goods, which is what makes deadweight losses (whether introduced by price floors, monopolies, distortionary taxes, or other factors) so maddening, since it means destroying value that could be had by mere allocative efficiency.

As the sneaker example makes clear, none of this is to deny there aren't considerations that one might consider overriding. The claim so far isn't that markets should always prevail, but that (under favorable conditions) we have something to regret when they do not. To illustrate with the case of children again, we may not want our kids swapping some goods, like those they receive for Christmas. There is certainly something unseemly about your progeny hastening to swap away the gifts you so lovingly selected for them. The point, though, is that in blocking this exchange (or in effect taxing it by forcing your kids into the behind-your-back blackmarket), you are destroying value, which you should regret. (It appears that between one-tenth and one-third of the value of all Christmas presents is deadweight loss because of impediments to trading them.)[9] More exactly, we should accept that there is moral reason to promote and avoid impairing markets that would otherwise produce value in virtue of exchange. This reason can be tied to respecting the liberty of the agents transacting, but also to considerations of beneficence and harm-avoidance. These are the same as in other cases of value creation and destruction, as when you simply enjoy playing tennis and I have it in my power either to promote or frustrate this good.

Before going any further, however, we should confront some fundamental doubts.[10] It will be pointed out that the virtues of markets only arise under *favorable* conditions, and that any reasons to promote them will depend on these being satisfied. Markets are known to malfunction in the presence of imperfect information, monopolies, or other barriers to perfect competition, externalities like pollution that affect others but aren't priced into exchanges, and public goods which are difficult to monetize since if anyone gets them everyone does, to name some of the usual suspects. Moreover, philosophers, at least, will want to highlight the fact that the logic of exchange only guarantees transactor-*perceived* benefits, which may be delusional. The value generated by a trade will depend in part on the objective nature of the things that are exchanged. People eagerly engage in trade in order to consume drugs, play video games all day, or gamble. Economists modestly prescind from rendering judgment on the objective value of such activities, but everyone else will find it odd to ignore the fact that some trade results in "benefits" that are actually bad for us. It's fine to focus on perceived benefits or abstract utility-functions for narrow technical purposes, but once we pull back to assess the virtues of exchange more broadly, we must scrutinize the actual quality of the results, not just perceptions.

On top of all this, according to an important but still underdiscussed theorem, we cannot infer anything very useful about what the second-best setup will be in the presence of market failure, and in particular we cannot infer that the closest approximation to a free market is always the next best option (in fact, it won't be).[11] Suppose that a company enjoys monopoly powers that we cannot immediately remove under the present regulatory regime, but that one of its upstart rivals enjoys a market-distorting state subsidy which we can remove. It is a fallacy to infer that market efficiency will be improved by at least killing the subsidy—the reverse may well be true—just as it is fallacious to reason that if our military lacks both bombs and bombers the second-best solution is at least to build the bombers. So we cannot be confident that when market conditions *aren't* favorable, the next best thing is to have the closest approximation to a free market possible. It may not seem, then, that there is much to recommend valorizing market transactions if they can be touted only if they satisfy an endless-seeming list of conditions, and if we cannot be confident that the closest approximation to a free market will be second best.

These observations are useful correctives to gauzy, ideological views of the market as panacea. But most of them are based on conditions that feature in proofs of how the market as a whole will behave, which means these criticisms don't tell us much about individual cases. The moderate claim I put forward was the specific and narrow one that we have reasons to promote and avoid impairing market transactions when they would otherwise produce value in virtue of exchange, which I take to be very often. This is so even when other considerations turn out to trump such reasons of liberty or beneficence. The moderate claim is thus immune to most of these general doubts about markets. The fact that they can fail under adverse conditions is important, but it doesn't show that we don't have reason to promote individual exchanges that allow agents to improve their positions.

In fact, even in actual instances of market failure, the moral reasons we've identified to respect exchange still hold. Suppose I hire you to fix my broken arm at the hospital, and that the local medical market exhibits all kinds of imperfections, like information asymmetries (I can't evaluate quality of care) and barriers to entry. This means that the exchange won't fit various models that can be used to prove what *must* be true under favorable market conditions. But those conditions are only necessary relative to the theorem; it is a fallacy to think that if they are violated, none of the market benefits *can* accrue. We mustn't confuse A and B:

A: Assumptions XYZ are necessary to prove that P *will* occur under conditions CDE.

B: Assumptions XYZ are necessary so that P *can* occur under conditions CDE.

The general tendency of market failures is of course to vitiate individual transactions, but that is consistent with the moderate claim I have made. Even in the imperfect medical market, I may very substantially benefit from the exchange in which you fix my broken arm for money. It may well be that this could or should occur in a more efficient manner, at a lower cost, etc., but all of these are consistent with it being value-destroying to block or discourage the actual exchange I am engaged in, if, say, my alternative is to live with a broken arm and the price, while high, is worth it for me. It is a non sequitur to point out the existence of widespread market failure and conclude that markets don't do much to help people improve their welfare.

We should also accept that when thinking about markets more broadly what matters are genuine benefits, not just personal utility functions. Efficient markets in opium dens aren't particularly worth celebrating, whatever their legal status. Classical liberals may be tempted to press hard on the respect we owe individuals' autonomy as at least *a* reason we have to respect delusional transactions, but this would be to make the moderate claim less moderate. In line with the overall argument I have been marshaling, I wish to avoid putting weight on an idiosyncratically strong view of individual rights or the relative importance of negative liberty. The moderate claim doesn't depend on an extreme view of letting people do whatever they want, or ignoring people's delusions about what is good for us. We can instead just accept that our beneficence- and harm-related reasons to respect market transactions are contingent on actual improvement in the parties' positions. This will still involve a great deal of deference to people's opinions in practice; most of us are better positioned to make sense of our own welfare than of others', and on some views the fact that we are satisfying a preference of ours gets at least *some* positive weight. But we needn't make the moderate claim that we have reason to respect exchange depend on championing opium dens.

And lastly, there is no need to neglect the unpopular truth that when markets are malfunctioning there is no simple recipe for the next best arrangement. Recognizing the destructiveness of market-impairing activities doesn't require us to urge the closest possible approximation to an ideal market, especially since the theory of the second best applies to systems as a whole, not to individual transactions.

We can get a better sense of how often the moderate claim will come into play or be defeated by adverse market conditions by reflecting on our own experience. Consider everything you bought in the past month. Now envision a third party considering whether to block those exchanges on grounds of some market imperfection, for instance that you were deluded about the nature of the good, or knew less than the seller, or were buying from a monopolist. How plausible is it that the moderate claim failed to apply in any of those transactions? It is likely that it really did fail in some of them, since we don't always get what we expected, and sometimes what we expected was the wrong thing to want in the first place. But this is likely to be true only rarely; most of our exchanges seem to us valuable—that's why we make them—and accordingly a third party would be destroying value for us if they interfered. (What is more likely is that

we consider *other* people in need of intervention, since we tend to hold condescending attitudes toward our benighted neighbors that we don't have of ourselves; readers should ask how often *they themselves* are deluded about their
exchanges and require guidance to show them the light.) If we arrive at this conclusion from within what is already a highly structured and regulated market, we
cannot, on pain of circularity, use it to protest those structures and regulations.
But all of us participate in highly imperfect markets frequently, markets in which
we buy with imperfect information over the internet, or use software created by
monopolists. And much of the regulation that protects us is mostly for show or
reduplicative; food inspectors make it to a tiny fraction of manufacturers, and the
real (financial) deterrent to unsafe practices is the existence of a news media and
consumer response to reports of injury.

Imperfect markets are sources of huge welfare gains to all. Markets aren't
panaceas, but they don't need to be for us to harm people by impeding them.

■ THE MORAL LIMITS OF MARKETS

Interfering with trade through taxes, regulations, or outright prohibition harms
people's interests. In the terms of figure 8.1, these prevent people from improving
their position by moving into the lens-shaped area toward the contract curve.
So averse are people to accepting these needless losses—needless in the sense
that the losses are incurred merely because of the inability to swap goods—that
they display an amazing tendency to foster markets despite extensive efforts to
eradicate them. Accordingly, there is very little that cannot be bought or sold,
and prohibitions often just produce black markets. Nevertheless, there are many
things that everyone agrees *ought* not to be for sale. Almost no one thinks that
murder, judicial outcomes, military leadership, grades, or captured human
beings should be for sale. What connects these "blocked exchanges"?

We should insist on seeing this question from the point of view of witnesses
to an exchange that the parties see as benefiting them, but which we propose to
frustrate by force or threats. The problem, we should remind ourselves, is not
whether we may try to use reason to persuade people not to trade—no controversy there. Nor is the issue whether it would be wise or decent or moral to trade,
at least not directly. Clearly there are all kinds of sales that no decent or wise
person would make, but which society doesn't and shouldn't block, like selling off
your deceased mother's diaries just to spite your siblings. No one disagrees that
many exchanges are immoral and that everyone is welcome to use persuasion to
prevent them. The question concerns the circumstances under which—to make
things vivid—we look out our window, see two parties wishing to make an exchange, and yet are justified in organizing those around us to use force or threats
to block the trade.

Critics have put forward a number of suggestions, but one should be ruled out
of order right away—criticisms of exchange that ultimately turn on distributive

worries. These are often couched in terms of fairness: it's unfair to let the market dictate prices for the subway or parking or college or healthcare, because the prices will impose burdens on the poor but not the rich, and so we should dismiss efficiency-based arguments that cheap parking, say, leads both to overutilization (there's nowhere to park), and failures in allocation (the people who really need to park are crowded out by those who don't). What is out of order here is not the general issue, the plight of those who cannot afford healthcare or parking, but advancing this concern in the form of an attack on free markets. The standard response to such concerns is vouchers, and whatever one makes of that proposal in practice, it makes clear the difference between distributive concerns and worries about some market per se. For even the possibility of a voucher system shows that what we really care about isn't blocking an exchange, but ensuring that distributive concerns are met. This is decidedly not the case when it comes to markets in organs or sex, where no voucher system will quell the doubts (if anything, they aggravate them).

Since a great many everyday objections to markets are ultimately objections to distributive unfairness, this restriction does somewhat divorce the discussion from the form it takes in popular culture. But to the extent that worries about the market really are just worries about distribution, relitigating them here would be duplicative, and if we aren't careful to recognize them as such, we end up with a form of dialectical double-counting. Moreover, channeling distributive anxieties as attacks on markets often has a pragmatic basis that shouldn't influence our own discussion. Vouchers make *clear* that what is occurring is wealth redistribution, and this is often unpopular and therefore infeasible, leading those with distributive worries to lodge objections to the free market instead. This allows them to achieve distributive goals without making these explicit and without facing the inevitable resistance from some quarters. (The result, alas, is bad for all sides, since it means inefficiently cheap parking or rent in order to subsidize the worse off in ways that are politically expedient but incredibly wasteful.)

Turning to proposals for why we should block trade that are in good dialectical order, some maintain that certain markets *corrupt* or degrade the goods that get traded; others say that they allow one party to *exploit* and victimize another; others say that they produce *social inequality* as money comes to spill over and dominate other social spheres; and still others say that markets *harm* either one of the parties or else third parties in the form of negative externalities. (The thought behind invoking externalities this time around isn't that they show markets aren't really beneficial, as above, but that we should block certain exchanges.) Let us develop these worries a bit, before stepping back to assess them.

To begin, should we let people sell their babies? Buyer and seller may advance their positions by exchanging a child, and who are we, mere third parties, to interfere? A natural objection is that selling babies is corrupting or degrading in some sense. According to Elizabeth Anderson, parties to a contract pregnancy "accept the legitimacy of parents' disposing of their children for personal profit.

These actions constitute a degrading treatment of children, a devaluation of them to use-objects that is inconsistent with parental love."[12] There are many variations on this theme applied to different markets. Michael Sandel suggests that "to decide whether college admissions should be bought and sold, we have to debate the moral and civic goods that colleges should pursue, and ask whether selling admission would damage those goods." More generally, "as markets reach into spheres of life traditionally governed by nonmarket norms, the notion that markets don't touch or taint the goods they exchange becomes increasingly implausible."[13] He cites a wide range of examples and research, including the (contested) negative effects of commercializing what were once freely donated goods like blood or legal services, which often has the paradoxical tendency to decrease the supply. There seem, then, to be two distinct worries here. One concerns objectionable attitudes of the traders (eventually influencing the social meaning of the good); the other concerns diminishing the quality or quantity of the goods. In one sense, tossing certain goods into the arena of commerce corrupts them because we come to treat and view them as mere commodities whose significance is exhausted by their cash value; in another sense, they are corrupted by becoming worse or diminished.

Exploitation, by contrast, occurs when one party to the trade is holding all the cards, and uses that fact to disadvantage the other. This may be because the other party is vulnerable, being desperate for reasons of genuine need, or because they lack a capacity to exercise effective agency in the market, perhaps because they are ignorant or lack skill in trading.[14] The market makes no distinction between trades occurring because parties have a yen for the item sold and because they really need it to survive or lead a decent life, and yet trades structured by the vulnerabilities or weakness of the one party often make us uncomfortable. The shantytown dweller who turns to prostitution with sex tourists may improve her position overall, and such trades may reflect the consensual acts of adults, but the background conditions against which such markets arise make the one party look exploited, and the other like they are taking advantage. If the exploited have needs, we may suppose those ought to be addressed outside of the market. Marx's account of labor markets, though couched in more grandiose terms, more or less boils down to charges of exploitation in this sense.[15]

Next, as the market assumes greater and greater importance in the distribution of goods, it becomes harder to assure social equality in other domains, for example to guarantee full political standing in the community. Initially, it is tempting to see in this worry another avatar of the distributive objection, but when we apply the voucher test, it isn't clear that the worry vanishes as we might expect. Michael Walzer comments that even in the presence of wealth equality we will need to prevent the sphere of the market from dominating all the others, even if such spillings-over reflect free choices:

> Because I am willing to do without my hat, I shall vote twice; and you who value the vote less than you value my hat, will not vote at all. I suspect that the result is

tyrannical even with regard to the two of us, who have reached a voluntary agreement. It is certainly tyrannical with regard to all the other citizens who must now submit to my disproportionate power . . . private trading is ruled out by virtue of what politics, or democratic politics, is.[16]

This isn't supposed to be a special point about the political either. Even in the domain of commerce or business, Walzer thinks that we should prevent individuals from accruing powers that hold a social significance that is properly vested in society as a whole. He refers to Roman roads and Egyptian irrigation systems; one imagines he would add server farms and the internet nowadays.

Finally, there are the simple harms, both individual and social, that some trades permit. In the individual case, there are trades that produce massive harm to the buyers, and the fact that these harms are supposedly internalized by the buyers may not impress us. Addiction, hyperbolic discounting, and social mania all may cause buyers to engage in irrational forms of consumption that are said to justify intervention. Charts-and-graphs economists sometimes say that the theory of "rational addiction" can account for this behavior, and that such purchases represent reasonable attempts to maximize overall subjective utility. But such theories are very difficult to reconcile with the flesh-and-blood experience of addiction.[17] Raving addicts who steal their mother's jewelry for another fix, then immediately regret it, who make endless vows which they immediately break, don't look like rational agents differing from us merely in their preferences. Even if they were, we are unlikely to accept their subjective utility functions as the final word on whether the downward spiral really benefits them. And of course many kinds of harm are social and so go uninternalized in the exchange, and these even more obviously suggest restrictions or regulation of exchange. Taxes are fine for pollution of a certain scale, but some kinds of externalities might call for simple prohibition. If fracking threatens an earthquake, getting the parties to internalize the cost of all our children dying may not be the right approach.

▪ MARKETS AND ROCK AND ROLL

A puzzling feature of these doubts about markets is that they don't seem special to markets. Corruption, exploitation, social inequality, and harm have many and diverse causes, and yet market skeptics write as if commerce posed a sui generis threat. Why don't doubts about trade apply to other domains by parity of reasoning? Art can corrupt the social meaning of goods. Personal relationships can lead to social inequality, as I show below. If the earlier doubts permit us to restrict trade, it is unclear why they don't let us to restrict these other things as well. Since few of us think invasive restrictions on art or freedom of association are permissible (with narrow exceptions), we should reject arguments for restricting trade that would have such implications. To be plausible, a case for blocking an exchange must *generalize*—it must survive the application to other domains. The doubts described above fail this test.

For now, assume that markets are on par with other human endeavors, and that arguments for interfering in the one are arguments for interfering in the other. Take the point about objectionable or degrading attitudes of buyers and sellers, and how these can come to influence the social meaning of a good and affect the supply and its quality. The same can be said of the arts. As Plato pointed out in the *Republic*, the arts have an enormous influence on what people care about, and so we all are affected by what people watch on TV or listen to on the radio. And many artists exhibit offensive or degrading attitudes toward their subjects, and this often has baleful consequences for the good in question. Jimi Hendrix's Hey Joe seems to glorify violence against women; Metallica's Fade to Black depicts teen suicide in a positive light; entire genres are dedicated to demonizing law enforcement, exalting drug addiction, and praising homewreckers. Political majorities may view many of these attitudes as corrupting and corrosive of various civic virtues, often on decent-enough evidence. The question is whether, if we judge someone's art to express degrading attitudes or otherwise to harm the community simply in virtue of shaping attitudes, we may intervene. If the community decides that someone's art poses a threat to social meanings we view as important, should we use threats or violence to suppress their work?

There have in fact been calls to suppress genres like heavy metal and hip-hop from time to time, but few intellectuals seem enthusiastic. The reasons against interference are various, ranging from Mill's canonical harm-standard in *On Liberty*, to ideals of state neutrality with respect to questions of ultimate value. It isn't important to pick a winner here, so I will simply state that in my view the argument for allowing pernicious rock and roll is twofold. First, setting aside utopian fantasy, no person or group of citizens will be a *reliable* judge of which interferences are warranted. We don't want our representatives determining which art is permitted and which is not because, even if there were a fact of the matter about which self-expression was pernicious, in practice, rulers are terrible at censoring wisely. This is an argument for giving individuals wide latitude in conducting their affairs, and interpreting intervention-justifying harm very narrowly.

More profound, though, is a second consideration. Different types of harm call for different types of redress. If I suffer by envying your success, the appropriate remedy isn't to prevent you from succeeding, but for me to practice meditation. It is otherwise if I suffer at the end of your fist. In general, the liberal and indeed the enlightenment ideal, tracing back to Socrates and the *Apology*, is that supposed harms that arise merely from people's changing attitudes are properly addressed by reason and persuasion, not by threats or hemlock. Taking one another seriously as co-citizens and as rational agents requires us to use reason and persuasion when we are at odds with one another's opinions; substituting violence is an impermissible end-run unless we're confronted with violence in turn. If rock and roll lures my neighbors into apostasy—they stop believing in the pope or in Marx or in bourgeois values—it is my duty to show them the light, but not by force, not even if I am adversely affected by their shifting attitudes. So we shouldn't ban art, even when it is harmful, if those harms proceed merely by shaping people's opinions. And the point of this line of argument is that the same thought applies to markets. Buyers and sellers may have corrupt attitudes, and they may undermine important social meanings or even produce a decline in quality or quantity of some good. But just as this is insufficient to warrant using force to suppress art, so too it is insufficient to warrant stopping people from swapping goods. The appropriate remedy is to *persuade* them that the sale in question is inappropriate.

Similar comparisons can be made for the other doubts about markets. Exchange can produce exploitation through the vulnerability of a party, but markets are hardly unique in this. In some societies, mothers-in-law exploit their social position over their daughters, often in horrific ways,[18] record producers make it known that sleeping with them is a path to fame, pressure groups compel vulnerable politicians to do their bidding or face a primary opponent, established artists exploit their understudies because they can. Evidently, those with power use it to promote their advantage, but this isn't a general argument for the state putting an end to exploitation. Looking at some of these examples, many reasons come to mind—intervening would often mean impinging on intimate and personal relationships, the machinery of intervention would be vulnerable to hijacking by interest groups, and in general, we're reluctant let political majorities determine when we are and are not making wise *trade-offs*, while recognizing that we are being exploited (as in-laws or understudies or interns). And it is unclear why these considerations wouldn't apply in the case of markets. The simple point about exploitation is inadequate to establish a case for prohibition without a great deal of further discussion. The shantytown prostitute is undoubtedly being exploited, but it would be absurd to conclude that this is enough to know what to do. It would be unwise in the extreme for neighbors to use force in order to reshape someone's consensual relationships with his in-laws, even if lives were being ruined; so too it would be rash to conclude that we are in a position to block the prostitute's exchange while ignorant of the trade-offs she faces, her family situation, her finances, her alternatives, or what the post-ban situation would be. At best, the point about exploitation is a point of departure, not a final destination.

Social inequality, likewise, does not require markets for its expression, or when it does the influence isn't always of markets spilling into other domains. As often as not, the influence is the other way around; it makes as much sense to talk of the tyranny of good-looking people with lots of friends as the tyranny of the market. Success in the domains of friendship or love or politics or religion has vast sway over success in the market, and again few seem interested in curtailing such influence. (How would we begin to do so? By taxing the gregarious and the holy?) And apart from domination of one sphere leading to domination of the others, it is worth reflecting on the sheer amount of intraspheric social inequality that has nothing to do with the market. Consider social interactions like friendship, marriage, or sex, and note the truly vast disparities produced in them by such random factors as facial symmetry, hair pattern, cheek profile, height, shyness, or religious upbringing. Many spend much of their lives as virtual pariahs, while others experience staggering welfare gains due to these and other factors. Simple freedom of association, as opposed to freedom of transaction, probably has the greatest impact on something deserving the label "social equality," and yet few think it wise to let majorities dictate such relations to their satisfaction.

When it comes to simple harm, focusing on the influence of markets seems even more myopic. We hurt ourselves, let us concede, in all kinds of transactions where we are blinded to the good or just succumb to irrationality, and often enough harm others in the process. But why is the point artificially restricted to exchange? A given community may have overwhelming evidence that individuals or even large classes make disastrous vocational or relationship decisions, many of them every bit as damaging as substance-abuse problems connected to markets in drugs. Many of these could easily be "fixed," for example by issuing judicial restraints on relationships that research shows to be misery prone, perhaps marrying young or after dating just a few weeks. (We already issue restraining orders and regulate visitation rights.) Research may reveal that those who major in fine arts or attempt to become rock stars become indebted and unhappy at overwhelming rates, and here too we could prevent self-harm. We should insist that paternalistic bans on trade be justified by general policies that we are comfortable applying to our relationships and our vocations. The same is true of externalities that harm others. Some, like dangerous engineering projects, undoubtedly warrant regulation or prohibition. But it is precisely cases like this that do generalize. Non-market activities that threaten to kill us all don't elicit fears about intervention. Unlike the comparisons we have been discussing so far, there is nothing embarrassing about generalizing from restrictions on an earthquake-inducing business to restrictions on a dangerous NASA mission.

There is something paradoxical about all of this. On the one hand, those concerned about the reach of markets warn us about the perils of "commodity fetishism," meaning the tendency to treat everything as if it were a mere thing to be bought and sold.[19] This suggests a healthy sense that there is far more to life than market goods—all those things we shouldn't be commodifying, like friendship and people. On the other hand, when it comes to explaining why we should block various transactions, all those non-market domains seem to melt away, and we're left to think that markets pose some special threat to us, and that, surprisingly, similar threats aren't present elsewhere, even though those other domains are so important. A sober appreciation of markets and their place in human welfare suggests rather that markets don't pose a sui generis threat, and that considering them in isolation tempts us to forget first principles about the use of force to get our way.

■ ARE MARKETS DIFFERENT?

I am suggesting that markets are like everything else, and that if we propose restrictions on exchange, we must take seriously invasive restriction on personal relationships and art as well. My suspicion is that liberal democracies would be reluctant to contemplate the relevant restrictions in non-market domains, and so we should worry more about restricting trade. All this depends, though, on the idea that markets are "like everything else," and this may be resisted.

One possibility is pragmatic. Corruption, exploitation, and the rest really are troubling wherever they occur, but we regulate or prohibit markets because we *can*. However objectionable, a culture of oppressive mothers-in-law isn't the kind of thing that can be effectively overseen by the state, at least not at acceptable cost, and so we reluctantly let such institutions be. By contrast, we can perfectly well forbid contract pregnancy or carbon pollution. A deeper suggestion is that the claims we have to free market transactions are weak or weaker, at any rate, than our claims to things like freedom of expression in art or in our relationships. Our liberty-interest in choosing a mate is dramatically stronger, it might be said, than our liberty-interest in tossing our wares into the market. It may just seem more invasive for our friends and neighbors to insert themselves into some aspects of our lives than others. Relatedly, we might suppose that the goods imperiled by others' exchanges are more important than the goods imperiled by restricting people's ability to buy and sell. Some of the examples we noted above are quite weighty indeed, since we are all affected if education becomes tainted as its social meaning changes, or when our homes are polluted.

None of these proposed asymmetries is persuasive, however. The pragmatic suggestion confuses our sense of what would be a terrible idea with what would be literally infeasible, our having reasons not to do something with sheer incapacity. This both underestimates the amazing lengths we are willing to go to stop various exchanges, and the lengths we could go to perform non-market interferences if we so desired. The state already has vast agencies at its disposal to shape all facets of our lives. The American Department of Agriculture alone employs over 100,000 people, and various state institutions already inject themselves into the most intimate details of people's lives, overseeing whether we can see our children or not, or be within 100 yards of our lovers. It is well within the state's capacity to shape the arts and our vocational decisions if we wish it to.

Nor is it easy to believe that the state's meddling in the arts is ruled out because the ability to trade is generally less important than other kinds of liberties, or that externalities from trade are more harmful than those generated by other activities. The fungibility of money means that markets are vehicles for attaining all the other goods and services people care about. Preventing trade is often *equivalent* to interfering in the choice of mate or other intimate decisions, since the one frequently requires the other. Stopping someone from contracting a pregnancy will often prevent her from marrying the person she loves, or living where she wants to live, or having a second child, or keeping her grandmother alive. It is incoherent to claim that interfering in markets is all right because market freedoms are less important than other goods, when market transactions are often *prerequisites* for those other goods.

More abstractly, it is worth reflecting on how much value is destroyed by interfering in markets—a topic critics of markets rarely dwell on. We can get at least a very rough sense of the answer by considering the extent to which government regulations reduce the amount of economic activity as reflected in real GDP. Between 1949 and 2005, the Code of Federal Regulations grew from 19,335 pages to 134,261 pages. Analysis suggests that this may have destroyed value measured in the trillions: "Federal regulations added over the past 50 years have reduced real output growth by about 2 percentage points on average. . . . That reduction in the growth rate has led to an accumulated reduction in GDP of about $38.8 trillion."[20] Some of the post-1949 regulations are ones we wouldn't want to do without, obscuring the baseline, but precision isn't important for our purposes. The fact that the impact is anywhere near a point of annual growth, and is thus to be measured in the trillions, is what matters. Combined with the earlier point that non-financial goods often require money, one can only conclude that interfering in markets has produced extraordinary harm. Some harms are permissible, so this doesn't settle anything in itself, but we cannot plausibly claim that our interest in exchange is trivial compared to others we have. Saying so would be like saying we don't have a serious interest in having double or triple our real income, or equivalently, the money to send our kids to better schools or buy better medical technology.

■ STANDARDS FOR INTERFERENCE

We should conclude that there is no special license to forbid or restrict exchange. Arguments about what we may collectively do to prohibit other people from improving their welfare as they see it must be general. The golden rule is a useful heuristic in this context. As Kant pointed out (in a footnote!) golden-rule reasoning has its limits; it doesn't capture beneficent grounds for action, and it has false implications for those who don't mind a regime of mutual interference.[21] The golden rule tells such people that they are licensed to interfere, which shows that ultimately we need an account of what we *should* want, not just the advice to do unto others as we *would* want. Still, reflecting on our expectations of others can be helpful. We should ask ourselves under what conditions we ought to accept our neighbors breaking down our doors or threatening us or fining us in order to prevent us from making some exchange. My proposal has been that the answer to this should be the same as our answer to the question under what conditions we would tolerate society preventing us from creating art that altered the social meaning of some good. I take this to imply standards that are quite high, even if they are difficult to make precise. Nevertheless, there are many occasions—in absolute terms, a vast number—on which we are within our rights forcing our neighbors to abstain from trade. These are cases in which the threats they pose, or other moral considerations, enable us to overcome the normal presumptions.

We can think of the simple cases of prohibition as having an a fortiori rationale. What permits us to prohibit has nothing to do with trade per se. Even if no exchange were involved, we would still be warranted in prohibiting, simply in virtue of the moral facts involved. Banning the trade would thus be permitted a fortiori, as a trivial corollary. Although this standard is high, it is by no means impossibly high. We would be justified in stopping our neighbors from dumping sludge into the river upstream that contaminates our drinking water, and so there is a fortiori a rationale for prohibiting business operations that have such an effect. The exact form such prohibitions should take is up for grabs, but environmentalism in this sense at least is perfectly consonant with the classical liberal state.

Similarly, we have a fortiori grounds to shut down Murder Incorporated, human trafficking, and forms of prostitution that involve violence, coercion, or fraud. And harder cases are at least illuminated by the a fortiori test. May we prohibit the sale of highly addictive drugs to nineteen-year-olds? This is harder to settle, but the difficulty arises for the right reasons, i.e., that we are sometimes of two minds about using force to promote other people's welfare. What we must not do, on this line of argument, is *generally* ban the sale of opiates without prohibiting other forms of life-threatening activity, such as climbing Mt. Everest or base jumping, unless these differ in relevant ways.

Some less obvious cases deserve more comment. We don't treat votes or justice or military leadership as goods up for sale, which is sometimes interpreted as a sign that we recognize the importance of preserving equality in these areas, or discomfort with sullying their purity with the dreck of commerce. But these too can ultimately be assimilated to concerns about harm and other rights violations. There is no need to invoke fancy conceptions of social equality. Notice, first, that these kinds of goods differ from those that individuals can have an independent claim to; one's vote isn't something one digs up in the vegetable garden or earns by paycheck. Whether people can sell their vote or issue a get-out-of-jail card is something that is properly determined by the polity. Some individuals will prefer a system that allows them to become richer by selling their vote, but it's easy to explain why most people will not. Putting votes up for sale would be equivalent to accepting the risk that elections and so laws and so our liberty might, without our knowledge or consent, be radically altered. In effect, putting votes up for sale means accepting the possibility of becoming someone else's slave, since the richest among us might just rewrite the laws accordingly. It is unsurprising that this isn't a risk most of us are willing to take on. Some people might be eager to sell their vote—my good-for-nothing students tell me they would happily sell their right to vote for $10,000—but creating such a market would be a threat to the rest of us for the reasons just given, and so majorities may reject it. (That doesn't mean such markets are absolutely forbidden. This would wrongly imply that we may not move to an uninhabited island and start a society in which votes are up for sale; there is nothing intrinsically immoral about such a scheme.)[22]

Goods like military command and criminal justice can be treated similarly, since selling these poses an obvious threat. However, criminal justice also highlights the role that moral considerations besides harm can play, especially the role of desert. When the polity decides how to dispense justice, it is morally required to avoid doing so in a way that is morally wrong. But get-out-of-jail-free cards would allow people to flout their just deserts, which is wrong. Therefore, polities ought not to put justice up for sale. This may look as if we're suddenly conceding that immoral transactions should be banned, whereas before I claimed that all kinds of exploitative and otherwise despicable behavior should be permitted as a matter of social policy. The difference is that before we were considering under what circumstances we may intervene to prohibit people from benefiting themselves in private transactions. There is a presumption that such transactions, which merely involve the exercise of two parties' freedom of action, should not be prohibited. Just as we may not stop someone's marriage or art short of some significant injury to the rest of us, there is no justification for blocking exchanges short of narrowly defined injuries to the rest of us. This is so even if one of the parties is doing something wrong. For example, if a transaction is cruel, or breaks a personal promise, or a married person betrays a vow, or someone's art gratuitously hurts people's feelings, that gives the *agent* a moral reason not to *perform* those actions. But the view I have been expressing, consistent with the tradition of liberal democracy, is that these are insufficient grounds for *third parties* to *intervene*, again short of very high thresholds of narrowly defined harms to the rest of us. But when it comes to goods that we the polity are jointly creating or constituting, there is no question of intervening against anyone. We ourselves are the agents. We are deciding what we ought to do—whether we should issue cards to flout justice, say. And we ought not to do what we ought not to do.

9   Luck and Opportunity

Our view of luck and its role in shaping income and wealth often plays an important role in our assessment of classical liberal ideas. Suppose that I am poor by sheer misfortune. Perhaps I found myself abandoned to the foster care system, attended lousy schools, and then came to majority devoid of skills and know-how. Not blessed with the rare bootstrapping genius to overcome such disadvantages, I am now forced to eke out a living as best I can. Meanwhile, trust fund heirs enjoy a life of luxury they have done nothing to deserve. Many hold that in these kinds of cases, misfortune confers on us a claim of justice against our fellow citizens, who owe it to us to make up for what circumstance or nature has left out. Leaving those worse off though bad luck to the face the free market unassisted would, on this view, be a distributive injustice. "It is bad—unjust and unfair—for some to be worse off through no fault of their own," as Larry Temkin puts it.[1] To the extent that libertarianism doesn't provide a remedy for misfortune, we may thus worry that it overlooks serious injustices.

In taking luck seriously, we needn't focus on a luck-inspired egalitarianism. For one thing, the proper response to bad luck need not be a sustained pattern of equality. It could, for instance, be a one-off payment to compensate for bad luck that is then allowed to dissipate as it is spent or as others make gains. Or luck might yield only a claim to a sufficient minimum rather than full equality. And luck egalitarians may wish to invoke luck in a less ambitious way than I am interested in. Nozick identifies a "negative" egalitarian argument according to which we *already* accept some version of egalitarianism, and the point about luck is then made to rebut claims that those who triumph in the market *deserve* their departures from an egalitarian rest-position.[2] In fact, it is striking how often those who are invested in appeals to luck seek mainly to explain the content of their claim—to clarify exactly what sort of misfortune matters and precisely who is entitled to what as a result—rather than to confront the basic question of whether bad luck produces any injustice at all if left unaddressed.[3] By contrast, I wish to confront the stronger claim that being left poor as a result of bad luck produces a *positive* case for redistribution (we can set aside exactly what form it would take). This, it strikes me, is truer to the intuitive worry raised by someone coming up through the foster care system ill-equipped to strike it rich. Any sensitive person must see in this at least a prima facie challenge to leaving distribution up to the market. Nevertheless, I claim we should be skeptical about considerations of luck supporting redistribution so long as (1) we take seriously common-sense morality as a constraint on the state, and (2) we don't make background assumptions about social justice that are so powerful and controversial as to render the point about luck otiose.

■ WHY DOES LUCK MATTER?

What difference does luck make when considering distributive justice? There are many ways to draw a connection between luck and redistribution, but let me emphasize a few that are especially notable.

(a) There is a standing reason to relieve people suffering deprivation. And that reason is *amplified* by the fact that the agents were unlucky in arriving at that state, since their lack of control implies they couldn't have been at fault.

(b) The distribution of goods ought to follow some non-arbitrary, morally significant pattern—perhaps of desert, or merit, or (hypothetical) choice, or need, or a weighted sum thereof—and luck disrupts that pattern in ways that call for redress.

(c) Everyone has a prior claim on some bundle of resources—perhaps some fraction of the fruits of social cooperation—and if luck deprives them of that bundle, society must compensate them.

(d) The role of luck shows that those who *aren't* poor have either no or only a weak claim to their wealth, making the case for transferring some of it to the poor that much stronger.

(e) Everyone ought to have some reasonable (or equal) opportunity for welfare, and to the extent that bad luck deprives people of that opportunity there is moral reason to correct for the misfortune.

These claims vary dramatically in how exactly luck enters the story, and in what is doing the work to get us from misfortune to redistribution. Claims (b) and (c), for instance, rely on a very powerful and controversial background picture in which it has already been established that everything ought to be distributed according to need à la Marx, or that national resources ought to be divided up evenly, or the like. Similarly, (d) relies on the view that our claims to wealth are weakened or destroyed by the role of luck, typically because luck is held to destroy desert. This may be true, but it is hardly something that those not *already* sympathetic to widespread redistribution are likely to agree with. Notice that it would be radically revisionary relative to our existent legal and moral practices; it is not a part of those as things stand to discriminate between what people get by luck under the Christmas tree and what they earn through hard work selling at the market, or between riches gotten mainly by working hard and riches gained by a fortunate shortage in what is being sold. Random strangers aren't thought to have a better claim to taking our money when it derives from the one than the other as things stand; we don't retract our recriminations of those who steal lucky Christmas presents rather than merited earnings. (To test your own beliefs, ask yourself whether you feel more entitled to confiscate your neighbors' money over their objections in order to send it off to charity if it was won in the office raffle, rather than earned by the sweat of their brow.)

For these reasons, the role that luck plays in pressing (b)–(d) is in a sense minor. When we announce that major redistribution is in order, accenting the role of luck seems out of place if the driver behind the relevant arguments is that Marx was right about everyone having a claim to what they need, or that national resources must be split up evenly, or that we ought to radically revise our legal and moral views of property. If they figure in the story, then it is *those* claims that ought to form the basis of a claim for redistribution, not the fact that some are more fortunate than others.

But things are quite different when it comes to (a) and (e). These may express comparatively modest claims. In fact, anyone who believes both that there are reasons to help those in need and that the force of those reasons is modulated to some extent by other moral phenomena like choice and desert is committed to (a). And (e) need only express the common feeling that it is a great pity to see social outcomes be "endowment-sensitive" rather than choice- or "ambition-sensitive."[4] Those who never get their shot because bad luck deprives them of opportunities evoke a sense of cosmic injustice as we contemplate what might have been, and we are likely to see a reason to help if we can. (It is harder to motivate this thought, perhaps, in contemplating those with bad luck in native talents or quality of will, than with those whose only obstacle is finding a ride to work or tuition for college.)

Of course, this modest reading of (e) could be ratcheted up into a much more ambitious proposal, one that places more weight on *equality* of opportunity and on, say, a contractualist framework. A contractualist might assert that it is unfair for anyone to enjoy more potential for welfare than anyone else merely as a result of native and social endowments: "As equal members of a cooperating society we all agree to share one's another's fate to the extent that we don't tolerate anyone being worse-off for morally arbitrary reasons like sheer bad luck."[5] But this would lead us back to the problem that luck would enter the picture only as a relatively trivial accoutrement to a powerful, revisionary claim. All the real work would be done in persuading us to accept the contractualist framework, implying that we must agree to share our fate. It might in turn be said that considerations of luck are in part what motivate this revisionary framework in the first place, but although that may be true initially and at an intuitive level, the elaborate nature of contractualist reasoning once again suggests that luck is playing at best a subsidiary role. The movement from luck through contractual reasoning to sharing our fate is too complex and controversial for luck to be the star of the story.

Let us, then, focus on a modest reading of (a) and (e) as the explication of what might bother us about bad luck condemning some to poverty. Fortunately, doing so is also consonant with our broader goal of capturing something deep and intuitive about cases like the foster child who comes of age ill-equipped to prosper in the market through little or no fault of his own. The natural thought in a case like that, it seems to me, is not anything so complicated as a radical revision of our system of property, or how to apply social contract theory. The thought is more plausibly construed as the simple one that the person in question is in a bad way, isn't responsible for being in that condition and is unable to realize the potentialities of his character and ambition, all of which naturally heightens our sympathies and lends a sense of at least a kind of cosmic injustice to the case.

■ LUCK, MORALITY, AND BURDEN-SHIFTING

Consider, then, the claim that those who are worse off by misfortune have a claim against their fellow citizens because of the standing reason we have to relieve the suffering of others amplified by the agent's innocence, and/or because there is reason to see that people's prospects aren't limited by their lack of opportunity. From the point of view I have been emphasizing throughout, the relevant question is whether these give us license to use force or threats against others. And as soon as we boil the question down in this way, the answer should be straightforward. As discussed in earlier chapters, we shouldn't be absolutists about this, and so if misfortune leads to a situation like the dying child who can be rescued only by harming third parties, this may sometimes be permissible (though only in ways that don't justify anything resembling a welfare state). But in the run-of-the-mill cases we are generally interested in—the impoverished youth emerging from the foster-care system—bad luck does not seem to permit using force against people in order to benefit others or ourselves. In general, common-sense morality doesn't support forcing others to share in our misfortunes; burden-shifting of this sort usually looks quite indefensible. To revert to an earlier example, if my car breaks down in the morning, I do not get to commandeer yours or to insist on a coin flip. Announcing that there is a reason for my neighbor to render aid in light of my misfortune, or that I will otherwise miss out on realizing my potential, doesn't do much to bolster my case. I don't get to shift the burdens of my foster-care upbringing onto you by forcing you to give me $1,000 toward college.

In these kinds of cases, my fate is my own, and I may not compel you to share it with me. None of this is to say that people of good will won't wish to offer aid, or that those suffering a misfortune haven't the right to make an appeal; but we need only envision the manner in which I would be expected to ring your doorbell and ask for a ride when my car breaks down to see how anything like everyday morality dictates such appeals be handled. Thus, common-sense morality seems to rule out inferring widespread redistribution for luck-based reasons, at least if we are careful not to invoke powerful background theories that would render luck beside the point. It is only if we specifically *avoid* applying the standards of common-sense morality that we can come to the conclusion that relatively mundane considerations like (a) or (e) could render it permissible to do what redistribution in fact does—to force some to make sacrifices for the sake of others.

The first person is the acid test in all this. Suppose I have children, and focus for a moment on the hard-to-resist slogan "Equality of opportunity for all!" Can I really say I wouldn't insist on equal opportunity for my own children? Would

I really tolerate *my* children not having the same chance of getting a nice job or becoming a senator as the kids down the road? But it's crucial to distinguish different *reasons* for differing opportunities. I wouldn't want my children disadvantaged because they were robbed or mistreated. But there are plenty of unobjectionable ways my children could suffer unlucky disadvantages that I don't believe that I, as a parent, would have grounds to complain about. Suppose that you subscribe to the "tiger mother" philosophy of childrearing and send your children to long-division camp for the summer, while I prefer to bond with my kids playing soccer with them.[6] These differences, multiplied many times over, lead your kids to do better in school and ultimately to earn more money than mine. It may well be true that I was literally *incapable* of doing what other parents do out of love for their children. But it would be wrong to think this gives rise to a complaint. In such a case, my children would not have an equal opportunity for success, and yet in my view I would have no claim of injustice to invoke, and in trying to compel the other parents to subsidize better schools for my own children to eliminate the disadvantage I would, I believe, wrong them. Children have a moral claim against their parents for a decent upbringing, but not against society for the same opportunities as those produced by the *maximum* parental investment associated with future income potential. What, after all, would be my justification in compelling you to subsidize nicer schools for my children just because you taught yours things I didn't teach to mine?

Naturally, friends of the slogan will wish to focus on other ways that inequality of opportunity arises, some of which are considered below. But if nothing else, thinking through the tiger mother case shows that there are perfectly respectable grounds for rejecting even the irresistible-seeming slogan of equality of opportunity.[7]

■ **THE HERITABILITY OF SOCIAL STATUS**

This may all sound rather glib so far. It's one thing to argue in the abstract that bad luck rarely permits us to use coercion against our neighbors; it's another to seriously confront the fact that many people's social outcomes are dictated by factors beyond their control. Let us then rub our noses in some of the more far-reaching effects of luck.

One way to gauge the effects of luck on the distribution of wealth is to consider social mobility. To the extent that children's social destinies may be predicted in advance by their parent's social status, we may worry that forces beyond their control determine what happens to them. Figure 9.1 displays an estimate of father-son income elasticity for selected countries.[8] Intergenerational income elasticity is a measure from 0 to 1 that signifies how much of an income difference in the parents' generation gets passed on to the children; an elasticity of .4, for example, means that if a rich father earns 100% more than a poorer father, we expect the rich father's son to earn 40% more than the son of the poorer father. Thus, in the

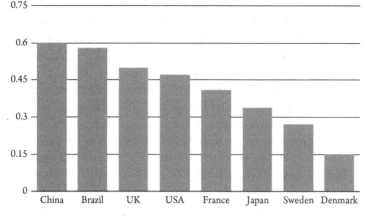

Figure 9.1 Father-son income elasticity

United States and the United Kingdom, about half of a father's income advantage may be expected to be transmitted to the son—more than twice the figure we find in what are usually viewed as more egalitarian societies, like Denmark. Another way of thinking about the matter is represented in table 9.1, which displays the probability of a son ending up in the same income quintile as his father.[9] One might hope that being born into the bottom or the top categories is likely to have been some sort of fluke and thus that the sons in those quintiles would be likely to converge on the mean, but that is so only to a surprisingly small degree. In the United States, in particular, children of the rich have a pretty good chance of following suit, and many of the poor will inherit their parents' poverty.

These figures are usually considered quite damning, but they in fact severely understate the case. A problem with these single-generation measures is that children who choose occupations with low pay but high social prestige get wrongly counted as downwardly mobile. A banker's daughter may become a professor or a diplomat, and her son, enjoying many privileges of educational opportunity and social connections, may become an attorney. Intuitively, this is a narrative of a single elite family maintaining status, but counting individual income correlations will miss that fact and see only the encouraging disconnect between parents' and children's incomes. A different approach taken by some economists

TABLE 9.1 *Probability of Son Occupying Same Income Quintile as Father*

	Denmark	Sweden	UK	US
Quintile 1	0.247	0.262	0.297	0.422
Quintile 2	0.249	0.225	0.228	0.283
Quintile 3	0.224	0.223	0.188	0.256
Quintile 4	0.223	0.217	0.247	0.252
Quintile 5	0.363	0.374	0.346	0.360

is to study rare surnames across many centuries and across varied measures of status in order to track the rate at which social status regresses and progresses to the mean, and then to calculate the implied parent-child correlations. Gregory Clark and colleagues use this method to study, for instance, the persistence of elite educational status among families across centuries at Oxford and Cambridge, and of wealth as recorded in probate courts, and of other measures of status like elite occupations. The results can be displayed in terms of how over- or underrepresented various surnames are over the period being studied, and how rapidly elites regress toward the mean and low-status families progress toward it. Since this is a relatively novel form of research, we should be cautious, and some economists have expressed skepticism.[10] However, since our interest is in social arrangements in light of the role luck plays, the exact values aren't important, and even if we regard this work as a kind of worst-case scenario, it is useful in calibrating our judgments. Briefly, Clark finds that status often persists for centuries—sometimes for a thousand years or more.

In figure 9.2, status as measured by attending Oxford or Cambridge is plotted against time. The y-axis shows how overrepresented individuals with rare surnames deriving from the Domesday book of the Norman conquerors of 1066 are (e.g., "Darcy") compared to their frequency in the population at large.[11]

In this case, the descendants of the conquerors have yet to sink into the population average in terms of status, nearly a thousand years later.[12] Moreover, the rate of regression is extraordinarily slow, implying an intergenerational correlation of .93. Other measures typically show faster regression rates, with correlations more often around .75, but these rates are nevertheless amazingly high—certainly far higher than conventional estimates, which is why it is useful to think of this as a worst-case scenario. Figure 9.3 displays the representation of various American groups as measured by surname in the elite occupation of

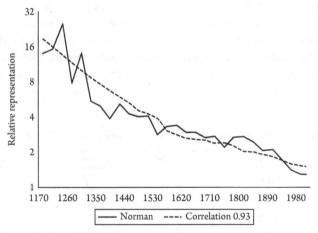

Figure 9.2 Normans invade Oxbridge

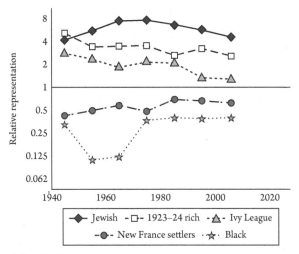

Figure 9.3 Physicians in America

physician.[13] The same pattern of very slow regression to the mean, which is to say status persistence, is apparent. In addition, it is clear that *progression* to the mean is roughly symmetric and thus comparably slow for groups like African Americans or descendants of northern French settlers. (Notice that the French settlers persist as an underclass despite the absence of any obvious discrimination against them.)

Of course, if these were idiosyncratic facts about Oxford, Cambridge, and American physicians they would be mere curiosities, but as Clark documents, the pattern is present in nearly any measure of status, including income and wealth, that it is easy to think of. Moreover, the same thing seems to occur in east Asian societies like China and Japan, and in socially progressive societies that have low Gini coefficients, such as Sweden.[14] And the historical onset of the welfare state and of progressive policies seems to have little effect on the rate at which underclasses or elites regress or progress to the mean. For example, graphing surnames characteristic of the Swedish nobility against elite education over the last few centuries produces a graph similar to figure 9.2. The descendants of samurai in Japan likewise display similar rates of status persistence, despite radical social change over the last century. In England, tracking the rate at which family estates enter probate (because they are sufficiently large) through rare surnames indicates no appreciable change in the rate of re- or progression toward the mean for rich or poor families between 1860 and 2010.[15]

Clark is officially agnostic about the exact causes of this status persistence, but notes that it is unlikely that the mechanism is just inheritance of wealth. As we have seen, the pattern is unaffected by wild swings in tax rates across the years—including very high inheritance taxes in some places and times—and persists even in places like Sweden. Wealth, in fact, isn't any better preserved than other measures of status, nor can wealth differences explain why members of different groups with the same affluence tend to regress toward different means. A Jewish family with an income of $90,000 and a descendant of French settlers centuries ago are equally fortunate, and yet they should be expected to fare quite differently in later generations. The French settler family is likely to regress toward a far lower population mean, while the Jewish family shouldn't be expected to regress at all, it turns out, $90,000 already being the mean of the group.[16] All this leads Clark to a remarkable rediscovery of Rawls, anti-libertarians will be pleased to see:

> If so much of social outcomes are determined at birth, then we can appeal to people's sense of justice in other circumstances to argue for more redistribution. For example, there is widespread support for the resource transfers necessary to ensure that people born with physical limitations are not thereby impoverished. If social success and failure are strongly ordained at birth, then, by analogy, why not provide more aid for those who are unlucky in the familial random draw?[17]

We should be tentative in our embrace of this work, but let us assume the worst-case scenario that maximizes the role of luck in social outcomes, and is thus most embarrassing for a classical liberal position that does little to correct for luck. This scenario is roughly as follows: most forms of social status, including wealth, are highly heritable, regress/progress to the mean slowly, and are resistant to manipulation through indirect policy changes in institutions like schools or the political system. For many people, we could predict with a reasonable degree of confidence what their social status will turn out to be at birth, just by glancing at their surnames or by researching their ancestors.

■ PREDICTABILITY AND INCAPACITY

The data on intergenerational mobility or its absence is sobering, to say the least. In the United States, sometimes this leads commentators to call into question the traditional self-conception of America as a "land of opportunity."[18] It's hardly a land of opportunity if outcomes are determined at birth, runs the criticism.

Let us consider this reasoning in more detail. The critic seems to reason as follows: If there were anything like equality of opportunity, then we couldn't predict outcomes at birth, but we can, and so the land of opportunity is a myth. Let us assume the standard to meet here isn't exact equality of opportunity for every single citizen. Could there still be reasonably high levels of opportunity despite outcomes—including bad ones—being highly predictable from the start? The critic seems to assume the following principle:

> *Predictability defeats opportunity*: if we are able to specify social outcomes with a high degree of accuracy in advance, then the people in question cannot enjoy much opportunity.

Why accept this principle? What is it that connects predictability and opportunity? The obvious answer is that we think we know enough about people to be confident that if they *did* enjoy opportunities, they wouldn't exercise them in a way that leads to bad social outcomes. The fact that we know that Smith will end up poor in all likelihood suggests that he is powerless to avoid it, since if he were capable of influencing the outcome, then he would. This amounts to another, deeper principle:

> *Predictability is evidence of incapacity*: the fact that we can predict poor social outcomes is evidence that those who experience them lack a capacity for avoiding them.

Another way of putting the matter is that a fixed proportion of poor outcomes might be bad, but it wouldn't be bad for reasons of diminished opportunity, since it might be the case that there are going to be winners and losers in anything resembling a free society, and as long as everyone has a fair shot at being a winner, things aren't so bad. (No doubt more would need to be said about what "losing" amounts to for us to feel reassured.) What is terrible about predictability is that the losers aren't just random, but never had a chance. Because predictability is evidence of incapacity, we know that those with poor outcomes never had a chance to succeed, and a fortiori they lacked anything like an equal or reasonable opportunity for success.

The problem is that it isn't true that predictability, in itself, is evidence of incapacity, that outcomes are beyond our control. I don't want to deny in the end that certain forms of incapacity do play a role in social outcomes, but how much is far from settled, and by opening with the assumption that predictability implies incapacity, we go wrong from the start. The fundamental confusion is between the epistemic question of what we can say about the future and the metaphysical question of what people are able to do at a given time in given circumstances. There are various fancy examples to illustrate this in the free-will literature, but for our purposes we can stick to some everyday examples:

> *Rope line*: at the airport, we predict with great confidence that people will walk along a particular circuitous path—the one laid out by the velvet ropes. Nevertheless, the passengers are free to step over the ropes any time they like. It's just that hardly anyone does. Predictability here doesn't imply incapacity, it's just that the passengers all have reason to exercise their freedom in a certain way.[19]

> *Fraternity*: over the years you have taught dozens of members of the fraternity AAA, and noticed that they tend to be highly intelligent, but very distracted by the extensive activities of their fraternity. In fact, they almost never get decent grades, despite being almost uniformly quite bright. You can predict with great accuracy that the next batch of students from AAA will not do well, and yet they don't lack capacity—if they tried to do well in your class, then they would.

> *Coach*: you have coached the neighbor's kid in little league, and know she has tremendous talent for soccer. But unfortunately her father has taught her all the wrong

things. She follows his instructions and never does well, despite her native talent. Knowing this, you can accurately predict she will be a poor player, even though if she just listened to your coaching she'd be a star.

Parents: Jennifer is a talented student who could easily attend a top school if she applied. However, no one around her mentions this as a possibility, and when the subject of her future comes up, her parents take for granted that she will have a child during or just after high school, and that she will be unemployed. As a result, Jennifer is both unmotivated to work hard and ignorant of her true potential. Her guidance counselor confidently predicts that Jennifer will have a poor outcome, but not for reasons of incapacity—if she made a few relatively simple decisions that other students similarly situated routinely make, then she would be far more successful.

As these cases show, it's false that predictability in itself implies incapacity, at least in any strong sense.

This may seem pettifogging to some: perhaps we need some more facts on the table, say that people desperately want to achieve success, but those facts combined with predictability might seem to imply incapacity. However, this isn't true either in at least one sense, as cases like Coach show. It is all too common to desperately *want* to achieve an outcome that is *easy* to achieve in your circumstances, and yet utterly fail to make any progress at all toward achieving it. Bad coaching, poor parenting, lack of adequate role models, lack of imagination, poorly trained-up motivational systems, and inapt beliefs can all come between our ambitions and social outcomes. The vignettes show that your destiny may be written in trivial facts like your fraternity or parents, and yet this is consistent with outcomes *not* being beyond your control in the following sense: if you made certain simple decisions that other people relevantly just like you make all the time, then the outcome would be different (i.e., far better).

Some will still be dissatisfied. There is a sense in which we may regard sheer ignorance or related deficits, such as those in our motivational systems, as constituting an incapacity of sorts. John Roemer points out that directly comparing the effort made by those growing up in fortunate circumstances to those who do not may be a mistake for related reasons:

> Children form views about the desirability of exerting effort in school by observing what others are doing and by making inferences about the value of education from observing adults who have and have not achieved education at various levels, and how their lives have consequently gone.[20]

Choices reflect antecedent circumstances, in other words, and so comparing the choices of those who are poised to cash in on working hard at school, say, to those who have never seen anyone like them succeed through the usual middle-class vehicles is unreasonable, since the latter may suffer from a kind of ignorance. Someone who has a golden thread is capable of turning at the appropriate forks in a maze and so of reaching the destination; someone who is lost in the maze *could* reach the destination with pertinent information, but is rendered *incapable* of doing so absent a thread or map, we might say. A more sophisticated version of the earlier worry about predictability would then go as follows: what is troubling about our foreknowledge of someone's likely poor outcome is that, given various plausible assumptions about what the person wants, this predictability is strong evidence of *incapacity due to ignorance* (or a related deficit). Such incapacities are subtler than what we can call *choice-defeating* incapacities, i.e., those such that even if the agent tried to do X he or she would still fail because of external impediments. But they remain incapacities, and to the extent that we are troubled by agents' social outcomes falling out of circumstances beyond their control, this is just as bad. Putting any special emphasis on choice-defeating incapacities is to think that your predicament on being locked in a dungeon is somehow worse than that of Theseus dropped into the Labyrinth no one can escape (without a golden thread). In terms of luck, both are equal misfortunes.

I don't wish to quibble with this retrenchment. We can simply underscore that the kind of predictability that leads us to think of someone as born into good or bad fortune need not be a matter of choice-defeating bad luck and may rather be a function of ignorance or other deficits that are quite different in nature, for instance poorly trained-up motivational systems. The main point I will want to make about this later is that incapacity due to ignorance may suggest a rather different remedy than choice-defeating incapacity.

■ THE EFFECTIVENESS OF CHOICE

This will all seem irrelevant if we doubt that, in fact, the worse off can do much to influence social outcomes. Distinguishing predictability and incapacity may make for subtle philosophy, but it hardly removes the sting if we're pessimistic about the effectiveness of choice in the first place. Unfortunately, it is difficult to observe choice directly. But one way of proceeding is to consider how *hard* it is to achieve a decent social outcome. For if it turns out to be next to impossible to achieve a decent living without the benefit of affluent circumstances, then it is safe to conclude that choice isn't very effective for the worse off.

Surprisingly, writers on social justice after Marx have shown relatively little interest in the question of how easy or hard it is to achieve a decent living. One approach, though, is to look at the conditional probability of various social outcomes. This means examining how likely people are to end up falling into a particular category of income or status, given that they have done X, Y, or Z. Depending on our assessment of X, Y, and Z, we can then form some rough idea at least of what it takes to achieve that status. Unfortunately, there is not much data of this form, and what we have is merely suggestive. But a few years ago, Brooking Institution researchers Ron Haskins and Isabel Sawhill reported

TABLE 9.2 *Likelihood of Poverty by Norms Observed*

	All three	One or two	None
Below poverty	2.0	26.9	76.0
Poverty—299%	24.2	47.9	17.1
> 300%	73.8	25.3	6.9

the conditional probabilities in the United States given in table 9.2 for the following social norms:[21]

- Obtain high school diploma or equivalent
- Work (≥ 35 hours per week, 40 weeks per year)
- Wait until 21 and marry before having children

The table shows the likelihood of being in a family that is below the poverty line or that earns a given multiple of the poverty threshold *given* that some number of these norms is attained by the head of the family. These figures thus suggest that the odds of being poor even by the standards of a rich country like the United States are vanishing if these norms are met—only 2%. This might raise the worry that observing such norms merely serves to move us just over the line of destitution, but no: complying with these norms makes it extremely likely (73.8%) we will lead a solid middle-class existence at 300% or more of the poverty level. Quibbling about the definition of "poverty" is correspondingly unhelpful. There is nothing magical about the official line, but the general point concerns the effectiveness of choice, and the evidence appears to bear this out, if only in a rough-and-ready way. Adding additional norms would obviously shift these numbers still further—they should be regarded as telling us about the *lower* bound for the effectiveness of choice—but it is difficult to find the data.

Other kinds of research support the gist of these findings. It is striking that very few households with anyone doing any kind of full-time work are (officially) poor in the United States—3.5% in 2007.[22] To a good approximation, an American in a family in which someone consistently works will not be poor. One may imagine that for a single worker to support a family would require him or her to find work that required significant qualifications or was otherwise difficult to obtain, but just one member of a household working as a janitor or hairdresser would put a small family beyond poverty in the United States. An average delivery truck driver would vault this family far beyond the poverty line.[23] (In fact, a good way of thinking about the problem of poverty in a rich country with low unemployment is this: what are likely to be the barriers preventing the relevant tens of millions of people from becoming delivery truck drivers [or the like]? I don't mean that the answer is obvious, but this at least provides some constraints.) Further research into these matters would be highly desirable. What, one wonders, is the *conditional* social mobility for people who meet various social norms? As it is, one can infer that such conditions must make a huge difference simply by observing the differential mobility rates of groups that are all initially poor, but have a greater or lesser propensity to meet some of the relevant norms, such as various poor but scholastically focused immigrant groups.

It is natural to object that the relevant choices themselves reflect social constraints. The environment may make it unreasonable to expect people to make prudent decisions about school, work, or family. But I again want to insist only that this is usually not a case of choice-defeating incapacity in places like the United States—if the relevant people simply made various choices, there is evidence that they generally would succeed at attaining a decent livelihood. They are free to succeed in that, admittedly restricted, sense. If poverty seems inescapable or even heritable, it is usually inescapable in the sense that the Labyrinth is inescapable without a thread, not as a dungeon. For reasons that I outline in appendix B, it is tempting to deny even this—it sounds *mean* to claim that people generally have a capacity to influence social outcomes when thinking about the poor, a bit like victim-blaming. But such a denial would involve insisting that something like the following claims are generally true (readers are invited to imagine these in the mouths of their own children facing unfavorable social circumstances, such as a lousy school system):

- "I can't help it that I skipped class."
- "It wasn't possible to do my homework."
- "I had no control over whether I had children."
- "There was no way I could have worked this past year."

It is important to acknowledge that for some people, these statements will be true. Mothers have children due to rape, classes go unattended because of gunfire or violence in the school, recessions destroy employment opportunities even for those who are highly qualified and persevering and willing to accept low wages. The point isn't that all poor social outcomes are blameworthy, but that *most* (not all) *people can exercise an enormous amount of influence* over whether they lead a decent life in the developed world, even when ignorance or other internal impediments bar the way. There are times and places even in rich countries in which it is unreasonable to expect anyone in a household to find work as an electrician, or driver, or assistant, or cook. But it is less plausible to suppose that, for most people in places like the United States or Europe, over the long haul, setting aside a bad year or two, it is just a matter of chance whether they meet norms like those above. The evidence suggests that predictability generally does not imply choice-defeating incapacity in affluent countries.

None of this speaks to the issue of equality of opportunity, strictly speaking, since, even if choice were generally effective for attaining a decent living, that wouldn't address differences in opportunities to move far beyond that threshold. It may be encouraging that there are relatively few external barriers in rich countries to reaching 300% of the poverty line—roughly the middle class—but that won't assuage worries about unequal opportunities to get rich (and to obtain the further perquisites of being rich). How important that gap seems will depend on how bad we think it is for people to reach the threshold of earning a decent living, of having *enough*, but perhaps having reduced opportunities to obtain more than that. On one view, passing some sufficiency threshold is what really matters when it comes to social justice, but this is contested by various egalitarians.[24] I can't settle the debate about whether enough is enough, but those who think it is have further reason to think things are not as bleak as Clark's picture initially suggests. And the conditional mobility point I alluded to offers still more grounds for optimism; if choice is generally effective for reaching the middle class in a single generation, presumably it will be increasingly effective for expanding opportunity across several generations, especially if they observe not just three norms but more besides.

▪ PROPER REMEDIES

Earlier, I denied that bad luck was a sufficient reason for using force or threats to take some people's resources and give them to others by the garden-variety standards of common-sense morality. We then asked if we could live with such a result, given the long arm of luck and the heritability of poverty and riches. (If the very question seems an embarrassment, it is worth pointing out that anti-libertarians rarely face up to the corresponding question of whether *they* can live with using force or threats to compel people to contribute to what they deem important ends.) The fact that at least in developed countries like the United States choice still seems to be effective for most people to attain a decent life removes some, though surely not all, of the sting of Clark's findings, in my view, especially if we are mainly worried about people having enough. Nothing can (or should) make us feel at ease over the fact that social outcomes might be predictable, at least in a rough and statistical way, sometimes across a thousand years. But confronting a kind of ignorance or motivational deficit is different from confronting choice-defeating incapacity in ways that matter. Apart from presenting a less pessimistic account of the situation, there are several further implications worth reflecting on.

First, cases of incapacity due to ignorance or motivational differences suggest different *remedies*. In cases like Parents or Coach, where someone is disadvantaged due to poor advice and rearing from others, it would be a mistake to press for harming third parties in order to compensate agents for their misfortune, say by cash transfers or in-kind benefits. The obvious remedy is education of a sort. The same is true of real-world cases. To give a concrete example, it may be that our subculture places less stress on educational attainment than other subcultures with which we are, in effect, competing, perhaps because of low historical returns on investing in education. If so, then we may in a sense inherit poverty, but not due to anything like choice-defeating incapacity, and choice might very well be effective. The appropriate remedy here is, in effect, to be educated about education, to be shown the effectiveness of choice, not cash compensation. The latter would merely harm those whose wealth was transferred without warrant and may well harm the recipients as well by setting up disastrous incentives effects.

Suppose that Ruritanian immigrants in 19th-century America earned less than other groups, and that this was largely because they had absorbed poor lessons about the effectiveness of being enterprising, industrious, and resourceful. (Feudal oppression had reduced the returns to those traits, let us say, making them less worthwhile to instill, with the result that Ruritanians were initially at a competitive disadvantage. Something like this story is a realistic proposal with respect to Irish and New French immigrants in the past.) What is the proper remedy for the Ruritanian who comes of age with comparatively few skills or interest in educational or vocational attainment? One option is to compensate him for this misfortune by transferring money to him from other groups. But such a remedy would be inappropriate both because of the unwarranted harms to the non-Ruritanians and because it would fundamentally fail to address the underlying problem. The underlying problem isn't the poverty of the Ruritanian, but the deficits that prevent him from effectively exercising his basic capacities. (If it makes us feel better, we can sternly blame these on the feudal aristocracy back home.) In fact, it's important to note that providing aid in the form of welfare payments may well *reinforce* these fundamental problems insofar as doing so continues to render returns on investment in entrepreneurial activity or education lower than they otherwise would be in comparative terms. To imagine otherwise is to think that the proper remedy for a Theseus is to transfer other people's wealth to him in compensation for his unfortunate position rather than to publicize the way out.

Second, we should absorb the fact that, according to Clark, social institutions have been remarkably ineffective in curbing the persistence of social status, and so in reducing the element of chance in the distribution of wealth. Clark takes this to be a reason for forced redistribution on the analogy of existing support for redistribution in cases of genuinely choice-defeating incapacity, such as severe disability. As I have argued, choice-defeating incapacity is probably not the right model in this context. But we should nevertheless reflect on what it means that focusing on social institutions as a means of empowering people to overcome bad luck has been ineffective. In places like Japan and Sweden, everyone has access to high-quality education (and the United States certainly spends vast sums), and yet, according to Clark, little has changed.[25] There has been as yet little discussion of whether this is true and if so how to respond. But this evidence does seem to count against emphasizing social institutions like the education system as the proper remedy for lack of opportunity (at least when it isn't combined with the meta-education urged above). This is just the flip side to the fact of status persistence in the face of violent institutional change.

Finally, we shouldn't neglect the perspective of the fortunate parents, rather than the less fortunate children who are at issue. The goal of many on the left is to eliminate disadvantage due to luck, but this can be redescribed as the goal of *eliminating the ability of parents to pass on their advantages to their children*. Put this way, the goal, it seems to me, is both more sobering and less obviously attainable. "We guarantee that no one will suffer by not receiving the same advantages from their parents as anyone else" may sound attractive; "we guarantee that no one will be able to *give* their children any advantages in life" less so. Even for the disadvantaged, it is unclear whether such a guarantee wouldn't have an ominous ring to it. For it would imply that, best-case scenario, those who extricated themselves from poverty and became successful would be unable to use the advantages accrued for the purposes they may care about most, i.e., benefiting those they love. Of course, the expected benefit of not *suffering* from disadvantage might be greater than the expected value of this drawback in *conferring* advantages, but this may not be a case where the worse off would wish to employ expected-value reasoning. The fact that a social scheme will maximize the chances of our getting a leg up, but at the cost of preventing us from doing what we would most want to get a leg up *for*, may not attract us to such a scheme.

10 Wealth, Disability, and Happiness

The free market worries those who disapprove of some of the exchanges the market permits, or the role that luck plays in the market. But another kind of doubt arises from stepping back and contemplating the nature of rich societies. When we survey the materialism that accompanies enterprise, when we reflect on how unhappy many rich people with houses full of gadgets are, and conversely on how tranquil those with simpler, more fulfilling lives can be, we may begin to ask ourselves, "To what end?" Capitalism and economic growth may make us rich, but should we really care? What matters in the end, runs the thought, isn't how rich we are, but how happy we are. Certainly there is no need for reflective people to be impressed by the relentless rat race that lies behind a great deal of commercial activity. To the extent that this, or something like it, is the reason that philosophers have tended to scorn the merchant class, perhaps they had a point.

We can pursue this idea by focusing on two related paradoxes. According to the *Easterlin paradox*, individuals within countries see their happiness affected by how their incomes compare to their fellow citizens', and yet both across countries and across time, vast differences in income don't make a difference to average levels of happiness. This looks like it might substantiate the doubts expressed just now. Why emphasize economic growth when it doesn't make us happier and when progrowth policies often come with painful trade-offs? On the other hand, according to the *disability paradox*, people who suffer from what look like severe health problems often don't feel as unhappy as healthy people predict. In fact, some of them don't seem unhappy at all: they have adapted to their condition in ways that the healthy, who overlook adaptive processes, neglect. Apparently, large differences in what we might call people's objective welfare don't always make for differences in people's subjective happiness.

This should give us pause, because to the extent we think we have reason to avoid disabilities, it suggests there may be more to what we care about than happiness. In fact, as I will argue, the anti-growth message that people sometimes read into the Easterlin paradox is mistaken, and we have reason to concentrate on economic growth even when it doesn't make us happier. The reason for this is that happiness is overrated. There are many categories of welfare that matter to us at least as much as happiness. In fact, we can go further: there are things that matter to us beyond our *welfare*, like the fate of humanity, or our attachment to individuals we love. The implications of this thought extend beyond narrow questions about libertarianism and the market; eventually they seem to lead to the conclusion that Aristotelians are mistaken to think that practical reasoning in general concerns pursuing what's best for us. I hope that the grandness of this theme will excuse a brief detour from assessing classical liberalism toward the end of the chapter.

■ HAPPINESS

What is happiness? In the research I will be discussing, it's clear that what is meant by "happiness" is something subjective in the sense that it concerns people's mental states, and I will stick to that usage here. Intuitively, the idea is to capture how good or bad someone's life looks from the inside; often the phrase "subjective well-being" is used. Of course, that's still rather vague, and there are many different ways of filling in the blanks. More fully fleshed-out theories of happiness in this subjective sense include simple hedonism (happiness is the preponderance of pleasure over pain), emotional state theory (happiness is possessing a preponderance of positive emotional states), and the life-satisfaction theory (happiness is just the judgment that your life is going well on the whole).[1]

This entire family of theories contrasts with what I will call "welfare," which refers to how someone's life is actually going, whether he realizes it or not. Intuitively, the goal here is to capture our judgments as well-informed, sympathetic observers about how people's lives are going for them. (Students of ancient philosophy will recognize this as related to Aristotle's conception of *eudaimonia* or human flourishing, which shares many of the features of what I am calling welfare.) This notion of objective welfare is thus broader than happiness, since our own feelings about how things are going for us are often misinformed or underinformed, and thus we seem to be fallible in our judgments about our own welfare.

That there is room for such a gap is controversial, since it can seem hard to understand why we would judge someone to have low welfare when he is perfectly happy.[2] The standard examples used to rebut such skepticism include the cuckold, whose whole life turns out to be a lie despite a blissful ignorance, or the scientist who spends his life toiling on a research program that turns out, just after his death, to have been hopelessly wrong. (They can be pleasingly combined, perhaps, in the figure of the cheerfully cuckolded string-theorist whose work turns out to be mistaken.) Another example is the happy serf, who accepts his condition and never thinks of what his life might be free from servitude; there is a sense in which such a life is not a good one. We can represent all this in a matrix, as in table 10.1. On this picture, happy persons whose lives are compromised in some way from the perspective of well-informed, external observers fit into the top-left box, while those in agony have lives that leave them unhappy and that we would judge of poor quality, placing them in the bottom left. The rare, lucky individuals who feel happy and whose feelings are apt fit into the top right, while the bottom right is empty. This is because presumably happiness is one

TABLE 10.1 *Welfare and Happiness*

		Welfare	
		Low	*High*
Happiness	*High*	Scientist-cuckold	Life feels and *is* good.
	Low	Migraines	

component of welfare: we don't think people's lives are going well for them if they themselves feel miserable. Of course, we might think people are wrong to be so unhappy, but if they really are persistently miserable, it's hard to see how their lives could be judged a great success from the outside.

I will be supposing that it's worth taking seriously the implications of some of the empirical research on happiness. This may seem worrisome to the extent that we have doubts about measuring happiness accurately, and indeed a great deal of caution is in order. But there are four considerations to bear in mind. First, for the most part I will be using the empirical research merely to illustrate philosophically important possibilities. Second, nothing turns on the relevant measurements being remotely precise or fine-grained. The issues turn on such general findings as whether huge gains in wealth have produced significant changes in how happy people are, or whether by and large disabled people tend to adapt. Third, even if we are skeptical about simple-minded surveys asking people about whether they are happy (or how satisfied they are with their lives, etc.) we might be willing to grant that these can be reasonably well *correlated* with whatever we think happiness really amounts to. It might not matter if the survey instruments are dead wrong about what happiness is, especially in view of the first two points. And finally, researchers have obviously invested substantial effort in assessing how reliable and valid their work is, and the results aren't completely discouraging, though there's certainly much room for improvement. It turns out that asking people about how they feel yields prima facie results of the sort we would expect, e.g., people generally look less happy after an economic crisis or after a divorce.[3] And in the cases I am interested in, the research usually (though not always) concerns large groups. Since the relevant measurements are from hundreds or thousands of people, there's less reason to worry about random error.

■ THE EASTERLIN PARADOX

The first half of the Easterlin paradox consists of the positive association between higher incomes and greater individual happiness within a country. The other half consists of countries getting dramatically richer without getting happier.[4] As one researcher describes it, "Our economic welfare is forever rising, but we are no happier as a result. The puzzle is that rising in rank on the income scale seems to improve one's chances of happiness, but a rise in one's income when everybody's income is rising does not."[5] This part of the paradox is supposed to be revealed in studies that compare either levels of happiness in a particular country across time, or else cross-sectional studies that compare countries at varying levels of development. For example, it is often claimed that while Japan underwent spectacular economic development in the postwar period, it made no significant gains in happiness, as revealed in surveys conducted over the years. Something similar, if less stark, is said to have occurred in the United States. Real GDP per capita in the 1920s was under $6,000; now it is over $30,000, an astonishing fivefold increase.[6] But none of this seems to have been accompanied by any dramatic rise in happiness as measured by the surveys, and those measurements seem to conform to most people's intuitive sense of how happy they are compared to their parents and grandparents. Few middle-class people think they are dramatically happier than their middle-class parents or grandparents were just because they are so much richer. Moreover, a little reflection makes it easy to understand why that should be. Among other factors, happiness may be a function of how one fares relative to one's (ever rising) expectations; one may become habituated to rising standards of living; we may walk on a hedonic treadmill it is difficult to escape for long; after a certain point our happiness may be dominated not by wealth but by relationships and other social factors like status or relative success.[7]

But these pessimistic views are contested. Some have claimed that there is no paradox and that in fact higher levels of income have almost always been associated with greater happiness. The star witness of Japan, for instance, may fall apart when the relevant survey questions are retranslated, revealing that the Japanese questions changed over time, influencing the results; and a more careful look at the cross-country comparisons, it is claimed, also shows a tendency for happiness to align with income. The skeptics even deny that there is clear evidence refuting the claim that more money is always good for national happiness, even after we are rich. (I.e., they "find no evidence of a satiation point beyond which wealthier countries have no further increases in subjective well-being.")[8] These counterclaims have in turn been contested, and thus no social-scientific consensus has been reached.

I want to insist, however, that there is a sense in which, despite the technical disagreement, some version of the Easterlin paradox must eventually be real. Barring catastrophe, it is inevitable that we will reach a point at which countries continue to get wealthier and wealthier in absolute terms without getting happier and happier. Assuming that our individual happiness continues to be affected by how our incomes (cars, homes, yachts) compare to those of our colleagues and neighbors (and the rest of our countrymen), the paradox will then hold. The question, in other words, can't be whether the paradox holds, but only *when* it holds—now or later. This is because our capacity for subjective well-being is rather limited, while our capacity for economic development is vast. That is, there is a sharply delimited upper bound on how happy we can be, given mundane facts about human nature and the kinds of societies one can readily envision. I take it, in fact, that many individuals living in the best-off, most favorable circumstances in the developed nations are at or near that upper bound. Making such people substantially happier just by increasing their prosperity simply isn't possible, both because of natural limits to how much happiness one can get, and because of ine-liminable social facts like envy, failures in love, or natural misfortune. By contrast, we are nowhere near an upper bound on economic development. Since such de-velopment is largely driven by increases in efficiency of consumption and produc-tion, there is no necessity of our reaching that upper bound any time soon. (The ultimate limits are probably tied to the energy output and computational capacity of the universe.) So the idea behind the Easterlin paradox can't be fundamentally wrong, though it might be too early for Easterlin to declare victory.

Moreover, it is worth bearing in mind that something like the Easterlin par-adox could hold true in particular cases, and the evidence suggests that it probably does. By this I mean that regardless of the general point about the relationship between development and happiness, *individual* countries might experience joy-less growth (or cheerful stagnation), and comparisons between particular coun-tries might reveal a similar disconnect, with impoverished nations seemingly content with their lot (or rich ones miserable). If there turns out not to be much difference between how happy the Japanese are and how happy Nigerians are (which is what I think we should expect), we can raise a modified version of the puzzle. Or again, on a scale of 1 (low) to 7 (high), with 4 set as neutral, American college students described their overall well-being as 4.9, while slum-dwellers in Calcutta offered a disturbingly close 4.4.[9]

Since the Easterlin paradox will be real soon enough and can apply in indi-vidual cases, we can set aside the social science disputes and turn to philosoph-ical questions. The central issue is this: if economic development turns out not to make us happier, why should we care about economic development as much as we do? And if economic development comes at the expense of other things that might contribute more to our happiness, why don't we attempt to shift our priorities toward those other things? In fact, if we are living under the Easterlin paradox, why do we work so hard and expend so many resources both to promote the economic development of poorer countries and to avoid slipping back our-selves to a lower level of development?

The view I have in mind here could take the form of calling for an aban-donment or at least a significant abridgment of the quest for economic growth, or at least a rebalancing that places much more weight on "gross national happiness."[10] I raise this mainly as a philosophical challenge, but it's worth noting that policy experts have actually mooted suggestions along these lines. The economist Richard Layard, for instance, claims that on a traditional economist's view, little harm is done by an occasional bust bringing "creative destruction" in its wake, because the long-run gain outweighs a small immediate cost. . . . But modern psychology leads to a different emphasis. The short-run psychological cost of fluctuations in employment is great, while the long-run gain from growth is relatively small because the value of each dollar becomes smaller and smaller as people become ever richer.[11]

This kind of reasoning leads him to advocate (or at least emphasize the advantages of) high taxes which might lead to lower growth rates, but which would deter the negative effects of emphasizing individual performance (the envy and dissatisfaction of the losers), as well as the habituating effects of ever-increasing pay. And many other dissident economists have at least urged that we pay less attention to national income and focus more on measures of happiness.[12]

But I want to point out that there is actually a simple answer to the questions raised above, an answer that endorses the grubby status quo of striving for high growth rates and bemoaning the low growth rates of the cheerful poor. This is just the contrast drawn earlier between happiness and welfare. On this view, prosperity makes us better off, even if it doesn't make us happier. Above, we noted that the stock examples used to motivate the possibility of a gap between happiness and welfare exploited values many of us have that we can be deluded about. Because we care about not being deluded, cuckolds and scientists can suffer welfare losses in the face of great happiness. Similarly, in the case of economic development there are values at stake that allow for happy people to be suffering a low level of welfare. Here are some examples of such values:

Life expectancy: Simple longevity needn't be reflected in happiness studies. If people don't reflect on and feel unhappy about their life expectancy, a population can be happy without living long. But life expectancy would be at the top of any list of welfare indicators. (The life expectancy of cheerful Americans in 1920 was under 60.)[13]

Health: It is implausible that chronic pain wouldn't affect happiness. But many other forms of sickness need not if such conditions are taken for granted, especially on the life-satisfaction view, despite making a difference to welfare. Examples include cognition-impairing malnutrition, developmental disorders, stunted growth, and generally speaking moderate forms of illness that incapacitate without being agonizing.

Welfare of loved ones: If our children suffer malnutrition or die in infancy, most of us think that makes *our* lives go worse, but in places where that is deemed the normal course of things, it may not affect one's happiness.

Perfectionist goods: Economic development enables such goods as acquiring an education, the advancement of science, and attaining knowledge of, e.g., the nature of the universe, the origin of species, and the history of the world. It also enables travel to see other peoples and places, and the creation of art. If it is taken for granted that these things are unavailable, their absence may not affect one's happiness, but many would consider them important components of welfare. We pity happy people living in utter ignorance of their world or of great art.

Realized potential: People's lives go badly for them if they are prevented from accomplishing worthwhile things they might otherwise have. But if few people around us realize their potential, we are unlikely to register this subjectively.

The claim, thus, is that there are goods we would lose were we to decline economically, even if we didn't experience losses in happiness, and that poorer countries suffer these losses now, no matter how contented with their lot they may be. And by simple extension, we should strive for economic development in the future even if we don't anticipate being made much happier thereby. Doing so will enable us to live longer, live more healthily, see our children better off, and to learn about the nature of reality. (To be sure, the benefits of such welfare gains must be balanced against negative side-effects like pollution and lost leisure time, which likewise affect welfare.)

We have a natural tendency to see our current level of development as normal, as perhaps not much worth improving on, especially if doing so comes at some hedonic cost in the form of, say, more work-related stress. But this looks a lot like status quo bias. Future generations will presumably look at the primitive state of our knowledge, of our healthcare, etc., in just the way we look with horror on the welfare levels of the past. Since we have reason to expect the welfare gains from future prosperity to be at least as great as those made in the past, our reasons to press for growth seem be great indeed. Economic prosperity may not bring with it happiness, but we have strong reasons to pursue it anyway.

■ THE DISABILITY PARADOX

Next, we can compare the Easterlin paradox to the disability paradox—the finding that the disabled are often less affected by their condition than the healthy suppose. The suggestion to be explored is that the lives of the disabled are in certain respects analogous to the lives of those living in less developed countries, and that there is a puzzle about why we wish to avoid disability given that the disabled are often about as happy as healthy people are.

We can understand the concept of disability very broadly to include any serious and long-lasting health impairment. In this sense, deafness, kidney disease, and a colostomy are all disabilities, and we should bear in mind that disabilities can be either congenital or acquired. A research summary of the paradox runs, "The preponderance of evidence suggests that many patients with chronic illness and disability are able to emotionally adapt to their circumstances and experience relatively high levels of mood and [quality of life]," though the author goes on to note that such adaptation is not always complete.[14] The relevant evidence includes findings such as the following:

- The disabled assign higher health utilities to their conditions than do the healthy, as established by multiple independent instruments.[15]

- Those *currently* disabled assign higher health utilities to their condition than do those who *were* disabled in the past in just the same way.[16]
- In studies examining what kinds of trade-offs the disabled would be willing to make in exchange for full health (e.g., would they trade a life shorter by X months for full health), many disabled are unwilling to make any trade-off whatever.[17]
- In general, there is evidence of a hedonic-treadmill effect, whereby major life-events affect us less than we would predict, and we tend to settle back into a set-point level of happiness. Spinal cord injuries are less terrible for us than we imagine; winning the lottery is less wonderful.[18]

On reflection it shouldn't be all that surprising the disabled or those suffering from medical problems aren't as devastated as we might casually predict. The standard explanations here include that we overlook habituation and adaptation processes, whereby we either get used to or adapt to our new circumstances, so that the status quo comes to seem normal and not some disastrous downward change;[19] or again, ex ante, reflecting on what it would be like to suffer a disability we're by construction *focused* on the bad change, whereas ex post we aren't—most of our days will be spent attending to everyday life events not involving our disability; and, finally, many of the health conditions at issue are just less bad than we imagine. We attach stigma to medical conditions, even when, as experienced, they aren't so terrible.

These mistakes on the part of the healthy are hard to eradicate, even when subjects are explicitly told about them. A researcher working on the focusing illusion just described writes, "across more than a dozen studies and more than 1,000 participants, people's predictions of what it would be like to experience these disabilities were either unchanged by the defocusing task or went in the opposite direction we expected, with people thinking these disabilities would make them even more miserable."[20]

Nor is the disability paradox merely a theoretical problem. It is central to the question in health economics of whether to discount the value of years lived under disability. On one view, we should assess the effectiveness of medical interventions in terms of quality-adjusted life years (QALYs), meaning that we discount the benefit of an operation, say, if that operation would leave patients disabled.[21] This could mean that the state would pay to save a life that would leave a patient healthy, but allow patients to die who would, were they saved, be left disabled. It would have this implication if an intervention was expensive and were judged not cost-effective in the latter case. QALYs could also mean failing to pay for life-sustaining interventions for the disabled, since their continued survival would be discounted by their disabilities. And the architects of the QALY apparatus seem to endorse some of these implications, i.e., they aren't the philosopher's far-fetched extreme. Speaking generally, people often seem comfortable with the first sort of discounting (discounting for disability when some intervention would leave otherwise healthy people disabled) and much less comfortable with the second (discounting the ordinary survival of, say, congenitally disabled people).

We seem hard-pressed to reconcile our conflicting attitudes toward the significance of disability, treating it as disastrous in some contexts, but in line with the subjective well-being of those actually disabled in others. This might look like a purely moral problem about how we treat others, but in fact the core issue is a conflict in our values that can manifest itself reflexively. Suppose that if I do nothing I face the gradual loss of my legs, perhaps because of a tropical disease that affects my nervous system. On the one hand, I might be willing to pay large amounts of money or incur significant risk of death for an operation that might save my legs, an attitude that may well fail to be extinguished by my doctor informing me that people with this condition eventually adapt quite well. These attitudes are at least consistent with the discounting embodied by QALYs. But on the other hand, I'm also likely to exhibit a panoply of attitudes suggesting a full valuation of my disabled years, particularly if I come to believe that I'll be pretty successful at adapting. Thus, I may well oppose medical policies that would disadvantage me in my future disabled state for the sake of benefiting me more while I'm still in good health, as a QALY-based system could. For instance, I might push for the development of drugs that would sustain my disabled life even at the cost of losing out on other drugs that would benefit me before losing my legs, even if doing so wouldn't make sense if the years added were discounted at the rate implied by what I would do to avoid becoming disabled in the first place. Or again, I'm likely to reject even small increases in the risk of death after my disability for the sake of gains now; if I were fully persuaded of discounting, I should be willing to drink more alcohol, eat worse, and save less if doing so would make me better off now at a risk of dying later, since those future years would be discounted (just as we might do all those things if our life expectancy suddenly dropped precipitously).

■ WELFARE AGAIN

A natural suggestion at this point is to once again draw on the contrast between happiness and welfare: our aversion toward becoming disabled is related to the loss of welfare, not of happiness, just as we can justify pursuing growth-oriented policies on the basis of considerations of welfare. We might, for instance, say that we don't want to lose mobility because there is something objectively valuable about being able to walk on our own, participate in sports, and access remote mountain views. Accessing those goods is valuable in itself, not because of how it makes us feel. We could then explain the attitudes of the disabled by conceding that they weren't much or any less happy than the healthy, and also leverage that point to explain why we seem to have conflicting attitudes toward discounting—when we focus on the objective goods lost we're for discounting, when we focus on what the felt experience of disabled life is like, we aren't.

However, this approach can at best be part of the solution. It just isn't plausible that all of the goods that disabled people lose are objective welfare goods that are detachable from the happiness they bring. Recall the paradigm cases of such detachment, such as the value we place on avoiding delusion, or having a long life, or attaining knowledge, or seeing our children succeed. What makes these cases persuasive is that two conditions are met: (a) it's fairly easy to see how one's happiness might not be affected by the loss of such goods, and yet (b) we really do value them independent of the quality of our experiences, or our judgments about how our life is going, or our positive/negative emotional states. But now focus on disability. In extreme cases in which people are, say, in constant pain or unable to leave a hospital room, (b) will be satisfied, but (a) will not be. So focus on more moderate cases, say people with reduced mobility in virtue of having to use a cane or being confined to a wheelchair, who have adapted fairly well and are about as happy as their healthy peers. Here, (a) will be satisfied, but what about (b)? The crucial question is whether someone with reduced mobility is losing out on goods that make his life less worthwhile just in virtue of the intrinsic value of those goods (independent of their effect on people's subjective well-being). A life of vast unrealized potential, lived amid ignorance and illusion, is less successful than the reverse, even holding happiness constant; but is the same true of a life (or many years) lived without running, or walking, or playing basketball, or enjoying attendant goods like seeing the views from remote mountain-trails?

In my view, there aren't any compelling reasons to think that these goods matter or matter much apart from their hedonic effects. Take the perfectly contented disabled person who just doesn't care all that much that he can't walk or play certain sports or access remote mountain views. "But wouldn't you prefer a cure if one were available?" we might ask him—"Sure," he may shrug, "but in my everyday life I'm just not hung up on it, and in the meantime I have a great family and rewarding work." (I am not claiming that all disabled people adapt this well, but many do.) It's just very hard to see what reasons we could give this person to convince him that he is *missing out*. There doesn't seem to be any reason to think that the mere fact of jogging or playing basketball or achieving certain mountain views is important, given that the subject is content to go without. Why would they be?

In positive terms, these kinds of goods seem to be subject to norms of satisficing, not maximizing. We care about them (in non-hedonic terms) only insofar as we care about attaining *enough* of the goods in some broader category. Some areas of knowledge are like this. We may care a great deal that our children have the experience of learning to play a musical instrument or delving deeply into literature. But it wouldn't be a tragedy if someone remained cheerfully ignorant of the clarinet or Faulkner while spending time mastering the piano and Henry James instead. (Nor would we think someone had failed to reach his potential just because he hadn't read Faulkner.) What matters here is getting enough of something in a certain category of good, not achieving the very narrow specific goods. (We can imagine a clarinetist insisting that his child absolutely *must* learn clarinet in particular, no matter that the child couldn't care less and already knows piano and violin. But what would we make of such a parent?) The same seems true of the disabled person. Maybe it's valuable to have experiences of moving one's body, getting about, seeing the world, experiencing the beauty of Planet Earth, but those broad goods can be realized in a wheelchair perfectly well, albeit only by trading remote mountain-trail views for wheelchair-accessible views, and basketball for wheelchair rugby. But if someone insists that, no, the welfare of the disabled will be impugned by failing to walk and play basketball *in particular*, this looks like a puzzling obsession with particulars (like the attitude of the pathological clarinetist).

Explaining away the disability paradox by invoking welfare doesn't look promising. To make progress, we need to extend our horizons beyond classical liberal themes and address some broader issues in the theory of ethics. This will make for a brief detour, but hopefully one that proves worthwhile.

▪ WHAT MATTERS TO US

Let us focus on how exactly the argument is supposed to go for thinking that we don't have much reason to prefer a life of full health to a life with a disability (which in turn calls into question discounting in the context of QALYs, and trying hard to avoid being disabled). So far, that argument has been left vague. What's obvious is the conclusion and one premise:

P2: Life with a disability doesn't differ significantly from life with full health in respect to either our happiness or welfare.

C: We don't have significant reason to prefer a life with full health to a life with a disability.

Many have focused their energies on challenging P2—either by claiming that there is something objectively bad about disability, or else claiming that the happiness of the disabled is (always? inevitably?) irrational or otherwise defective. But another option is to note that the major premise is clearly missing. The only obvious way to supply that premise is P1:

P1: If states of affairs X and Y don't differ significantly in respect to our happiness or welfare in them, then we don't have significant reason to prefer X over Y.

P2: Life with a disability doesn't differ significantly from life with full health in respect to either our happiness or welfare.

C: We don't have significant reason to prefer a life with full health to a life with a disability.

On the approach I want to explore, we grant that P2 may be true, at least in a broad range of cases, but we go on to reject P1.

The basic problem with P1 is that it assumes a false picture of what matters to us. On this picture, the particulars of *how* we come to reach a given level of happiness or welfare is entirely immaterial. The reason this picture can be tempting, of course, is that it seems obvious that what we really want, in the end, is to be happy/well-off, in line with the Aristotelian tradition that everything we do (rationally) we do to promote our flourishing. Given this summum bonum, we then leap to the conclusion that different ways of realizing that aim are fungible; P1 seems to follow from thinking about our own lives in something like the way utilitarians think about the lives of others. But this is a mistake: different ways of attaining happiness or welfare are not all alike to us—not even when we're discussing ourselves so that morality is off the table—for there are particular attachments to people and activities, inter alia, that are all-important to us.

The obvious cases involve love. I might be equally happy and equally well-off married to various other women besides my wife, or raising children other than Kate and Brian, or accepting another country and culture as my own, but of course I'm not indifferent as between those states of affairs and the status quo. On the contrary, I would do almost anything to avoid some of these changes, even if they would happen gradually and involve no unhappiness or lost welfare to myself or others, and even if there were no moral duty to resist such a change. Couples work to foster and perpetuate relationships that might otherwise run their course and be replaced with equally satisfying new relationships. I don't care merely about the part of the good life that stems from rearing children, I care about that satisfaction being associated with Kate and Brian in particular.[22] Many relationships are such that even if we knew we'd be happier—even if we knew *everyone* would be happier—we'd prefer to continue on with our particular attachments, suboptimal though they may be from the point of view of happiness and welfare. As Jeff McMahan puts it, "There are . . . cases in which a person can *rationally* be glad that his life has gone the way it has, even when he recognizes that it would have been better for him if it had gone differently," for instance cases in which a wife comes to see that she would have been happier had she married someone else years ago, while nonetheless being fully in love with her husband.[23]

The same goes for the goods lost with a disability, I believe. I enjoy playing basketball and being able to hike up to the Hanakapiai Falls. My life wouldn't be less successful if I substituted other goods of the same type—their meaning to me at that level isn't token-specific. But I have attachments to those particular activities in virtue of having engaged in them enthusiastically over the years, and having thus embedded them in my life in the form of interconnected memories, emotions, or friendships. The idea, then, is that we resist even adaptive disability because adaptation is no guard against particular losses. In effect, adaptation is no more an argument for assigning full value to life with a disability than it is to a life without my wife or children. Basketball and hiking are valuable to me in a way that resists substitution in the same way, if to a lesser degree, that other things and people we love can't, without loss, be substituted with other members of the relevant class. We have reason to avoid changes that would destroy the things we care most about.

This account explains our conflicted attitudes. We're averse to disability for the reasons just described, but once we take up the point of view of ourselves postadaptation, we don't value *that* life any less. That point of view is analogous to contemplating remarrying and having new children after our first family's death in a car crash. Again, we would do anything to avoid such a change, even quite apart from the agonies preceding adaptation, but once we got there we wouldn't value that life any less.[24] This yields the result that, for reasons that are evident even within the first-person, non-moral point of view, we feel we have reason to avoid disability, without discounting our lives after we're injured (let alone discounting the lives of those already disabled).

There remains the question of whether we might not just announce that particular attachments are themselves welfare goods. Perhaps we should just say that losing your spouse makes your life go much worse, even if you adapt fairly quickly, and similarly that losing your mobility amounts to a welfare loss despite adaptation and the absence of any great loss in happiness. If so, we could lump together the stories about wealth and about disability, and let the moral of it all be that we mustn't neglect the role of welfare as against happiness in our decision-making. But the intuitive idea behind welfare, recall, is that sometimes we assess lives (usually other people's lives, but sometimes our own) from a detached, third-personal point of view, and ask ourselves such questions as, "How well is his life going for him?" quite apart from how things may look to the agent from the inside. And if we take adaptation seriously, it's unclear how particular losses could be welfare losses. Someone who has suffered such a loss but recovered, and now sees himself as flourishing, doesn't seem to have a life that's going particularly badly, assuming the other kinds of goods we flagged earlier are to be had. It's true that some of his strongest preferences have been thwarted, but this too is of dubious significance. Ordinarily, we would count thwarted preferences toward an assessment of welfare when the agent later *regrets* those preferences not having been satisfied; the person who desperately wants to avoid moving to Oregon (the rain, the fog), but then comes to adore the place (the hills, the forests) once he is forced to, doesn't look like a candidate for downgraded welfare. And our cases of adaptation are by construction cases where the result isn't one that realizes the sort of fears that were built into (or presupposed by) our ex ante preferences. So for these reasons, it doesn't seem to me plausible to gloss the preceding account of resistance to adaptive disability as a welfarist account.

In sum, part of what is interesting here, I submit, is that we can apparently have very powerful reasons to act despite its not making a difference to our welfare. This is at least as striking as the earlier, more familiar conclusion that we have reasons to act beyond our happiness. And together they yield the claim that contrary to a great deal of our everyday thinking about these matters, large tracts of our decision-making shouldn't be governed by considerations of either our happiness or our well-being more generally, even when we have only our own lives in view. That result is possible because welfare and happiness can both come apart from the things we care about. There is sometimes a superficial reflex to cram what we care about back into either what makes us happy or welfare more generally, but I've argued that we should reject that impulse.

■ PRACTICAL REASONING AND WHAT WE CARE ABOUT

Cases similar to that of disability have sometimes been thought to support part of a broadly Aristotelian picture of ethics, but I wish to conclude by urging the opposite. Joseph Raz, for instance, argues against a distinctive moral domain whose considerations are different in kind and in normative authority from self-interested considerations (which might leave us with a kind of standoff, as encapsulated in Sidgwick's "dualism of practical reason"). Instead, he suggests what he takes to be a more classical approach, according to which there are simply *reasons*, whose force isn't related to any particular difference in domain or general provenance. The fact that we don't view substitutions within a given domain with indifference—Raz considers a dancer who resists becoming a director when that would leave him just as well off—is evidence that it's the particular reasons that matter, not the domain. And others have even claimed that our welfare is largely irrelevant to grounding decisions we make, since what we care about are the particular goods and bads at stake, not the fact that something will promote our welfare as such. Or again, it's said that we can make sense of *self-sacrifice* in self-directed terms, for example when we give up leisure and fun for the sake of research projects that make our lives seem more worthwhile or interesting.[25] In all of these views, there is the thought that we should focus on particular reasons and the considerations that ground them rather than the categories they fall into, and that in turn is said by some to support the Aristotelian picture which de-emphasizes the sharp divide and possible conflict between the moral and non-moral.

But the Aristotelian upshot of blurring the moral and non-moral is often thought to be that practical reasoning is fundamentally concerned with welfare or "human flourishing." And our reflections on wealth and disability, as well as the very claims just described, seem to show that this view is mistaken; a great deal of practical reasoning is directed toward things that have nothing at all to do with our flourishing. It's not just that the categorization doesn't matter much to us, it's that the range of our concerns is vastly broader than our welfare. And other familiar cases buttress these claims. Causes and movements provide one set of additional examples, again connected to what we care about: religious people perpetuate their faith even in the face of evidence that a gradual fading away of their beliefs would result in an equally satisfying life. And then there's morality. Although many aspects of our moral lives can perhaps be subsumed under some eudaimonist heading, there lingers the suspicion that this agglomeration is at best incomplete. Perhaps making nice with my friends and neighbors is part of a broad strategy to lead a life I find worthwhile and fulfilling, but every now and then there's the sharp, dividing case—the grenade to be jumped on, local practices to denounce at the cost of exile. Aristotelians have their thoughts about such cases,[26] but as the number and variety of non-welfare-promoting activities proliferate—perpetuating love, retaining fundamental abilities, keeping faith, acts of pure altruism—one's suspicions only grow. Thus, far from suggesting that we return to a broadly classical outlook on practical reasoning, reflection on wealth, disability, and structurally similar cases seems rather to point toward a fundamental defect in the classical picture, for it isn't true that happiness, or our welfare, or human flourishing, lies at the root of our practical reasoning.

Moralists are routinely scolded by Aristotelians and their friends for failing to see that there's more to life than morality, as a narrowly construed other-regarding practice; perhaps it is time that moralists and *their* friends take up scolding Aristotelians for failing to see that there's more to life than the broad concern for human flourishing.

11 The Epistemology of Popularity and Incentives

We are accustomed to thinking about markets in terms of their practical effects for good or ill, but markets are also relevant to epistemology, the theory of knowledge. For example, a tradition associated with Friedrich Hayek emphasizes the role that markets play in distributing knowledge in a society, as we have seen. Before leaving markets behind, it is worth taking a look at the individual level as well, at the microepistemology of markets. Principles pertaining to popularity and incentives are especially interesting in this context, as is the question of why people often seem reluctant to employ them. Because of this reluctance, we can take as our goal the relatively modest one of highlighting the relevance and importance of these principles, not of offering a fully fleshed-out account of how they are to be deployed. The main idea is that evidence from popularity and incentives counts in favor of shifting our beliefs, and that we tend to underutilize this evidence from the marketplace.[1]

■ BUYERS AND SELLERS

Assume that other things being equal, the popularity of a seller (a restaurant, a doctor) is evidence that service will be good, and vice versa. Assume, moreover, that other things being equal, sellers respond to incentives, and that by extension the fact that a seller faces strong incentives to focus on the service relevant to the consumer is evidence that service will be good, and vice versa. Both kinds of evidence are of course highly defeasible, since many sellers are popular for reasons irrelevant to the buyer, and the seller may respond to irrelevant incentives that drown out those the consumer cares about. But conversely, the force of these signals can be amplified when the seller is popular *despite* providing reasons *not* to buy, or when the seller has little or no incentive to respond to any incentives but those the buyer cares about. Duly cautioned, rational consumers will reason that they generally have grounds to patronize a seller when (a) he is popular, (b) when his popularity isn't due to irrelevant factors, and when (c) he is popular despite countervailing factors ("popularity" for short); and when (d) he has an incentive to provide good service, when (e) those incentives trump other kinds of incentives, and (f) he has few incentives besides those relevant to the buyer ("incentives" for short).

This advice about popularity and incentives may seem abstract, but it captures the guidance often given by such homely social epistemologists as food critics, as the economist Tyler Cowen's work brings out.[2] Assuming we're interested just in the quality of the food at a given price, these principles tell us (other things equal) to patronize restaurants right after opening since they will be eager to establish a reputation for good food, whereas once they actually have such a reputation, their incentives for good food diminish since their sales are in part a function of that (sticky) reputation. They also suggest avoiding restaurants in scenic locations or full of good-looking people, Cowen points out, which reduce the incentive of restauranteurs to rely solely on quality of food and weaken the evidence due to popularity (since they will then be popular in part for food-irrelevant reasons). Instead, foodies should eat at places in obscure, ugly locations or featuring lousy atmosphere, say aggressive and alienating religious art. Once again the incentives work in the buyer's favor, and against-the-tide popularity is an especially strong signal in this context. Here, fashionable cynicism is supported by sound epistemology that draws on the two pieces of evidence that are among the most commonly available to discerning buyers. It's hard to know if the cook was recently replaced or what experts say about some establishment while drifting through Barcelona; it's easy to observe that the restaurant is on the main square and full of attractive hipsters, portending culinary disaster.

The restaurant case is a light-hearted illustration, but an important question is why this kind of information is not more widely utilized by rational consumers of services like medicine, art, and politics. Perhaps the answer is that it's difficult to say much about how powerful this sort of evidence really is in absolute terms. But we can often bypass this worry by focusing on matched pairs, where the potential sellers are about on par, or where we simply don't know anything else besides popularity and incentives. Here are some examples.

Hiring: suppose we're looking to hire an accountant, doctor, executive, or professor strictly for professional competence and that we face two candidates roughly on par. Much of our evidence reflects a kind of popularity: recommendations, previous hirings, and many accomplishments ultimately reflect the fact that people thought highly of the candidate. How should this popularity influence us? Empirical evidence indicates that irrelevant personal attributes like beauty or warmth influence this kind of popularity to a startling degree, and accordingly we should discount for it. (The lifetime wage premium for being above average in attractiveness has been estimated in the hundreds of thousands of dollars.)[3] Conversely, we should favor those swimming upstream against such attributes. (Point (c) above.) Faced with otherwise similar candidates, then, we should count it against someone that he is good-looking, tall, confident, warm, extroverted, or well connected, just as foodies should eat at the same-priced, equally popular restaurant in the rotten part of town rather than the scenic square. In roughly pair-matched hiring situations, it's rational to pick the stout introvert over his more likable rival. After all, the rival is likely to have prospered in part due to these irrelevant factors, and the introvert succeeded despite swimming upstream, meaning his work must have been especially strong. And incentive effects suggest better work in the future from the latter, who will be less able to draw on the advantages of popularity, and will thus be forced to produce better work. (Point (f) above.) Of course, popularity and incentives are only two signals among many, but they can be important ones about the quality of service we can expect from those we hire.

The arts: suppose you are interested in two writers and only have time to read one of their novels. X is a well-connected schmoozer publishing her third novel; Y is a reclusive first-novelist. Both popularity (in the form of garnering the attention of a publisher and any praise by third parties) and incentive effects suggest reading Y. The same goes for movie sequels or spin-offs that can draw on name recognition instead of quality, or classical music albums that feature suspiciously attractive performers in suggestive poses on the cover (when one should hope for a rotund sexagenarian with a large wart).

Voting: voting is complicated because it's harder to sort out what counts as relevant; if being tall and attractive helps a politician pass legislation because of people's poor epistemic skills, then that is paradoxically a genuine reason for the voter to count such attributes as relevant. (It's reasonable to hire a good-looking litigator to persuade the unreasonable jury.) However, often we face two candidates, one of whom is tall and charismatic and the other is, say, corpulent and inarticulate, yet equally successful thus far (perhaps the two are successful governors). Other things equal, here we have evidence that the latter candidate possesses some kind of unusual talent and has the incentive to rely on it. This is only one signal among many for a voter to consider, but it's at the very least grounds for deep reflection on how the candidates became successful, and what kind of difference the talent at issue might make in office. One should expect complex, mixed feelings in reasonable voters about the charisma and height of the one candidate, and in specific cases that should count against their vote.

In these examples I have emphasized not just plumping for the popular worker, novelist, or politician. Instead, following the restaurant critics' suggestion, we should look for evidence that the seller's popularity and incentive structure are *pure*, in the sense that they are as closely aligned with our interests as buyers as possible. And to that end, we can leverage the fact that if we and others care about trait T, and there exists a bias against some other trait B, then in a pool of candidates that exhibit both traits to varying degrees, the fact that X is popular despite exhibiting B to a high degree is strong evidence that X is popular for the right reasons, and that his incentives will be aligned with our interests, since otherwise we would expect X to have been less popular.

It's useful to compare ethnic discrimination. There is evidence that Asian students in the United States require significantly higher qualifications than others in order to be competitive at elite universities. Research suggests that Asians require a Scholastic Aptitude Test score of 1540 (out of 1600 at the time studied) in order to have the same chance of admission as a white student with a score of 1400, holding all other quantifiable qualifications constant.[4] Natural experiments with states that do or do not require race-blind admissions similarly display large disparities in Asian admissions, as do secular trends in the composition of the applicant pool (the Asian share rises, but admission levels plateau). This isn't conclusive evidence of bias, since Asians might be worse qualified in unquantifiable respects such as references or extracurriculars, but suppose for argument's sake there does turn out to be an Asian penalty or de facto quota. That bias means that Asians will tend to be more qualified than others; in fact, determining how much more group X is qualified than others in some selected-for population is a good way of *measuring* bias for or against the group. (We could thus compare bias levels against Asians and Jews or African Americans in the present or past by noting by what proportion their qualifications had to exceed those of others in order for them to advance, or vice versa.) The popularity principle, at least in respect to (b) and (c), is just the same point in a different guise. Of course, publishers don't think of themselves as "discriminating" against sullen first-time authors who must produce superior work in order to succeed, but in effect they are, and that tells us that such authors who nonetheless clear the same hurdles as previously published schmoozers are likely to be special in a way the discerning book-buyer cares about.

We might wonder whether this point about popularity really is distinct from the one about incentives, or whether we aren't in fact double-counting. Are there really two separate reasons here for buyers to consider, one being that the seller's popularity suggests quality service, and another being that his incentive structure suggests the same? Double-counting would be a problem if popularity were merely a reflection of the seller's incentives, but it isn't. Popularity tells us something about how other *buyers* feel about the service, which is useful information for us to the extent that our interests align with theirs, whereas incentive structures tell us something about the *seller*. The two are correlative insofar as a seller will often be popular because of how he responds to his incentives, but that doesn't mean that the two pieces of evidence aren't distinct. To see that they are, note that in unusual cases they will come apart, as when a seller is very popular because he acts contrary to his incentives (e.g., he foolishly sells too cheaply), or when he is unpopular despite acting on them. The situation is analogous to that of establishing motive and opportunity for a crime as well as providing evidence like fingerprints. The fingerprints may reflect, in a sense, the motive and opportunity of the criminal, but that doesn't impugn the independent evidentiary value of both. Jurors should raise their probability on the defendant's guilt upon hearing his fingerprints were at the scene of the crime; hearing that he had motive and opportunity, they should do so again, since the conditional probability of guilt is higher on that evidence plus the fingerprints than on the fingerprint evidence alone.

Finally, it is worth noting that these principles can be extended beyond literal markets. Consider the assessment of other people's opinions about you or your work. Usually there is a social dimension to your interaction with opinion-givers, i.e., they would benefit or be harmed by your liking them, hating them, or feeling sad around them. The social dimension gives us an incentive to say nice things to people that will make them feel good, and an incentive to avoid saying mean things. We have social reasons to lie to people about how they look in that sweater, how good their presentation was, how much we liked their book, how much fun their party was. By contrast, there is much less reason to falsely tell them they look terrible and aren't interesting, setting aside special cases, as when we wish to insult our enemies. This suggests that when people tell us mean things we don't want to hear, they are nearly always true, but when people say nice things to us, they are often lies. Accordingly, we should pay little attention to the nice things people tell us and focus intently when their remarks are painful and unflattering, since these are more likely to be true or at least sincere.

■ FOOT-DRAGGING

Why is it unpopular to invoke such evidence, even at the margins, even as one signal among many? Why is it rare to hear anyone talk of rejecting a candidate in part because he is warm and handsome? Faced with a pick of accountants at a firm, sound epistemology suggests barreling past attractive, polite workers and urgently seeking out the ugliest, shortest, most boorish ones available, yet this strategy is rarely considered.

There are several objections to this kind of reasoning that might support ignoring it. To begin with, perhaps the parameters I've set seem unrealistic. How often is it irrelevant to us whether someone we hire is fun to be around? Being fun or attractive can be useful for things like teamwork and collaboration, which are in turn important dimensions of professional life. There may be some scope for this kind of consideration, but to see how much weight it really deserves, consider making things explicit: "I propose the department reject Professor X's candidacy because she isn't as warm and fun as Professor Y" or "I think you should choose Dr. Schmidt as your cardiologist because he's taller than Dr. Geary" or "I want someone good-looking to take care of my retirement plan." These preferences look embarrassing once we spell them out. There may be the occasional gray area generated by our concern for positive social interaction, but by and large this explicitness test doesn't seem to support dismissing popularity and incentives as signals.

Another objection is that the practical application of these principles will turn out to be at best murky. Two difficulties present themselves. On the one hand, this may all seem to depend on getting hold of empirical information that we can at best have some hunches about. Earlier, I noted the existence of at least some such information, but it's difficult to imagine knowing exactly how much good looks help political candidates, or how much less motivated a movie studio is to find a good script for a sequel. If we can't get hold of empirical information of this sort, are we simply to guess? And even if we do get some information in the form, say, of wage premiums, it's hardly obvious how to incorporate that information into a function for updating our beliefs. More subtly, how can we know that we've accounted for all such influences on the popularity and incentive structure of a buyer? And if we factor in the information we have while ignoring what we don't have, we seem to risk worsening our epistemic position rather than improving it. On the other hand, when we *are* confident about how popularity and incentives factor in, we're likely to see a lot of conflicts, since the evidence rarely stacks up neatly in favor of one view, leaving us back where we started. One job candidate will be charming, another handsome, one governor has a disfavored ethnic background, the other comes from a disadvantaged social class, and we might wonder whether such conflicts can be resolved in a way that leaves us with any useful guidance at all.

These problems are real, and there are some specific things to be said about them below. But the first thing to stress is that they aren't special to popularity and incentives. And insisting that everyday epistemic principles in general avoid such problems would be optimistic indeed. Consider testimonial evidence. If eyewitnesses agree that they saw that X, then that generally counts in favor of believing that X. But of course we are beset with problems in making sense of such evidence. We rarely have access to fine-grained information about how probative various forms of testimony are. What we have is a random hodgepodge—the occasional terrifying experiment on eyewitness fallibility or selective recall, and otherwise just intuitions and life experience.[5] We recognize that testimony can be more or less reliable under various conditions, but we have only a rough sense of the extent that this is so, despite drawing on testimony constantly for very important decisions. And here, too, it's not obvious how exactly to incorporate such data as is available into our updated beliefs, and we cannot be sure that the testimonial evidence that we respond to is representative of all such evidence that is out there. (We can hardly assume, in a trial say, that the testimony we hear is an unbiased random sample of all that was witnessed.) And even if we did have such evidence, in everyday life testimonial evidence often conflicts in various ways that are hard to net-out.[6] But in the case of testimony it's obvious that these are grounds for caution, not for doubting the existence of such evidence, i.e., that appropriate testimony really does count in favor of believing certain things, and that consequently we ought to pursue it as best we can, duly mindful of the pitfalls. We muddle through, informally trying to determine how much weight to accord a given piece of testimony, and sorting out conflicts by seeing where the balance lies in net, or whether such conflicts cancel the value of such evidence altogether. There's no reason to think popularity and incentives are any worse off than testimony in these respects.

Apart from this general response, notice that the specific information relevant to (a)–(f) is hardly obscure or unattainable, even if our knowledge of it remains intuitive and hard to quantify. Determining how popular a job candidate or book or politician is often presents no serious obstacle. Determining, more subtly, the extent to which buyers discriminate against irrelevant features of the seller requires simply that we estimate the extent to which buyers punish such traits as shortness or obscurity or a lack of charisma. (Sometimes it will be more natural to think of this in the equivalent terms of rewarding height or fame or charm.) This, too, seems far from hopeless. Knowing a popular restaurant is down an alley off the square is helpful; knowing that people perceive it as a *rather dangerous* alley strongly amplifies the signal, given our background information about how patrons feel about dangerous alleys. All we really need to know is how much people prize or dislike the relevant traits, and allow such feelings to influence their market behavior.

Perhaps the hardest information to come by is the extent to which sellers are moved by incentives. Here, we need to know to what extent sellers will attempt to make up for drawbacks to their services by improving quality in other ways. Although it is difficult to have any very precise knowledge about this, all we need is a sense of how much harder, say, a writer will work to produce high-quality work as against someone famous following up on several previous bestsellers. This is something we can get a sense for after reconnoitering the relevant market a bit. To give an example close to home, in academia professors just before and just after tenure face different incentive structures, and we might have insight into how productive such people respectively are at our institution. (As this example shows, the incentives at stake may be complex; academics [and others] are motivated by pride, envy, a sense of role-related responsibility, and many other concerns besides money or fear of being fired, making the question a serious and open one.) Overall, I see no reason to doubt that popularity and incentives give us one more kind of reason to add to the epistemic mix, about on par with other kinds of everyday evidence in respect to tractability.

I have been rejecting various explanations of our foot-dragging when it comes to popularity and incentives. But I have two positive alternatives to propose. One is simply that while it's obvious that popularity at a given price is evidence of quality, and that people respond to incentives, the point about *discounting* for irrelevant popularity, and the one about *diminished* incentives, are less obvious. It requires slightly more abstraction to see the point about choosing between equally popular restaurants, one of which has attractive clientele or scenery; similarly for the point about the seller's incentive to focus on what the buyer cares about when the seller's sales are impacted by other factors as well.

Second and more interestingly, there is something disquieting about "punishing" a job candidate for a non-job-related personal attribute, as it may seem to us. Telling someone, "You lost the job because you were attractive" intuitively feels not just wrong-headed but perhaps even discriminatory and unethical. Something like this, it seems to me, explains some of the resistance to the social epistemology I have laid out. However, there are several ways in which this reaction is, I think, a mistake. First, it makes it sound as if we do have the right *epistemic* responses, but then refrain from implementing them out of ethical delicacy. As a descriptive matter, that sounds much too optimistic to my own jaded ears. What the examples given above and our reactions to them suggest is rather resistance to admitting the epistemic situation, not to admitting it but virtuously abstaining from its application. Second, we can concede that institutional hiring involves distinct policy questions. It may be a bad idea to write into the official hiring procedures that we prefer short introverts. Avoiding resentment and rancor may take priority, and perhaps institutions have special reasons to insist on high and publicly available evidential standards for the criteria applied to candidates (though institutions often ask applicants to give evidence of hardships overcome, which can be an example of swimming-upstream reasoning).

But on the core normative question of whether it is unfair to discount for charm and beauty, the objection seems to me confused. The usual ground for objecting to employer discrimination is that it rests on prejudice against a group and/or has a deleterious effect on a victimized class. But neither is true here. Correcting for the misperception due to irrelevant popularity isn't a form of invidious discrimination but the removal of a distortion in judgment. And considering incentive effects is no more unfair in the labor market than when insisting on paying a painter by the job instead of by the hour. If anything, it seems unfair to the stout and sullen candidate *not* to frame one's hiring decisions in the way suggested, since he will otherwise be harmed by a competition that is judged in an unreasonable manner. Framing popularity and incentives in terms of "punishing" the tall and attractive is entirely optional; we can equivalently describe the process as "proactively boosting the prospects of the less attractive." The "punishing" perspective assumes that the current status quo is the right frame of reference, but the epistemology of popularity and incentives suggests that it is not.

A related concern is that focusing on the biases of others interferes with the aim of avoiding biases of our own. There is increasingly an awareness that market participants ought to avoid prejudices influencing their decision-making, with an attendant rise in blind refereeing, orchestral auditions behind opaque screens, and anonymized résumés. A renewed emphasis on the irrelevant characteristics of applicants may look like we're going backward. And it is certainly true that there are procedural conflicts that could arise: if an orchestra auditions behind an opaque screen to avoid bias, then the judges cannot simultaneously discount for beauty. Efforts to avoid our own bias may make it harder to counteract the bias of others, and there's no reason to deny that the former may sometimes take precedence over the latter. It is also true that the strategy outlined above depends on other people succumbing to various prejudices, which may seem inconsistent with our own efforts to avoid bias. But there is a higher-level consistency at work, I think. Buyers are looking for good service, and in the process are rewarding sellers for quality. Discounting popularity for beauty is one way of connecting with high-quality sellers and in the process rewarding them for their service, while avoiding one's biases in hiring is another. Both are attempts to purify the connection between buyer and seller so as to ensure that the buyer gets what he or she really wants and sellers are appropriately rewarded for their quality of service.

PART THREE

History

12 Justice and the Wealth of Nations I

If capitalism is so bad, why has it worked out so well?

Activists and intellectuals continue to express doubts about the capitalist panoply of free markets, joint stock companies, private banks, speculative investment, consumer culture, and the science and technology they finance and motivate. But why, then, have several centuries of this system produced such impressive results, including for the worst off? It was under this system, after all, that we went from Malthusian conditions to widespread abundance—in *one one-thousandth* part of human history. Embracing these results might naturally be accompanied with suggestions for further improvement—tinkering with the tax code, pointing out abuses—but critics of the capitalist panoply have more in mind than tinkering.[1]

Crude and imprecise though my opening question may be, it lies at the core of many disagreements about social organization between classical liberals and their critics. And yet philosophers rarely grapple with it in detail, say by reviewing the effects of economic growth on human welfare. Facing up to history raises problems for market enthusiasts too, though, and especially for libertarians. For a natural response to our question is to point to devastating global poverty, and to associate that poverty with the injustices of the rich countries. "Things have worked out fine for violent empires and purveyors of unequal treaties," one might quip. And even if we draw a less jaded lesson, it may be tempting to turn the question around—if moderate *socialism* is so bad, why has *it* worked out so well in places like northern Europe (and perhaps even the United States, if we look closely), and why does that fact of history not trouble libertarians more than it does? This chapter and the next address these questions.

▦ GROWTH AS A SPECIES-HISTORICAL PHENOMENON

We are so used to exponential economic growth that we scarcely notice it, save for when it teeters or fails, and the timescale on which it operates is one we have trouble registering. And yet even modest growth in the 1%–2% per year range (in real terms) is historically aberrant and completely transformative.[2] The norm for the last 200,000 years, after all, has been little or no sustained growth and subsistence-level conditions. As with all forms of exponential change, we forget that the incremental units aren't fixed but a function of the ever-increasing base, which produces unintuitive results, as with the old saw about folding paper (42 times gets us to the moon, 103 times outstrips the universe). "Meager" 1.5% annual growth in incomes means that in one generation of 30 years, we can witness change equivalent to $50,000 turning into nearly $80,000, and $150,000 over a lifetime, in real terms. Average incomes won't always keep pace with overall GDP growth, but it is still useful to reflect on the difference in lifestyles afforded respectively by $50,000 and $150,000, and the fact that modest growth can shift the average from the one to the other in a single life-span. And just this is what we have in fact seen in the rich countries over the last few centuries, which have gone from clawing at the dirt to survive to skyscrapers and ubiquitous computing. It may be protested that median incomes in countries like the United States haven't advanced much since the 1970s. But on the timescale of centuries that is relevant to philosophy, the Great Depression, much less stagnation, is a trivial blip, barely visible on a graph. Writing about the wonders of growth in 1932 would have seemed perverse, but would have been perfectly reasonable from a wider perspective.

Consider figure 12.1, which plots per capita GDP against time for the United States, United Kingdom, and Japan, which are representative.[3] Beginning at the birth of Christ is, of course, arbitrary. The horizontal axis could in fact be extended leftward at the same or a lower level back to the dawn of the species. Taking per capita GDP as a rough proxy for prosperity, all available evidence suggests that the first 200,000 years of human history produced little sustained improvement in material conditions for average people. Most lived at or near subsistence levels most of the time. To avoid exaggerating, we should acknowledge life could be good for Roman aristocrats or the urban elite of Song-era China,

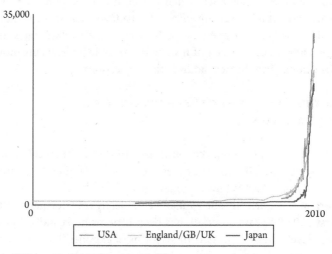

Figure 12.1 GDP/capita (1990 international $)

who had access to vast, bustling markets.[4] But most of us would be horrified at the prospect of living as average people generally have until recently.

Of course, figure 12.1 wouldn't mean very much if per capita GDP were an empty formalism. But consider the more qualitative evidence that supports taking it as a rough proxy for features of well-being we care about. As table 12.1 shows, until recently, your body may well have been stunted due to nutritional deficiencies and disease, making recent growth in stature a vivid, physical analogue to economic growth.[5] Not surprisingly, the benefits of growth are also reflected in life expectancy, even if we set aside infant mortality, which we shouldn't: American life expectancy in the mid-19th century was 38, and lower still in preindustrial England. These are just a few examples of the general improvement in actual welfare that has tracked economic growth. Growth isn't important in its own right, but there is no reason to doubt the overwhelming impression that it is growth that has ultimately brought about goods like increased health and life expectancy, not to mention the ability to travel the world, build universities, reduce child labor, and increase leisure time.

Nowadays the environment is sometimes raised as a counterexample, but the historic tendency is for richer countries to improve the environment in important ways once they can afford to do so. Trends in air pollution, water quality, forestation, and many other metrics tend to get dramatically better once nations emerge from initial industrialization.[6] Very few citizens in countries that have grown economically live in areas that are environmentally hazardous or unpleasant, and air pollution, which does still contribute to premature deaths in some areas, is the focus of intense abatement efforts. On the contrary, it is countries that have not managed to grow that often face severe problems like indoor air pollution or impure drinking water, and plenty of static, pre-growth societies have suffered environmental devastation.[7] Of course, this could all change, and if we fail to respond to climate change, it could end in disaster. But there are perfectly sensible plans for responding to this problem, most obviously by introducing a carbon tax that takes into account both risk and losses from risk avoidance.[8] If disaster ensues, it won't be because growth is inconsistent with sound environmental policy, it will be because political dysfunction or social malaise blocked timely action, just

TABLE 12.1 *Selected Estimates of Height of Adult Males*

Location	Period	Height (cm)
Europe	Mesolithic	168
Denmark	Neolithic	173
Greece	1700 B.C.	166
Worldwide	Modern foragers	~165
United States	1750	172
United States	1900	170
United States	1930	176
United States	Modern	177

as it did in many non-growth societies. Blaming this on growth would be like blaming auto manufacturers after we steer into a tree.

Since figure 12.1 refers to averages, we might worry about within-country distribution. And there are of course disparities in rich societies that growth tends to exacerbate. But from an absolute-scale perspective, things look quite different. As one economist sums up, "economic historians agree that the [within-country] poor have benefited the most from modern economic growth." The bottom fifth of Americans has seen real wages increase by a factor of *20* since 1890, not to speak of earlier times.[9] Data on wages for unskilled workers at the bottom of the social pyramid over many centuries suggests the same.[10] The gains depicted in figure 12.1 didn't simply redound to the benefit of the elite; the gains for unskilled labor have kept generally pace with the exponential schedule of economic development, as predicted by Adam Smith.[11] And once again, brute, physical measures like stature, caloric intake, etc. reflect that massive and sudden rise in welfare for the poor. The rise in median (as opposed to average) wages tells a similar story, once again confirming that what figure 12.1 captures is real, robust, and widespread. This doesn't negate the disparities between rich and poor, but it suggests that they need to be interpreted carefully. In particular, it's a terrible mistake to infer from the persistence of inequality that the currents of history haven't enormously benefited all.

None of this is to say that poor countries can't, through wise stewardship, bring about some of these goods as well, even if in practice they rarely do. Amartya Sen has made the example of Kerala in India famous, though even here, none of the technologies that are crucial to advancement would be possible without large-scale industrialization and immense national wealth somewhere. Kerala's hospitals, power stations and mobile phone networks are chock-full of materials, machines, and practices (like X-ray machines, drugs, and surgical techniques) that required expensive research and a massive industrial infrastructure somewhere in the world. Kerala-type examples of pursuing welfare without growth are thus illusory insofar as they just push the connection one step back. (Such cases can still illustrate how the welfare differences between two states might be related to things besides growth, such as emphasis on education or political participation.)

Turn next to the differential outcomes evident in figure 12.2.[12] A glance reveals what has come to be known as "the Great Divergence" between the fortunes of rich countries like those of Western Europe and the United States, and poorer countries like China, India, and those in Africa. There are several interesting features of the Great Divergence. One is its staggering magnitude, reaching income ratios of 400 to 1 and higher. But this is a huge change from just a few centuries ago, when that ratio was more like 5 to 1, and for countries like China or India more like 2 to 1.[13] In fact, Song dynasty China (10th–13th c.) was far ahead of Europe and wealthier by any measure, though still poor by contemporary standards. Song dynasty China is special in that respect, but of course it

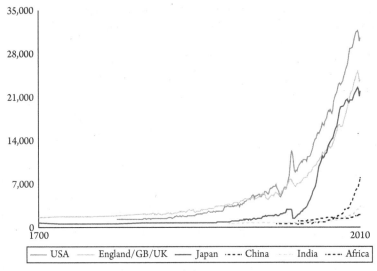

Figure 12.2 GDP/capita (1990 international $)

follows from the general poverty of the past that the ratio of richest to poorest was close to 1 in the past.

What figure 12.2 renders vivid is that the rich countries got rich by pulling away from the poor, who were originally on par. The poor countries, in turn, became "poor" simply in virtue of holding steady, or, more often, merely by failing to grow as fast. Similarly, the less rich became less rich by failing to grow as quickly. Note the difference, for example, between the United States and the United Kingdom, which was first to begin growing, but settled into a slower long-term growth rate. Figure 12.2 also displays a more positive phenomenon, the lately commenced Great *Con*vergence, most spectacularly in the case of postwar Japan. There is reason for guarded optimism that at least a significant portion of the gap will be closed within a few decades or centuries in much of the world.

To sum up: the last few centuries of economic growth represent an astonishing shift, significant at the species-historical level. (If that sounds overblown, notice that space exploration and artificial intelligence owe as much to economic growth as to science.) The rise in quality of life, including for the within-country poor, has been literally exponential. It bears repeating that unplanned economic growth has done more to improve people's lives than all of the intentional beneficence of the world combined. Unfortunately, not all countries have grown simultaneously in the same one-thousandth part of human history, and thus some remain mired in poverty, but poverty in this context simply means growing less quickly than others.

Not everyone will share this "good news" approach to recent economic history. In fact, there is a remarkable propensity to ignore or deny the good news presented above. A large literature documents an anti-market bias and a pessimism bias behind that tendency.[14] Because the gains, though vast and rapid, have occurred on a timescale that is out of proportion with our everyday concerns ("Will I make next month's mortgage payment?"), these gains can be easy to overlook or downplay. Our everyday moods are dominated by the short term and of course are often strongly influenced by factors unrelated to absolute economic gains, like how our relationships are faring or what our relative positions are. And it's difficult to move beyond anecdotal impressions to getting a picture of what is going on. When one imagines the unregulated, market-dominated period 1850–1900, for instance, one often pictures the bleak existence Marx or Charles Dickens portrayed (to some extent accurately, since the earlier phases of the Industrial Revolution were undeniably brutal in the cities).[15] And yet this was a period of a 10-year gain in life expectancy. William Blake's "dark satanic mills" were making people better off; Wagner's industrial Nibelungen were forging a better world. Even the age of cinema struggled to make sense of what was happening. Chaplin's *Modern Times* (1936) captures something of both the costs of early industrialization and its possibilities, but Fritz Lang's *Metropolis* (1927) once again misses the big picture, and the phantasmagorical scene of Moloch eating the workers is in many ways representative of the obscurantism that surrounds this topic.

■ JUSTICE AND GLOBAL POVERTY

Why then do activists and intellectuals often seem skeptical of the capitalist panoply? One obvious reason is that there is massive global poverty, which is widely perceived to be a rank injustice, a kind of stain on the riches just described. Among philosophers, this view can be found in writers like Richard Miller and Thomas Pogge, who think that rich countries like the United States and the global economic order they "impose" are to blame for the plight of the poor.[16] Miller speaks of "vast and morally unjustified harms" to the poor emanating from the United States, and Pogge writes that "features of the present global order [imposed by the rich countries] cause massive severe poverty."[17] The grounds of these criticisms are extremely heterogeneous and include allegations of economic, political, and military injustices all over the world. It is hard to encapsulate the charges, but to give some of the flavor, Miller writes that "structural adjustment [imposed as a condition of International Monetary Fund loans] is an exercise of the domineering influence of the United States by multinational means," and he points to "the vast gains to the United States from the structural adjustment process" on the backs of the poor. He goes on to reference UN reports suggesting that billions hang on trade negotiations in which the United States is said to be "bullying" the poor in order to protect agricultural and other subsidies that harm desperately poor overseas farmers by making their goods uncompetitive, even as workers in Western-owned factories toil under exploitative conditions.[18] Pogge cites medical patent regimes that benefit corporate tillers but not the poor, and claims that these and other transnational agreements amount to an "institutional order that foreseeably produces a reasonably avoidable excess of severe poverty and of mortality from poverty-related causes" which thereby "manifests a human-rights violation."[19] Miller, Pogge, and others on the left conclude that radical compensatory action is required to address these injustices that they say are responsible for the poverty of the poor.

All people of good will should join Miller and Pogge in their horror at global poverty. People of good will can disagree only about causes and remedies, not the existence or appalling nature of global poverty. But as I interpret it, the important question concerning global *justice* comes down to whether it is true that

(a) the rich countries have caused or significantly contributed to the poverty of the (across-country) poor, and that
(b) they have violated some moral constraint in doing so.

Both of these are important: I may be responsible for your poverty in some thinly causal sense in virtue of beating you in a race or getting a job for which you were the other candidate, but that doesn't make me guilty of an injustice, since there wasn't anything wrong with those acts in the first place. And of course, although violating a constraint is always wrong, if doing so doesn't cause you to suffer poverty (or other significant harm), we arrive at an injustice that is at least less interesting. (It would be a mistake to blame me for your poverty, if I've merely pocketed some of your change.) Observe, too, that the stress isn't really on justice per se as I wish to develop the problem. So far as I'm concerned, as long as (a) and (b) are met, and we are thus squarely in the domain of violating constraints, I'm content to speak of an injustice in these cases of international disparities. If that should turn out to be a conceptual mistake and we should instead speak of some other species of wrongdoing, I don't wish to rest anything on that fact. It is important to emphasize, however, that talk of "constraints" is intended to contrast with other normative concepts that we're setting aside. The issue is not supposed to be one of acting uncharitably, or merely failing to maximize utility, or of inadequately expressing the virtue of kindness. The conduct we should focus on is abdicating one's moral duties in the process of making others much worse off.

Are, then, rich countries responsible for the poverty of the poor countries in some constraint-violating sense? It clearly is true that rich countries have and continue to commit injustices, as do most nation-states. (To the extent that Pogge, Miller, and others identify specific injustices, we should join them in their condemnation.) But are these injustices the fundamental reason for vast disparities that mean the difference between living amid plenty and struggling to survive? This sort of view doesn't initially seem very plausible in light of the previous section. What seems to have happened is that after thousands of years of universal poverty, a small number of countries managed to stumble on economic growth, while others simply stayed where they were. Then, a little later, more and more countries managed to grow. Unsurprisingly, however, not everyone managed to grow at precisely the same time and at the same rate, and thus some were left behind in conditions that the rich, from their uncharacteristic and entirely novel perspective, find abysmal. But this state of affairs, it's important to emphasize, was inevitable. What, after all, were the odds that the millennia-old status quo would be overturned everywhere at precisely the same time and rate, given that the causes of growth were obscure and elusive? To put it another way, if the poor countries begin to grow within the next few centuries, that will still yield a degree of simultaneity of 200,000/500, or 1 part in 400.

Critics of the rich countries typically ignore this account altogether; there is little or no attempt to make sense of graphs like those in figures 12.1 and 12.2. There is, to be fair, discussion of whether it makes sense to assess the justice of international institutions against various historical baselines, but there is no attempt to grapple with (or even mention of) the Great Divergence, the historical origins of inequality in asymmetric growth, or the simple point about simultaneity made just now.[20] Perhaps that is because these deep facts about the origin and nature of inequality are (surprisingly!) irrelevant to justice. We can pursue this by considering the two broad options open to the critics for identifying the relevant violations of moral constraints. They can either claim that the problem lies (1) in how the rich enriched themselves, or (2) in how the poor stayed poor (or both). The first kind of objection would apply if the rich got rich by stealing from the poor. The second would apply on the theory that although the rich got rich by endogenous processes, they suppressed growth among the poor, say by violent subjugation or unfair trade practices. Let us take up these suggestions in turn.

■ GETTING RICH AND STAYING POOR

Consider figures 12.1 and 12.2 once again in conjunction with the first strategy, of locating violations in the way the rich got rich. A striking feature of the Great Divergence is that it strongly suggests that the current disparities are a part of a single, centuries-old process that is still unfolding. That process was underway many centuries ago—by 1600 the divergence is already pronounced in figure 12.1, though perhaps not yet "great"—and by 1800 there is a radical inflection point that all but guaranteed vast disparities if then-current trends held. The process leading to current global disparities thus has been marked the following structural features:

- Commencing in the distant past
- Long term, with a smooth, rarely interrupted curve persisting for centuries
- International and cross-cultural
- Independent of any specific technology platform

- Independent of colonial or other foreign policies beginning, ending, or never occurring
- Robust against revolution and radical shifts in culture

Historians widely share this assessment, although they can't agree on what exactly the long-term process undergirding exponential growth has been. The usual suspects include political and economic institutions, science and technology, bourgeois social norms, the emergence of a culture of innovation, demographic/fertility changes, or some combination thereof.[21] And the problem now is that neither these candidates nor any others that it's easy to think of both plausibly explain how the rich got rich, and involve significant constraint violations, i.e., satisfy both (a) and (b) above. Getting rich through the adoption of good institutions or bourgeois values, or by pursuing technological innovation or undergoing the so-called demographic transition, isn't obviously wrong. Once we realize that the current disparities were generated over a long time, not by policy decisions of the last few decades, but by some cross-generational, cross-cultural process that wasn't affected by initiating and then abandoning a multitude of domestic and foreign policies (including radical changes in regard to mercantilism, democratic governance, and colonialism, none of which had any significant effect), but rather by something that must have been much more abstract and powerful, it's not easy to see how that process could be something morally wrong.

We can sharpen the point a bit by particularizing: whatever the high-level explanation of rich-country affluence, it must fit Britain, Germany, Switzerland, Denmark, and Japan, 1800–2010, allowing for some differences between original and catch-up growth and implementation details. What is the right explanation of how these countries got rich, such that they massively violated moral constraints? Specifically, what moral abominations did the Swiss indulge in in order to get rich, and if the answer is that they followed some innocuous process, why doesn't that explanation apply to the United States, United Kingdom, and the rest of the group? It is hard to see what explanation could apply only to countries like Switzerland without turning out to explain growth in the others as well, and it's hard to see what the process explaining exponential growth for a Switzerland (or Canada or Singapore or Australia) could be that would have been constraint-violating in the sense of (a) and (b) above.

Of course, even if the macro-level explanation of affluence is morally inert, it will inevitably be the case that there were particular injustices inflicted along the way, and no doubt some of these are significant and important to address. We can all agree there was little to be said for, say, the Philippine-American war. But as long as they aren't connected to the historical process (whatever exactly it was) that shaped the economic trajectory of the rich countries across the last few centuries, such complaints will ultimately fail to support the claims emanating from the critics of global capitalism cited above. It remains true that current disparities are fundamentally a function of the Great Divergence and the long-term processes that underlie it.

Next, recall the other strategy for condemning current disparities, by locating constraint violations not in the gains of the rich, but in suppressing the growth of the poor. Here it's worth reviewing the very form of the Great Divergence. The general pattern of growth can be characterized as a long initial period in which two groups (the future rich and poor) have close to nothing, followed by explosive growth by the one group, and perpetuation of the status quo for the other. Call this abstract pattern of growth branching growth, and contrast it with another pattern, whereby two groups are both initially already at a high level, but then the two groups diverge, with the one growing rapidly and the other not maintaining the status quo, but sinking rapidly, as in figure 12.3. An example of this pattern would be the share prices of two rival companies that initially are both successful, before the one company starts to gain market share at the other firm's expense, causing a Y-shaped divergence (e.g., Apple vs. other gadget makers 2010–2012). Call this forking growth. There is nothing logically impossible about branching and forking growth having similar causal explanations. Just as an instance of forking might be explained by the grower gaining at the decliner's expense or by an unrelated process of causing the other party's decline, so too an instance of branching might be explained in just the same way. The grower may, for instance, siphon away all of the gains the non-grower makes as soon as they are generated or otherwise suppress growth, thus creating a false impression of inertia on the non-grower's part. But although these kinds of explanations come quite naturally in cases of forking growth, they're much less natural in cases of branching. In fact, they make for some quite puzzling coincidences and lacunae.

Suppose the view is that the grower grew at the non-grower's expense, by simple theft, say. It's then startling that the gains of the grower are so vastly out of proportion with the losses (if any) of the non-grower. After all, the grower is rising at a rapid clip, while the non-grower isn't declining much at all. To explain this would require some sort of further epicycle, perhaps a theory about offsetting gains to the non-grower masking the effect. Alternatively, one might concede that the grower grew endogenously, but say that the grower independently suppressed growth in the non-grower, say by destroying valuable output

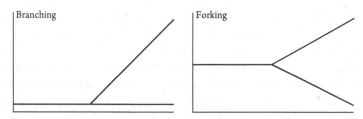

Figure 12.3 Branching vs. forking growth

in aggressive warfare. But this story implies that the non-grower was poised for explosive growth at or near the point of branching (if not, a Great Divergence was beckoning), only to see all that growth somehow suppressed before it could manifest itself, and without markedly depressing the non-grower from the status quo. That implies some remarkable coincidences.

Both of these suggestions involve the kind of elaborate explanations we usually try to avoid. Cases of branching growth are easiest to explain with a simple change/no-change model in which the grower experiences changes permitting departure from the status quo, while the non-grower continues as before since nothing has changed. And in the case of the Great Divergence, as we've noted, several candidates for such changes are widely discussed in the literature. And on the other hand, there isn't much evidence that the non-growers in the Great Divergence were poised for growth. Nothing in the record suggests that Africa or South America or Indonesia was on the verge of UK-style growth in the period 1600–1800 or before European contact. There is, to be fair, some discussion of China's and India's prospects, though this requires us to believe either that technology wasn't important for growth or else that there wasn't much of a science-technology advantage in post-Newtonian Europe.[22] And even then, it's a further step to the claim that growth was successfully suppressed. (It's instructive to consider that Britain did try to suppress growth among its European rivals through various anticompetitive practices, but in vain.) Again, it would be an impressive coincidence if other nations were poised for growth, but never managed to take off, specifically because European nations arrived at the right moment to suppress growth, but in a way that didn't much depress the preexisting flat line either. We should keep an open mind given the murkiness of history, but one might reasonably be suspicious of this kind of story.

A natural interpretation of the staggering inequalities is thus one that doesn't involve violation of constraints: growth took a branching form, the poor remained in the status quo by economic-historical inertia, while the rich grew because of a macro-level process or processes, the most promising theories of which aren't obviously constraint-violating. This suggestion is distinct from both the claim that poverty is due to current mismanagement or domestic malaise among the poor, as well as from the claim that the poor are poor because the rich are oppressing them.

■ OPPRESSIVE INSTITUTIONS

Now consider three objections, arising respectively from the relevance of the Great Divergence, from colonialism, and from the existence of feasible alternatives. The first worry is simply that none of the foregoing shows that the rich countries aren't in the process of committing injustices at *present*, and wasn't that the main point of the critics cited earlier? Does anything really hang on the dusty history I've been emphasizing, especially when the critics tend to reject appeals to historical baselines of poverty? However, conceding the possibility of past and present injustices is compatible with my claim that the fundamental reason for the gross disparities we observe has nothing to do with such injustices, and this really is an important fact. It's one thing to assert that the loan policies of the IMF or the worldwide patent regime is unjust (neither of which is obvious, of course); it's another to claim that these have anything non-trivial to do with the disparities that we observe. It's morally important to note this distinction because the concept of injustice has a special normative significance, and so it matters whether we conceptualize the gross disparities we observe as tragedies (possibly calling for charitable aid) rather than injustices. There is also a practical question. If we become convinced that what needs to be fixed is fundamentally the oppressive policies of the rich countries, we will generate pressure to pursue a particular set of policies—those focused on liberation from oppression. If, by contrast, we focus on the factors that are plausible explanations of growth that fit the bullet list of features above and that fit figure 12.2, then we will be more likely to think about promoting endogenous growth. Again, the two aren't mutually exclusive, but reading the critics I have cited one hears almost nothing about the latter.

This response may not seem persuasive. Even if I am right about the historical process leading to the present disparities, it is possible that current policies are preventing a rapid *convergence* of the sort that is only slowly and very selectively occurring in places like China. But few economists take such a position seriously. Paul Collier, former director of the World Bank Development Research Group, writes, "Citizens of the rich world are not to blame for most of the problems of bottom billion; poverty is simply the default option when economies malfunction."[23] Another economist studying growth states:

> Barriers to trade on manufactured goods and in many services are at a historic low in rich countries. . . . It would be hard to identify any poor country whose development prospects are seriously blocked by restrictions on market access abroad. Any country with a sensible development strategy has the opportunity to grow its economy, with assistance from trade.

Or again:

> Most sensible estimates suggest that complete trade liberalization . . . would produce a net gain to the developing world of one percentage point of their income or less—a meager impact that the World Bank and the WTO do their best to hide behind more impressive-sounding claims.[24]

Even if this is wrong by a factor of two, or five, or 10, there isn't any serious evidence that the deep problem lies with policy details, not the centuries-old factors underlying the Great Divergence.

Moreover, the beneficiaries of many of the suggested changes in policy would likely be middle-income, not desperately poor, countries.[25] This is because the former enjoy vast advantages in infrastructure, economies of agglomeration, and labor-force quality, which tend to swamp differences in labor costs. Poor farmers in Malawi or garment manufacturers in rural India simply aren't well positioned to reap the benefits compared to Mexico and Malaysia. To overcome this problem would require a sophisticated and probably unfair strategy of blocking middle-income countries from soaking up the new opportunities, perhaps through highly targeted tariffs. It's unlikely the middle-income countries would tolerate this, but in any case it is hardly constraint-violating of Europe to fail to punish Mexico with enormous import tariffs so as to offer a window of opportunity for businesses from Bangladesh.

However, setting all this aside, and supposing that the relevant policies did make a significant difference for the worse, it would remain to show that they were foreseeably wrong, as opposed to simple mistakes. This is far from obvious. Notice, first, that there is a broad trend among rich countries toward realizing the non-zero-sum nature of trade, albeit with lurches in the other direction.[26] The trend is evident in efforts like the Marshall Plan and corresponding initiatives under MacArthur in Japan, which resulted in the losers of World War II seeing greater economic growth than the winners.[27] This isn't to ignore local exceptions (mercantilism, for instance, in an earlier epoch, or particular cases of special-interest capture leading to indefensible subvention policies in the United States or European Union). But there's a clear pattern over the long term of recognizing the non-zero-sum nature of trade interactions, and thus no reason to think rich countries wouldn't want to see the poor exit their desperate state. Even if only for the kind of self-interested reasons that led the Allies to aid their hated enemies just a few years after total war, there's every reason to believe it in the rich countries' interest (and perceived interest) to build up trade partners who would be in a position to buy American or European goods and services. This, after all, was Adam Smith's anti-mercantilist counsel from the very beginning of the capitalist epoch. Western developed countries got rich together, then got richer together with Japan in the postwar period, and are in the process of getting richer still together with a broader swath of Asia. There simply isn't any motivation generally to resist growth among the poor, always allowing for local exceptions and special-interest capture. Granting that rich-country policies are dominated by greed and ambition, why wouldn't greed and ambition generally favor richer neighbors who can pay more for rich-country products? This, again, suggests that even conceding that policies such as those of the IMF are mistaken, it is far from clear that they are or were intentionally so.

■ COLONIAL VIOLENCE

The second objection relates to colonialism. I stated earlier that the evidence suggests growth occurred independent of violating moral constraints. But this may seem puzzling in light of colonialism and other extended episodes of violence. It may sound awfully convenient for the rich countries to absolve themselves of that despicable, violent history now that it has begun to draw to a close, and announce that that history had nothing to do with the respective positions of poor and rich.

I can't address this large topic in detail, and some of what should be said will be left to the discussion of reparations. But it is worth making a couple of specific points in addition to the more general ones made earlier, i.e., that the structural features of rich-country growth don't fit a constraint-violating picture, and that the very form of the divergence charted in figure 12.3 is inconsistent with a theory of the rich keeping the poor down. We can break our discussion into four parts.

The Curse of Windfalls

Few economic historians have concluded that colonialism was the key to achieving exponential growth, or suppressed imminent growth among poor countries, though inevitably there is some disagreement. In part, this is because the wealth generated by the colonies was rarely more than a fraction of that generated by internal trade. Moreover, huge windfalls of the sort reaped by the iniquitous conquistadors often turn out to be curses in disguise. The problems with such windfalls are various, and can include financial complications due to currency appreciation and concomitant collapse of export competitiveness ("Dutch disease"), as well as more straightforward problems with corruption, and skewed incentive effects, as countries are temporarily insulated from pressure to be productive. Spain, the central example of early colonial aggression, displays this problem effectively, since it made enormous lump-sum gains from bullion stolen from the Americas. Despite these gains, David Landes's assessment runs, "Its new wealth came in raw, as money to invest or spend. Spain chose to spend—on luxury and war. . . . Spain spent all the more freely because its wealth was unexpected and unearned. It is always easier to throw away windfall wealth."[28] He continues, "Spain, in other words, became (or stayed) poor because it had too much money," and concludes, "that Europe needed these acquisitions for capitalism's sake, is simply nonsense. Some businessmen made money in these strange and distant places; many more did not. But European economies as economies gained little if anything." The key to getting and staying rich appears not to be natural resources or windfalls but fostering a climate of productivity and innovation.

Colonial windfalls may be compared to the "resource curse," whereby wealth from oil or other natural resources paradoxically inhibits growth and produces social-political pathologies.[29] (Nigeria is often mentioned in this context.) It is worth pointing out that the resource curse is both broader and subtler than is sometimes appreciated. Philosophers sometimes associate the curse simply with the fact that the money from the resources often goes to illegitimate or corrupt governments and not their impoverished populations. This then leads to an emphasis on the role of rich countries in facilitating the trade in what are seen as stolen goods, and a plea for institutional reform to put an end to this. ("The resource curse results from a failure of institutions.")[30] But the viewpoint which blames international buyers ignores the endogenous dynamics at work, such as the reduced incentive to create a productive and innovative workforce. As the case of Spain shows, the problem isn't isolated to the trade practices of other countries. The trouble for *Spain* wasn't, at root, that Italians and others were willing to take their money; it was that they lapsed into a nation of comparatively unproductive consumers and pursued ruinous wars. Similarly, in contemplating the instructive fact that Israel and Japan—largely devoid of natural resources—both enjoy a higher per capita GDP than Saudi Arabia, it would be misguided to focus exclusively on political pathologies and corruption. The basic problem isn't that petrodollars *don't* reach the people, it's at least in part that they *do*.

Conquest

As alluded to earlier, many rich countries became rich without engaging in imperial designs, and violent conquests conversely failed to enrich many peoples; there is no obvious pattern here beyond those with power exploiting those without. The first group includes countries like Switzerland, Korea, Taiwan, and Iceland. And the list could be extended still further by countries that did engage in imperial conquest, but did so in a manifestly fitful, inept, and impecunious manner, such as Germany, Japan, and Italy—no one thinks Germany got rich by invading Namibia. Clearly across wildly varying times and social conditions it's quite possible to get rich without colonial aggression, making it less compelling to attribute the growth of the rich colonizers to their colonizing activities. It would be an odd coincidence indeed if Germany, Britain, and Switzerland all grew rich more or less in parallel, but that the engines of growth systematically diverged, such that Britain wouldn't have grown rich but for its colonies, when this proved completely unnecessary for the other two. The second group—that of ill-fated conquerors—includes imperialists like Spain and the Ottoman Empire, which grew poor despite a history of widespread, unjust aggression against their neighbors.

Onset and Withdrawal

Moreover, the key test of onsets and off-ramps of colonizing activity doesn't seem to show any significant impact: growth to the colonizers when the colonizing spigot was shut off rarely shows any significant disruption. Looking back to figure 12.2, we see that Britain went from strength to strength throughout the ups and downs of its world-leading colonial activities; the parallel graph for the Dutch would show the same thing; and to the extent that the United States has been described as a colonial power or empire and certainly in respect to slavery, US growth shows no significant impact arising from fluctuations in those domains. Over the long run these grave injustices were simply trivial relative to the real drivers of growth. (Critics should, in a way, welcome this point; it makes it all the more egregious that those practices were maintained.)

Anti-colonialism

Lastly, on the point that this all sounds awfully convenient, it's worth remembering that many of the brightest minds were urgently calling for abandoning the colonial project as soon as it began. Adam Smith not only derided mercantilism, but insisted that colonial holdings and the associated trade monopolies were both unjust and net money-losers. His advice from a strict prudential perspective was simply to give up on the colonies (the "golden dream") and to enjoy the far greater gains that were to be made by engaging in trade, while shrewdly acknowledging how unlikely it was that his advice would be followed in the near term:

> No nation ever voluntarily gave up the dominion of any province, how troublesome soever it might be to govern it, and how small soever the revenue which it afforded might be in proportion to the expense which it occasioned. Such sacrifices, though they might frequently be agreeable to the interest, are always mortifying to the pride of every nation, and what is perhaps of still greater consequence, they are always contrary to the private interest of the governing part of it.[31]

■ FEASIBLE ALTERNATIVES

Finally, there is a third objection to the claims I have been making. Pogge and other critics of the global economic order emphasize the availability of alternative systems, and view the mere existence of such alternatives as indicative of a prima facie injustice. It would be "Panglossian," they say, to claim this is the best possible system, and point out that it's all too easy to envision a patent or property regime that would be more favorable to the poor. If this were true, then even if my argument so far were right, it could still be claimed that the existence of feasible alternatives points to an injustice. As Thomas Nagel puts it, "If there are possible alternative arrangements that would reduce the inequality without drastically harming productivity, then such a system is illegitimate."[32] But remember that to make the case for rich countries bearing responsibility for the state of the poor, as I have interpreted the issue, we need to establish that constraints are being violated—it's not enough to say that we are failing to maximize utility or that the virtue of charity is being inadequately expressed. Thus, the claim would have to be that the existence of feasible alternatives that would substantially improve the welfare of the poor (and whose existence is or ought to be apprehended) in itself violates some moral constraint.

It would certainly be Panglossian to deny that there is an alternative that would make the less developed nations much better off. But this is completely trivial. It follows from the possibility of an alternative system that would, say, require rich countries to give poorer countries lots of money, or (equivalently) a medical patent system that would require rich countries to transfer intellectual breakthroughs to anyone worse off and in a position to benefit. Similarly, there are feasible alternatives to current *intra*national social arrangements, including some that would benefit the worse off. For example, there is the alternative policy that business owners must always give workers the most generous deal possible at whatever cost to themselves. Nevertheless, I can see no reason for thinking that it is constraint-violating for owners to resist such an alternative and not to volunteer to implement it.

A more serious question is whether developed nations violate a constraint in promoting an international order that favors *their* interests—for instance, one that protects medical inventions—but I don't see any reason to accept this either. For what could the constraint be that they violate? There is no general constraint on favoring one's own interests. Turning into the open parking space on a busy street favors my interests and disfavors yours even if I got there first and you're still down the block, and doing so may be as arbitrary as can be insofar as no deep moral rationale supports this outcome, yet parking in Manhattan doesn't violate a constraint. And although many other moral facts start to shift as we adjust upward the costs to you in losing the spot, I don't think rising costs can produce a constraint out of thin air. (A constraint against what, exactly?) At most those rising costs indicate that my failing to put your interests ahead of mine is mean or perhaps even cruel, but these are quite different from committing an injustice. If it is true that institutional arrangements could be changed at little cost to rich countries and produce vast gains to poor countries, we can all agree there are moral reasons to do so (though I cited various doubts about this earlier). But that still wouldn't make the status quo an injustice, and that difference matters. If northern Italy is richer than southern Italy, there may be all kinds of things the northerners have reason to do to assist their southern countrymen—favoring them in the allocation of infrastructure projects, perhaps. But it makes a difference whether the situation is described as *having moral reasons to aid* or as *correcting a vast injustice* the northerners have visited on the southerners.

The claim at issue might be stronger. We might accuse rich countries of exploiting a dominant position to *force* a deleterious system of rules on others. (Compare, say, drawing up rules to a novel card game being played for money, and threatening to harm the other players if they don't agree to rules that help you win.) Here, I believe, there is common ground. If it were true that rich countries exploited their power to force poor countries to accept an international order that was bad for them, that would clearly be wrong. But of course that is quite different from the claim that the mere existence of feasible alternatives or favoring one's interests implies the violation of a moral constraint; it is this that I have been denying. Whether the rich have actually forced the poor to accept deleterious systems of rules is a question I won't address here, except to note that answering it would probably require a complex argument. To give an idea of the complexities, notice that it would not be sufficient to show that, say, IMF conditional loan policies or medical patents were bad for the countries involved, and that they faced harrowing alternatives. That would leave open inter alia whether these agreements involved offers or threats. There is often nothing wrong with offers, even when the outcome would be bad for the recipient and he has no good alternatives. (If I get myself into a bind and ask you to buy my car, and you can only afford half its value, you do no wrong in making me such an offer, which of course I can just refuse without being any the worse off. What you may not do is threaten me if I refuse to give you a discount.) Sorting this out would then require investigation of the circumstances of the supposed offer, the alternatives open to the recipients, who was responsible for the baseline position of the recipients ex ante, and the like. It strikes me that very little has been attempted, much less demonstrated, in this arena at the relevant level of complexity and with due attention to distinguishing threats from offers.

13 Justice and the Wealth of Nations II

We have been considering what lessons to draw from economic history and the prosperity enjoyed by countries that have seen growth. Some have concluded that global poverty must be the result of the injustices of the rich, and I have tried to show this judgment to be unfounded. On the contrary: capitalist-style economic growth has been one of the best things ever to happen to humanity, and those who neglect this history miss the deep story behind how countries like Germany or South Korea went from subsistence conditions to affluence. In this chapter I consider three more lessons that people have drawn from the history of economic growth, each of which sheds light on the classical liberal view of political economy.

The first is that many countries have curtailed the capitalist panoply and festooned it with supposedly inefficient welfare transfers, but enjoyed prosperity all the same. "If Swedish-style socialism is so bad, why have things worked out so well for *them*?" we might ask. Focusing on these cases might lead us to wonder whether there isn't something crazy about a libertarian state that is perversely committed to giving away what amounts to a "free lunch." The second lesson is supposed to be that the only things that make capitalism tolerable, let alone work out "so well," are precisely the anti-capitalist appurtenances of the modern welfare state. The capitalist panoply, on this view, only works because it is significantly curtailed. In fact, it is claimed that it will need to be hemmed in ever further if we are to avoid a return to the Gilded Age—the belle époque that was a nightmare for non-rentiers.

These two points can be combined: libertarianism sets itself against those features of the status quo that alone make it tolerable, even though the ameliorating welfare programs come at no real cost. I will attempt to respond to these criticisms in a few of their guises, and more broadly address a strain of Rousseauian pessimism toward free market growth. This pessimism accounts for many of the differences between European and traditional American approaches to social organization.

Finally, I conclude with a third lesson, which draws on the role of economics in Kant's "universal history." On one interpretation of that history, important features of a market-oriented society are unavoidable, because rivals are doomed to failure. This proposal stands apart from the others and asks us to consider whether, whatever our doubts or enthusiasms about capitalist-style growth, the pressure to grow is ultimately irresistible and thus some aspects of progrowth capitalism are inevitable.

■ REJECTING A FREE LUNCH

To motivate the free-lunch idea, notice that the long-term association between growth and taxation levels (as a proxy for the expansive state libertarians oppose) isn't very suggestive, as in figure 13.1 which covers the period 1970–2004.[1] Although there is of course an enormous amount of detail that could be wielded to press the point in various directions, on the whole there doesn't seem to be a clear consensus about the relationship between growth and taxation within the ranges we care about. (Studies of "the relationship between the level of taxation and economic growth, which attempt to hold constant the impact of other determinants of growth to isolate the tax effect, have come to no consensus.")[2] This suggests that the effect, if any, is relatively small and tends to be dominated by other factors, at least within the ranges we need take seriously. And in an unusually detailed study, Peter Lindert makes the case that the welfare state does amount to a "free lunch," inasmuch as inefficient social spending that should,

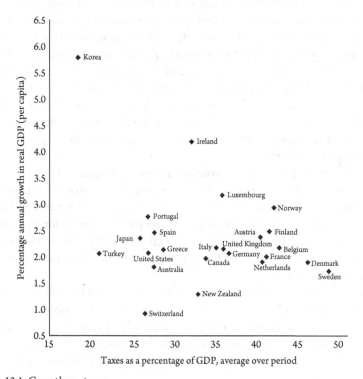

Figure 13.1 Growth vs. taxes

from a charts-and-graphs perspective, result in devastating effects on growth simply doesn't.

> If the welfare state countries of Europe are now spending between 25 and 35 percent of their national product on less productive people, and are taxing the more productive to pay for it, doesn't this damage economic growth? . . . Yet the history of economic growth is unkind to this natural suspicion. . . . Nine decades of historical experience fail to show that transferring a larger share of GDP from taxpayers to transfer recipients has a negative correlation with either the level or the rate of growth of GDP per person. The average correlation is essentially zero.[3]

These findings can be (and have been) contested in detail or read more pessimistically in light of the ongoing international pension crises and the like. And the free lunch isn't really free, since there seem to be persistent problems like high unemployment and especially youth unemployment associated with many of the European welfare states Lindert has in mind, problems which few have managed to curb consistently. "Free" here needs to be understood narrowly to mean only that the impact on growth doesn't seem to be large. More interestingly, some have argued that the free lunch depends on *someone* or other pursuing a more aggressive, high-risk/high-reward approach that motivates innovations that others can then copy and benefit from. "Someone gets to be Sweden, but not everyone can be," runs the thought.[4]

Still, the fact that a case for a free lunch of sorts can be made at all is significant— as Lindert points out, one would think that paying people not to work or to retire early would have devastating consequences clearly visible and beyond dispute. And even if growth rates are lower compared to some conjectured minimal state, absolute levels of growth and prosperity matter. Just as trying to deny the positive story of growth in the capitalist epoch seems desperate at this point, inconvenient though it may be to one's ideology, so classical liberals should grant Lindert's central point. There is nothing inconsistent between prosperity and growth on the one hand, and a welfare state with inefficient transfers on the other. Certainly if the comparison is between actual, observable states, it would be willful to deny a narrow free-lunch effect. Sweden, Germany, and other countries have had to make reforms and will continue to do so, but they aren't nearing collapse. We should accept that there is a sense in which the classical liberal state may give away a free lunch, or at least a lunch whose costs are surprisingly low compared to what is achieved by forgoing it.[5]

But not all free lunches are morally compelling or even permissible. In essence, the free-lunch idea is a point about efficiency—it seems wasteful to turn down value that doesn't cost "us" anything. But this point is the mirror image of Pareto-efficiency arguments on the right, urging us to focus on social changes that benefit some and harm none. Both have the superficial appeal of systems that seem to create no losers. The one urges a political economy structured by the pursuit of changes that are better for some and worse for none, the other one structured by the pursuit of changes that benefit some with no loss to the rising tide of growth—the free lunch. But in both cases, the no-losers appeal is ultimately deceptive. Pareto efficiency, as is well known, glosses over the initial starting points of the people involved and any unfairness in those positions; the free-lunch argument glosses over the fact that the free lunch won't be free to those on the wrong end of the necessary transfers. What is free is only the overall growth, not the losses to individuals.

To see this more clearly, consider how the free lunch works. Two mechanisms seem to play important roles: high-transfer societies may reduce anti-growth policies elsewhere in the system (say, by structuring their tax policies more efficiently), or else the transfers themselves may aid growth (say, because childcare investments pay social dividends down the road). Lindert mentions examples of both mechanisms, attempts at compensation as well as genuine payoff, but the former type of effect seems to be, if anything, the stronger.[6] It is difficult to give a simple interpersonal analogy without being misleading, since many of the effects involved are intergenerational and societal. But in general, if I force you to make transfers to your neighbors, we can hardly call it a free lunch for *you* just because you make up for it by working harder or by squeezing out efficiencies, or because the neighbors receive offsetting benefits. On the contrary, this is terrible for you, even if the group as a whole experiences a rise in income. We cannot show that there is no loss to you in virtue of *others* doing better as a result, or even in virtue of your responding to your initial losses in ways that make up for them.

This point is similar to one we can make about healthcare debates, where it is said that "inefficient" private models tend to spend lavishly on life extension to little effect in terms of quality-adjusted life-years, while "efficient" public models prioritize spending on things like primary and preventative care with greater gains for the same money.[7] The public model may or may not be correct, but it would be misleading to describe it as more efficient on these particular grounds; the free lunch once again consists of transferring money from individuals who otherwise would spend (privately) on prolonging their lives, and giving it to others to (publicly) improve theirs. Perhaps this is right, and perhaps prolonging one's life slightly by expensive means is unwise, but in any case we shouldn't describe gains achieved with other people's money as a free lunch for *them*.

In sum, just as it is misleading to present the Pareto principle as best for everyone, so it is misleading to criticize deontic theories of the state for rejecting the free lunch. Instead, proponents of entitlement states should stick to the negative strategy of denying that such states are doomed to stagnation, which is evidently untrue or at best speculative.

■ SOCIALISM MAKES CAPITALISM WORK

Alternatively, a critic of classical liberalism might take the lesson of economic growth to be that it is the non-market, statist forces that have made capitalism work and that will be required to prevent it from collapsing in the future. There are two versions of this idea. The basic version is that what recent growth shows is that the sort of minimal state that libertarians are committed to is actually *inimical* to growth. A truly minimal state with fanatical attention to property rights would quickly disintegrate amid financial crises, monopolies, environmental collapse, or social unrest in the absence of various forms of social insurance. The more speculative variation is that without socialist moderation, a capitalist society will turn into a nightmare of inequality in which rentiers and aristocrats lord it over ordinary citizens who have no recourse. We can think of the first version as denying that pure capitalism will produce long-term growth, and the second as saying that without socialist moderation, capitalist society won't be the sort of place we would want to live in.

The first idea begins with the observation that every successful, high-growth state in the last 200 years has been forced to resort to a statist panoply to complement the capitalist panoply I outlined earlier. It consists of such institutions as a national education system that promotes human capital; a national banking system that intervenes in financial crises, shapes interest rates, and insures private banks; and a heavily regulated business environment that includes consumer protections and antimonopoly provisions, environmental protections, and much else besides. The 20th century was as much about the defeat of the classical liberal state as it was about the demise of communism, the argument continues. Modern states have converged upon a blueprint that is good for growth in an advanced mass-society, but which no longer bears any resemblance to the classical liberalism of an earlier era. The key to this convergence has been collective action problems that simply cannot be solved without a coordinated statist approach—the Great Depression is the obvious example. In fact, the critic continues, observe that advanced societies have come to implement many of the items on Marx and Engels's program as laid out in the *Communist Manifesto*, including progressive taxation, child labor laws, and mass education, and that the state has a very significant role in financial and transportation oversight even where it has deviated from the communist prescription of a state monopoly.[8] The irony of libertarians trumpeting the miracle of growth is that such growth is no longer sustainable on a libertarian basis, the critic concludes.

There is much that is right in this argument, and we will have occasion to continue grappling with the observations about convergence below. But the critic both exaggerates the association between statist policies and prosperity and underestimates the resources of a moderate libertarian political philosophy. As figure 13.2 shows for the United States, the convergence on a welfare state isn't really associated with improvement in growth—it merely hasn't led to the collapse some might have predicted (the free-lunch point).[9] If anything, growth since the postwar boom period appears to be decelerating, though there are many reasons for this. Although the uncertainties rise as we go back in time, if we view the

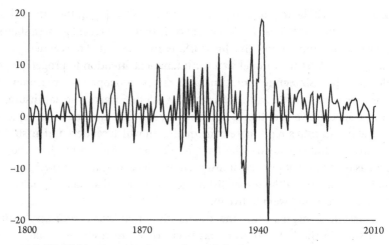

Figure 13.2 US GDP/capita annual growth rate (%)

graph as even a very rough guide, it doesn't really suggest that the rise of statism unlocked growth previously untapped. This is even clearer in figure 13.3, which shows per capita growth in logarithmic scale.[10] There are a few trend lines we might discern—one through the early 1800s, another in the mid-19th century, and then an acceleration in the late 19th century produces a slight increase in slope continuing through the 20th century, with some flattening of late. The underlying forces of growth do not show any obvious association with the vast changes wrought in most advanced countries in the first half of the 20th century. Convergence on the welfare state is better explained by the free-lunch observation, plus the willingness of voters to think about wealth transfers in broadly utilitarian fashion, perhaps unsurprisingly in light of the horrific disruptions of the Great Depression.

Those disruptions and their attenuation up to 2008 in the "great moderation" are themselves important, however. (Notice how the gyrations in figure 13.2 abate toward the right.) Stability may be part of what the critic has in mind in saying that state intervention at scale has become a necessity. But here it is unclear that moderate libertarians cannot endorse the relevant institutions. Financial crises and massive volatility in the business cycle are similar to fires or other natural disasters whose prevention is in many respects like a public good, subject to what I described earlier as the anti-free-rider principle. This says, loosely, that if we cannot reasonably avoid providing a service to all that will attract free-riders, we are within our rights compelling others to pay for such services. Earlier, I left vague how much this principle might cover, and I still don't wish to enter into the details of how far exactly it might be stretched. The important point was that there is a clear difference between, say, a healthcare program that is merely a transfer program in disguise—a difference that emerges when we reflect on

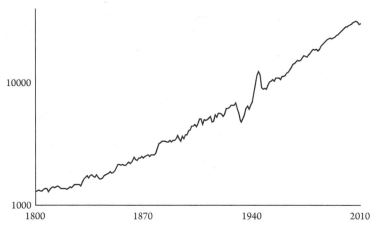

Figure 13.3 US GDP/capita log scale (1990 international $)

why we cannot simply provide people with an exit option—and one that is not, as when fighting an epidemic in which all must be covered. The relevant question is whether the establishment of institutions like a central bank might be covered under something like the anti-free-rider principle, and without settling the matter, it certainly isn't obvious that it is not so covered. An argument could be made that we are permitted to force banks on a certain scale to comply with various conditions, including funding a bailout program or taking out deposit insurance, on grounds similar to compelling all to cooperate in stopping or preventing an epidemic. How far such an argument might extend toward other institutions and other forms of social insurance is a tricky question, but then it is equally unclear to what extent the system most states have converged on is integral to stability and growth; as we've noted, there isn't a particularly compelling case to be made from past growth, and states have often converged on political-economic systems that turned out to contain either gratuitous or plain awful features (e.g., European mercantile imperialism).

■ SOCIALISM MAKES CAPITALISM BEARABLE

The second sense in which socialist policies might be taken to be required for capitalism to work is that they make a laissez-faire system bearable (if indeed it is bearable!). A remarkably enduring French tradition stretching from Rousseau to the present is skeptical of classical liberal pillars like property rights, free markets, and in general the capitalist panoply, particularly on egalitarian grounds. This tradition holds that capitalism left to its own devices produces intolerable inequalities that must be corrected for.

The economist Thomas Piketty, for example, asserts that in the long run, returns on capital eclipse overall economic growth in general and returns on labor in particular, and that especially in times of slow growth this has enormous effects. In his view, we have wrongly come to see the postwar period as normal, when it was in fact an unusual interregnum in which capital had been destroyed on a massive scale by two wars and inflation that wiped out the fortunes of rentiers, and this unusual state was then perpetuated by left-leaning taxation and social policies. Now, he points out, inequality seems to be rising again toward early 20th-century levels. On the income side, he points out that income inequality keeps rising, mostly due to the "working rich," the top managers whom he suspects of paying themselves vastly more than they are worth.[11] And reviewing the historically common distribution of wealth, he says that "the top 10% of the capital income distribution always owns more than 50% of all wealth . . . whereas the bottom 50% of the wealth distribution owns nothing at all, or almost nothing."[12] Elsewhere, he writes "from 1877 to 2007, we find that the richest 10% appropriated three-quarters of the growth," and he decries "the considerable transfer of US national income . . . from the poorest 90% to the richest 10% since 1980."[13] Looking ahead, Piketty makes the quasi-Ricardian prediction that rentiers will inherit the earth as the fraction of the national income composed of returns on capital rises—rises to levels that weren't unusual in the past if not for cataclysms and left-leaning policies.

Yet again, some of these claims have been contested. Even the broader trends Piketty points to have been denied, for example by questioning whether he adequately takes into account risk to capital, which is what its high returns generally reflect—one man's base rentier is another's swashbuckling risk-taker—or the many bubbles that puncture those returns regularly, or the diminishing returns on capital as profitable investments become harder to find.[14] But to press these criticisms here would be petty, since we are interested in the broad, normative assessment of capitalism and inequality. We should again grant at least the outlines of Piketty's picture of persistent income and wealth inequality, if not his dystopian prognostications. Piketty, after all, is just the latest avatar of Rousseau's perspective, and the French tradition is responding to something real about inequality that there is no point in trying to evade on technical grounds.

Earlier, I pointed out that the evidence suggests that even the worst off in developed countries generally have it in their power to lead a decent life, and I urged that this is what matters. The Rousseauian tradition rejects this because it views inequality as intrinsically unacceptable. In this respect it is telling that Piketty, unlike Marx and Engels, makes virtually no attempt to examine the powers of citizens to attain a decent living, to examine how standards of living have improved over time, or to consider the absolute level of welfare of the people he is concerned for. No newspaper reports of children being worked to death here.[15] He does point out that 19th-century novelists depict a world in which an income of 30 times the average of the day was required to feel comfortable and not to suffer some form of real indignity—living at average levels was unthinkable for Jane Austen or Balzac.[16] He then acknowledges that this has completely changed, while noting that contemporary TV shows often depict well-educated experts, which he attributes to a dubious myth of meritocracy. But nowhere is there reflection on *why* Jane Austen's attitudes would no longer make sense, even though we're supposed to be on the verge of the return of the rentiers. It is worth pursuing this theme. A modern Jane Austen story should focus on a romance between someone living "decently" and a high-powered lawyer or doctor or manager who is rich. Helen Fielding's *Bridget Jones' Diary* (1996) self-consciously follows *Pride and Prejudice* and still serves as a plausible mirror of our society. The protagonist starts off as a publishing assistant whose salary is not given, but whose world fits comfortably in the range of average incomes. Adjusting for her single status and fudging her salary and lifestyle a bit doesn't make much of a difference. What matters is that a modern novelist can depict something vaguely average without either seeming disingenuous or depicting some great horror—unlike Jane Austen. Marrying an international human rights lawyer would of course be nice, but living as Bridget Jones already does just isn't all that appalling. The inequality may not have changed very much, but it's misleading to ignore massive changes in absolute levels of welfare. Austen's picture as Piketty presents it is as relevant to us as is Fritz Lang's industrial Moloch in *Metropolis*.

Nor is there any real evidence that the inequalities Piketty refers to go back to the kind of unfairness that Marx and Engels were concerned with, whereby those with capital could force workers to accept injustices. Piketty tries to suggest such an unfairness with zero-sum phrases like "appropriated three quarters of the growth" and the "transfer of US national income" to the richest, but these are deeply misleading. "Appropriating the growth" just means that the rich got richer at a faster rate than the less rich; there was no fixed sum up for grabs that the rich somehow stole for themselves. Income was "transferred" only in the sense that the rich made more money in the relevant period, which doesn't mean that there was some fixed, independent stream the poor might otherwise have received. The rich, the less-rich, and the poor are not in a zero-sum competition for national income falling from the sky. In most of the kinds of cases Piketty has in mind, it was the activities of the rich "supermanagers" that generated the additional wealth that was "transferred" to them. There aren't more than a few casual references in Piketty to instrumental reasons to avoid inequality. The focus is *pure* inequality. (This is particularly salient in the emphasis on the partitioning of inequality toward the top—the concern that even within the top 10%, the top 1% are further segregated, which can only matter for reasons of pure inequality.) The Rousseauian thought is that there is something morally objectionable about the very idea of some being richer than others; in philosophical terms, egalitarianism in this guise isn't a vehicle for prioritizing the worse off, but for inveighing against the very existence of a gap.[17]

Perhaps Lockeans, with their classical liberal bent, and Rousseauians are constitutionally incapable of reconciling their differences, particularly the weight that pure inequality should get. What is puzzling from the Lockean perspective, though, is that the Lockean approach has led—with ups and downs and plenty of pathologies—to broad prosperity. Again, if the capitalist panoply is so bad, how come it has worked out so well in absolute terms *for the worst off*? Figure 13.4 displays the real wages for unskilled and production workers in the United States for the last few centuries.[18] There is plenty to worry over in detail, especially the recent stagnation in wages, but the long term nevertheless displays the staggering, indeed exponential, gains to the worst off in the capitalist epoch, in the country Rousseauians like Piketty are most exercised by. This same period saw the life expectancy increase by *decades*. Some got even richer obviously, but surely those other facts do not deserve to be glossed over lightly, and it seems telling that the argument has shifted so dramatically from Marx and Engel's focus on the actual quality of life of workers to handwringing over pure inequality. And we should remember that even when we do focus on a class of people, "the rich," this class is fluid across individual lifetimes, with many attaining "riches" at some point, and few staying there very long. In the United States, about 70% of the population will spend time in the top 20% of the income distribution (60% for two or more years), and only about 20% will remain there for 10 years or more.[19]

It is worth further stressing how inequality can increasingly result from processes that are not obviously unjust in themselves. Consider the significance of the size of the market. Globalization and development abroad mean that certain forms of labor are worth more, merely in virtue of scale. To see this, consider the difference between local and potentially global workers, the difference between those who can market a product or service to the entire world, like a software engineer, and those who serve only a local market, like a daycare worker. Global workers can take advantage of increasing scale in a way that local workers cannot, both directly by selling to more people, and indirectly as firms

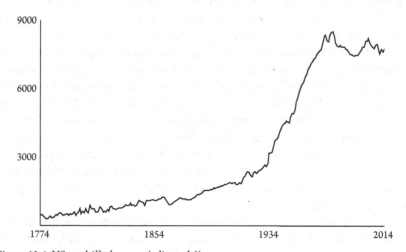

Figure 13.4 US unskilled wages (adjusted $)

are capitalized at ever higher levels and pay more for slight differences in skill or experience. (Being a skilled programmer is worth more to Google the more customers the company has.) Moreover, those reaping the benefits of global scale no longer require as many employees; Henry Ford's factories required more workers per dollar in revenue than Facebook or Google do. How strong an influence these factors are on wage gaps is of course an empirical question, but my point is only that these and similar factors can create large inequalities without any obvious wrongdoing. The fact that more people want to buy your stuff than mine is not the sort of thing it is easy to describe as an injustice (which isn't to say that it might not be an important social problem).

■ BRAUDEL AND ROUSSEAUIAN HISTORY

We have been considering the Rousseauian tradition that says capitalism creates a dystopia which only socialist correctives can render tolerable. But we have yet to mention perhaps the most important exponent of that tradition, the historian Fernand Braudel. (*Civilization and Capitalism* is surely among the most illuminating and profound works touching on political economy.) No serious discussion of capitalism and its history can afford to neglect his ideas.

Braudel shows that capitalism in one sense is eternal and has always been with us: "the whole panoply of forms of capitalism—commercial, industrial, banking—was already deployed in thirteenth-century Florence, in seventeenth-century Amsterdam, in London before the eighteenth century."[20] A financial and merchant elite probably existed in antiquity in places like Phoenicia, since it is hard to see how else their manifest enterprises could have been viable, but in any case, medieval Europe displays all the sophistication of insurance, money exchanged by paper bills, speculation on futures, the obsession with information to be turned to profit, gambling and risk, and international networks of trade. In a sense, Braudel's central claim is that nothing ever changes, that capitalism is in part defined by its protean tendency to seek out opportunity by exploiting whatever the current "game" happens to be by a "counter-game." The world has always been ruled by a dominant economic power, he says, usually focused on a single city, and within that by "a handful of privileged people. . . . Everything invariably falls into the lap of this tiny group: power, wealth, a large surplus of production";[21] he gives detailed analyses of Italian city-states like Venice and of Amsterdam in their periods of dominance to show that even then a strata of 1%–10% ruled the city and thus much of the world, in line with Piketty's and other Rousseauians' preoccupation with the tiny group of elites atop the social pyramid. (It is easy to see these individuals even now—they are hanging in our galleries in the sections by Titian and Frans Hals.)

In part, Braudel arrives at this result because he *defines* capitalism as a morally dubious process of economic exploitation at scale. The little shop where you buy your newspaper cannot be called a capitalist enterprise, he says, "though if it belongs to a chain of shops, the chain could be said to be part of capitalism." European trade he views as an "octopus grip," bills of exchange are "key weapons in the armoury of merchant capitalism," central banks are usually viewed as lenders of last resort, but "seem to me to have been above all instruments of power and international domination," and "any reinforced form of domination secretes capitalism."[22] The peroration runs:

> We are still being told today that capitalism is if not the best, at any rate the least bad regime. . . . It is argued that human nature is unchangeable, therefore that society is unchangeable too; that it has always been unjust, unequal, subject to hierarchy. History is dragged in to testify. Even the old myth of the "hidden hand" of the market, adjusting supply and demand better than any human intervention, will not lie down and die.[23]

There is no attempt to conceive of capitalism, however vaguely, in neutral terms of structures like savings, investment, the firm, markets, and R & D. It is characteristic of the Rousseauian worldview to see such conceptions as banal and naive. Of the many demonstrations of the ills of capitalism that motivate such an approach, this account of what is nowadays called "corporate welfare" is representative:

> [Capitalism] has, as it always did, burdened the state with the least remunerative and most expensive tasks: providing the infrastructure of roads and communications, the army, the massive costs of education and research. Capital also lets the state take charge of public health and bear most of the costs of social security. Above all, it shamelessly benefits from all the exemptions, incentives, and generous subsidies granted by the state, which acts as a machine collecting the flow of incoming money and redistributing it, spending more than it receives and therefore obliged to borrow.[24]

One can only concede much of the specific texture Braudel is responding to. Enron was corrupt, and corrupt in a way that has a very long history; firms do prefer the state to pay the bill for health insurance and an educated workforce; companies do shamelessly seek out monopolies and handouts that benefit them, as Adam Smith already complained. As we'll see in more detail in the next chapter, violent merchant-capitalism was in fact a scourge on the earth (that financed a lot of those Titians and Halses). Both Braudel and Piketty rightly stress the eternal aspect of people seeking economic advantage, and the concentrations that emerge. It is implicit—and sometimes even explicit—in the clay tokens and envelopes of Mesopotamia and in the grid-lined papyri that anticipate our spreadsheets.

However, two flaws ultimately vitiate this Rousseauian analysis. One is now familiar: Braudel, too, tends to ignore the actual condition of the worse off, and how it changes over time and under capitalism. Like Piketty, Braudel displays little interest in the actual welfare of the people he discusses, as against their relative status. It would be entirely possible to read all three volumes of *Civilization and Capitalism* and come away thinking that the worse off were living at about the same qualitative standards in 1960 as in 1580. A brief discussion of growth is included, but nothing would indicate that this produced astonishing gains in lifespan or health, or that the capitalist panoply had taken people who were literally stunted and brought them to the point that *over*nutrition was their major health problem. (One may criticize Coca-Cola for fattening up the youth, but let us do so with a sense of reverential awe.) Tracing the commonalities in economic systems across time is misleading when uncoupled from the actual effects they have, and the changes in those effects. As evident in the swipe at Smith's invisible hand above, Braudel seems to reject the very idea of unintended benefits to society in the form of capitalist enterprises that pool investments and enable vast and efficient production. This may be because he is determined to define capitalism as the "nasty" part of commercial enterprise, but of course this starts to look circular. Most social institutions will come off badly if we insist that the nice versions thereof "don't count." And as we have seen, once we do consider real effects and change over time, it is unclear why we should be fulminating rather than celebrating.

The other flaw is to ignore the means that particular capitalist enterprises adopt. For Braudel, giant multinational corporations are but the latest incarnation of an eternal force with the same inhuman agenda. But the means by which elites arrive at their elite status and manage to produce huge concentrations of wealth surely matters. Getting rich by a piratical monopoly licensed by the state is different from making a gadget that everyone wants, and yet the Dutch East India company is treated as somehow on par with modern-day firms in the Rousseauian tradition. In a sense, this is right. The Dutch East India company and Apple are both joint stock companies with immense power across the world and are indeed the face of the inequalities Rousseauians decry. But it is misguided to overlook the way in which that power is deployed. None of this is to void incrementalist criticisms, say of worker conditions in Chinese factories, but failing to cognize the moral gulf that remains can only obscure things. Apple's employees and its investors are not fundamentally rich because they have undertaken moral depravities from which others would shrink. The same is true of individuals who come into vast holdings. Zeal for underlying continuities becomes misleading once we fail to distinguish the fortunes of merchant-conquerors, and say Nathan Rothschild, who came to hold a non-trivial fraction of the entire wealth of England by supplying Wellington with the bullion to wage war on Napoleon, and making huge bets in the bond market on the effects that peace would have.[25] Some will decry the resulting inequality, but that still wouldn't make it useful to run together thinly veiled conquest and peaceful trade.

The same distinction between permissible and impermissible means applies to the idea that capitalist enterprise has managed to organize society around its aims, offloading unremunerative tasks like education and healthcare onto other institutions, while shamelessly looking for handouts and tax dodges. On the one hand, there are the corrupt practices, say the company that secures favors and loopholes by bribes or campaign donations. But the more general idea of getting others to pay your expenses is hardly limited to capitalist enterprise. Public choice theory suggests that individuals of all stripes will band together and seek to bend the state toward their will. Theories like this are sensible if depressing, but singling out specific groups vying for favorable treatment is more dubious and tends ultimately to reflect one's ideological sympathies, rather than principled concern for justice. To see this, notice that the elderly form a powerful political constituency, albeit one that is harder to scold than the dreaded multinational. It is easier to denounce the pinstripe suit than the cookie apron, and yet from a public choice perspective, the pressure, say, to enact intergenerational transfer policies looks no different than pressure to subsidize weapons manufacturers or agribusiness.[26] In other words, it makes sense to criticize the outright corruption one sees in occasional scandals nowadays or in the merchant capitalism of the past; it also makes sense to criticize at a grand, philosophical level the fact that democracies succumb to interest groups of all shapes and sizes; it does not make sense to subject enterprise to scrutiny while ignoring pay-as-you-go entitlement programs with a net-expropriative structure. Yet Braudel's criticisms rely on this sort of invidious distinction.

■ CAPITALISM AND THE IDEA OF A UNIVERSAL HISTORY

This chapter on economic history has inevitably focused more on economists and historians than philosophers, but I want to close with Kant, since he was among the first to propose that economics helps to determine the shape of history. It seems to me that he was right on the whole, and that the kinds of constraints on successful societies that he gestures toward offer us insight into the range of feasible social-economic arrangements. These constraints provide another useful lens through which to view the claim that capitalism and free markets push us in a direction we should fear or regret. For better or worse, there might be something *inevitable* about at least some features of market-dominated societies.

Kant suggested that it might be possible to discern a pattern to history, that there might be a hidden structure to the seeming chaos—an idea more often associated with Hegel or Marx.[27] Three central motifs structure Kant's "Idea for a Universal History with a Cosmopolitan Purpose." First, he conjectures that people's free choices over time unintentionally produce outcomes that follow lawlike regularities. This thought is remarkably similar to Smith's invisible-hand suggestion made just eight years earlier. Kant writes,

> Individual men and even entire peoples give little thought to the fact that while each according to his own ways pursues his own end—often at cross purposes with each other—they unconsciously proceed toward an unknown natural end, as if following

a guiding thread; and they work to promote an end they would set little store by, even if they were aware of it.[28]

This just is Smith's point, applied not to the economic realm, but to history as a whole. (Compare "Every individual . . . intends only his own gain, and he is in this . . . led by an invisible hand to promote an end which was no part of his intention. . . . By pursuing his own interest he frequently promotes that of the society more effectually than when he really intends to promote it.")[29] To fill in the proposal, Kant then makes two additional suggestions—one about the end that history does in fact unintentionally tend toward, and a second about the mysterious mechanism whereby this occurs.

The end that Kant suggests is that "All of a creature's natural capacities are destined to develop completely," though for us humans, "natural capacities directed toward the use of his reason are to be completely developed only in the species, not in the individual." More concretely, Kant foresees a "universal civil society administered in accord with the right" which will enable us to realize the full potential of reason.[30] (Later, in "Perpetual Peace," he seems to backpedal from global governance toward a federated league of nations, though many of the details of his thinking are obscure.)

The mechanism that Kant proposes for fixing the arrow of history toward these ends is in turn "antagonism" or competition, as people are driven to develop their capacities by the desire for "honor, power, or property," and thus to "secure status." Our species, as it were, knows that conflict and competition are good for us: "thanks be to nature for the incompatibility, for the distasteful, competitive vanity, for the insatiable desire to possess and also to rule. Without them, all of humanity's excellent natural capacities would have lain eternally dormant."[31]

It is at this point that Kant's argument touches on capitalism in a way that is illuminating. In some ways Kant sounds fantastical, almost mystical in his talk of an end, a telos, for history, and in his oracular suggestion about our capacities being developed in the species as a whole. But a sober gloss is that Kant simply has a prescient awareness of invisible-hand mechanisms and of how powerful they can be. The idea can be put in terms of natural selection: competitive forces pit individuals and ultimately societies against one another, and so compel them to change in ways they would never have chosen freely. And since there are patterns to the kinds of changes that are selected for in such clashes, there is an arrow fixing the direction history takes. And Kant seems surprisingly clear that individual liberty and commerce ("free enterprise" in the literal sense) are one or perhaps even the crucial factor in this universal history:

[C]ivil freedom can no longer be so easily infringed without suffering after effects in all areas of endeavor, especially trade, in which event a nation's power in its foreign relations will diminish. If one hinders the citizen from pursuing his well-being in whatever ways consistent with the freedom of others he chooses, one hampers the liveliness of enterprise generally and, along with it, the power of the whole.

He also touches on finances and their relation to war:

> In the end, even war gradually becomes not only a very artificial undertaking, so uncertain for both sides in its outcome, but also a very dubious one, given the aftermath that the nation suffers by way of an ever growing burden of debt (a new invention) whose repayment becomes inconceivable. At the same time, the effect that any national upheaval has on all the other nations on our continent, where they are all so closely linked by trade, is so noticeable that these other nations feel compelled, though without legal authority to do so, to offer themselves as arbiters.[32]

We can accept a suitably modest version of Kant's thesis without prematurely celebrating an "end of history." Certainly there are obvious examples of nations progressively altering their social systems under the kind of selection pressures that Kant describes. One is the opening of China under Deng Xiaoping, who wrote, "No country that wishes to become developed today can pursue closed door policies," recalling that "in the early Ming Dynasty in the reign of Yongle when Zheng He sailed the Western Ocean, our country was open. After Yongle died, the dynasty went into decline . . . through 300 years of isolation China was made poor, and became backward and mired in darkness and ignorance. No open door is not an option."[33] And in truth, far before Kant, rulers who grasped the connection between money and power said as much, notably the merchant kings of Venice, the doges who saw that "looking after one's ducats, dwellings and doubelets was the road to true power."[34] World War II is the most impressive example of a war decided largely on economic grounds, but there are many others, meaning plenty of selection pressure to operate on the social variations as Kant describes.

Kant's thought is ultimately that enlightenment is power, and that this means that all people will eventually be grudgingly brought toward an enlightenment state. Enterprise and individual liberty play an important part in his reasoning, though not one we should exaggerate (and not one that is incompatible with tax-and-transfer regimes). Kant might just as well have predicted that mass education and science were critical to a powerful state and that these and many other features that aren't directly related to enterprise would have to become staples of successful societies. On the other hand, it is striking that in the ongoing experiments with different social arrangements, there has been, if anything, greater convergence on more or less free enterprise than there has been on political liberties or enlightenment values like freedom of speech, especially in places like China or Singapore. And many of the specific social features that market economies dictate are especially interesting as selection forces that compel the adoption of otherwise unpopular norms.

It is worth noticing some of the items that would have to feature in a list of economy-related attributes of a society that are now mandatory for Kantian reasons:

> *Luxury*: it has been a common fallacy to suppose that economic might lies in production, not consumption. But apart from an initial period of frugal export-growth, all

successful societies have been ones that prize what are now barely even recognized as luxuries (houses full of stuff, restaurant dining, fresh produce year-round, international travel, fashion, yoga lessons, etc.). This isn't just a byproduct of wealth. Consumer demand motivated the voyages of Columbus, da Gama, and Magellan (seeking cloves and pepper), and textiles and nice clothing drove the industrial period. Now it is information technology and frivolous gadgets and social networks. A society that lived as early Christians, Buddhists, Spartans, Aristotle, or secular utilitarians have suggested we ought to live could not win its wars, whatever its other virtues. (Hume was one of the first to see this, in his neglected essay "Of Commerce.")

Flux: many political philosophies broadly oppose change, innovation, and social dynamism, including most ancient Western and Confucian philosophers. (Stability is a leading note of the *Republic*, for instance, and respect for one's elders a pillar of the Confucian worldview.) But creative destruction is of the essence in a capitalist system. Capital is allocated and deallocated; the average life span of the powerful firms on the Fortune 500 is just a few decades.[35] People move constantly, must relearn their jobs with new skills; their life experiences can become irrelevant overnight. This requires not just technical or business change, but social change as well. It tends to rule out tradition and a gerontocracy that cannot adapt to radical changes like introducing women into the workforce, or becoming tolerant and cosmopolitan (as great capitalist centers like Amsterdam and London have always been). It tends to favor adaptive youth-culture, and neotocracy. The result is a Heraclitan system in which little is fixed for long.

Bourgeois virtues: societies with good formal institutions won't succeed without an economically viable culture—the customs and mores the very poor generally cannot afford, and the aristocracy can afford to ignore. Such bourgeois virtues include timeliness, reliability, contractual honesty, thrift, and ambition. (Try envisioning a successful workforce that is lazy, shows up to work at random hours, cannot be trusted with contracts, and doesn't care about advancement.) These virtues come in different wrappers, sometimes that of the Protestant work ethic of a Benjamin Franklin, sometimes the Japanese culture of excellence. And not all of these virtues are violently opposed by competing ideologies. But the evidence does suggest that they are distinctive, non-obvious traits that are routinely flouted, and yet essential to economic success. Identifying cultures as less honest or comparatively lazy has a politically incorrect quality that generates resistance, but no one who has traveled widely could deny that there is a spectrum of likelihoods that the average worker will, say, be late for a meeting, nap in the afternoon, renege on prior agreements, or spend rather than save, even when doing so is imprudent.[36]

Not everything in this list is desirable. A society of constant upheaval and change presents obvious costs, especially to the old, the traditional, the rural, the technologically unsophisticated. One way of putting it is that the economic growth rate is a major factor in the rate of generalized social change. And if we ask ourselves if we want the rate of social change to be as high as possible (new manners, customs, expectations every year), we can only answer No, and so we should be skeptical that having the highest possible growth rates is always best. A reasonable conjecture might be that the optimum growth rate varies across the absolute level of welfare, and steadily diminishes. (Recent slowdowns in growth may be a "mixed curse.") Thus, Kant was focused on the enlightenment virtues of his vision, but there are many costs he doesn't mention.

There is obviously a range of permissible values within the constraints we've recognized. There are more and less humane ways of dealing with a redundant workforce. Japan, for instance, has traditionally resisted many of the more extreme features of capitalist society one sees in the United States, say by trying to provide lifetime employment, and constraining CEO/worker pay ratios. But lifetime employment is starting to fade even in Japan; such choices are hard to sustain in the long term, and in any case the range of permissible values that remains is still remarkably narrow overall. Japan, after all, tore up its social fabric in the Meiji reforms and considered changing the national language to English.[37] On the whole, Kant seems right that these kinds of features, desirable or not, shape what does and will constitute viable or at least globally competitive societies. And in aggregate, it is a remarkable fact that Kantian considerations rule out most societies favored by thinkers of Western antiquity, medieval Christianity, traditional Islam, Confucian China, and what at least some secular utilitarians have suggested. Even this fragment of just the economic element of Kant's idea thus has sharp teeth indeed.

Being ruled out might not be so bad, of course. Kant was surely exaggerating when he spoke of *all* nations conforming to some model; if one is willing to be vulnerable to one's neighbors' depredations (or fortunate in their meekness), and doesn't mind a relatively impoverished backwater status, the foregoing can be ignored. One should expect *holdouts*—peoples preferring to hold on to tradition or repelled by flux or luxury or incapable of developing institutions to manage them. (Or, in a more interesting variation, countries themselves may vary dramatically in the degree to which they conform to the list—one thinks of different regions in Italy or the United States. Holding out is made easier when surrounded by friendly non-holdouts, and it is an open question if the holdouts *would* hold out if not subsidized by the non-holdouts.) Nor should one chortle too loudly at holdouts—to test one's own stomach for flux one must look not at those struggling to adapt, but to a future in which *we* would need so to struggle—say by considering transhuman cyborgs decamping for Mars (no more far-fetched than suburbia would seem to Charlemagne). Kantian reasoning can only fix the direction of the arrow, not fix the nature or proportion of holdouts.

There is thus a paradoxical element in Kant's cosmopolitan thinking we should allow for: as countries become enlightened (in Kant's non-religious sense), they become less rapacious, more attentive to the costs of war, more cognizant of the wisdom of Adam Smith and others that wealth lies in trade and innovation, not in robbery and conquest. The Roman Empire's approach to victory was plunder and triumphs; the Allies' was the Marshall Plan and some nice parades. This makes being a holdout successively easier, as the selection pressure drops. How significant this effect might be is hard to say, though; it depends on such factors as whether societies are content with peaceful stagnation, or whether, say, internal pressure to be as rich or culturally innovative as other peoples will pressure them into adapting even without external threats. The Eastern bloc seems to have unraveled mostly because of jeans and rock and roll, not because of bombs.

This last hedge notwithstanding, Kant's reasoning seems plausible with a little squinting. Why, then, are there so few liberal democracies around, and where is Kant's enlightenment state or at least a non-farcical league of nations? The obvious reply is that we are moving in the direction Kant sketched, but slowly and incompletely. China and Japan are the most dramatic examples: after centuries of resistance to economic liberalization, both adapted for specifically Kantian reasons—both recognized the threat they faced was existential. Part of what is praiseworthy in Kant, though, is the recognition that economic forces matter a great deal, and precisely this means that there is less pressure in other domains, like politics or rule of law. Successfully adapting economically makes it possible to be a holdout on republican government and the rest. Kant seems to have underestimated this effect.

Still, we must not forget how dramatic the Kantian change we observe has been on the whole. Recall the now-mandatory role of luxury, flux, and the bourgeois virtues. These are clearly visible in Dallas, Bremen, Tel Aviv, Bangalore, Shanghai, and Osaka. And yet it is difficult to think of *any* society widely exhibiting them before 1800. (Hume and Smith had to produce elaborate defenses of rising incomes and access to luxury goods—and they were living in the vanguard.) A somewhat decadent capitalist society in constant flux and surrounded by some holdouts doesn't seem doomed, as Marx suggested, but inevitable.

14 Reparations, History, and Nietzsche

Classical liberals stress property rights, and I have insisted that claims to property have a distinctively moral basis. But this may seem faintly absurd once we reflect on how the actual distribution of land and other property was arrived at. Jonathan Swift described his times as "a heap of conspiracies, rebellions, murders, massacres, revolutions, banishments, the very worst effects that avarice, faction, hypocrisy, perfidiousness, cruelty, rage, madness, hatred, envy, lust, malice, and ambition, could produce."[1] Growth aside, subsequent history has not been an improvement. Why should we take the resulting distribution of assets seriously, unless we have corrected for historical injustices through extensive reparations?

Libertarians tend to admit that reparations are reasonable in theory, but then go on to ignore them in practice. In order to take the question of reparations seriously, I propose first to acknowledge historical injustices in some detail, and then to take up two leading approaches to reparations. The first is the narrow, moral argument for transfers—whether of cash or land or in-kind goods. The narrow question of reparations is whether standard moral reasoning of the sort familiar to us in everyday life supports such transfers even in the relatively distant past. The second approach to reparations is broader, and concerns symbolic forms of atonement, most obviously in the form of an apology, or else other kinds of gestures. Here, the key question is whether anyone is left to offer a credible apology on behalf of the wrongdoers of the past—a connection that makes it possible to say, sincerely, "*We* did this."

I will argue both that many forms of reparations are still owed, especially to still-living victims, and that the two approaches to reparations just outlined are difficult to support as we look further back in time. The central reason for this is that claims to reparations *fade* over the years. Explaining why that is in a way that doesn't just express a love for the status quo and impatience with history is an important task. I conclude with a broadly Nietzschean suggestion, that discussions of reparations often don't seem to be based on the neutral application of principles of justice. Instead, they often seem to be motivated by categorizations of who counts as an underdog or victim and who does not.

▦ THE COMPENDIUM OF EVIL

The behavior of the American and European powers in respect to colonialism and slavery can only be described as a compendium of evil. That the immediate object of their rapacious endeavors were initially spices (followed by the "drug foods" of sugar, coffee, and tobacco) only aggravates the case against them. The Dutch East India Company achieved its clove and nutmeg monopoly (of all things) by destroying all the plants growing outside of its control, and making war on the native populations in order to obtain low prices. Company leader Jan Coen infamously declared that "trade cannot be maintained without war, nor war without trade," and acted accordingly.[2] King Atahualpa of the Incas was garroted by the Spanish, who proceeded to rip the gold off the native temples with crowbars, and sent thousands of tons of gold and silver back to Europe over the next decades. Bartolomé de las Casas records, often in eyewitness form, a staggering litany of evils, including natives being "grilled" alive, or forced to dive for pearls amid sharks until they spat blood, or being massacred by the thousands.[3] Another European eyewitness records his opinion that it was "absurd, for the sake of drinking rum, and eating sugar, to persevere in the most unjust and diabolical barbarity."[4] As late as the early 20th century, in the Belgian Congo under King Leopold severed hands were a de facto currency, since they were the payment demanded for those not making their rubber quota.[5] And in between, of course, came the massive expropriations of millions of people's land, and the simultaneous importation of millions of captured slaves. In Fernand Braudel's formulation, "Europe was beginning to devour, to digest the world," both literally and figuratively.[6]

In order to make this compendium more concrete and to expand on the latter kinds of cases, we can consider a specific narrative, fictional but historically rooted:

It is the 18th century. Slavery is widely practiced around the world, and is native to Africa. The Asante (indigenous Africans) make war on the Akyem people in what is now Ghana, and sell a vast number of war captives as slaves, as was common practice, generally independent of European meddling and influence, though these sometime contributed to both the wars and slavery practices, in proportions that varied over time. One of these slaves is marched for days to a British fort maintained at Annamaboe on the Gold Coast, in cooperation with African elites who profit from and support the slave trade. After languishing there a while, the slave is loaded onto a British ship for middle passage, first to Barbados, then Charleston.[7]

On arrival, he is sold to a slave holder who exploits his labor by violence, despite initial resistance and attempts to free himself. One of his children is taken from him and sold to a slaver in the Mississippi delta. There, he is tortured and abused for decades, exploited for his labor, separated from his children, and dies prematurely. Several generations of his descendants are treated similarly, and each provides free labor that enriches his or her slave holder.[8]

Eventually, a descendant is freed following the Civil War, and moves north to find work. Thereupon, several generations face continuing discrimination, fraud and outright theft that prevents them from realizing their economic potential. Even in the

Civil Rights era, descendants of the first slave experience explicit discrimination in the job market and in housing, as descendants are prevented from buying in high-value neighborhoods or obtaining favorable interest-rates or attending high-performance schools. Government agencies contribute to the formation of the ghettos in which some descendants grow up.[9]

At the end of this violent history, an older African American wishes to make a claim for reparations, having lived through explicit discrimination in the housing market. She is at the median African-American income of about $35,000, which compares to a median white American income of about $58,000, and a GDP/capita in Ghana of about $1,500. She has the median net worth of about $11,000, compared to $142,000 for white Americans and next to nothing for Ghanans. Her life expectancy is about 75 compared to 78 for white Americans, and about 65 for Ghanans.[10]

Similar stories could be told in connection with Native Americans, Indian castes, Arab slavery, European imperialism, the "Greater East Asia Co-Prosperity Sphere" of Japan, and many other instances of historical injustices. For now, though, let us focus on the case of American slavery and the question of reparations it raises.

Two responses should be widely shared in light of this narrative, beyond the moral outrage any sympathetic reader will feel. First, reparations are clearly owed. If nothing else, it is clear that the state itself harmed still living African Americans like the individual in the vignette, who are owed compensation for wrongs they themselves suffered. They are owed compensation in the same way that Japanese victims of internment or Holocaust survivors have in fact been compensated.[11] Indeed, this is something critics of the overweening state on the right, and people on the left, should be able to find common ground on. Second, trying to arrive at a more detailed accounting of the past that features in the above narrative will inevitably be extremely difficult in light of how complex it is. Those professing great confidence in such matters have either far more or far less wisdom than the rest of us. Even addressing the broad principles that are at stake—the modest ambition here—calls for fear and trembling, and is unlikely to produce neat results.

▪ NARROW THEORIES OF REPARATIONS

Some claims to reparations are narrowly concerned with obtaining payments or other asset-transfers in light of past injustices. These can themselves be broken into two categories. The traditional approach is one of *rectification*, and involves trying to reshape the world in the present so that it resembles what the world *would have* looked like had justice prevailed in the past.[12] (Sometimes this is also called the "counterfactual" theory, but this is confusing since the alternative turns out to be just as counterfactual.) This suggestion comes naturally to us, since our first instinct when confronted with a historical injustice with ongoing ramifications is to hit rewind, so to speak, and to replay history from the point where it went wrong but with some editing. And the first step is often reasonably easy, since averting injustice will often have involved simple omissions—not participating in the slave trade, say. The problem, though, is that the next part of the story looks hopelessly opaque. With the repairs made, what does the replay of history actually look like?

Three problems emerge. First, there is the essential obscurity of the counterfactual scenario. What would Africa or the United States or Singapore have looked like without British or American involvement? What would the distribution of wealth look like under the alternative scenario, such that we ought to achieve that distribution? Answering this question seems impossible, and so there is an epistemic objection to the idea that we should rectify injustices by undoing history's wrongs.

Second, it's often unclear whether the counterfactual story is even coherent, since the people to be compensated in the present may well not have existed sans the injustices at issue.[13] This will be so if the injustices were far-reaching enough to disrupt who met whom, parental lineages, and genetic identities. And of course it is just these pervasive injustices like the Holocaust or colonialism or slavery that we are interested in repairing. Reparations may be owed, but they cannot be grounded in a redo of history if the redo would preclude the reparee's existence, meaning we cannot identify the existing reparee with anyone in the counterfactual redo. Notice, though, that this non-identity objection also cuts against a strain of *anti*-reparation theory. The earlier vignette (and associated references) makes clear that contemporary descendants of slaves are in many respects better off than contemporary citizens of Ghana. This may tempt us to say that such descendants are better off as things are than had slavery never occurred. But this, too, is incoherent, since the individuals involved would not have existed under the counterfactual scenario in which slavery does not take place and different people mate and produce genetically different individuals.

On the other hand, once we set aside these non-identity issues, this point about benefiting from an injustice really does raise a (third) problem. In such cases, undoing the past would make the victims *worse* off, as when colonizers, let us imagine, steal indigenous subsistence farmers' land but also make them wealthier as they integrate into a modern economy. (Assume that their lives are better overall once they transition away from backbreaking labor.) A literal undoing of the past would mean giving back the land but also *taking* their money. Of course, the victims could just waive their right to rectification, but the objection is that they are owed compensation for being wronged (in addition to getting their land back) despite having *benefited* on net. Explaining this reaction isn't altogether easy, but the underlying idea seems to be that when wrongdoers produce a mix of harms and benefits for their victims, victims are entitled to keep the benefits for "free," while demanding compensation for the remaining harms. If I plow into your garage exposing a cache of hidden money, I can't get out of paying for the garage by pointing out that my actions benefited you on the whole, though at some margin it may be ungenerous of you not to waive your claim. Or again, if you meet the love of your life while unjustly imprisoned, this cannot be used as a defense against compensation claims because you benefited on net. The reasoning here seems to be that what we owe those we harm is precisely not rectification per se but rather the *option* to be made whole for any *specific* (not just net) harms inflicted. Sometimes this will coincide with undoing history, but in the case of the garage, it will rather entail compensation for repairs.

The rectification approach echoes Fitzgerald's Gatsby in insisting that we can somehow "repeat the past," but just as in the novel, this turns out to be an illusion.

▪ THE INHERITANCE ARGUMENT

For these reasons, reparation theorists have tended more recently to pursue a different strategy, one focused on what Bernard Boxhill calls the *inheritance theory*, which he explains in relation to American slavery:

> [T]he slave holders harmed the slaves. From this fact it follows . . . that the slaves had titles to reparation for some portion of the estates of the slave holders. . . . it also seems true that the slaves had titles to reparation for some portion of the estates of . . . those who assisted, concurred or consented to their transgressions against the slaves. . . . Assume finally that present day white US citizens are the heirs of slave holders and those who assisted, concurred or consented to their transgressions, and that the present day African Americans are the heirs of the slaves. In that case it would seem that present day African Americans have titles to a part of the estates white US citizens have inherited from the slave holders and those who assisted, concurred or consented to their transgressions.[14]

Moreover, Boxhill goes on to assert that "a people's failure to express dissent from their government's unjust acts gives tacit consent to these acts," meaning that "slaves had titles to reparation against the estates of practically the entire white population." Since each succeeding generation of whites inherited the wealth passed down either by slaveholders or tacit consenters and "specified that only whites of the succeeding generation were permitted to own or compete for the assets" left behind, this is said to imply that slave descendants now have a claim to a significant fraction of the total assets currently held by white citizens.[15] Finally, Boxhill insists that this applies to recent immigrants, not just direct, lineal inheritors, since they "came to take advantage of opportunities, funded by assets to which the slaves had titles. . . . If I laboriously grow valuable crops on your fields, not knowing they belong to you, I am entitled to keep my earnings, but surely I must give you back your fields!"[16] If successful, the inheritance approach would sidestep the non-identity problem, as well as other obvious worries about reparations, such as the fact that those harmed are deceased, and that those paying for reparations did no wrong. For the inheritance approach says only that all current white inhabitants of the United States are in possession of ill-gotten gains that ought to be transferred to others, not that they must compensate people for wrongs committed.

Let us avoid nitpicking, and focus on the core issues that the inheritance approach raises. An initial worry is that it's unclear whether we recognize the inheritance approach in our ordinary moral reasoning, especially when the assets are or become nontangible. Many of us have ancestors who were wronged, and yet it is exceedingly rare to find either formal or informal recognition of a principle of reparation in such cases. If one of your grandparents stole $1,000 from one of my grandparents, there is no generally recognized norm whereby you owe me that sum—not even if both your grandparent and parents left inheritances in excess of that amount. On the legal side, in most jurisdictions such claims need not fall afoul of the statute of limitations, which tend to take effect only after the claimant has knowledge of his grounds for the claim, which might be the present day. It is just that few jurisdictions seem to take seriously the idea that you have a claim against those who are said to have economically benefited from other people's wrongs in the past.

On the moral side, this legal feature isn't hard to fathom. In order to transfer someone's property, we generally wish to be assured that what is being transferred really belongs to the recipient, i.e., that the person has title. But establishing that some fraction of the wealth you hold is really *my* wealth in virtue of your inheritance is difficult in such cases. It is far from obvious how to show that, because of your grandparent's theft and subsequent inheritances, a thousand of your dollars are really mine. For there are once again obscure counterfactual questions that would need to be settled, like how much of the money your grandparent held at the end of his or her life was due to the earlier theft, and how much money you now hold is in virtue of that fraction of your inheritance. To the extent we find these questions nebulous or even unanswerable, we will be reluctant to claim that I am morally entitled to your money. It may be easier to cross this barrier in very extreme cases in which a people is entirely expropriated and left with nothing, so that the next generation starts from zero—here we can be pretty sure that but for the injustice they would have had *something*. But at any rate, if the idea is to take familiar moral reasoning and extend it to reparation cases, we must acknowledge that there is such a barrier.

On the other hand, claims involving specific, tangible goods may be easier to establish. If you have inherited a stolen car from your ancestors, it is easier to envision both a moral and a legal claim. Some courts have recognized this in cases like art stolen by the Nazis:

> The Court acknowledges that Defendant acquired the Painting through no wrongdoing on her part. Defendant's predecessor-in-interest, Wilharm, however, as a result of the acquisition of the Painting through the forced sale, did not acquire good title to the Painting. . . . Legal title to the Painting remained in Dr. Stern and was transferred to the Stern Estate upon Dr. Stern's death. Because Defendant's predecessor-in-interest

did not have title to the Painting, Defendant cannot lay valid claim to ownership of the Painting. This Court concludes, therefore, that Defendant is in wrongful possession of the Painting.[17]

Other courts have decided similar questions differently, and it is interesting to note that in general, common-law jurisdictions tend to hold that theft cannot effect a transfer of title, while civil law systems are less strict on this point.[18] Even so, decisions like these and the moral intuitions underlying them prompt the question of why claims for tangible assets tend to be more persuasive than intergenerational claims to nontangible, misappropriated wealth.

The answer involves the difference between *restitution* claims for specific objects (land, art, a car) and *reparation* claims for money or other nonspecific assets. Restitution means returning the very object at issue to the person entitled to it; reparation (as I use the term) means transferring money (etc.) to the victim of some injustice, because *some* such asset is owed in light of the moral facts. Because restitution involves concrete particulars, the counterfactuals involved look more tractable. Showing that a painting was likely to come to you but for a past injustice is much more straightforward than showing that you would be $1,000 richer but for your grandparents suffering a $1,000 theft. Neither case can be made airtight—perhaps the painting would have been destroyed in a fire had it not been stolen—but at least we can meaningfully trace the movements of the physical object through space and time. Wealth, by contrast, cannot be easily traced, and alternate scenarios whereby money gets sidetracked are far easier to construct. Because of this difference, the Nazi art case seems to me to count against, not in favor of, the inheritance argument; the features that make restitution seem plausible are precisely the ones that are absent in cases of reparations. In sum, the inheritance strategy seems to share many of the discouraging features of the rectification approach.

■ ARE PROPERTY CLAIMS CONTINGENT ON THE DISTANT PAST?

A deeper problem emerges if we reflect on the structure of the inheritance argument. Initially, it sounds like the argument is this:

1. Slaves had claims to reparations.
2. Present-day whites are heirs to those owing reparations.
3. Therefore, present-day descendants of slaves have claims against present-day heirs to those owing reparations.

Waiving quibbles about premise 2, the problem is that the conclusion doesn't follow; there is a missing premise. What is needed is something like premise 3:

1. Slaves had claims to reparations.
2. Present-day whites are heirs to those owing reparations.

3. If X has an unfulfilled claim against Y, then the descendants of Y are liable for those claims to the descendants of X for all eternity.

4. Therefore, present-day descendants of slaves have claims against present-day heirs to those owing reparations.

Of course, premise 3 could be stated more modestly to avoid mention of eternity. But the time-scale needs to be (a) long enough to sustain the relevant reparation claims (so centuries), and yet (b) not just arbitrarily limited. It is hard to see how to meet those conditions without a claim that is in perpetuity. How plausible, then, is premise 3 or anything like it?

Suppose we generalize a bit, and take seriously the idea that no one is entitled to anything that was originally misappropriated, or that is owed to others as the sort of compensation Boxhill outlines. All wealth and lands are to be transferred to those who would possess them had their ancestors succeeded in bringing just claims against those who wronged them. Suppose, that is, that we generalize the inheritance argument, subject to generous qualifications if we like. Let us assume, for instance, that claimants must leave those they make claims against enough to make a living, or in the case of territorial disputes, that claimants must leave current occupants a reasonable amount of space so that they aren't left stateless. Even with these qualifications, it is obvious that generalizing the inheritance argument throws a significant proportion of the world's wealth and property into doubt because of what may have happened in the distant past. At least in principle, what the present-day Greeks are entitled to will depend on whether the ancient Greeks, thousands of years ago, were entitled to sack the sacred citadel of Troy.

The worry this inspires is not merely practical or epistemic. Suppose that a combination of genetic testing and archaeological research reveals that some Anatolians are the descendants of the Trojans, and let us suppose they were wronged by the Achaeans. (Helen ran off with Paris of her own free will, and the Greeks were after the gold, it turns out.) The real worry about bringing a claim against the modern Greeks is that the claims of descendants to property owed their ancestors *fade* over time. The denizens of Troy had a good claim against the Greeks (let us grant), but their descendants thousands of years later do not, because, against premise 3, claims of the relevant sort weaken over the years. To see this, remember that the inheritance strategy is not to claim that the living owe reparations as compensation for past wrongdoing that they did not commit or condone. Nor is the strategy to say that debts can be passed on to innocent generations, like biblical iniquities. What motivates the inheritance strategy is precisely to avoid such dubious moral claims. The idea is rather that past generations owed part of their wealth to others, and that the present generation has inherited wealth from the past that it has no title to (in part or whole), since it is money owed to others. But this means that the inheritance strategy depends critically on assuming that *the current wealth of the Greeks is significantly inherited from the heroes of Troy.* To the extent that we doubt this, the inheritance arguments fails, for premise 3 will turn out to be false because the Anatolians won't have a claim against the descendants of Agamemnon and the gang. And, on reflection, over time it becomes less and less clear that a person's or group's wealth *is* substantially inherited from the distant past.

We can bring this out by imagining that the Greeks suffered some post-Iliadic cataclysm (as seems in fact to have happened in the late Bronze Age). Assume that wealth went back to zero, with widespread famine and chaos, and that the Greeks were forced to start over again in small city-states that had long lost track of whatever was stolen from the Trojans, or was inherited while owed to others. In this story, the caesura between epochs prevents us from claiming that the Anatolians have a claim to the Greeks' money, since it is no longer the case that Greeks have illegitimately inherited goods that were in fact owed the descendants of Hector and Priam, even granting these to be existent and identifiable.

And on reflection, there are many mechanisms by which the inheritance claim may be undermined or moderated in this way. We can list some, starting with the one just outlined:

Breaking: cataclysms like wars, famines, or civilizational collapse rupture the line of inheritance (e.g., the late Bronze Age collapse or the World Wars). To this should be added absolute poverty; most people in most times, including 19th-century America, have had little or no net worth to pass on, exempting them from claims.

Branching: if there is population growth, then after several generations, descendants may outnumber wrongdoers by such an extent that the fractional inheritance is completely trivial.[19] For each time descendants have several children the inherited wealth branches. E.g., you wrong me, we and our descendants each have two children, and 10 generations later there are 1,024 descendants each. My descendants' claim on your descendants may well be nugatory if the original property has been divided 1,024 times.

Dilution: immigration can diminish claims to inheritance by substantially diluting the antecedent population (e.g., all but one family of the original population of wrongdoers die, and then a thousand new ones move in). Alternatively, newcomers may dilute the wealth that is at issue (e.g., the wrongdoers contribute one unit of money to their descendants, who are joined by immigrants bringing 10,000 times that sum not subject to descendants' claims). It may be that some of the immigrants come to inherit wealth from descendants of the wrongdoers, but in any case that wealth will be diluted across a larger population, and many will inherit little or nothing, or be affected only in some very attenuated way.

The next two mechanisms pertain to interest. Under growth conditions, the nominal amount owed is likely to be small relative to the present day, unless interest of some sort is included. The appropriate interest rate is figured by determining the victim's opportunity cost—what they lost out on because they were unable to make use of the compensation they were owed. In everyday cases, bank interest is often a reasonable approximation of opportunity cost, though forgone wages and other measures may be relevant as well. When the timescale is intergenerational, though, bank interest is less relevant than overall economic growth.

Differential growth rates: often there will be reason to assign an interest rate to reparations that is lower than the growth rate among descendants of wrongdoers. This will be so if there is evidence of a divergence in growth rates. If you steal from me and owe me restitution, you also owe me interest at some rate or other, but if you get lucky in the stock market and make millions, you owe me restitution plus some standard rate of interest, not the millions gained by your exotic strategy for growth. A real-world example: Japan's past colonial aggression raises claims among those who were wronged, but Japan's growth rate has been far higher than that of China and other relevant countries over most of that period. This is evidence that the appropriate interest rate to be applied to compensation will be relatively low.

Growth insensitivity: growth introduces two additional subtleties. One concerns how much present-day wealth can be said to have been *inherited* from the distant, pre-growth past; the other what descendants of the wronged would have *gained* had there been compensation. Both matter: the former tells us how much of what the one group has constitutes ill-gotten gains; the other tells us what the appropriate interest rate is for compensation. If growth turns out to dominate initial wealth differences, and if growth effects turn out to be relatively insensitive to initial capital, then it makes less sense to attribute gains to wrongful inheritance in the distant past, and the interest rate should be adjusted downward, possibly toward zero. For in that case, the wealth or income of a present-day worker descended from wrongdoers will tend to be derived mainly from working in a rich, high-growth society and not from relatively small wealth-difference arising from his ancestors' failure to compensate. (He is likely to be comparatively rich because he works in a rich country, not because his great-great-grandparents were 119 times poorer than he is rather than 120 times poorer had they paid compensation.)

And, on the other hand, the wealth or income of a worker descended from the wronged is likely to reflect not the relatively small difference compensation would have made to his ancestors, but the fact that he works in a rich, high-growth society. (It is unlikely that, had his ancestors been compensated, he would have been 120 times richer than they, rather than only 119 times.) There are many historical examples of growth being insensitive to initial capital over time. E.g., the relative impoverishment of Spain following the Age of Discovery as against Holland and England wasn't due to differences in capital, and vice versa for Japan or Singapore as against China or Argentina. To put it another way, winning a modest lottery in 19th-century Georgia was unlikely to make a difference to the wealth or income of present-day descendants, as empirical research confirms.[20]

These mechanisms are not mutually exclusive, of course; over time they are likely to combine, since branching, say, is often accompanied by economic growth. On the other hand, we should acknowledge that these mechanisms don't inevitably nullify descendants' claims; it is just that over time they will tend to grow weaker to the extent that these mechanisms operate. Over the short term, things like growth and dilution can be safely ignored, but as decades turn into centuries, they usually cannot. In addition to the more obvious epistemic and practical worries, these mechanisms explain why we can reject the suggestion that what the Greeks are entitled to is a function of the distant past, or that they now owe the Anatolians a vast fortune.

In a case like American slavery, the evidence of the operation of these claim-diminishing mechanisms is mixed. Branching and dilution clearly have been in effect, since there have been many generations and a great deal of immigration, but it is less clear what to make of breaking, differential growth rates, or growth insensitivity. And of course many further complications could be raised, for instance compensation for Reconstruction-era violence and theft, the extent to which "the entire white population" condoned slavery and later abuses, or the many practical and epistemic difficulties implementation would involve. However, I do not believe wading into these would provide additional clarity. The bottom line is that making the inheritance argument stick ultimately requires us to show that wealth levels of present-day Americans are to a significant extent a function of wealth levels in the distant past. In light of the preceding, this looks like a formidable task. Certainly reasonable people will be able to conclude that, while reparations are clearly owed to African Americans in light of still-recent injustices, due attention to historical wrongs doesn't imply massive redistribution of the sort we started the chapter worrying about.

■ LAND AND THE RESTITUTION REGRESS

So far we have been considering monetary reparations, but of course there is also the question of land. Here, too, the perpetuity of the claims generates problems. The key observation is that those favoring land transfers to victims of historical injustices will generally face a dilemma. On the one hand, they cannot accept that continued and long-standing occupation of territory (perhaps accompanied by other factors, like improving it) can gradually produce a title to the land, so that over the centuries land that was stolen in the past can come to be rightfully held. In my view, this is the only position consistent with anything like our settled beliefs about who is entitled to what, for reasons discussed in chapter 4. But accepting this view would obviously tend to undercut arguments for restoring lands to preconquest possessors except in the relatively recent past. Therefore, proponents of land restitution must instead defend a more radical doctrine of title, something to the effect that once land is rightfully held by some group, then its descendants have a claim to it in perpetuity. Explaining and defending such a principle would, of course, be difficult, though it is notoriously difficult to defend any view in this area. At a minimum, much more would need to be said about the extent of proper original claims; presumably a small clan cannot claim a gigantic continent for its descendants in perpetuity by first occupying some part of the land and then announcing a policy of rejecting immigration. But let us simply accept the legitimacy of some such radical view of ownership that implies that land must be transferred back to the descendants of the rightful owners for all eternity.

The problem then becomes that title will belong not to the most recent victims of expropriation, but to whoever can produce the earliest evidence of rightful ancestral occupation. Lands stolen in colonial aggression will not revert back to the indigenous victims of the colonizers if it turns out that the indigenous peoples in turn conquered the land from their neighbors. For example, the Spanish under Pizarro violently conquered the empire of the Incas. But the Incas had in turn violently subjugated others, as had the Aztecs, who were widely despised for doing so.[21] The Incas, in fact, were a tiny, distinct ethnic group that ruled as imperialists over millions of their subjects across far-flung regions by Babylonian-style depopulation and resettlement policies. (Both empires, it so happens, were quite recent at the time of the Spanish conquest, and part of why the Spanish were successful was that they allied themselves with native groups hostile to those empires.) There is no prospect that those conquered in the recent past were autochthonic; they were "only the latest in a long series of kingdoms and empires that had risen and fallen in the Andes and on the coast for more than a thousand years."[22] Perhaps a few exceptions may be found here and there (Australian aboriginals come to mind), but surely not many, and even then, such claims must be assessed in terms of the validity of relatively small populations staking claims to large landmasses.[23] Asia, Europe, the Americas, the Arab world, Africa, and much of India have been intermittently the scene of marauding hordes looting and conquering for millennia, making it unlikely that arguments for land restoration will terminate in convenient fashion, with a transfer to just the latest round of victims. Thus, on the second horn of the dilemma, those favoring restitution must accept that the land will often go to obscure groups living who knows where, that can produce historical, genetic, or archaeological evidence of rightful possession centuries or even millennia ago.

A certain crudeness can cause us to overlook this point. Sometimes the victims of colonial aggression are conceived of as a monolithic bloc ("the Native Americans"), when the peoples see themselves as a diverse group riven by divisions and ancient hostilities. Think, for instance, of the Tlaxcalan-Spanish alliance against the Aztecs, or later the widespread support of Indians and slaves for the Spanish crown against Bolívar and independence. These complications unsettle us, and so we tend to ignore them. The question for restitution isn't whether even a genuinely aboriginal population *group* has occupied a territory continually, but whether the specific *individuals* being ceded control of the land have title to it on whatever theory is said to motivate restitution in the first place. If Europe had been more thoroughly subjugated by Islamic or Mongol powers in the Middle Ages, fomenting large-scale population shifts, it would hardly have made sense to give back Italy to the French as an act of restitution, on the theory that the land belongs to "the Native Europeans." (If the Italians could no longer be identified, there would presumably be no claim to restitution at all.) A distinction thus too rarely drawn is between aggressor and aggrieved on the one hand, and those with title to land and those without it on the other. European powers invading Islamic-ruled territories in the Maghreb may have been aggressors and the Islamic peoples the aggrieved, but native Berber populations who had been overrun by Arab invaders in the past would still be puzzled why some act of restitution wouldn't deliver the lands to them, and of course other claimants would be right behind them in the queue.

These implications make it hard to accept a theory of landownership that doesn't, over time, ratify ownership, at least under some conditions. Just as claims to reparation fade out over time, so claims to ownership can fade in.

■ BROAD THEORIES OF REPARATIONS

We have been considering narrow claims for reparations based on the kind of reasoning we commonly accept in such contexts as the law or interpersonal morality. But the discussion so far may seem cramped. Perhaps the narrow moral principles we have been examining aren't what is really at issue when it comes to grandiose conflicts between peoples and their resolution in history. It may seem inadequate to address convoluted legalisms to the descendants of Holocaust victims or colonial aggression. The 1952 agreement between Germany and Israel, for example, did reflect narrow moral arguments concerning the costs of repatriating Jewish refugees and the theft and violence of the Nazis, but it would be a mistake to frame the underlying motivations in such narrow terms. During the lead-up to negotiations with Israel, for instance, Chancellor Adenauer spoke to the parliament of "unspeakable crimes" requiring "moral and material reparations [*Wiedergutmachung*]" in order to bring about "a spiritual alleviation of infinite suffering"—hardly the language of a narrow or legalistic framework.[24] And often what is wanted isn't a legal settlement with payments in cash but an apology or some other form of acknowledgment and recognition; compensation may even be insulting if the wrongs are incommensurate with the money.[25]

There is, then, a second, broader dimension to reparations that consists of something more elusive than mere transfers—something that is better thought of as communicative than transactional. We can think of this second dimension as a kind of symbol or gesture of atonement. Gestures can express a recognition of both the need to make up for a wrong and the inadequacy of any material compensation. The point of the gesture is to indicate something about one's own feelings in the hope the offended party will in turn find resolution, or at least see that there is a shared moral framework connecting the two parties, that the offender accepts the significance of what he, she, or it has done. If reparations do take the form of cash, this may be viewed as mainly symbolic. The money is a symbol of the recognition that has taken place and of the sincerity of the wrong-doer, who might otherwise be suspected of seizing on gestures as a cheap way out. The symbolism may be even deeper when it takes the form of in-kind goods, as when Germany sent industrial equipment to Israel in the 1950s, and more recently submarines widely reported to provide nuclear second-strike capability, manufactured by ThyssenKrupp.[26] "Atonement," with its religious connotations, captures the deeply serious nature of wrongs like mass enslavement or killings or lootings that are at stake. Not just any wrong rises to the level of reparations in the broad sense. It also captures the quasi-religious sense in which offenders attempt not just to appease claimants or to satisfy narrowly moral duties to others, but to answer an external demand. This can come in the form of making things right with God, as in a traditional religious conception of atonement, or simply in satisfying one's own sense of impersonal justice that would produce a claim even if no one was asking for an apology, like the Greek Erinyes.

To be sure, in practice there is often a cynical aspect to these gestures. For they facilitate two aims of an offending state: to draw a finish line, so that the issue doesn't become an ongoing political liability ("We consider the matter closed"), and transferring blame by defining who committed the offenses ("Mistakes were made, but not by us"). Adenauer himself announced that the reparations agreement served as a "conclusion to what is for every German the saddest chapter of our history," while insisting that the vast majority of the German people "abhorred the crimes against the Jews and did not participate in them"—in fact, he emphasized how many Germans had heroically *helped* the Jews at their own peril! Reparations, he made clear, were paid because of what was done by the Nazis in the name of (but not through the agency of) the German people.[27] Critics are apt to find fault in these hedges that perhaps mar the purity of reparations, but one must remember how unpopular they are in the first place; apologies that reflect the political reality of a grudging and surly electorate should probably be seen as second-best solutions requiring real courage in their own right. "Apologies of purest self-abasement or nothing!" would be an unhelpful international norm.

In the case of 1950s Germany, there is little doubt that there was sufficient continuity between past and present for it to make sense to talk of atoning for what "we" did. Certainly there were discontinuities in government, but the relevant individuals were mostly still alive, as were specific firms and other social structures. But this question of continuity becomes murkier with time, and eventually the relevant identities break down. For example, it doesn't make sense for the present French government to apologize for the Napoleonic invasion of Russia. At this point, both the governments and the peoples are too different for this to be appropriate. A French citizen will feel differently reading about these events than will a Spaniard, and patriotism will inspire a sentimental resonance or even sympathy for one's ancestors. (One can feel this way as a classics major reading about the Roman republic.) But what matters is that the structure of the state, the deepest values of the people, the social and economic institutions underlying and flowing from the act, are all lost in the past now. If the reasoning behind the invasion were advanced in a contemporary setting (say, in a speech by the president proposing another invasion of Russia or Austria), French citizens wouldn't just dismiss it out of hand, they would be bewildered by the very terms of the argument. All this robs statements like "*You* did this to us" or "*We* regret what *we* did" of sense. They might serve some political purpose, but history wouldn't substantiate them.

The case of American slavery perhaps falls somewhere in between obvious 1950s German continuity and obvious 21st-century French discontinuity. In the American case, there are massive *dis*continuities of government, of peoples in the form of migration, and of values, but some have pointed out economic continuities. These are sometimes inflated into the claim that American prosperity has depended in some deep way on slavery and the cotton-industrial complex.[28] Maybe so, but it is striking that (a) cotton slavery only lasted about 60 years at industrial scale, (b) for most of that time cotton itself didn't represent a large share of national economic activity (5% of GDP in the 1830s), and (c) abolition had no long-term effect on cotton production or prices.[29] Textiles were of course an important related industry, but there is little to suggest that there weren't alternatives to slave labor to be found—and after abolition they were found (all of which, of course, only makes slavery the more odious). Colonialism and slavery seem to have been similar in this respect. Deirdre McCloskey points out that most of European colonialism produced little benefit for the countries involved ("India itself, one can show, yielded no economic benefit to the average person in Britain. Imperialism had therefore no national economic point.")[30] Fernand Braudel states that 80% of Dutch trade at the height of Holland's commercial empire was of the insipid, intra-European variety.[31] None of this is conclusive, but it might be wiser to make the point about economic continuities in a more moderate fashion, and to focus on the more recent past as a target for atonement. Since there have been wide-ranging injustices related to housing, education, and criminal justice in the relatively recent past, there would still be plenty to apologize for.

▪ NIETZSCHE AND REPARATIONS IN PRACTICE

A common response to demands for atonement among those reluctant to atone is the grumbling reply, "We just did what everyone else did back then." In Japan, for instance, it has often been pointed out that there was something odd about Western demands for penitence and reparations.[32] (Japan did, in fact, pay reparations to dozens of countries, including Switzerland and Spain, but not China, which waived its claims.) To the extent that these were for violent imperialism, hardliners noted that Japanese leadership was explicitly modeling itself on the Western example. It was puzzling to them how they could be exhibiting abominable behavior requiring abject apologies when presently or not long before the Allied powers were colonizing Southeast Asia, fighting opium wars, and forcing the Philippines under America's thumb. If atonement was in order for such things, there ought to have been an orgy of international reparations. The inconsistency was taken as evidence that what was at stake wasn't a sincere yearning for justice, but a political desire among the winners to humiliate the losers.

We can set aside the merits of the Japanese hardliner views (rejected by many of their fellow citizens). The important lesson is a cynical one Nietzsche might have sympathized with: expressions of moral rectitude often mask baser motives that are their true source.[33] Saying this risks opprobrium, since it threatens to pierce the righteous indignation of those issuing the moral judgments. But, as the Japanese case shows even without entering into its merits, this Nietzschean theme is an important one to confront in making sense of history. It is at the very least a challenge that the righteously indignant ought to confront, and in some cases it may even be true. One must resist temptations on all sides. Entering into the viewpoint of the Japanese and entertaining the possibility that bias leads one to overlook hypocrisy isn't easy or popular. On the other hand, giving into Nietzsche's spirit of polemical cynicism altogether can be a mistake as well—we need not take up his moral nihilism to take on board some of his suspicions. One might accept that there was a certain Western hypocrisy toward Japan without accepting a false equivalence between the Japanese occupation of Nanking and American attitudes toward colonialism in the early 20th century.

The application to reparations theory is not, of course, that those pressing for reparations harbor base motives. Nietzsche thought that Judeo-Christian morality was a smokescreen for a deep hostility, and nothing like that is remotely true of reparation theorists. But we might wonder, in tamer fashion, whether both demands to re-examine sordid histories and the concomitant calls for reparations aren't suspiciously selective. If it turns out that national histories are pretty unflattering all around while talk of reparations is highly specific, then we might wonder whether there isn't another layer to the morality of reparations worth considering. And history *has* been pretty unflattering all around when it comes to practices like slavery, colonialism, and violent conquest. As I suggested in the opening vignette (and accompanying references), most American slaves seem to have been captured by native African groups before being passed on to Europeans merchants on the coast. In fact, by the time the Europeans arrived in Africa, slavery was already "endemic in Africa, part of the structure of everyday life"; the Portuguese found well-functioning slave markets in Benin upon their arrival.[34] Large numbers of slaves had been sold internationally for centuries, especially in the Islamic world. Other world civilizations without a presence in Africa practiced slavery as well, such as China and India, and the slave trade across the Indian Ocean probably exceeded the Atlantic trade.[35] Mention of these extra-European practices sometimes evokes defensive hairsplitting among more or less malign forms of slavery, but apart from the evident brutality of many non-Western versions, there are plenty of other gruesome and presumably reparation-worthy practices to consider. Human sacrifice was practiced on a significant scale in Africa,[36] and of course at the time of the Spanish conquest, the Aztecs were busy fattening up their enemies' children in cages, only to rip their hearts out while they were still alive and subsequently eat their limbs with a tasty *chilmole*. These practices were routine and on a massive scale, with tens of thousands of victims, probably far more.[37] Nor were non-Western forms of slavery rare or only intermittent. It is especially noteworthy that according to historians, Muslim slavers based in northern Africa enslaved significant numbers of Europeans (and some Americans), probably over a million people. These Italians or Americans or Englishmen often wound up living in horrific conditions as galley slaves or sexual slaves in harems, and were routinely snatched by "barbary coast pirates" from towns (not just ships) throughout the Italian coast, and as far away as Ireland.[38]

None of this diminishes the unique horrors of the European-American slave trade. And nothing could be more infantile than to toss about rival catalogs of horrors in order to suggest that they somehow cancel out or relieve anyone's obligations of redress. The point is rather to underline the broadly Nietzschean thought that there is something peculiar about the selective focus on reparations from the United States or Europe or Japan, and not from North African or South American peoples—say from Morocco to Ireland or Italy in virtue of the Barbary Coast slave trade, or from Arab slaveholding countries to either descendants or the countries of origin, or from the descendants of slave-making Ghanans to slave-descendants. Even if monetary compensation isn't made available, a gesture of atonement readily could be. Specifically, the suspicion is that this selective focus is explained not by the principles of justice governing reparations, but by whether we categorize groups as winners or losers, underdogs or overdogs, victims or aggressors in history. Since it is difficult to view rich, powerful countries as victims, it is difficult to see Italy as a victim and relatively poor Morocco or Algeria as an oppressor, whatever the complicated history of Mediterranean slavery. I propose that it is these psychological features of groups like rich, white Italians (unworthy of sympathy) or relatively poor, former Maghreb colonies (worthy) that is expressed in the selectivity of the reparations debate. Certainly, an inspection of the fairly comprehensive Oxford *Handbook of Reparations* underscores how rare it is to find reparations claims rooted in impartial justice that "feel" wrong because the claimants don't have the attributes of stereotypical underdogs.[39]

Such suspicions are nevertheless difficult to verify, and Nietzsche's claims about our tendency toward moral hypocrisy are often met with scorn for this reason. I have noted many challenges for making good on particular claims to reparations, and one might simply argue that Italian claims on Morocco fail on some technical ground. Perhaps the narrow claims to compensation fail due to the many breaks in government, and perhaps requests for some broader symbolic gesture are inappropriate because of a lack of identity between the past and the present. These kinds of objections in fact strike me as quite plausible, since as I have argued much the same kind of point seems to undermine many of the claims against European or American states. The idea, though, is that there is an *inconsistency* in how reparations claims come to be made, not that Morocco really ought to pay up. This can in turn be resisted on technical grounds by insisting that there is some important asymmetry between the various cases, so that it turns out that it is always those whom we naturally feel a great deal of sympathy for who have claims and those we don't feel particularly sorry for who do not. This is possible. But it sounds too good to be true. It is like the research suggesting that jurors in civil cases are mainly driven by a need to satisfy their feelings of outrage, not the many complicated factors that ought to matter when assessing damages. Subjects appear willing to punish the wrong people, to produce more pollution, and to endanger the public in order to respond to their outrage, yet we rarely admit the lowly, humbling roots of this part of public justice.[40] One imagines Nietzsche laughing at us. Similarly, reparations do respond to a genuine need for justice, but it looks as if opinions about who counts as victim or oppressor, itself a function of such dubious factors as current social status, drive the application of reparations theory. We should take seriously the possibility that, in a world soaked in universal violence and blood, the quest for reparations often reflects something besides the impartial principles of justice.

■ REPARATIONS IN PERSPECTIVE

We began by noting a strong, obvious case for reparations in many instances, and to the many still-living African American victims of state-sponsored injustice in the United States in particular. We can reaffirm that case here— nothing said in the interim upends it. The fact that reparations theory is often selectively applied doesn't show that no one is owed reparations. However, I have also argued that people of good will, sensitive to history and its moral bearing on the present, can reasonably deny that past injustices delegitimize much of the status quo. The inheritance argument runs into trouble when it comes to nontangible assets and the fact that claims can fade over time, and proponents for the restitution of land rarely consider how far back such restitution would have to go. Calls for symbolic atonement, while important, depend on the backing of history, which likewise tends to fade. And it is rare to find any acknowledgment of the political layering on top of reparations discourse that some Nietzschean reflection uncovers.

PART FOUR

Theory and Practice

15 Dilemmas of Political Correctness

It is difficult to discuss classical liberal themes without saying things that will seem offensive to some. Many of the assertions and reactions that crop up in considering personal responsibility and poverty, reparations for slavery, or European colonialism seem to have a politically (in)correct cast to them. Someone who announces that in the rich countries poverty is often the result of not doing enough work is likely to encounter not just empirical disagreement, but moralized outrage some will think of as manifesting political correctness. This makes political correctness an important theme in political philosophy, since it has a major impact on our discourse. Indeed, political correctness is in some ways central to the politics of our time, which (alas) revolve around the media, the attention economy, and cycles of internet outrage. For this reason, I propose to consider the phenomenon quite broadly, without restricting the discussion to its narrow application to libertarianism.

Debates about political correctness often proceed as if proponents see nothing to fear in erecting norms that inhibit expression on the one side, and opponents see nothing but misguided efforts to silence political enemies on the other.[1] Both views are mistaken, as I see it. Political correctness is an important attempt to advance the legitimate interests of certain groups in the public sphere. A default norm that entrants to public discourse shouldn't threaten the acknowledged social status of women or minorities or gay people or the poor is a reasonable response to the history of injustices these groups have been subjected to. There can be good reasons for taboos. However, this type of norm comes with costs that mustn't be neglected—sometimes in the form of conflict with other values we hold dear, but often by creating an internal schism that threatens us with collective irrationality. Political correctness thus sets up dilemmas I wish to set out (but not, for the most part, resolve). The cliché is that political correctness tramples on rights to free speech, as if the potential loss were merely expressive; the real issue is that in filtering public discourse, political correctness may defeat our own substantive aims.

■ WHAT IS POLITICAL CORRECTNESS?

Political correctness, as I will understand it, is the attempt to establish norms of speech (or sometimes behavior) that are thought to (a) protect vulnerable, marginalized, or historically victimized groups, and which (b) function by shaping public discourse, often by inhibiting speech or other forms of social signaling, and that (c) are supposed to avoid insult and outrage, a lowered sense of self-esteem, or otherwise offending the sensibilities of such groups or their allies. The concept, we should note, is one used by its enemies; dubbing something politically incorrect implies there is something worrisome or objectionable at work, though not necessarily that the politically correct option is wrong all things considered. But to avoid verbal disputes, let us simply take on board the language of "political correctness" and concentrate on the substantive merits of the doubts that are implicit in the pejorative tone.

According to this characterization, merely advocating for substantive policy changes is not itself a reflection of political correctness, except in a vague, by-association sense of the term. Criticizing someone for referring to an administrative assistant as a "secretary" is a manifestation of political correctness, but advocating for higher wages for assistants is not; demanding that we talk about migrants in certain ways and not others can again be a form of political correctness, but voting for particular migration policies cannot. Certain fringe environmental positions (tree-hugging, etc.) might themselves be loosely dubbed "PC" views, but I suspect this is only because the people who adopt such positions often advocate politically correct norms alongside. Symmetrically, it isn't politically incorrect to make a donation to fight gay marriage—though of course many would respond to doing so with outrage—but it is politically incorrect to write an op-ed making a careful, dispassionate argument against gay marriage. Political correctness thus isn't about private choices deviating from some norm; the notion doesn't refer to a distinctive personal morality, but to a system for molding public discourse.

The norms involved are mainly, if not universally, negative and inhibitive, and many cases that initially seem positive are more complex, as when campus advocates urge multicultural curricula that move away from the Western canon, or argue for including more women or minorities on syllabi, which doesn't initially seem inhibiting. But the underlying goal, even in these cases, is to avoid the sense that certain groups are marginalized or devalued because members of their group aren't represented in the canon or syllabus. What is being resisted in this kind of case is a certain *implication* that would otherwise inform public discourse, an implication that proponents of political correctness wish to eliminate. We might worry that this isn't what is happening when people simply point out that the Bronze Head from Ife, say, has intrinsic aesthetic merit that warrants study on par with comparable European art, but then this doesn't look much like an appeal to political correctness. The account, it's important to emphasize, isn't supposed to capture just any revisionary or vaguely left-leaning policy, but rather those with the flavor of responding to the sensibilities of marginalized groups by blocking an offending element. Making a case for the Ife head as envisioned above is an aesthetic argument motivated by independent, positive enthusiasm for the features of the work; appealing to the negative effects on the self-esteem of certain students when asked to study Phidias, Michelangelo, and Picasso is an appeal to political correctness. The same goes for historians' arguments for the revision of inaccurately jingoistic textbooks versus those concerned with avoiding any implication that certain groups are inferior or that their grievances aren't worth addressing. (Of course, the distinction can be a difficult one to draw.)

On this definition, moreover, it is significant that what makes a statement politically incorrect is not whether it in fact serves to promote the interests of certain people overall, but whether it threatens their public standing, as typically manifested in a sense of insult and outrage, or a lowered sense of self-esteem and inclusion. Notice, for instance, that no one is willing to retract judgments about what look like politically incorrect statements if they later turn out to promote the interests of the groups in question. If the president of the university says, "Members of group G are underrepresented in field F because of unflattering trait T," this may well be judged politically incorrect, and that judgment won't change if it turns out that this was just what G needed to hear. The objective likelihood of advancing the cause of G is beside the point when it comes to political correctness. The air of political incorrectness is brought about by the insult itself, and thus the usual way of overcoming substantive criticism—by showing that the local harm of the insult was outweighed—is ineffective. Calling someone by some group epithet does not become less politically incorrect if that turns out to be motivating and helpful to the individual, as insulting a friend at a tennis match ("Come on, you jerk!") can evade criticism if it turns out to be helpful overall. That is because the target of political correctness is the insult itself (along with the corresponding threat to the public standing of the group), not the overall interests of the people involved.

This might be resisted on grounds that there is evidence of "stereotype threat," i.e., that issuing politically incorrect statements like the university president's often negatively impact the actual performance of members of marginalized groups, simply by raising the salience of their group membership and the perception that members are less good at a given task. (Subtly reminding test takers that they are members of a marginalized group may cause them to perform worse than control groups that take the same test without a priming cue.)[2] My characterization may then seem to suggest that the concern is for something trivial-sounding ("not hurting people's feelings"), whereas the ultimate concern is to prevent the real and documented damage that the relevant speech and behavior does. However, my claim is not that politically incorrect speech cannot have objectively damaging effects on others, or that such effects might not motivate politically correct norms. The idea is that what *makes* something politically incorrect is a certain kind of offense in virtue of undermining public standing, not that offending people in such a way need be trivial or that blocking such offenses might not have a deeper underlying motivation—just the opposite, as we will see.

As a final elaboration, my gloss emphasizes marginalized groups as the intended beneficiaries of politically correct norms. It is this aspect that leads me to differ with the economist Glenn Loury's otherwise searching analysis. Loury treats political correctness as a far more general phenomenon than I have, suggesting that as "an implicit social convention of restraint on public expression, operating within a given community," it applies to any such restraint, left or right, including, say, fascist censorship.[3] The key for Loury is that political correctness, left or right, culminates in a kind of *self*-censorship through a feedback loop in which, first, there are sanctions for those who violate the communal norms, and then those who are willing nevertheless to risk such sanctions come to seem especially refractory:

> Suspicious speech signals deviance because once the practice of punishing those who express certain ideas is well established, the only ones who risk ostracism by speaking recklessly are those who place so little value on sharing our community that they must be presumed not to share our dearest common values.[4]

Loury emphasizes such examples as the German politician Phillipp Jenninger, who fell into disgrace after a speech that engaged rhetorically with the perspective of Nazi-era Germans, even though it was unambiguously clear that both the speech and Jenninger's prior life and work were devoid of Nazi sympathies or anti-Semitism. It is worth noting that after Loury's article was published, a Jewish leader gave the same speech in a synagogue in order to demonstrate what he rightly predicted would be the nonresponse.[5] The worry, clearly, wasn't the substance of what Jenninger had to say but the *signal*, Loury would underscore, that is sent by a German politician (but not a Jew in a synagogue) being willing to take up, if only for rhetorical purposes, the perspective of Nazi sympathizers *after* it has been established that taking up the Nazi-era point of view is taboo.

Loury is surely right about the impressive degree of self-censorship political correctness can achieve or demand. But although self-censorship is a kind of ultimate victory for those wishing to eliminate some form of expression, actual censorship of various sorts is on the table as well, for example in the form speech codes. And of course it's natural to start with formal censorship in order to induce self-censorship. More importantly, I believe there is something distinctively *left* about political correctness, something connected to the concern for victims' groups. This may sound semantic—Loury and others could just announce their conception of political correctness is a bit broader than mine. But there are important differences between how and why various norms shaping public discourse originate and are enforced that are worth recognizing.

Take right-wing attempts to delegitimize opposition to war by suggesting dissenters are insulting "the brave men and women who fight on our behalf," or attempts to shape discourse concerning torture by insisting on Orwellian euphemisms like "enhanced interrogation." Such maneuvers are important to analyze in their own right, since they may work to inhibit speech in disastrous ways, often with outcomes far worse than anything to emerge from petty

TABLE 15.1 *Norms Inhibiting Speech*

	Left	Right
Motive	Sympathy	Security
Target	Offense	Weakness
Response to violations	Outrage	Contempt
Accusation	Cruelty	Disloyalty
Danger	Backfire etc.	

squabbles over how to refer to an office assistant. But that doesn't make the cases any less distinct. What motivates these right-leaning efforts, baleful though they are, is usually different from and nearly opposite to what motivates norms against questioning affirmative action or syllabi with too many dead white men. In a typical case, what motivates an effort to suppress dissent about war or torture is concern for security, not sympathy or feeling sorry for marginalized or oppressed groups. And the target of the norms is typically what is seen as a display of weakness rather than insults or offenses against the sensibilities of those marginalized, while the response tends toward contempt for the weak rather than outrage at the insult; accusations of disloyalty or spinelessness are more likely than those of being insensitive or cruel. There is a common danger that these attempts at molding discourse will backfire in ways we'll explore below, but these subdifferences, summarized in table 15.1, still result in an important overall difference in the character of what takes place.

Political correctness, then, is far from unique in trying to influence public discourse and in trying to compel people to speak or think in certain categories or terms. In discussing the problems associated with political correctness we are not singling out left-leaning concerns for special scrutiny. All kinds of social institutions, both left and right, shape which arguments get made, including libel and national security laws, and informal conventions that govern clubs or associations, each with their own profile of burdens and benefits. But political correctness *is* distinctive, and a distinctively left phenomenon, I want to insist. Those attempting to shape discourse on the right are rarely moved by feeling sorry for some group and rarely make corresponding objections focused on avoiding offense. And when they go wrong and undercut their own aims, as when their attempts to shape debate about a war turn out to undermine national security in the long run, they do so by exhibiting a characteristic series of mistakes that are distinct from those most common on the left.

▪ LEGITIMATE ENDS

Political correctness is dismissed by its opponents as if it were either a bizarre and trivial insistence on redefining words, or else an insidious attempt to advance an ideology by silencing the competition. "Yes, but . . ." is not the typical response of those with reservations. Loury, for example, speaks of the "superficial moralism" of political correctness. This certainly applies in some cases, but it is less easy to dismiss, say, the taboo on the N-word (herewith observed), harder still to dismiss certain taboos regarding racial science, and impossible, I think, to dismiss the underlying worries animating such strictures.

Consider research on race and IQ and on occupational gender skew. Since much of this research is controversial on purely scientific grounds, there is plenty of detached scientific criticism in these debates. But it is easy to demonstrate that politically correct norms and taboos play a role as well. In the case of IQ, it is striking is that there is little outrage about research into the cognitive *advantages* that Ashkenazi Jews or certain Asian groups are sometimes said to enjoy (in scoring higher on average on certain kinds of tests), or the flip side to such research, which is that various European groups are inferior in some respect. There is to be sure scientific scrutiny and disagreement, but there isn't the collective shock of a taboo being breached and the accompanying outrage, public shaming, excommunication, and so on. No one will be fired for discovering that Jewish people are smart. By contrast, similar research that produces unflattering results for politically sensitive groups is subjected not only to scientific criticism, but widespread outrage—firings are a real possibility. Of course, it is possible that all research that produces "nice" results is done well, and all research that is "nasty" is poor, but that seems unlikely. Political correctness is a better explanation for the asymmetric treatment of parallel work that does or does not threaten the status of politically sensitive groups. Discussions of occupational gender skew display the same asymmetry: there is no taboo on discovering that women are *superior* to men as stock traders, say, because of population-level differences favoring women (e.g., distinctive attitudes toward risk). But the reverse is not something greeted warmly in polite public discourse.

This much theorists of political correctness get right—political correctness is not a myth.[6] But they neglect the perfectly good *reasons* for cultivating and enforcing various politically correct norms. In the case of race, the root concern is clearly that there exists a horrific record of violence and injustice directed toward African Americans and other minorities, as well as a record of promoting such violence by superficially respectable means (including racial pseudoscience), and enlightened moral thinking has thus converged on a *default norm against advancing ideas associated with the oppression or marginalization of minorities*. A similar story applies to gender and occupation. Political correctness thus represents the evolution of public standards with the praiseworthy tendency to protect and promote the interests of historically oppressed groups. These standards work by introducing a *high barrier of entry* to those wishing to enter public discourse in a way that that threatens to undermine moral progress. By maintaining the norms, we acknowledge that such threats exist and that it is important to us collectively to signal to new entrants into public discourse that they must observe the norms carved out to protect the status of groups potentially under threat. And what is true in this case is true of many other examples of political correctness, such as censoring stereotyped depiction of Asians, the German anxiety over displays of sympathy for National Socialism, calls for including more women and other groups on syllabi, or suggestions that the poor are to blame for their plight.

In this respect, I am entirely in agreement with Richard Rorty that political correctness has made "the casual infliction of humiliation . . . much less socially acceptable than it was," and even that "encouraging students to be what mocking neoconservatives call 'politically correct' has made our country a far better place."[7] There is no case for denying that having norms such that by default we avoid insulting or otherwise attacking the status of women or gay people has brought huge benefits, and critics of political correctness who ignore them are simply mistaken. There are, to be sure, limits on the pursuit of these worthy ends, and inevitably disagreement about where to locate those borders. Barriers to entering the arena of public discourse can be higher or lower—at one end of the spectrum are minor conventions, next are downright taboos, the sense of collective shock when someone "dares" to utter certain things, and at the far end are explicit laws governing speech, which may themselves be narrowly or broadly defined. One may acknowledge the legitimate ends of political correctness without endorsing any and all barriers to public discourse.[8] And of course any particular instance of political correctness may be wrongheaded or petty, just as individual applications of patriotic norms may be. We must not, as Rorty ultimately does, lose sight of the potential drawbacks to political correctness, and try to arrive at a reasonable estimate of what, all-in, we gain and suffer, in upholding these norms.

These, then, are legitimate ends for political correctness. Proponents of PC norms aren't confused to think that racial pseudoscience has had enormous, damaging effects in the past; they aren't mistaken to regard any revival of racial science as potentially disastrous and in any case accompanied by huge costs. It is not true that opposition to any such revival is (or need be) rooted in mere "superficial moralism," and there are good reasons for maintaining collective default-norms that signal certain kinds of discussion out of bounds in the normal course of things. It might seem surprising that the norm to evolve was one that focused on offense and not simply on promoting whatever was in the people's objective interest. But this is again similar to other norms, like love of country. In both cases there is a core goal of promoting the interests of some entity, but part of this is taken to involve discouraging insults and other threats to the publicly recognized status of the people or thing in question. Failing to acknowledge the values in question by a lack of reverence or deviance from certain standards are thus punished, even when what is at stake seems superficially to be only symbolic. Political correctness is one face of a deeper concern for the oppressed comparable to the dimension of patriotism associated with denouncing insults to country, like flag-burning.

∎ DILEMMAS

There is nothing wrong with promoting a presumption that historically oppressed or marginalized groups should not be insulted or subjected to discourse
threatening to undermine their status, and it is puzzling that critics of political
correctness seem frequently unwilling to acknowledge its legitimate ends. That
leaves the door open to a second kind of criticism, the misguided application of
the relevant norms. But whatever the damage to individuals losing their jobs or
being publicly anathematized (perhaps when they call something "niggardly"),
it cannot be said that the mere misapplication of values raises interesting philosophical problems. It is rather a third kind of problem with political correctness
that should anchor our attention, the problem of *conflicts* among values, whether
between those associated with political correctness and other things we care
about, or even internal conflicts within the former. We can note several different
kinds of dilemma-engendering conflicts.

Orwellian discourse: One kind of conflict occurs when politically correct
norms lead to the abuse of language that Orwell criticizes in "Politics and the
English Language." As he points out, the vague and imprecise use of terms like
"fascism" can come to serve as a "defense of the indefensible."[9] Instead of using
reason and persuasion, political leaders can short-circuit debate and delegitimize
opposition. Contemporary versions of this on the right are easily recognized, as
when policies are justified with reference to a nebulous and never-ending "war
on terror," but political correctness seems to involve a similar tendency. Loury
draws attention to phrases whose "linguistic imprecision impairs analysis" by
design, in order to avoid controversy and debate.[10] "Diversity" has come to have
this quality. Reasonable people oppose terrorism and favor diversity, but there
is little attempt to pin down what this really means. A naive newcomer might
suppose that promoting diversity means a leg up for underrepresented religious
minorities like Mormons or Buddhists who have viewpoints different from most
people, but in practice this is not what it means. The exact contours of what diversity really amounts to could probably be sketched by institutional leaders, but for
Orwellian reasons they typically decline to do so—justifying decisions in virtue
of diversity (like fighting terrorism) is easy; explaining why diversity of viewpoint or of opinion often gets short shrift in institutional settings is harder.

Another example is the increasing tendency to reject official government terms
like "illegal alien" in favor of "undocumented immigrant" or "undocumented
citizen," with the implication that refusing to do so implies reactionary or hateful
views. These campaigns aren't just the one-off ideas of random individuals; the
phrase "undocumented citizen" is encouraged by administrators at universities
in the United States, and others urge that the statement "America is a melting pot"
constitutes a form of "microaggression."[11] Regardless of what the right immigration policy is, and notwithstanding the legitimate interest in avoiding various
forms of marginalization, this kind of discourse once again "impairs analysis."

"Undocumented immigrant" is meant to make it harder to focus on the fact that there are laws and procedures governing entry to the country that were flouted by the persons in question, while the Orwellian "undocumented citizen" seeks to present a political aspiration as a fait accompli. To the extent that we recognize both the legitimate ends of political correctness and the undesirable effects that Orwell drew our attention to, we should see these as cases that present a dilemma.

Causal structures: More substantively, fears of politically incorrect stereotyping threaten to subvert our understanding of the world even without Orwellian word-games, as when there is resistance in the public sphere to the suggestion that a stereotypical trait is causally implicated in some negative outcome. The stereotype of deference to authority in many East Asian (and other) societies and its role in causing accidents is an example.[12] When the Korean airline Asiana had a plane crash in San Francisco in 2013, the suggestion was made that such deference made a difference, as the pilot was relatively junior and was being supervised by an instructor, possibly leading the pilot to be reluctant to assert the need for a go-around. This suggestion was in turn widely derided for succumbing to cultural stereotypes. (*The Atlantic* introduced the claim under the heading "Confucius in the Cockpit," alongside a comical depiction of the sage.)[13] What appears to be at work here is anxiety about reinforcing stereotypes. The important thing for our purposes isn't whether deference to authority actually did play a role, only that politically correct norms threaten rational analysis of the cause of a plane crash, assuming that public ridicule counts as a cost those analyzing such crashes must reckon with. But as it happens, "Interviews with pilots indicate that Korean culture may have played a role in the crash. . . . Captain Lee told investigators that any of the three pilots on the plane could have decided to break off the approach, but he said it was 'very hard' for him to do so because he was a 'low-level' person being supervised by an instructor pilot."[14] The NTSB report states that "the PF's [pilot flying's] deference to authority likely played some role in the fact that he did not initiate a go-around."[15]

Against this, the fact that there are sources to cite discussing the role of cultural differences in accidents may seem to undercut the idea that there is some politically correct taboo surrounding the subject. But politically correct norms are graded—some topics are widely off-limits in public discourse, but others merely get subjected to "heightened scrutiny." These introduce a filtering effect. The thought isn't that it is impossible to discuss publicly the arguments involved, but knowing one will be subjected to moralized criticism introduces a penalty or tax, serving as a partial filter on public speech. Similarly, no one thinks it was impossible to criticize the Iraq war, but patriots seeding suspicion of dissent in effect raised the barrier to entry into the public debate. And it's worth observing in passing that the barrier introduced by stereotype aversion extends beyond political correctness strictly speaking, to avoiding stereotypes more broadly, again with worrying effects. Neanderthal research, at least any that informs public discourse, is inevitably along the lines of, "Surprising new study upends stereotype that Neanderthals were dim-witted." This in itself might seem to reflect a random piece of scientific progress. The trouble is that it is difficult to imagine an article title, let alone a newspaper headline, along the lines of "Neanderthals: As Dumb as We Thought." Such research would thus need to overcome both bias in favor of novelty and the bias against reinforcing stereotypes.

Backfire: Other conflicts are internal to the concerns the community has for those marginalized, particularly conflicts arising between the public-facing desire not to insult or offend, on the one hand, and the substantive concern actually to advance people's interests on the other. We see this in the case of patriotism when jingoistic zeal interferes with frank and open attempts to improve the life of the country. Dissent in war is the obvious case, but there are many others, as when critics on the right refuse to accept "revisionist" histories that attempt to wrestle with an ugly past so as to improve national culture, or when national pride leads to a denial that core values are being undermined by various policies. These conflicts represent a set of norms backfiring against those who apply them so that the core values the norms emerged from are actually undermined as a result.

A possible case of political correctness backfiring concerns the European Union. Consider a German public figure pondering criticism of closer European integration and of specific measures like a currency union in the 1970s or 1980s. Many of the arguments that might be deployed in such criticisms would have a politically incorrect flavor. The basic point would be that over the long term, advanced, northern economies fundamentally had their act together in a way that less developed, southern economies in places like Greece or southern Italy did not. In light of the war, as well as the implications of impugning the productivity or innovativeness of southerners, it would be difficult to make such arguments without striking up against various taboos and thus incurring the penalties for breaking them. And once again, there are good reasons for having such norms. However, this would have the tendency to suppress dissent to further integration and a currency union, even if it turned out to be true that currency union without political union would be a disaster. And recent history suggests that there really were serious problems with the currency union, as revealed in the Greek debt crisis from 2009 on. On one reading, this sort of crisis is evidence of backfire, since norms of discourse prevented the airing of disagreements that resulted in institutions which, once they malfunctioned, produced precisely the sort of animosity that integration was designed to prevent. Of course, this interpretation might be debated. Critics would claim that the crisis was manufactured by flint-hearted German bureaucrats, who in turn pointed out that Greece has more or less been in default since 1832, and that an "unconditional transfer-union" is unsustainable.[16] But whatever we make of the particulars, it illustrates the possibility of backfire, and the danger that politically correct norms can pose.

Another possible case again involves occupational gender skew, which in some circles is considered off-limits except to condemn discrimination against women. This makes it impossible to confront any possible endogenous factors, such as gender differences in interests, if there should be any. Yet this dynamic may well prove harmful for women, for instance if they end up underrepresented in important occupations because endogenous factors go unaddressed. And in the United States, there is a taboo (again, in some circles) against discussing affirmative action programs, despite a body of research suggesting that as currently structured they may be harming the intended beneficiaries. This research could turn out to be false, of course, but the taboo creates the possibility of backfire.[17]

It is important to emphasize that I am not claiming that those enforcing politically correct norms in these cases are wrong, all things considered. The point is rather that doing so comes with *costs*, setting up a *dilemma*. My central contention isn't that we ought to do away with the supposed superficial moralism of political correctness, but rather that we ought to focus on the dilemmas political correctness introduces, and face up to the costs incurred in being gored on either horn.

■ NORM-DEPENDENT RESPONSES AND REVERSE HYPOCRISY

It is difficult to tally up or even to compare the costs of having or not having politically correct norms, but it is clear that both can be high. To dwell on the costs of enforcing them, in a high-cost scenario they can lead to what Timur Kuran calls widespread "preference falsification" in which what people believe in private becomes increasingly detached from what is spoken in public, which in the case of Eastern bloc communism made it impossible to discuss pervasive dysfunctions urgently requiring reform. Worse, Kuran identifies an "intergenerational process through which the unthinkable becomes the unthought," making such dysfunctions unidentifiable even if they could be discussed.[18] Alternatively, Loury points out that preference falsification can lead to polarization, by a process analogous to Gresham's law, whereby the bad money (extreme opinion consonant with politically correct ideology or else violently opposed to it) drives out the good (moderately heterodox opinion), and so comes to dominate what circulates in public.[19]

This is the high-cost scenario for political correctness. We can illustrate it in the arena of distributive justice, which offers ample scope for the relevant norms. As I point out in appendix B, attributing poor social outcomes to factors external to the person (to society, the state, etc.) sounds "nice," since we don't feel like we're blaming underdogs for their already unpleasant position; attributing them to factors internal to the person (e.g., to poor choices or maladaptive culture) sounds "mean" and is likely to trigger charges of "blaming the victim." This makes the latter less politically correct. And on the international stage, claiming that poor countries are in part worse off due to endogenous factors like institutions or culture similarly has an un-PC quality to it that blaming multinational corporations or the rich countries does not. Since there is a long and ugly history of rich countries invading poor countries and an even longer history of richer citizens taking advantage of poorer citizens in politics, law, and business, it isn't unreasonable to accept a norm discouraging theories threatening to undermine the status of the poor. But against this, if it turns out that people are capable of significantly influencing social outcomes in the course of educational, fertility, or work decisions, and that absent these, statist policies are likely to be ineffective, it will be disastrous for such facts not to inform public discourse, or for them to face ridicule. (Similarly in the international variant.) The high-cost scenario in these cases, then, is one in which there is a widespread belief that, say, social pathologies play an important role in explaining bad social outcomes, but there is reluctance to discuss that belief; or in which the thought doesn't seem even a live option to many (it is "unthought"); or in which damaging polarization sets in because those with moderate views face penalties for voicing their opinions in the public arena.

This high-cost scenario seems to me more than overblown fear-mongering, though it would be difficult to establish the extent to which it is or may be realized. Instead, let me make two specific suggestions about how to think about the costs. First, there is a curious problem that arises when one is concerned to promulgate norms so as to avoid insult or offense, but that very act shapes how these are interpreted. In some cases, promulgating the norm will sensitize people to the insult, making things worse. If some children are making fun of a foreign student, a well-intentioned teacher may decide to give a stern lecture in front of the class, urging norms of respect. ("No making fun of his accent!") But this may backfire, both by sensitizing the victim and making him feel worse, and by drawing everyone else's attention to the matter. There is evidence of a similar phenomenon in relation to serious trauma. Victims of sexual abuse and combat veterans fare worse the more they see their traumatic event as a central, defining moment; norms tending to *downplay* the importance of the event would thus be more helpful.[20] A *New England Journal of Medicine* piece on victimhood and resilience points out that immediate counseling after trauma, which tends to highlight that the victims *are* victims who should be expected to feel traumatized, often seems to make things worse, increasing the likelihood of mental disorders.[21] Given all this, we must be cautious in thinking about how to assess the costs of promulgating norms against insult and offense, e.g., with training programs focused on "microaggressions" or other initiatives that raise the salience of injury and offense.

A second point about the costs of political correctness concerns "reverse hypocrisy," or not preaching what you practice, which we touched on in chapter 7.[22] This is the phenomenon of applying high standards in one's private life, especially toward one's children or other loved ones, while publicly promulgating low standards for others, either explicitly or by withholding public criticism. Reverse hypocrisy is evidence of something like Kuran's preference falsification. The savvy Communist Party member publicly signals agreement with low standards for productivity, urging that the state should provide for everyone's needs without anyone doing "extra" work not officially assigned to him; but privately he urges his kids to work long hours in the informal sector and to accumulate savings. Examples closer to home include private insistence on personal responsibility in domains like fertility decisions or work ethos, while ignoring or even mocking these as public norms. In this sense, it's reverse hypocrisy to make it clear that you expect your children to make sensible decisions about family and to work hard in school whatever the excuses they are tempted to make, while lampooning old-fashioned-sounding public norms to the same effect.

It might be objected that there are substantive reasons to uphold different standards in the public arena than in the personal. A liberal tolerance for differences or even just politeness might seem to dictate as much, and of course if one judges that others are less fortunate in their capacity for making the relevant discriminations, or are less well positioned to act on them, it may seem inappropriate to uphold what would be unreasonable standards. Arguments from liberal toleration or etiquette are less persuasive, though, when the stakes include the well-being of someone else's family. And the view that *we* or those close to us can adhere to high standards that will promote our well-being, but *they* cannot, has a worrying ring of condescension. Short of extreme circumstances, many successful families simply will not tolerate children doing poorly in school (let alone not finishing), making poor fertility decisions, or failing to work. But many of the same people are reluctant to assert these as public norms or to issue criticisms based on them. Since asserting such norms would often involve criticizing marginalized groups, this sort of reluctance looks like a good measure of political correctness, and its prevalence would be a useful barometer of what I called the high-cost scenario.

16   Utopia and the Real World

> If the horsemen don't bring us down, the philosophers will.[1]
>
> —SIMON BOLÍVAR

Suppose libertarianism were true. That would mean much of the contemporary political world was upside down and should presumably be "fixed." But that sounds like a utopian scheme with little practical import. Realistically, we are not going to dismantle the welfare state anytime soon, it might be said. More importantly, even if we could implement classical liberal ideals, doing so could have consequences that even proponents of such ideals would regret. (If I could press a big red button that would—somehow—induce a revolution and bring about the libertarian minimal state overnight, I wouldn't press it.)[2] Suddenly upending decades-old social understandings would likely have far-reaching and possibly dangerous ramifications—such changes are risky. So why should we be interested in the classical liberal ideal, except perhaps as an arid academic exercise?

Any political philosophy that deviates substantially from the status quo is bound to seem both impractical and threatening, whether it be libertarian or for that matter Confucian. The demands of justice aren't easily set aside, and yet if justice requires vast changes to the social safety net, or to the structure of pensions, or the operation of markets, we are apt to suppose that such radical changes threaten social upheaval, and are in any case unlikely to see any uptake in what non-academics like to call "the real world." But on the other hand, if we simply accede to the status quo and the constraints of political feasibility, what room is left for acknowledging serious injustices that *ought* to be corrected whether or not it is "practical" to do so? What room is left for acknowledging room for vast improvements? Abolishing the slave trade may have been in a sense unrealistic in 17th-century Portugal, but that hardly made calls for justice pointless or wrongheaded. There is thus a tension between our need for ideals that capture truths about justice—sometimes distant and far-out truths—and the sense that there isn't much use in projecting ideals that would crumble on first contact with brick and blood. It is this tension that we must come to grips with if we wish to address the opening challenge.

We can approach the problem by considering the various parameters of utopia. Each parameter can be thought of as a slider that we can move up or down along a particular dimension of idealization. The positions of all of the sliders will determine a particular view of how ideal or, in one sense of the word, how utopian our project is. In particular, it is worth examining assumptions about people's *moral dispositions*, about their *nonmoral dispositions*, about *social systems* like markets and political institutions, and finally *transitions*—whether we can get "there" from "here," regardless of whether a particular system is practicable in absolute terms. By taking up each of these dimensions we can get a grip on what it means to idealize in political philosophy. By the end it should become clear that in this domain we must aim for a moderate position in which we do idealize, but only within certain natural bounds we may mark out, at least in rough terms. I do not believe that the arguments for a classical liberal state exceed these bounds.

■ MACHIAVELLI ON MORALITY AND UTOPIAN SCHEMES

Hardheaded no-nonsense types will sympathize with Machiavelli's critique of utopian political thought:

> For many authors have constructed imaginary republics and principalities that have never existed in practice and never could; for the gap between how people actually behave and how they ought to behave is so great that anyone who ignores everyday reality in order to live up to an ideal will soon discover he has been taught how to destroy himself.

These reflections are in turn informed by a view of our moral dispositions:

> For of men one can, in general, say this: they are ungrateful, fickle, deceiving, avoiders of danger, eager for gain. As long as you serve their interests, they are devoted to you. They promise you their blood, their possessions, their lives, and their children.... But as soon as you need help, they turn against you.[3]

Machiavelli emphasizes that his frequently shocking advice to the prince is contingent on a particular understanding of people's moral character, and that devising a political system founded on an unduly optimistic picture of what people are like would be disastrous.

These observations, however, are less far-reaching than it may appear, since they apply only to *actualized* political systems. There is surely some eye-rolling contempt in Machiavelli's remark that "imaginary" republics are destined to remain imaginary, but he doesn't pretend to show that there might not be good reasons to consider an ideal *as* an unactualizable ideal. On one view, we should think about how to organize society by assuming, initially at least, that people will be motivated by justice, so that any ideal institutions that we put forward will be ones we can count on the citizens observing and cooperating with.[4] This in effect involves assuming that the people for whom we are devising a social system have benign moral dispositions, at least insofar as justice is concerned. (It needn't involve assuming perfect beneficence.) But it is important not to misunderstand the rationale for such an assumption. Some writers, like Rousseau, simply have very optimistic factual views of what we are like: "Nothing is so gentle as man in his primitive state, when, placed by nature at an equal distance from the stupidity of brutes and the fatal enlightenment of civil man . . . he is restrained by natural pity from needlessly harming anyone himself."[5] But a theory like John Rawls's that assumes people comply with the dictates of justice needn't be predicated on optimism about how people actually will respond to various social situations; it need only assume that it's worth exploring what social institutions would look like if people *were* to be motivated by justice. And there are plenty of reasons we might be interested in such an ideal, even if we didn't make Rousseauian assumptions about people's actual propensities.[6]

To name a few, we might think that having a transcendent ideal could serve as a beacon in the distance, telling us how far we are from the mark we're steering toward; or we might require the ideal to help us judge civil disobedience that is motivated by the gap between ideal and actual institutions; or we might think that our moral natures are within limits malleable, and that it would be unduly limiting to consider social institutions only given the present state of moral motivations. (There was a time when it would have seemed pointless to discuss a society in which everyone agreed that people have the same intrinsic worth, but it wouldn't have been crazy for far-seeing thinkers to imagine institutions for such a society.) Of course, one might deny that transcendent ideals are useful even for such theoretical purposes as these; Amartya Sen has argued that we'd be better off focusing on *comparisons* of justice—on whether we can envisage improvements rather than on an absolute ideal.[7] But this sort of objection is in any case quite different from the Machiavellian objection to Rousseau, i.e., that he is confused about what people are like (even under reasonably propitious circumstances). An ideal-theorist like Rawls isn't liable to that objection.

An analogy may help: we are often moved by unimplementable ideals of moral or intellectual character. I may find it illuminating and useful to sketch out an ideal life of moral behavior that I am not really capable of entering into without courting disaster. Suppose the ideal involves sobriety and faithfulness, while in reality I am a drunken philanderer. Attempting to implement these ideals might go horribly awry. If I lead the life of the sober and faithful spouse while having my actual dispositions, I may buy beer for the party and invite my former flame. The ideal would handle both well, but I will end up ruining my life. If I cannot implement these ideals, what purpose might they serve? Again, there are several possibilities: if nothing else, they may shape my normative conception of myself—of how worthwhile my life is and has been, if only reflecting in bed at night; they may serve as a compass indicating direction even if moving more than very modestly toward the goal would be unwise; they might ground the assessments of others and serve to evaluate criticism and disapproval. Norms can be useful without being immediately practical.

We can make the point more sharply: it isn't an objection to a theory of justice that says slavery is wrong that the citizens have such depraved notions that abolition cannot feasibly be implemented. Just the opposite is true, we can assert—it's a test of the adequacy of a theory of justice that it *does* condemn slavery *even* under such conditions. Suppose the ancient Athenians were utterly unwilling to abolish slavery because doing so would make the silver mines unproductive, which would threaten the state with ruin. We can even imagine, if we like, that the slaves agree that abolition would be unwise, if, say, this would lead to civil war and their likely deaths. None of this would show that slavery wasn't unjust or that a plan of state ought not to include abolition. The trouble with Rousseau's methodology of "taking men as they are and laws as they might be"—setting aside the irony of Rousseau's implausible vision of what people are like—is that this threatens to make justice a hostage to the wickedness of men.[8] Unless we are careful and quite broad with what we mean by "as they are" (now? later? essentially?), we run the risk of losing our grip on what is supposed to be normative about justice.

In fact, with a strong enough "real world" constraint that insists that our picture of justice reflect what our contemporaries are willing to take seriously and how they are likely to behave, it becomes less and less clear that what we are doing is theorizing about justice at all. There is, after all, a distinction to be made between a theory of the just state, and pragmatic suggestions about how to exercise power effectively. Plato and Rawls are quite clearly attempting to picture a just society, whatever one may make of their results; writers highly sensitive to real-world constraints like Machiavelli and Hobbes aren't clearly engaged in the same enterprise at all, despite the misleading tendency to lump them under the generic heading of "political philosophy." Machiavelli's suggestions about how to destroy one's political enemies do not look like rival attempts to accomplish what Plato was trying to accomplish in spelling out plans to ensure his *kallipolis* was ruled by sages; similarly for Hobbes's advice to establish an all-powerful regent against whom the citizens had no recourse in order to stave off perpetual "war of all against all." These resemble rather the philosophical cynicism that *disavows* appeals to justice, as portrayed by Thucydides's Athenian ambassadors in the Melian dialogue:

> For our part, we will not make a long speech no one would believe, full of fine moral arguments. . . . Instead, let's work out what we can do on the basis of what both sides truly accept: we both know that decisions about justice are made in human discussions only when both sides are under equal compulsion; but when one side is stronger, it gets as much as it can, and the weak must accept that.[9]

It would be naive to interpret the ambassadors as putting forward a rival theory of justice on all fours with Plato's. Like Thrasymachus's similar suggestion in the *Republic*, the act of redefinition serves rather to dismiss genuine claims of justice altogether.

We should not, then, follow Machiavelli in dismissing theories of justice that cannot be implemented without disaster, since these can play useful roles even without being fully practical, and since asserting stringent real-world criteria threatens to remove us from the realm of justice entirely.

■ CONSTRAINED IDEALISM

Against all this, it might be urged that if we're going to help ourselves to generous assumptions about people's moral qualities, there are no longer any constraints— we might as well appoint a supreme dictator whom we can assume to be perfectly benign, and do away with law enforcement and juridical institutions while we're at it, since they're only needed for dealing with the crummy state of our actual moral natures. Idealizing along this dimension, says the critic, is to miss the point of theorizing about how to structure the state, since the goal is essentially to address the fact that we are flawed creatures living in a rotten world, disposed to conflict, drawn to temptation. If we weren't, benign anarchy or dictatorship— it wouldn't matter much which—would serve well enough, and no elaborate schemes of governing would be required. Any form of government (including none) and any institutions will do if we help ourselves to sufficiently utopian assumptions about how people will behave.

I take this, and not the earlier point about implementation, to be the best way to advance Machiavellian skepticism about idealized polities. And the core insight that there must be some constraints on the table to make the discussion worthwhile is surely right. However, idealizing along moral dimensions isn't incompatible with reasonable constraints. The obvious suggestion is that we should avoid projecting radical changes in fundamental features of human nature, in particular by assuming large shifts in basic drives and motivations. There is simply no point in proceeding on the assumption that people will adopt the selflessness of eusocial insects, any more than doing our engineering on the assumption of a perpetual motion machine. What is tricky is explaining why the assumption that people will by and large behave justly doesn't violate that constraint. The key distinction to draw, I believe, is between *what people of good will can be expected to do simply in virtue of changing their opinions,* and *what requires radical, non-conative changes in their basic drives and motivations.* There is a fundamental difference, that is, between envisioning people treating women as political equals, abandoning factory-farmed meat, or abandoning the welfare state, on the one hand, and assuming people will not be self-interested, love distant strangers as much as their own children, or never succumb to temptation and weakness of will. In part, this distinction simply marks the fact that although a given shift in public opinion may be unlikely in the near term, there isn't anything that fundamentally bars people simply changing their minds in response to arguments put to them (or more likely still, novels, movies, or songs that make a point). No one predicted the sudden shift in American opinions about gay rights in the early 21st century, and similar shifts in British opinions about the slave trade have likewise been relatively sudden and difficult to predict. By contrast, it is less useful to discuss utopian polities that make sense only if we come to resemble the eusocial insects; there is no pathway toward the latter, or if there is one it involves so much change (and science fiction) that it is unclear what value thinking about such a society would have.

But there is also a deeper reason to recognize the difference between people changing their moral opinions and changes in what people fundamentally care about. Typically, a part of what we are doing when we offer a blueprint of the just society is to give *reasons* for the principles that ideal-theorists are assuming the citizens will accept. The presentation of the blueprint usually integrates an attempt to argue for its contents. This means that the assumption that citizens will be just is essentially the assumption that the arguments being advanced won't fall on deaf ears, that the participants in the debate will respond to reason and persuasion. Naturally we may reject these arguments, but it is reasonable for someone making the case for a certain view, the plausibility of which partly depends on how people respond to the very arguments he is making, to suppose those arguments won't just be ignored. Otherwise, we are collectively in the position of rejecting someone's reasoned proposal just because it depends on our accepting certain views that we refuse to accept, without actually responding to the arguments. We may decide that the arguments aren't cogent enough to persuade us, rendering the plan a dangerous one since it depends on our going along, but we cannot reasonably announce, independent of rejecting the arguments, that the plan is no good because in order for it to work we would have to be persuaded by it!

Plato famously compared the structure of the state to the structure of the soul, but a better comparison is to couples therapy. Suppose a marriage is on the rocks and the couple is seeing a counselor who suggests they deliberate about how things might work going forward. There are two ways *not* to go about this: first, by ruling out of bounds discussion of, say, the husband's refusal to do his share of the household chores, even if he has an incorrigible habit of behaving in this way. A couple thinking about their relationship would be crazy not to spend at least some time thinking about how their relationship *ought* to work. But it would be equally absurd to announce that such deliberations should proceed on the assumption that husband and wife will behave like angels, or radically change in their fundamental motivations and drives. The sapient counselor will suggest a constrained idealism, and conduct at least part of their discussions on the assumption that the husband will do the right thing, while including plenty of advice about what to do when someone loses their temper, say.

In summary, theories of the just state are subject to legitimate anti-utopian criticism when they get lazy about how the various problems a polity faces are to be solved. Proposing a vision of the state in which citizens have changed their minds (relative to us) in response to arguments is aboveboard, and indeed simply accepting the "realistic" view that people will continue with their injustices is unacceptable. But helping ourselves to magical changes in human nature is a

260 Theory and Practice

wrongheaded and utopian approach to justice, which is the truth in Rousseau's methodological maxim. And the two points can interact, as when we acknowledge that changing people's minds doesn't mean that *everyone* will change their moral opinions, or change them immediately, or that individuals will always follow their own moral ideals. Imagining a society that doesn't practice de jure discrimination doesn't mean pretending no discrimination will ever occur.

Thomas More's *Utopia*, appropriately enough, illustrates the wrong way of handling both sides of the coin. On the one hand, he proposes an idealized version of slavery. More's fictional and sometimes satirical work shouldn't be confused with an academic treatise, but his, or rather his mouthpiece Raphael's, suggestions about a slightly less grim institution of slavery seem to have been serious ("The Utopians enslave prisoners of war only if they are captured in wars fought by the Utopians themselves. . . . The children of slaves are not automatically enslaved").[10] This is a remarkable and disastrous concession to realism, since it wouldn't have taken much imagination to see one's way past that institution in 16th-century England. On the other hand, More succumbs to magical thinking when he wrestles with pathologies of rapacity and greed. The Utopians, he tells us, despise wealth and use gold mainly to manufacture their chamber pots. He says this because he is frustrated by the question, "What kind of justice is it when a nobleman . . . or someone who makes his living by doing either nothing at all or something completely useless to the public, gets a life of luxury and grandeur?"[11] It is reasonable enough to wish to respond to this familiar sentiment, and imagining greed out of existence provides an easy solution. But in doing so, More presents us with a less compelling project, one that ultimately is entertaining but intellectually barren. Imagination is no substitute for the hard work of devising mechanisms to deal with our inveterate flaws. And at the risk of mixing high and low, it is interesting to observe much the same in pop-culture depictions of ideal societies. This suggests that the mistake at issue is pervasive and temperamental, not just intellectual. Gene Roddenberry's *Star Trek* represents an approach to trade and money that bears a depressing resemblance to More's. One encounters such suggestions as, "The acquisition of wealth is no longer the driving force of our lives. We work to better ourselves and the rest of humanity," where the context makes clear that the idea isn't just a modest one about keeping things in perspective, but a rejection of any desire to earn money or possess luxuries.[12] And yet such luxuries are one of our oldest legacies, going by the archaeology of burial sites; the stubborn texture of humanity is once again imagined away instead of being dealt with. The television show *The West Wing* is another example, where systemic and institutional problems of democratic social organization are implied to be solvable by appointing a kind of economist-king as president, surrounded by a court of selfless geniuses. If we help ourselves to such leadership we can imagine things going rather well, but this is to think through the happy consequences of solving the problems, not to think through how actually to solve them.

■ INTELLECTUAL CAPACITIES AND SOCIAL SYSTEMS

The tendency of citizens to comply with the dictates of justice has become a standard feature of debate about ideal and non-ideal theories of justice among philosophers, but our nonmoral capacities and, more subtly, our social systems are parameters just as susceptible to varying degrees of idealization. The two are connected because utopias like communism or Plato's ideal city rely on optimistic assumptions about both certain kinds of social systems and the expertise required for them to work. Plato famously insisted that the just city was to be ruled by philosophers, meaning that it was ruled by men and women who could "find the being itself in each thing" and "grasp the good itself" (532a).[13] Given such a useful class of people, arranging a new-fangled social system that was workable would naturally be a great deal easier. Plato's sanguine forecasts for these rulers include that they will be "by nature good at remembering, quick to learn, high-minded, graceful, and a friend and relative of truth, justice, courage, and moderation" (487a). More recently, communist systems intended to curtail free markets on a significant scale have had to posit expertise in organizing the production and allocation of goods, since this wasn't to be accomplished by individuals responding to market signals. The classic Hayekian response, of course, is that the requisite knowledge is socially distributed and unattainable by individuals or small groups of individuals, and that we therefore require market-based price-signaling systems both to broadcast this information and to generate an incentive scheme ensuring people respond to it.[14] The expertise posited is thus said to be both unavailable and useless.

In order to shed light on justice, we should avoid making heroic assumptions about the capacity of experts to assemble the relevant knowledge and to motivate others to respond to it, and we should likewise be realistic about the ability of social systems to solve critical problems. Positing a civil service system composed of well-educated technocrats tasked with managing a limited range of government functions (e.g., wildlife management) and a congruent social system is reasonable enough; positing philosopher-kings with direct knowledge of the good, or central planners capable of determining efficient production and allocation schedules, is not. Hayek and others have made obvious how various incarnations of socialist doctrines are likely to go wrong in this respect, but market enthusiasts aren't exempt; there is no use in pretending that vast social problems like monopoly, inequality, and the destructive part of "creative destruction" will be eliminated by free markets, or that lower taxes will always result in more revenue.[15] A sober approach to these problems must involve recourse to extra-market remedies in the form of government action, or else emphasize the badness of the alternatives if, say, vast swaths of creative destruction and the attendant social ills are simply to be tolerated. Disposing of these problems with optimistic prognostications about a particular social system looks like utopian daydreaming.

Another way of relating human nature and social systems is to engineer the latter to correct for deficiencies in the former. On this approach, we acknowledge various moral and nonmoral limitations we are subject to, but then adjust our social systems in order to work around them. In the case of our moral limitations, the dreamer concerned about poverty helps himself to deep changes in our level of other-concern; the sober visionary projects institutional mechanisms to fill in for our limited altruism. The welfare state is an example of this. Tax schemes take the place of generosity, mandatory insurance schemes take the place of prudence, the estate tax takes the place of Morean fantasies about our attitudes toward money. This strategy is a good one as far as it goes, but of course it merely shifts the utopian critique from assumptions about people to assumptions about social systems and our ability to manage them. These can only be evaluated on a case-by-case basis. Still, we shouldn't pretend that it's any less tempting to imagine away the difficulties introduced by social schemes like the welfare state than it is to imagine away the limitations introduced by human nature. It is as tempting to close our eyes and imagine a world in which welfare systems don't get hijacked by political factions that threaten to bankrupt the state as it is to imagine one in which people all love one another.

Education represents another social system for coping with our limitations, or perhaps even overcoming them entirely. Plato's philosopher-kings aren't supposed to emerge spontaneously; the *Republic* delineates an elaborate educational system designed to produce them. This, too, represents a natural strategy for dealing with our individual limitations, but it just shifts the focus to the system level. Plato surmises that it will be necessary to start with individuals who are blank slates, and accordingly that we must expel everyone older than 10 from his city, and then somehow develop and maintain a staggeringly complex pedagogy that lasts for decades, while utilizing propaganda and misinformation in order to ensure compliance. Systems of education or other mechanisms of social transformation may make change seem more plausible, but assuming that such a system will function perfectly, won't be hijacked, corrupted, or rejected is no less utopian than helping oneself to radical shifts in human nature.[16]

■ POLITICAL TRANSITIONS
AND PATH-DEPENDENT JUSTICE

Another utopian parameter concerns change across time. So far we have been considering synchronic factors, but there is also the diachronic question of whether an otherwise feasible polity is one we could actually *access* from the status quo, and if so, how and how quickly. "That sounds like a fine society you have described, but not one that *we* could ever arrive at, at least in the foreseeable future" is the gist of the anti-utopian objection. Some political transitions may simply be infeasible in the real world, rendering certain pictures of the just society unfruitful for *us* to think about. Others might require slow change in order for us to arrive in one piece. When Solon was asked whether his laws were the best that could be given to the Athenians, he replied only that they were the best they would *receive*.[17] There is the possibility that justice is, in a sense, path-dependent, that history constrains the kinds of changes that are possible for us to make, at least with acceptable costs. There may not have been any feasible path from sixth-century Athens to a European-style parliamentary democracy. The failure to acknowledge this may once again raise worries that our theorizing has become detached from the grim realities.

We can illustrate the problem through a range of cases:

Gradual: some blueprint for justice requires that prevailing communist institutions be abolished and converted to a free market system. (Or the reverse—pick the direction of change you find most appealing.) But our advisers indicate that making this change overnight would lead to social chaos and that the economy would likely collapse à la 1990s Russia. They suggest that gradual change over 20 years would greatly reduce these problems.

Delay: same as above, except that the problem is that social change would produce winners and losers, and rapid change would massively increase the losses to the losers. Moreover, many of the losers will be unpersuaded that the losses are just, and will consequently resist change, threatening social upheaval. On the other hand, delaying change by 20 years so as to prepare carefully, reduce losses to the losers, and persuade them of the importance of change would greatly reduce these problems.

Never: some blueprint for justice requires abolishing the American constitutional structure of government, and replacing it with internet-based direct democracy and a council of experts with veto power. But implementing these changes would produce widespread and very costly resistance because of attachment to tradition, reasonable fear of change, and disagreement about the benefits of the shift. The proposed alternative would have been feasible (without transition costs or utopian assumptions) if instituted from the beginning, but cannot be introduced in medias res without catastrophe.

These kinds of scenarios suggest that anti-utopian objections can indeed take a diachronic form, and that to avoid them we must consider not just the intrinsic features of the just society, but dynamic questions of transition. These are often ignored, though they feature at least implicitly in some of the deeper utopias; Kant, for instance, projects such astonishing changes as the emergence of a United Nations in "Toward a Perpetual Peace," but incorporates various forms of wise gradualism with respect to, e.g., the abolition of standing armies.[18]

None of this is to renege on our earlier assumption that people will respond to moral arguments, and that we can count at least on widespread changes in people's moral opinions. Nothing in Gradual depends on moral disagreement or on the assumption that change is "unrealistic" in the face of intransigence. Russia fell apart in the 1990s despite (or perhaps in part because of) a general openness to radical experimentation with social change. Delay does invoke the attitudes of some of the losers, but denying that massive losses to a large group will produce substantial social friction *in the short term* would involve heroic assumptions about human nature; we can count on something like widespread success in making moral arguments, but not that these will persuade everyone all at once, nor that the remaining resistance might not be enough for catastrophe. Likewise, Never doesn't hinge on moral stubbornness, but on the inevitable resistance to change in institutions that people have become accustomed to, depend on, and fear undermining. Ignoring such attitudes would once again render the discussion otherworldly and barren.

The main objection to path-dependency is rather resistance to the idea that justice may be subject to constraints based on costs. If we delay or deny a vision of justice because of social or economic disasters that loom before us, that may seem tantamount to denying justice because we're cheap. This resistance can already be felt when the social costs are felt by all, but when they accrue to groups who *ought* to lose—the unjust landholders in a feudal aristocracy, say—we may be especially repelled by the thought of taking these costs into account. And at some margin this objection is surely right: if the question is one of freeing serfs at a merely financial cost to be paid mainly by the landlords, talk of gradualism would be misplaced. But the claim isn't that we should consider only Pareto improvements when it comes to social change, it is rather the converse—that at *some* margin, it would be crazy *not* to consider gradualism, delay, or even ruling out a blueprint for justice indefinitely. And nothing prevents us from attending to differences in whom the various costs accrue to; any plausible account will be sensitive to them (and not merely to the point of Kaldor-Hicks efficiency). The only obvious reason for stubbornly rejecting even this, for rejecting any and all appeals to cost, is thinking that justice is a *dominant* value, one that trumps all other considerations. We might draw a parallel to the view that moral values dominate all considerations of self-interest. There is no amount of money that defeats the moral reason you have not to kill your uncle for the inheritance, and so we might think that there are no social costs that defeat considerations of justice. Rawls compares the significance of justice for social institutions to that of truth for systems of thought; both represent a kind of "first virtue" whose absence no other type of perfection can compensate for.[19] (A theory of quantum gravity that is *false* cannot win us over by being unusually parsimonious.)

I find this claim to dominance deeply implausible, and it is notable that we find it tempting only in the abstract, while detailed consideration of particular cases quickly inspires doubt. You may not kill your uncle for any amount of money, but we can't infer from that case that an unemployed person may not break a casual promise to meet us for lunch for the opportunity to get a job and feed himself. A society may not execute the innocent to save a few dollars, but that doesn't show it may not accept a minor injustice for a few years to stave off economic catastrophe. Cases like expensive emancipation which resist gradualism or delay cannot be generalized to say we may *never* put justice on the back burner. It all depends. Political amnesties and truth and reconciliation commissions in places like South Africa are testament to the value we place on goods besides justice, at least when it comes to short-term transitions; such devices suggest that we rec-ognize that sometimes the costs of a rigid and instantaneous implementation of justice must yield to broader concerns. More mundanely, even in the domain of simple criminal justice we are willing to pay a great deal to make our justice system rapid and accurate, but not just anything, and not at just any margin. More money would buy us less delayed and less inaccurate justice, but we don't always pay, nor do we think on reflection that we (always) should. Thus, in prac-tice we often price justice, if only as manifested in forced-choice situations that confront us when resources are scarce. "Justice delayed is justice denied" is our pious public maxim—the Magna Carta, etc., etc.—and we rightly squirm at each report of wrongful conviction; "Justice costs money, and so do education and snow-plowing" is the grubby retort of the appropriations committee.

But let us assume all this is mistaken and that justice is a dominant value after all. Another strategy is to emphasize that the truths of justice are often vague. On this approach, justice always wins, but its dictates are vague enough to permit at least gradualism and delay. Suppose that justice dictates enfranchising recently liberated serfs. Such a dictate leaves unspecified exactly how rapidly this must be accomplished. Suppose that the serfs are largely illiterate and are in danger of being manipulated by certain political factions to vote for policies detrimental to their own interests, and that in light of this it is proposed to prepare for enfran-chisement with a literacy program, delaying their voting privileges by a decade. The point is that this isn't obviously inconsistent with recognizing the broad principle at issue. However, we should once again recognize that not just any kind of cost will be recognized as counting in favor of gradualism or delay. We cannot plausibly affirm that justice is dominant while putting it off for the sake of promoting other values that presumably are non-dominant, say the preservation of pristine wilderness. What lends force to the serf case is that the considerations favoring delay are in a sense *internal* to the claim of justice in a way that costs associated with preserving a nice canyon would not be. (Readers worried at the thought that we might be forced to fill in the Grand Canyon for even a rela-tively trivial consideration of justice may wish to reconsider their allegiance to the dominance of justice.) On this approach, the fact that enfranchising the serfs in a particular way would be disastrous for the serfs themselves is relevant to the implementation of justice in a way that environmental losses (or the dilution of political influence among the feudal aristocracy) are not.

How long of a delay and how gradual of an introduction is compatible with recognizing a principle of justice in good faith while insisting on the dominance of justice? Could this strategy justify the Never vignette by way of permanent delay? Even this doesn't seem to me out of the question, as long as the relevant considerations really are internal ones. We might affirm that justice is dominant and that justice requires internet-based direct democracy, but go on to accept both that delay is permissible on internal grounds and that such delays may in principle be permanent or very long term. We might think that the right course is to review the relevant proposal every 10 years, evaluate how damaging the transition was likely to be (especially for people it was intended to benefit), and decide against switching indefinitely. And if such a procedure wasn't feasible and a decision needed to be made on the spot, it is possible that one would come to a like conclusion. Solon was asked to forge a workable system for a polity of extremely poor and landless thetes as well as the rich; his policies (the details of which are obscure) seem to have involved splitting the difference in various respects, for instance in canceling all debts while refusing to redistribute land, the former of which benefited the poor and the latter the rich. One reconstruction is that rigidly enforcing some view of justice he may have had would have led to immediate and catastrophic civil war of the sort that had haunted and would continue to haunt the Greek city states. It is sometimes even conjectured that his permitting the thetes to serve as jurors while leaving the laws vague enough that many decisions were likely to be settled in the courts was a calculated attempt to alter the power balance, but only in the very long term. The historical accuracy of such a reconstruction isn't important here, but it illustrates the intrinsic possibility of a justifiable indefinite delay in implementing justice, and its path-dependent character.

Finally, acknowledging transition costs and incorporating these into our thinking about whether a conception of justice is objectionably utopian shouldn't be confused with conservatism. In the course of criticizing the French Revolution Edmund Burke admonishes us,

> [I]t is with infinite caution that any man ought to venture upon pulling down an edifice, which has answered in any tolerable degree for ages the common purposes of society, or on building it up again, without having models and patterns of approved utility before his eyes.[20]

And elsewhere he expresses pride that "Thanks to our sullen resistance to innovation, thanks to the cold sluggishness of our national character, we still bear the stamp of our forefathers."[21] But the riskiness of change and the possibility of high transition costs count in favor not of conservatism (in the literal sense) but of slow, incremental changes, of what Karl Popper calls "piecemeal engineering" rather than risky revolutionary leaps.[22] There is nothing advantageous in a sluggish national character unless we assume that in general the status quo is preferable to even small, incremental steps whose effects are monitored and adjusted. The former looks more like status quo bias than sensitivity to transition costs and the risks that sudden shifts bring. Such a suspicion is amplified when, for instance, Michael Oakeshott talks of change—mere change—as a "threat to identity" and "an emblem of extinction." When we are young we fail to grasp this, he says, since we are lost in a kind of "dream" in which "Nothing is specified in advance. . . . Since life is a dream, we argue (with plausible but erroneous logic) that politics must be an encounter of dreams, in which we hope to impose our own."[23] We can cheer his enthusiasm for crushing the dreams of youth, but the appropriate grounds for such crushings are either that the dream is wrong, or else that the dreamers tend to neglect transition costs, not the mere fact of change. The objection to a utopian proposal that we transform society overnight, setting aside its contents, isn't mere love of the present, but a preference for gradual, piecemeal shifts, and an insistence on focusing not just on the finished utopian product but on what the path getting there will look like.

■ LIBERTARIANISM IN THE REAL WORLD

We now have some criteria for assessing the sliders that define how utopian a political project is. Some blueprints for justice are flawed in virtue of assumptions that are too otherworldly to be useful, while others envision a society radically unlike ours in ways that are nonetheless worthy of our utmost consideration. How does the classical liberal society fare by these benchmarks? The welfare state looks more or less etched in stone and is wildly popular, and so we might wonder how useful kicking against the pricks really is.

It is an obvious virtue of the libertarian picture that it makes very conservative assumptions about our moral natures. I have made no claims to the effect that we may rely on beneficence to solve social problems, or that the minimal state will somehow makes us kinder or more generous. There may be some disagreement surrounding how effective private aid or mutual assistance would turn out to be in the absence of government support, but none of the preceding arguments depend on such an assumption. In fact, it is precisely the absence of such assumptions that is likely to generate the opposite type of objection, far more serious in my view, namely that the classical liberal picture married to a modern economy will result in an unappealing society of vast inequality and widespread poverty. But whatever the justice in that sort of charge, it arises from distinctly *dys*topian considerations. (It is strikingly difficult to devise a political philosophy that doesn't seem either wildly utopian or horrifically dystopian!) It is true that the classical liberal view has fallen on hard times and that arguing for it may seem, in popular terms, "unrealistic," but this is only so in the sense that I have argued we should ignore. If Machiavellian realism were mandatory then we would have condemned Mill's feminist arguments and Bentham's concern for animal suffering.

On the other hand, it may seem far more tempting to accuse market enthusiasts of being unreasonably optimistic about certain types of social systems. Those they champion typically don't require heroic assumptions about nonmoral capacities such as expertise—that is the point behind emphasizing invisible hands and extended orders—but they may still seem unduly cheerful about the prospects for free markets to solve any and all social problems. Politicians depicting themselves as libertarian frequently suggest that shrinking government, slashing welfare programs, or cutting taxes will somehow have uniformly positive effects. Whether this charge sticks depends entirely on how libertarians respond to those problems, however. There are in effect three options: to help ourselves to convenient assumptions about the effectiveness of markets; to admit their limitations and confess that government or other solutions will be required; or to admit their limitations while explaining why we either should or must accept the resulting problems. Strictly speaking, I have invoked at various points a mix of all three, but I have been very sparing with the first, which is the only option that should attract utopian criticism. As noted, this kind response has the drawback of increasing pressure elsewhere, since if markets are *not* assumed to solve all of our problems, we may go back to grousing about the problems themselves and end up worrying about a libertarian dystopia. But here it is worth adding that in a sense this worry is the one I have been hoping to elicit and foreground. I have never pretended to refute utilitarianism. And to the extent that our rejection of the classical liberal state rests on the view that it produces consequences dire enough that we may threaten or use force against our neighbors, we have at least made some clarifying progress toward the understanding what our real view is.

Finally, there is the reasonable thought that, although a state respecting the moral powers of individuals would be all right in principle and was all right in the times and places that it existed, that time has passed, and attempting to move back toward it would be disastrous for path-dependent reasons. This, I believe, is the best anti-utopian objection to arguments for libertarianism, but it is also one that can be accommodated. The moral harms that are involved in the welfare state are serious ones, as I have argued—often tantamount to stealing large amounts of money. But I have also stressed that the rights that are infringed shouldn't be conceived of as absolutes, and so sufficiently strong path-dependency reasons could overcome the moral force of those rights. And in that case we could simply concede the objection and allow that there are strong reasons to move toward a minimal state, while allowing we should do so in piecemeal fashion. It was a bad idea to dismantle the French aristocracy and national religion overnight; it would be a mistake to press for an end to populist welfare institutions overnight.

Two considerations make this accommodation more plausible, despite the seriousness of the moral wrongs libertarians associate with the welfare state. First, what is at stake is gradualism and delay for the sake of achieving features of a society that existed until relatively recently. That makes it unlikely that the delays would need to be perpetual, at least at first blush. Historical processes can be strongly asymmetric; the energy required to break an egg is dramatically less than that required to put it together again. The response to losing a social entitlement is far stronger than not having it in the first place. Thus, we cannot infer from the mere fact of a state's obtaining a short time earlier that moving back toward it might not be difficult. Still, the situation is one of aiming for a known system whose likely problems and "approved utility" are fairly well understood compared to introducing a radical new vision of society whose ramifications might not be well studied, and whose implementation might therefore be expected to take far longer. Presenting the implementation of justice as a gradual process designed to smooth over the transition is obviously less objectionable than substantively rejecting it in part or whole.

Second, the costs that favor gradualism and delay are, in the above sense, internal to the cause of justice. They mostly likely would accrue not only to those who benefit from the current regime, but to everyone who stands to benefit from holding social chaos in abeyance, which is to say everyone, period. Significant political change is always risky, and thus those wronged by the status quo have strong reasons to accept incremental change, even while they reject Burke's prescription of "sullen resistance to innovation." Although this represents an accommodation by the classical liberal to the anti-utopian, I think it is a happy one. For it allows him to present his arguments as, in effect, reasons for avoiding further wrongs by the state, and for making piecemeal efforts to restore justice over the long haul. This means that the sincere beliefs of the classical liberal are in harmony with a sober and practical approach to political change. To put it another way, what the libertarian should ask for is the same as what he or she actually wants. The private individual owed $10,000 asks for the full sum, but may only demand staggered repayment on an installment plan; the wise respecter of the moral powers of individuals wouldn't want radical change in social arrangements overnight even if he could get them.

The classical liberal state is not utopian except in the sense that it urges (some of) us to change our opinions in dramatic fashion on moral grounds. It is no more utopian, in that sense, than contemporary calls to end factory farming or the calls for Rome to return to republican government in antiquity. In a way, this may seem disappointing to those (lonely few) who do think modern states are upside down in the sense that classical liberals suppose, for the view we have arrived at makes radical change imposed from on high difficult or impossible. But on reflection there is a deep inner consistency here. The central objection the New England libertarian has to the contents of the expansive welfare state is that it seeks to promote a vision of the good by means of force and threats rather than reason and persuasion. If reflection on utopianism leads us to conclude that we must wait on reason and persuasion to achieve justice, perhaps that should not come as a surprise, since this is merely to conclude that the contents and the method of achieving justice both must place reason and persuasion at their center.

Utilitarianism as Self-Deception

There are many people who call themselves utilitarians, and yet few of them exhibit much utilitarianism. In the main text I argue that this cannot be explained as a simple human failing; the lack of revisionist utilitarianism on display cannot be explained in the same way as the lack of weight loss among those on a diet. We should expect many books urging us to steal from our friends and neighbors and giving that money to charity; we should expect revisionist utilitarians teaching their children to do a lot of lying and cheating for the greater good.

Revisionist utilitarians can reply that it turns out that observing standard moral prohibitions on harm, theft, lying, etc. almost always *are* what promotes the greater good. But revisionist utilitarians are the ones who do not think that utilitarianism is self-effacing, that it collapses into common sense morality in practice. They do not, for example, claim that we should follow only those general rules that promote the greater good, and then argue that such rules must be relatively conservative. Revisionist utilitarians think that morality often dictates taking radical action, for example by becoming vegetarian. Given that, it is suspicious that utilitarians exhibit so little utilitarianism in practice when it comes to violating conventional moral constraints, or in their writings, or in their advice to their children. In the main text I suggest that this is because their doctrine is in some sense unlivable. But how could intelligent people avow a doctrine that turns out to be unlivable? Wouldn't they have noticed?

Self-deception about what we really believe, however, is surprisingly common. Atheists often make this point about theists, claiming for instance that the theist's beliefs have a strange, anomalous character that casts doubt on their status as genuine, full-fledged belief-states.[1] Those beliefs often don't respond to evidence in the way that other beliefs do, it is said, and they often don't have the influence over us that we would expect—as when those around us die, and the theist doesn't have the elated or horrified response he should according to the content of his beliefs about what comes next. Turning to another case, my undergraduates all tell me that they think morality is "subjective" and/or "relative," but when we discuss gay rights or female genital mutilation it turns out they believe no such thing. Other students report to me that they are adherents to various Eastern mystical traditions, or are Buddhists, or many other things they turn out not to be, even when the facts that exclude genuine adherence to these doctrines are readily available to them. (They are not simply confused about what Buddhism *is*.)

A diagnosis of these cases is as follows: we see that some consideration supports a certain belief, but fail to observe that, nevertheless, we haven't actually formed that belief, perhaps because of some countervailing consideration we don't focus on. For example, we notice that there is a great deal of disagreement about morality, and we feel that this cannot be explained unless morality is in some sense "subjective." This leads us to conclude not only that morality is subjective, but that we now *believe* it is. Meanwhile, we have overlooked that this would imply a number of things that we cannot accept, which blocks our supposed belief-state from functioning like one. This manifests itself, for instance, in our refusing to assume the subjectivity of morality for purposes of further reasoning or action. Hence the puzzling phenomenon of people confidently declaring that they think morality is subjective, while implying the opposite in their conversation and behavior. Essentially, we feel intense pressure to draw some inference, and this leads us to insist we actually *have* made that inference, even when we have not.

Revisionist utilitarians, runs the hypothesis, are involved in a similar misunderstanding. Impressed by the powerful arguments for utilitarianism ("How can it be wrong to pick the better of two outcomes instead of the worse?"), they avow a doctrine which they are not really prepared to integrate in their mental and practical lives. At some level, utilitarians simply are not prepared to jail the innocent or steal from their friends when doing so promotes the greater good, or to advocate this as an ideal, and so the official belief is left dangling like a cog that fails to connect with the rest of the machine.

There is no way to prove such a hypothesis true, but we can briefly compare the rival suggestions. Revisionist utilitarians claim that they do believe that, in theory, it would be okay to execute the innocent or steal from their children, but they almost universally insist that it just so happens that doing so would hardly ever promote the good. That is, despite emphasizing at great length how many lives could be saved with comparatively little money of ours, which in turn generates an enormous obligation for us to give, nevertheless these many lives are said not to generate permission to steal in any everyday circumstances. They don't even seem to give rise to an obligation to advocate stealing as an ideal to be imparted to our children. In favor of the utilitarian suggestion, there is the deference we should generally give to people's self-understanding—people are usually better positioned to know what they believe than we do, though there are exceptions, as we have seen. What favors the self-deception interpretation are chiefly (a) the suspicious reluctance of utilitarians to display much utilitarianism, especially when it comes to violating others (in ways that cannot be accounted for with a deontic threshold); (b) the refusal to embrace at least the corresponding *ideals* in writings or conversation; and (c) the asymmetry in treatment of common-sense moral options and moral constraints—it is suspicious that utilitarianism is said to apply in just the straightforward, obvious way one would expect when it conflicts only with our relatively modest beliefs about the option to favor ourselves, but mysteriously fails to conflict with the much more stringent beliefs we have about violating others.

In comparing these interpretations, it may help to consider a similar scenario involving a deluded classical liberal. Imagine encountering someone who insisted that he was a promarket libertarian, but who steadfastly refused to contemplate a smaller state with fewer wealth transfers. To be sure, he advocates lower tax rates and fewer tariffs, and eagerly presses theoretical concepts like individual rights. But whenever it comes to seriously considering classical liberal proposals like resisting egalitarian wealth transfers or devolved governance, he constructs elaborate reasons why these must be rejected. Redistributive schemes must stay in place because of complicated facts about how those specific policies would interact with people's rights; devolved governance is impossible because this somehow presents a threat to liberty. We might accept a couple of these dodges. But after a while, such a classical liberal would invite a diagnosis of partial self-deception. He would seem to us like the enthusiastic naïf proclaiming himself a Buddhist. We should consider whether something similar doesn't apply to revisionist utilitarians.

Victim-Blaming and Moral Modus Tollens

It is obvious that moral judgments are influenced by causal judgments, but the reverse is true as well: moral judgments inform views of causation, especially when conceptualized in terms of *the* or *a* specific cause of an event.[1] If we ask what caused someone to be robbed in the park, we are likely to cite the fact that the perpetrator decided to rob the victim, not that the victim decided to take a walk in the park. Even though both are necessary conditions for the chain of events that ensued, our moral evaluation leads us to focus on the morally salient fact of deciding to rob, not the nonsalient fact that the victim took a walk. This, of course, isn't surprising. We think of striking the match as the cause of its catching fire and not the presence of oxygen, since singular causal judgments serve in part to flag salient or counter-normative conditions. What we regard as normal tends to be relegated to the status of background conditions. Slight variations in moral narratives bring this out, as when we ask whether *leaving the door to the museum ajar* was a cause of the robbery. If the last person out was a visiting grandmother who had no idea she should close the door, and if a security guard was tasked with checking the door but didn't, we are less likely to attribute the robbery to the grandmother than to the guard. An insurance report is likely to cite him, possibly even as *the* cause. The difference in moral status affects our willingness to attribute the outcome to the agent.

Because moral judgments influence causal judgments, we can use causal judgments to infer people's moral beliefs. If we were confused, we could infer from people's responses to the grandmother vs. the security guard what people's attitudes were toward the responsibilities of each party. More interesting are cases in which moral attitudes shift. It is no longer acceptable in liberal societies to attribute a rape victim's attack to her being intoxicated, even if this turns out to have been a necessary condition of the events that ensued. This, we may infer, is because for independent moral reasons we deem the assailant's behavior (horrifically) counter-normative in a way that the victim's behavior was not, similar to the park case. Members of illiberal societies, present or past, take different views of the causal structure of the events because they have different (and we believe mistaken) moral views of how people ought to act.

One way of capturing this phenomenon is in terms of *moral modus tollens*:

1. If S caused Y, then S would be blameworthy or bad.
2. S isn't blameworthy or bad.
3. Therefore, S did not cause Y.

Usually, our judgments in these matters are intuitive and automatic, but this schema represents the implicit reasoning in such cases, and on occasion we do more or less consciously employ something like this. Thus, the robbery victim is certainly not blameworthy, and so we infer he must not have helped cause the attack, even if his actions were necessary conditions for (but-for causes of) what ensued. More worryingly, this schema can serve as a pattern for self-deception or denial, as when we reason (if only implicitly) that we did not cause our divorce, despite the endless hours in the office, since we are confident that we are not a bad person or to blame. It is easy to think of similar examples involving our relationships with friends, children, or parents.

Moral modus tollens can be employed to avoid *praise* as well as blame.

1. If S caused Y, then S would be praiseworthy or good.
2. S isn't praiseworthy or good.
3. Therefore, S did not cause Y.

An interesting feature of successful nonviolent protest is that it usually requires strong moral norms on the part of the oppressors. For if these are more powerful in material assets—which is generally why nonviolent protest is called for in the first place—then their ultimate reason for not employing those assets is broadly moral. Nonviolent protest against the Assyrian overlord Sennacherib would probably not have been effective, since the Assyrians lacked the moral sensibilities required to make such a protest succeed—presumably, a community issuing such a protest would simply have been butchered all the more easily. A positive example is the British colonial occupation of India. Nonviolent protest could only work because the British were ultimately unwilling to use sustained military force to keep up the occupation in the manner of Sennacherib. This is easy to overlook in light of British brutalities such as the massacre of Amritsar. But although horrific, these massacres weren't on the scale required to enforce the occupation. (Those resisting the rule of Sennacherib were skinned alive.) But despite this, we recognize the British colonial enterprise as morally repugnant on the whole by enlightened liberal standards, and so by moral modus tollens, we attribute the end of the occupation to the efforts of Gandhi and others, and not (even in part) to the moral code of the British, even though this played a crucial role from a dispassionate historical perspective.

Consider now how we treat causal attribution when it comes to distributive justice and poverty. One process that is at work, I conjecture, is that saying someone worse off was capable of exercising agency in a way that would have improved his condition seems to imply that he is culpable in a way that we independently want to deny, which in turn leads us to reject that agency. In other words, the following reasoning is (implicitly) in play:

1. If someone's (in)actions caused him to be worse off, then he would be blameworthy or at least less worthy of sympathy.

2. The worse off aren't blameworthy and merit great sympathy.
   Subassumption: it's wrong to blame the victim.
3. Therefore, the (in)actions of the worse off are not (even in part) a cause of their condition.

More generally, moral modus tollens will lead us to want to rule out factors internal to the agent's will when making sense of social outcomes since doing so allows us to maintain the moral judgment implied by premise 2.

What lies behind premise 2? I believe that it is in part our reluctance to "blame the victim." The worse off are often downtrodden, marginalized, and in other ways suffer deprivation. There are poor but contented surfers, or cheerful members of religious communities that aren't rich, but these aren't the standard cases, and in any event not the cases that inform our judgments. This naturally leads us to see them as victims in the sense of suffering harms we would not want to suffer, harms that elicit our sympathy. And that in turn makes us reluctant to issue judgments that would tend to imply blame or raise questions about the worthiness of sympathy for the people involved. Something terrible has happened to them as it is; saying anything tending to imply blame seems both wrongheaded, since we find it hard to understand why people would fail to remedy their situation were it in their power (despite knowing that we ourselves constantly fail to do so), and cruel, as if piling on. And given premise 2, we then are reluctant to accept anything like the evidence mentioned in chapter 9, to the effect that in most rich countries most of the time poverty isn't due to choice-defeating incapacity.

It is worth stressing how damaging moral modus tollens can be in this respect. Almost any attempt to attribute poor social outcomes to endogenous factors will tend to evoke a sense of blaming the victim, which in turn activates moral modus tollens. To some extent this is healthy, since it spurs us to look for exogenous factors, like oppressors keeping people down, and there are such oppressors. But many social outcomes are a complicated mix of the internal and external, with the external forming a convenient, easy-to-scorn enemy. If there are endogenous factors at work, moral modus tollens makes these harder to identify and discuss. If a community in Appalachia is struggling in part because of oppressive coal companies, but also partly because families insufficiently attend to the liberating possibilities of education, it will be disastrous if the latter are taken off the table as a target for improvement. Our understanding of colonialism is impoverished if we are not allowed to invoke the positive moral qualities of an empire to explain the success of nonviolent protest; our understanding of bad social outcomes is impoverished when we neglect endogenous factors.

I conclude with a more general observation about ideology and causal explanations. It is striking that those on the political left and right lean toward different styles of causal explanation for poor social outcomes, with the left usually preferring exogenous and the right endogenous explanations. (Roughly: "Social conditions and the environment are to blame" vs. "He didn't exercise personal responsibility.") In a typical case, the right will blame a troubled school system on internal cultural factors like attitudes toward schooling or individual responsibility, while the Left will tend to attribute the poor outcome to inadequate institutions and insufficient funding. In fact, for the perfect ideologue, there is no such thing as an endogenous (or exogenous) outcome; it's their preferred style of causal reasoning everywhere, all the time.

Matters are further complicated by fact that the relevant causes are what John Mackie called INUS conditions—complex sets composed of factors that are individually Insufficient but Necessary conditions, while the set as a whole is Unnecessary but Sufficient for the effect.[2] (Striking the glass with a hammer isn't by itself sufficient to cause the glass to shatter, since the glass must be cool enough to break and not flex (etc.), and the whole complex is unnecessary since there are other conditions that could lead to the shattering of the glass.) This means that each side in an ideologically charged dispute can *correctly* claim that the things they emphasize could solve the relevant social problem, since INUS conditions are sufficient, and that individual suggestions (e.g., more funding) are in a way *required* to solve the problem. Moreover, they can usually claim that specific suggestions of their opponents are at present inadequate, since many of the other conditions constituting the opponents' full INUS condition will be as yet absent. This produces a dynamic in which both left and right seem naive to each other ("We aren't going back to the 1950s!" vs. "Just throwing more money at the problem won't solve it!"). Further consideration of the role of preferred causal explanations and patterns of inference like moral modus tollens could help us arrive at a deeper understanding of ideological disputes in general.

◼ NOTES

◼ Chapter 1

1. See, e.g., Wright et al. 1992; Cohen 1978 and 1988; and Elster 1985.

2. For an overview of classical liberalism and its intellectual history, see Tomasi 2012, esp. chs. 1–2.

3. Emerson 2000, 133; Thoreau 1997, 112–114, 13; Cp. Emerson 2000, 386

4. Thoreau 1997, 1–73

5. Stanton 1997, 85

6. Thoreau 1997, 300. I abstract from the fact that his stay at Walden was a short-lived publicity stunt.

7. I am grateful to Kevin Vallier for discussion of this and many other points throughout the book.

◼ Chapter 2

1. Jaspers 1953, 1–21

2. Thucydides's Melian dialogue is often read as advancing a brutal realpolitik (the moralizers end up dead, their children enslaved) (1993, 103), but the fact that the poles of debate were articulated so clearly suggests a wide-ranging debate underway. Qian 1995, 80–81.

3. Roth 1995, 17; see also Foster 2005, 128.

4. See, e.g., Portmore 2011, ch. 4.

5. Bentham 1988, 259; Sidgwick 1966, 450–451, 474–475

6. James 2000, 24

7. Nozick 1974, 30–33

8. This may call to mind Rawls's "overlapping consensus" (1993, 11–15, 133–172). But my goal is in part to show that various political institutions are precisely not "free-standing," and do depend on various moral truths—they just happen to be widely shared.

9. As suggested by his views toward famine relief and the moral status of disabled infants, for example. See, e.g., Singer 1994, 130.

10. Scheffler 1994 14–40; Kagan 1991, 1–10

11. Rawls 1971, 26. In this and other references to Rawls's earlier work I am referring to the ideas as presented in that work, not subsequent revisions and reinterpretations. My interest lies in the ideas as presented at the time, not in biography or intellectual history.

12. Singer 2006

13. For an unusually candid appreciation of tensions between common-sense morality and the political liberalism exhibited in the welfare state, see Scheffler 2001, 12–31.

14. Heath 2014, 162

15. See Rawls 1971, 7–8. For more discussion, see Cohen 2008, ch. 3.

16. This is how Nozick (1974, 204–206) interprets Rawls.

17. Cp. Heath 2014, 146

18. The view I sketch here is inspired by McMahan 2009, criticizing the type of just war theory espoused by Walzer 1977.

■ Chapter 3

1. See Vallentyne and Steiner 2001, esp. Brody's "Redistribution without Egalitarianism," and Otsuka's "Self-Ownership and Equality: A Lockean Reconciliation," and Cohen 1995, chs. 3–4.

2. Arneson 2011; Nagel 1975, 141–142

3. Cp. Mack 2006

4. 1974, 30n

5. Cp. Thomson 1990, 149–175

6. Cp. Kagan 1998, 78–93

7. For gory details I blithely ignore, see Temkin 2012, esp. ch. 2 and pp. 101–108.

8. Slote 1984

9. Arneson 2011, 29; emphasis added. Arneson congratulates Nozick on achieving a "transcendental deduction of a non-fact" in his discussion of individual rights (p. 28).

10. See McDowell 1978.

11. For similar cases and further discussion, see Feinberg 1978, esp. pp. 102–103, and Mack 2006.

12. See Dancy 1993, ch. 4 for further discussion.

13. 109 Minn. 456, 124 N.W. 221 (1910). For philosophical analysis of this case and themes germane to this chapter, see Hampton 2006, 113–115, and Coleman 1992, ch. 18. The history and law behind the case is fascinating in its own right. See Sugarman 2003.

14. Boorse and Sorensen 1988

15. See, e.g., Newhouse 1996 and Baicker et al. 2013. There is, to be fair, debate about the interpretation of these results.

16. Sanger-Katz 2014; Mitchell et al. 2012

17. For an overview, see the works collected in DePaul and Ramsey 1998, and Booth and Rowbottom 2014.

18. Cp. Cappelen 2012, 148–163

■ Chapter 4

1. Proudhon 2011, 91; Rousseau 1983, 140

2. For an overview of some of the problems, see Lomasky 1987, 113–119. My account is Lockean in spirit, but I don't intend any contribution to the study of John Locke. For Locke's actual views, see Waldron 1988, ch. 6; Simmons 1992, chs. 1–2; and Sreenivasan 1995, chs. 1–3. Simmons notes that Locke wasn't just offering a conservative defense of the status quo; his arguments called into question, e.g., the possessions of the idle aristocracy (2001, 205).

3. See Honoré 1961 for the classic discussion of extensional issues, albeit narrowly focused on the law. For further discussion of the "sticks" in the legal "bundle" approach to property, see Epstein 2011.

4. Gibbard 1976. See also Lomasky 1987, 116–119.

5. Waldron 1988, 266–271

6. Locke 1980, 19

7. Nozick 1974, 174–175

8. A distinction still not sufficiently attended to. See Munzer 1990, ch. 10 for an appeal to desert, and Christman 1994, ch. 5 for an attack on private property predicated on desert.

9. See, e.g., Cohen 1995, ch. 12, and Christman 1994, pp. 56–61.

10. Locke 1979, 2.27. Locke was really concerned with sameness of consciousness, but I adopt the usual oversimplification.

11. Cp. Parfit 1984, 205

12. Murray Rothbard points to the broader category of *use*, but this still excludes many morally relevant categories (2009, 169–175).

13. For a much deeper discussion of the economic significance of discovery, and its application to the marketplace, see Kirzner 1989.

14. Russell 2004 offers a subtle reading of Locke that emphasizes the directive quality of labor that turns a potential resource into a resource, without requiring effort per se.

15. Locke 1980, 20–21, 28–30. Locke's "enough" is frequently misquoted as "as much" by writers, myself included, alas.

16. This is a standard assumption of many theories of property that stress the plurality of motivations for recognizing private property, such as Munzer 1990. Munzer, however, is somewhat nuanced in treating the contribution of utilitarian inputs to property (pp. 224–226).

17. Aquinas 1948, Bk. II, Pt. II, Q66, A7; Nozick 1974, 180. It's a little unclear whether Nozick means that we lose ownership or only the right to charge whatever we want for the water.

18. This bypasses worries like those in Waldron 1988, 260–262 and Sreenivasan 1995, 106–111.

19. Cp. Simmons 2001, 214

20. Hume 1978, 491. For commentary, see Mackie 1980, 82–96.

21. See, e.g., Buchanan 1975, 24–25 and Friedman 2000, 47–56.

22. Jeremy Waldron suggests that this makes his theory "bottom-up" rather than statist or "top-down" (2013, 8), but this seems to me dubious. As long as my property-conferring actions with respect to an asset can be nullified by changes in convention, things don't look very "bottom-up," at least not if morality is at the "bottom."

23. See Gauthier 1986, esp. ch. 10, for more on Hume's conventionalism, and for Gauthier's own distinctive contractualist view of how norms emerge. For an attempt to find an intermediate view of property as partly social but limited by our moral natures, see Lomasky 1987, 120–124.

24. See Simmons 1992, 90ff., for a deeper discussion of "natural" in this context.

25. Hume somewhat inconsistently declares the state of nature to be both a philosophical fiction and short-lived (1978, 493).

26. For an example, see Eldeib 2016.

▪ Chapter 5

1. Rawls 1971, 15. Again, our interest lies in the ideas as expressed (here, in the early Rawls), not in intellectual biography.

2. Cp. Rawls 1971, 273–274

3. Murphy and Nagel 2002, 32–33. For a similar point, see Holmes and Sunstein 1999, 43–44, 61, noting that even negative rights are expensive to monitor, enforce, and remedy.

4. See Gaus 2010 for a different but complementary view, according to which justifying social institutions even within something like Rawls's framework will require respecting those who oppose the high levels of coercion introduced by socialist taxation.

5. Rawls 1971, 61

6. Rawls 1971, 101

7. http://www.cbsnews.com/news/elizabeth-warren-there-is-nobody-in-this-country-who-got-rich-on-his-own/.

8. Smith 1994, 745. For more recent discussion, including implications for libertarianism, see Morris 1998, 273–284.

9. Cp. Huemer 2013, 22–24

10. Cp. Jan Narveson's distinct reflections on insurance systems favored by large majorities (2001, 245–257).

11. Insurance arguments are sometimes used as purely formal models to determine the *content* of egalitarian principles, without attempting to supply any justification for adopting such principles in the first place, since they don't explain why the state would be authorized to charge us for the insurance. See Dworkin 2002, ch. 2 for an example.

12. Cohen 1995, 185

13. See Gibbard 1976. It's a little unclear whether Gibbard is writing in his own voice or merely exploring the consequences of what he calls a "hard libertarian" position about rights.

▪ Chapter 6

1. Locke 1980, 20–21

2. Locke 1980, 29 and 26–27

3. Nozick 1974, 174, 180, 181, 179

4. 1995, 72–90, 173–188

5. 2003, 20. See Brody 2001 for a similar approach.

6. http://data.worldbank.org/indicator/NV.SRV.TETC.ZS. For discussion of the general concept of economic sectors, the history of such classifications, and modern debate, see Kenessey 1987. Some would further subdivide *services* into additional categories, but I set aside such complications here.

7. To get a sense of what "services" means for econometricians, consult the United Nations classification of economic activities, the so-called ISIC. The service divisions are 50–99. See https://unstats.un.org/unsd/cr/registry/regcst.asp?Cl=27.

8. See Caselli and Coleman 2001 for tables and narrative covering the last century or so.

9. See, e.g., the US case, http://www.bls.gov/emp/ep_table_201.htm.

10. http://www.eia.gov/cfapps/ipdbproject/IEDIndex3.cfm?tid=5&pid=57&aid=6. I conservatively assume a price of oil around $100/barrel.

11. Very roughly, $15 trillion at the lower bound. See the Federal Reserve statistical report, http://www.federalreserve.gov/releases/z1/Current/z1.pdf. I follow the procedure described by Matthew Yglesias for deriving the number cited, http://www.slate.com/blogs/moneybox/2013/12/20/value_of_all_land_in_the_united_states.html. For an estimate of $23 trillion, see Larson 2015.

12. Piketty 2014, 165

13. Thomas Piketty points out that the rise of wealth inequality in the United States is due mostly to "supermanagers," i.e., the working rich (2014, 302).

14. Buera and Kaboski 2012

15. Cohen 1995, 72

16. David Schmidtz: "Original acquisition (and its justification) remains a contemporary issue. Indeed, it is more important than ever since the property being discovered (or created) is more valuable than land ever was" (Schmidtz and Goodin 1998, 28). For a challenge to Lockean theories of strong intellectual property rights, based on the idea of an intellectual commons, see Shiffrin 2007.

17. Brody 2001, 43. Despite my gloss, Brody thinks of this as a *non*-egalitarian justification of redistribution, insofar as it ostensibly draws on a compensatory rationale not directly related to egalitarian concerns.

18. 1995, 45–49

19. Schmidtz and Goodin 1998, 29–33

20. Nozick 1974, 160–164

21. Piketty 2014, 277, 405

22. Rognlie 2015 claims that housing explains the entirety of the increase in capital's share of aggregate income that Piketty and others have written about. Even this increase is a bit confusing—it involves esoteric accounting concepts like imputed, nonactual rent that homeowners pay themselves.

23. George 2008, 403–407; Orszag 2015

24. Another approach I set aside for the sake of space is to treat jobs themselves as a form of natural resource to be equalized. See Van Parijs 1995 and Moller 2017 for a response.

25. See Kenessey 1987 for discussion of classificatory schemes of wealth production, and the possible emergence of quaternary and quinary sectors.

■ Chapter 7

1. Thoreau 1997, 69

2. See Moller 2009 and 2006, and Valentini 2011 for some criticism.

3. E.g., Singer 2015 and Cullity 2004, though note pp. 37–53.

4. 2006, 4

5. For discussion, see Sachs 2006 and Easterly 2002. For criticism of international aid approaches to Africa, see Moyo 2009.

6. Donadio 2012. For recent empirical work on culture and economic growth, see Guiso, Sapienza, and Zingales 2006.

7. A leading theme in that great study of institutional malaise, the television show *The Wire*.

8. See, e.g., Shi 2016.

9. 2009, 137

10. For an overview, see Wilde 1998, and Houston and Richardson 2007.

11. Murray 2012, 293–295

12. Lichtenberg 2014, 23, 24

13. Lichtenberg 2014, 26

14. I am offering a very loose gloss on Kant, 1964, 89 (Academy ed. p. 421). Others will of course choose to use these terms slightly differently.

15. Wong 2013

16. Buchanan 1987, 570. In fact, this is only one interpretation of those arguments that Buchanan offers; I set aside the other here.

17. See Feinberg 1984 for a classic discussion of issues of enforcement from a Millian harm-based perspective. Non-physical harms to friends or lovers pose a challenge to such a view.

18. See May and Hoffman 1991 for work on collective responsibility. See Beerbohm 2014, 176 for discussion of the importance of a guarantee.

19. Nagel 1975, 145

20. See Cohen 2000, 168–177 for discussion of some of these distinctions.

21. Narveson 2001, 248–251

22. Murphy 1993

■ Chapter 8

1. These include Montesquieu, Hume, Mill, and of course Adam Smith himself. More recently there are such works as Brennan and Jaworski 2016; Heath 2014; Tomasi 2012; and Schmidtz and Goodin 1998.

2. The *Phaedrus*, with its Egyptian references, would have made an apt occasion for such an acknowledgment, except for the dim view of writing it expresses.

3. Walzer 1983, 107; Anderson 1993, ch. 7; Satz 2010; Sandel 2012

4. See Hayek 1945, further developed in his 1988, esp. chs. 5 and 6.

5. As Brennan 2014 points out, these kinds of considerations would make markets vital even in a utopia devoid of scarcity. For a broader overview, see Friedman and Friedman 1980.

6. Gibbard 1985, 24–25

7. See, e.g., Kreps 2012 for more.

8. See Gibbard 1985, Sen 1985, and Varian 1975 on the philosophical relevance (and irrelevance) of these theorems.

9. Waldfogel 1993

10. For a classic compendium of these skeptical themes, see Kuttner 1999.

11. Lipsey and Lancaster 1956. For discussion, see Heath 2014, 175–181 and 2009, ch. 3.

12. 1993, 172

13. 2012, 112, 114

14. Satz 2010, 110

15. Marx 1976, 353–367

16. 1983, 22; the point below is on p. 122.

17. See Becker and Murphy 1988 and Elster and Skog 1999, esp. ch. 9.

18. See, e.g., *The Economist* 2013.

19. See Anderson 1993, 165 and throughout.

20. Dawson and Seater 2013, 168. For a finding that regulation has little impact on entrepreneurial dynamism on the other hand, see Goldschlag and Tabarrok 2014.

21. Kant 1964, 430

22. I thus agree with Brennan and Jaworski (2016, 183–194) that there is nothing intrinsically wrong about selling votes insofar as we can dream up scenarios in which doing so would be permissible, but I want to insist that it is rational of majorities to ban it all the same. We should not put votes up for sale.

■ Chapter 9

1. Temkin 1993, 13

2. Nozick 1974, 224

3. Samuel Scheffler: "Many discussions of luck egalitarianism are primarily directed to other egalitarians" (2003, 13). Works like Temkin 1993; Roemer 1998; Dworkin 2000; Arneson 2004; and Cohen 2011 tend to take this approach. It is worth noting that even critics of luck egalitarianism have by and large tackled the question from the left, e.g., Anderson 1999 and Hurley 2003, and thus passed over many of the issues I go on to raise.

4. In the language of Dworkin 2000.

5. Cp. Rawls 1971, 102

6. Cp. Chua 2011

7. For thoughtful criticism of this view, see Brighouse and Swift 2014, 127–132.

8. Corak 2016, 11

9. D'Addio 2007, 38. For more recent work using other data, see Chetty, Hendren, Kline, and Saez 2014 and Chetty, Hendren, Kline, Saez, and Turner 2014.

10. For some preliminary doubts, see Solon 2015 and Vosters 2016.

11. Clark 2014, 83

12. I cannot here do justice to Clark's methods, or answer obvious concerns about, e.g., non-Normans adopting Norman surnames, or maintaining status through the halo effect of the name itself, though Clark discusses these issues at length.

13. Clark 2014, 58

14. Clark 2014, 38

15. Clark 2014, 97

16. Clark 2014, 125

17. Clark 2014, 274

18. That self-conception "doesn't entirely square with the facts," as Haskins, Isaacs, and Sawhill put it delicately, 2008, 4.

19. I adapt the example from Nelkin 2005.

20. Roemer 1998, 34

21. Haskins and Sawhill 2009, 71. The data source is US Census Bureau, *Current Population Survey, Annual Demographic Supplement* (2008), table Pov 06.

22. Haskins and Sawhill 2009, 93. The American Census Bureau reports a 2.4% poverty rate for those working full time in 2015 (Proctor, Semega, and Kollar 2016, 16).

23. The average salary for janitors and hairdressers was in the mid-$20,000s in the past few years, according to *US News and World Report*. http://money.usnews.com/careers/best-jobs/janitor/salary. Glassdoor.com gives the salary for FedEx delivery drivers as just under $40,000 (as of July 17, 2017).

24. See Frankfurt 1988; Crisp 2003; and Temkin 2003.

25. According to the National Center for Education Statistics, the United States spends nearly 30% more per pupil than the OECD average. http://nces.ed.gov/programs/coe/indicator_cmd.asp. The Washington DC, public school system—not famed for the quality of its schools—spends significantly more than the national average per pupil, and vastly more than the OECD average. For more on this theme, see Mayer 1997 and Dahl and Lochner 2012.

■ Chapter 10

1. For an overview of philosophical theories of happiness, see Haybron 2008, part II.

2. See, e.g., Feldman 2010, 169–173.

3. For a defense of empirical happiness research addressing issues of reliability and validity by leading practitioners, see Diener 2009, ch. 6. For a more skeptical view, see Feldman 2010, ch. 12.

4. The original paper was Easterlin 1974. For a more recent overview, see Easterlin 1995 and Weimann, Knabe, and Schöb 2015, ch. 3.

5. Scitovsky 1992, 135

6. Maddison Project 2013

7. See Scitovsky 1992, 135–145, and the discussion of the hedonic treadmill below. Sometimes diminishing marginal utility is added to the list. But we can just restate the puzzle: how come the utility of money diminishes across countries (or across time) but not, or not as much, across income brackets within countries? Or again, how come America's going from the salary of today's day laborer to today's average desk-worker didn't have the same effect as an individual getting a raise of the same amount?

8. The quotation is from what is perhaps the most impressive work on behalf of the skeptics: Stevenson and Wolfers 2008, 1. Easterlin replies in Easterlin and Angelescu 2010. For a more detailed review of the economic literature, see Frey and Stutzer 2002, ch. 4.

9. Flanagan 2007, 153

10. Bhutan has seriously pursued the notion of measuring gross national happiness, with the aid of international professionals, novel survey instruments, and government working groups.

11. Layard 2005, 171

12. Among the more interesting is Scitovsky 1992. See also Gilbert 2006, 217–220.

13. CDC National Vital Statistics Reports, vol. 54, n. 14

14. Ubel et al. 2005, S60

15. Smith et al. 2006

16. Smith et al. 2006

17. Nord, Daniels, and Hamlet 2009, S10; Drummond 2009, S32

18. For reviews, see Lucas 2007 and Diener 2006.

19. For an accessible overview of this point, see Gilbert 2006, ch. 9. On the next point, see Kahneman and Schkade 98.

20. Ubel et al. 2005, S61

21. For an introduction to the theory and measurement of QALYs and similar measurements, see Brazier 2007.

22. See Frankfurt 1999, 166 and 169

23. McMahan 2005. McMahan's discussion is in several ways cognate with mine, though his target concerns parents bringing disabled children into existence. I follow McMahan and before him communitarian writers in using the language of "particular attachments."

24. Cp. Brock 1995

25. See, respectively, Raz 1999, esp. 315–320; Scanlon 1998, ch. 3; and Wallace (contesting Raz's view in part), in his 2004.

26. E.g., Annas 1993, 223–329

▦ Chapter 11

1. Prediction markets represent another field of market epistemology. See, e.g., Sunstein 2011.

2. Cowen 2012 discusses food critic lore, including the advice that follows, and its relationship to incentive structures.

3. Hamermesh 2011, 47. The effect of height alone for males is estimated at several percentage points of annual wages per inch difference in adolescence, according

to Nicola Persico et al. 2004. See also Harold Kelley's classic 1950. A complication involves covariation. Persico et al. argue that the vehicle of the height premium is largely adolescent social activity, not employer bias; if so, it's not so much a height premium as an adolescent-social-activity premium, and it's at least slightly murkier whether *that* trait is irrelevant.

4. Espenshade and Radford 2009

5. To experience some of the terror, see Loftus 1996.

6. See Coady 1992, 172–173 for some thoughts on dealing with non-cohering testimonial evidence.

■ Chapter 12

1. I am thinking of both academics like Cohen 1978, 1995 and others cited below, and popular writers like Klein 2000, 2007.

2. Piketty 2014, 95

3. Data from Maddison Project 2013 (building on Maddison 2007). Maddison's work has been superseded at a level of detail that doesn't matter here; see Broadberry 2013 and Fouquet and Broadberry 2015. Other overviews look similar. See, e.g., Ian Morris's development index 14,000 B.C.– 2000 A.D. in his 2010, 166. Needless to say, the uncertainty in the distant past is great, and we should use these estimates only to formulate a general picture.

4. See van Bavel 2016 for detailed study of pre-modern economic "success" stories, though he ultimately finds a cyclical pattern of decay.

5. Clark 2007, 48–49 and Richard Steckel, "A History of the Standard of Living in the United States," on the Economic History Association website, at http://eh.net/encyclopedia/article/steckel.standard.living.us.

6. See Goklany, 2007, 103–234 for extensive analysis.

7. See Diamond 2011 for examples.

8. See, e.g., Nordhaus 2013.

9. McCloskey 2010, 72. Clark 2007 offers a detailed investigation of who reaped the gains of growth. Inventors and owners of capital as a group were surprisingly ineffective at capturing those gains.

10. See, e.g., Clark 2005, table A2, helper's real wage.

11. "The increase of revenue and stock is the increase of national wealth. The demand for those who live by wages, therefore, naturally increases with the increase of national wealth" (Smith 1994, 79). Even more remarkably, Smith goes on to take up the question of whether, as elites of his day claimed, these increased wages weren't a *bad* thing, since they caused the poor to take up "luxurious" living and to demand outrageous sums for their services; Smith makes a fervent case for welcoming higher wages for the poor as a happy consequence of growth.

12. Maddison Project 2013. The details are subject to dispute, since even past-population estimates vary widely for countries like China and India.

13. Landes 1999, xx

14. See, e.g., Caplan 2007, chs. 2–3; Easterbrook 2004, chs. 1–3.

15. See Mokyr 2009 for discussion, esp. pp. 279–308, 338–348, and 449–474. I am grateful to Mark Koyama for insights on this and many other topics.

16. See Miller 2010 and Pogge 2002, 2007, and 2010. For further proponents of (and dissenters to) Pogge's view, see Jaggar 2010 and Shue 1996. For criticisms of this strain of

thought with which I am in broad sympathy, see Risse 2005 and Cohen 2010. For an overview setting the stage for many of the relevant disputes, see Beitz 1979 and Rawls 1999, esp. pp. 115–120.

17. Miller 2010, 181; Pogge 2007, 30

18. Miller, 2010, 154, 78

19. Pogge 2002, 183–184; 2007, 30

20. See Pogge 2010, esp. 39–40.

21. See Acemoglu and Robinson 2012; McCloskey 2010; Comin, Easterly, and Gong 2010; Maddison 2007; Clark 2007.

22. See Pommeranz 2001 on China and Parthasarathi 2011 on India. Both argue that the science-technology differences have been exaggerated. Pommeranz proposes that the Americas were crucial to staving off ecological collapse in Europe, and this, along with poor coal reserves in southern China, is said to have led to the East-West divergence. Parthasarathi argues that divergence is explained by the response to different competitive and ecological pressures. He further tries to show that the British did indeed suppress Indian growth (pp. 125–131, 251–258). These works merit close study, but seem to me to imply a series of incredible coincidences.

23. Collier 2007, 157. Note that Collier does suggest changes to various rich-country policies (including advocating selective military intervention).

24. Rodrik 2007, 222

25. See Collier 2007, ch. 6.

26. A point developed in Reitberger 2008.

27. For more, see Bernstein 2004.

28. Landes 1999, 171. He quotes a contemporary Spanish source that is eerily prescient and unconsciously damning: "Let London manufacture those fabrics of hers. . . Holland her chambrays; Florence her cloth . . . all nations train journeymen for Madrid . . . all the world serves her and she serves nobody" (p. 172). The following quotations are from p. 173 and p. 429 respectively. It is worth comparing McCloskey's discussion in her 2010, ch. 21 ("by 1800 Spain was among the poorest countries in Europe," p. 181), and Ian Morris's account of where New World bullion wound up, tracing it from the conquistadors, to the Hapsburg rulers, to Italian merchants financing European wars, and ultimately to China, which mainly wanted silver in its trade with the European states (2010, 460–461).

29. For an overview, see Humphreys, Sachs, and Stiglitz 2007. For detailed discussion of the case of Spain, see Drelichman 2005. Collier 2007, ch. 3 emphasizes that it makes a world of difference whether the resources become available before or after efficient institutions have taken root.

30. See especially Wenar 2008, p. 9, following in the tracks of Thomas Pogge and others.

31. 1994, 666. Smith anticipates Dutch disease (1994, 548) and concludes the entire book by once again pleading with his countrymen to do away with the money-losing colonial project.

32. See Pogge 2002, 209, and Nagel 2008, 55.

■ Chapter 13

1. Selmrod and Bakija 2008, 117, 119

2. Selmrod and Bakija 2008, 118

3. Lindert 2004, 16–18. See esp. chs. 10 and 18.

4. See Acemoglu, Robinson, and Verdier 2017, for a version of this idea.

5. For more analysis, see McCloskey 2010, 444–445; for a theoretical model that explains how the taxation effect might be low at moderate absolute levels, but very high through nonlinear effects as taxes rise, see Jaimovich and Rebelo 2017.

6. Lindert 2004, 234–263

7. Lindert 2004, 259

8. Marx and Engels 1978, 490. Marx and Engels list 10 items, of which advanced countries routinely implement perhaps two to four items wholly or at least in part, and several of the rest are obscure or anachronistic, like harmonizing rural and urban workforces.

9. Data from Maddison Project 2013. The wild swings of World War II are hard to measure and interpret accurately.

10. Data from Maddison Project 2013.

11. Piketty 2014, 24

12. Piketty 2014, 244

13. Piketty 2014, 297

14. Cowen 2014

15. By contrast, see Marx 1976, 353–367.

16. Piketty 2014, 411–414

17. For the distinction between prioritizing the worse off and pure equality, see Parfit 1997. For discussion of whether mere equality is morally important, see Frankfurt 1988; Crisp 2003; and Temkin 2003.

18. Data from Officer and Williamson 2015, deflated using their consumer price index (wages: 1860 = 100; prices: 1983 = 100). Given the historical uncertainties attaching to inflation, only the general shape can be given much weight, but that is all that matters for our purposes.

19. Hirschl and Rank 2015, 6

20. Braudel 1992 III, 621

21. Braudel 1992 II, 466

22. Braudel 1992 III, 629, 29, 66, 295

23. Braudel 1992 III, 625

24. Braudel 1992 III, 623–624

25. Ferguson 2008, 82–86. The same author opines elsewhere that France's loss of European primacy in the 19th century (which Braudel laments as its "backwater" status) came about because it consistently put equality above liberty, that "In sum, they chose Rousseau over Locke" (Ferguson 2011, 154).

26. Mueller 2003, 472–500

27. For more on universal histories, see Fukuyama 1992, 55–70.

28. Kant 1983, 17 (Academy pagination)

29. Smith 1994, 485

30. Kant 1983, 18, 22

31. Kant 1983, 21

32. Kant 1983, 27–28

33. Quoted in Ferguson 2011, 48

34. Braudel 1992 III, 121

35. Foster and Kaplan 2001, 11

36. I borrow Deirdre McCloskey's phrase "bourgeois virtues" and the positive connotations thereof, but not, on this occasion, her emphasis on the non-prudential virtues (like faith and love). See, e.g., McCloskey 2006, 126–138. The prudential bourgeois virtues listed above actually strike me as more distinctive of successful capitalist societies than the seven canonical virtues, which were after all identified and prized by notably *unsuccessful* medieval societies. For an interesting discussion of dissenting views, see Braudel 1992 II, 580, who cites Benjamin Franklin–style lists and apothegms from antiquity. These dissenters seem to confuse necessary and sufficient conditions for success.

37. Jansen 2000, 462

■ Chapter 14

1. Swift 1973, 207

2. Braudel 1992 III, 218; Bown 2009, 9–56; on the drug foods, see the classic Mintz 1985.

3. De Las Casas 1992

4. Stedman 1988, 168

5. Hochschild 1999, 165

6. Braudel 1992 I, 457

7. Sparks 2014, 122–132; Heywood and Thornton 2007, 109–168; Thornton 1999, 127–147; Thornton 1992, 98–125

8. Johnson 2013, 151–175

9. Coates 2014; Hirsch 1983, 1–39

10. Figures from 2013 (latest available) Census Bureau, the World Bank, and Pew Research. See https://www.census.gov/content/dam/Census/library/publications/2014/demo/p60-249.pdf, http://data.worldbank.org/indicator/NY.GDP.PCAP.CD, and http://www.pewresearch.org/fact-tank/2014/12/12/racial-wealth-gaps-great-recession/.

11. For an overview of some precedents and legal arguments, see Posner and Vermeule 2003 and Ogletree 2003.

12. Nozick 1974, 152–153

13. Morris 1984

14. Boxhill 2003, 74. For a similar suggestion and additional discussion, see Sher 2005.

15. 2003, 76

16. 2003, 77

17. *Vineberg v. Bissonnette*, 529 F.Supp.2d 300 (2007), 5

18. Turner 1999

19. I owe this point to Christian Tarsney.

20. Bleakley and Ferrie 2013

21. Morris and van Hagen 2011, 22–40; Davies 1987, 38–68 ("After each of these wars, the victorious Mexicas unfailingly purloined large tracts of lands," p. 40).

22. MacQuarrie 2007, 40

23. Waldron 1992, 21

24. Speech to parliament, September 27, 1951. http://www.konrad-adenauer.de/dokumente/erklarungen/regierungserklarung9.

25. Satz 2012, 130

26. *National Interest*, April 7, 2015, http://www.nationalinterest.org/blog/the-buzz/will-israels-new-advanced-submarines-carry-nuclear-weapons-12567

27. Speech to parliament May 4, 1953, http://www.konrad-adenauer.de/dokumente/erklarungen/erklarung-abkommen-israel?highlight=luxemburg%20israel.

28. Williams 1944; Baptist 2014; Beckert 2015

29. For data on production and price histories, see Ferleger 1990, 356–357; Watkins 1908, 21–35; and Beckert 2015, ch. 5. For GDP data see Baptist 2014, 321.

30. McCloskey 2010, 232. For a more detailed accounting, see O'Brien 1982 and 1988. For a more mixed assessment taking into account both private and public investment, see Offer 1993.

31. Braudel 1992 III, 266

32. Buruma 2001, 195–208

33. See, e.g., Nietzsche 1989, 33–56.

34. Braudel 1992 III, 435–436; Ferguson 2011, 130

35. Levathes 1994, 37–38; Heuman and Burnard 2012, 57

36. Thornton 1999, 129

37. Thomas 1993, 25; Diaz 2012, 414 ("they ate the flesh with *chilmole*")

38. Davis 2003, 23

39. De Greiff 2006, parts II and III

40. Sunstein summarizes some of the relevant studies (2005, 538).

■ Chapter 15

1. Earlier philosophical debates illustrate this. See, e.g., Friedman and Narveson 1995.

2. For a summary and discussion, see Gendler 2011, 48–51. See also research on the possible impact of emphasizing native talent or brilliance (Leslie et al. 2015).

3. 1994, 430

4. 1994, 436, italics omitted

5. *Die Welt* 1995

6. For various doubts about political correctness, see Feldstein 1997; Wilson 1995; and Fish 1994. These authors are generally responding to culture-war polemics from the right (e.g., Feldstein 1997, 116–120; Wilson 1995, 10–15; Fish 1994, 53–79), not careful analysis such as Loury's, and so their doubts should perhaps be taken in that light.

7. 1998, 81–82

8. See Waldron 2012 for an argument that the state should in fact pursue heavy-handed tactics like hate-speech laws in pursuit of the sort of legitimate ends I have been acknowledging.

9. 1946, 162

10. 1996, 447

11. "Undocumented citizen" occurs, for example, in an official publicity campaign of the University of Maryland, which places "illegal alien" alongside expressions like "retarded" and "no homo." http://thestamp.umd.edu/multicultural_involvement_community_advocacy/programs/inclusive_language/phrases. The "microaggression" point is from "Tool: Recognizing Microaggressions and the Messages They Send," part of the materials for a leadership seminar sponsored and extensively promoted by UCLA. http://www.ucop.edu/academic-personnel-programs/programs-and-initiatives/faculty-diversity-initiatives/faculty-leadership-seminars.html. For more details, see Volokh 2015.

12. For a review of how accurate stereotypes are, see Lee et al. 1995. For an accessible historical survey focusing on Asian aviation safety, see Gladwell 2008, ch. 7; I focus on a more recent example.

13. http://www.theatlantic.com/technology/archive/2013/07/confucius-in-the-cockpit-and-other-items-to-read-and-ignore-on-asiana-214/277703/

14. *New York Times* 2013

15. NTSB/AAR-14/01, 92

16. Reinhart and Rogoff 2009, 99; Bundestag debate of January 7, 2015

17. Sander and Taylor 2012; Arcidiacono and Lovenheim 2016

18. 1995, ch. 13 and p. 186

19. 1996, 435–436

20. Robinaugh and McNally 2011. See also Lukianoff and Haidt 2015, who describe attitudes of overprotectiveness, often with paradoxical effects.

21. Wessely 2005. For philosophical reflection on our propensity to underestimate resilience in the face of trauma, see Moller 2007.

22. Murray 2012, 293–295

■ Chapter 16

1. Arana 2014, 269

2. By contrast, Murray Rothbard claimed he would (2000, 242).

3. Machiavelli 1994, 48, 52

4. See, e.g., Rawls's pursuit of "ideal" rather than "non-ideal" theory, where the former involves "full compliance" on the part of the citizens (1971, 8–9).

5. 1983, 144

6. See Estlund 2014 for further development of this thought, and "utopophobia" in general. See Gauss 2016, 11–41 for additional discussion. I encountered these works too late to integrate them further into this chapter.

7. Sen 2009, 5–27

8. Rousseau 1983, 17. For a contemporary version of this point, see Cohen's objections to departures from egalitarianism motivated by appeals to the incentives people require in the real world, which appeals, he notes, neglect "open possibilities that were closed by human choice" (2008, 33). See also ch. 6, where Cohen generally denies that normative principles are grounded in (non-normative) facts.

9. 1993, 103

10. 1992, 59

11. 1992, 82

12. Captain Picard in *Star Trek: First Contact*. The only group interested in money in the broader *Star Trek* universe is the loathsome Ferengi. The television equivalent of Machiavelli is *Game of Thrones*; a noble instance of non-utopian theorizing is the rebooted *Battlestar Galactica*.

13. Grube/Reeve translation, Plato 1997

14. Hayek's critique of expertise, it's worth noting, extended to macroeconomics in general, whose viability and utility he viewed as a "delusion" (1988, 98).

15. See, e.g., Trabandt and Uhlig 2009.

16. Plato seems aware of some of this, and notes that his utopian sketch would be worth it for the sake of illustrating the general character of a just city even if it should turn out to be unrealizable (472cd).

17. Plutarch 2001, 115

18. 1983, 345

19. 1971, 3

20. 1993, 61

21. 1993, 86

22. 1962, 158–163. Also worth noting is Hayek's rejection of conservatism: "by its very nature it cannot offer an alternative to the direction in which we are moving" (1960, 520).

23. 1962, 410, 436

■ Appendix A

1. Rey 2006 defends what he calls "meta-atheism."

■ Appendix B

1. For empirical research into this phenomenon, see Hitchcock and Knobe 2009.

2. Mackie 1974, 62. I omit many qualifications and niceties in Mackie's theory, such as the "causal field," etc.

Acemoglu, Daron, and James Robinson. 2012. *Why Nations Fail.* New York: Crown.

Acemoglu, Daron, James Robinson, and Thierry Verdier. 2017. "Asymmetric Growth and Institutions in an Interdependent World." *Journal of Political Economy* 125, 1245–1305.

Anderson, Elizabeth. 1993. *Value in Ethics and Economics.* Cambridge, MA: Harvard University Press.

———. 1999. "What Is the Point of Equality?" *Ethics* 109, 287–337.

Annas, Julia. 1993. *The Morality of Happiness.* New York: Oxford University Press.

Aquinas, Thomas. 1948. *Summa Theologica.* Allen: Christian Classics.

Arana, Marie. 2014. *Bolívar.* New York: Simon & Schuster.

Arcidiacono, Peter, and Michael Lovenheim. 2016. "Affirmative Action and the Quality-Fit Tradeoff." *Journal of Economic Literature* 54, 3–51.

Arneson, Richard. 2004. "Luck Egalitarianism Interpreted and Defended." *Philosophical Topics* 32, 1–20.

———. 2011. "Side-Constraints, Rights, and Libertarianism." In *The Cambridge Companion to Nozick's "Anarchy, State, and Utopia,"* ed. Ralf M. Bader and John Meadowcroft. Cambridge: Cambridge University Press.

Baicker, Katherine, Sarah Taubman, Heidi Allen, et al. 2013. "The Oregon Experiment: Effects of Medicaid on Clinical Outcomes." *New England Journal of Medicine* 368, 1713–1722.

Baptist, Edward. 2014. *The Half Has Never Been Told.* New York: Basic Books.

Bavel, Bas van. 2016. *The Invisible Hand?* Oxford: Oxford University Press.

Becker, Gary, and Kevin Murphy. 1988. "A Theory of Rational Addiction." *Journal of Political Economy* 96, 675–700.

Beckert, Sven. 2015. *Empire of Cotton.* New York: Knopf.

Beerbohm, Eric. 2012. *In Our Name: The Ethics of Democracy.* Princeton, NJ: Princeton University Press.

Beitz, Charles. 1979. *Political Theory and International Relations.* Princeton, NJ: Princeton University Press.

Bentham, Jeremy. 1988. *The Principles of Morals and Legislation.* New York: Prometheus.

Bernstein, William. 2004. *The Birth of Plenty.* New York: McGraw Hill.

Bleakley, Hoyt, and Joseph Ferrie. 2013. "Shocking Behavior: Random Wealth in Antebellum Georgia and Human Capital Across Generations." NBER Working Paper No. 19348.

Boorse, Christopher, and Roy Sorensen. 1988. "Ducking Harm." *Journal of Philosophy* 85, 115–134.

Booth, Anthony Robert, and Darrell Rowbottom. 2014. *Intuitions.* Oxford: Oxford University Press.

Bown, Stephen. 2009. *Merchant Kings.* New York: Thomas Dunne Books.

Boxhill, Bernard. 2003. "A Lockean Argument for Black Reparations." *Journal of Ethics* 7, 63–91.

Braudel, Fernand. 1992. *Civilization and Capitalism*. 3 vols. Trans. Siân Reynolds. Berkeley: University of California Press.

Brazier, John, Julie Ratcliffe, Joshua Saloman, and Aki Tsuchiya. 2007. *Measuring and Valuing Health Benefits for Economic Evaluation*. Oxford: Oxford University Press.

Brennan, Jason. 2014. *Why Not Capitalism?* New York: Routledge.

Brennan, Jason, and Peter Jaworski. 2016. *Markets without Limits*. New York: Routledge.

Brighouse, Harry, and Adam Swift. 2014. *Family Values*. Princeton, NJ: Princeton University Press.

Broadberry, Stephen. 2013. "Accounting for the Great Divergence." LSE Economic History Working Papers 184/2013.

Brock, Dan. 1995. "Justice and the ADA." *Social Philosophy and Policy* 12, 159–185.

Brody, Baruch. 2001. "Redistribution without Egalitarianism." In *Left Libertarianism and Its Critics: The Contemporary Debate*, ed. Peter Vallentyne and Hillel Steiner. New York: Palgrave.

Buchanan, Allen. 1987. "Justice and Charity." *Ethics* 97, 558–575.

Buchanan, James. 1975. *The Limits of Liberty*. Chicago: University of Chicago Press.

Buera, Francisco, and Joseph Kaboski. 2012. "The Rise of the Service Economy." *American Economic Review* 102, 2540–2569.

Burke, Edmund. 1993. *Reflections on the Revolution in France*. Oxford: Oxford University Press.

Buruma, Ian. 2001. *The Missionary and the Libertine*. New York: Vintage.

Caplan, Bryan. 2007. *The Myth of the Rational Voter*. Princeton, NJ: Princeton University Press.

Cappelen, Herman. 2012. *Philosophy without Intuitions*. Oxford: Oxford University Press.

Caselli, Francesco, and Wilbur Coleman. 2001. "The U.S. Structural Transformation and Regional Convergence: A Reinterpretation." *Journal of Political Economy* 109, 584–616.

Chetty, Raj, Nathaniel Hendren, Patrick Kline, and Emmanuel Saez. 2014. "Where Is the Land of Opportunity: The Geography of Intergenerational Mobility in the United States." *Quarterly Journal of Economics* 129, 1553–1623.

Chetty, Raj, Nathaniel Hendren, Patrick Kline, Emmanuel Saez, and Nicholas Turner. 2014. "Is the United States Still a Land of Opportunity? Recent Trends in Intergenerational Mobility." *American Economic Review* 104 (5), 141–147.

Christman, John. 1994. *The Myth of Property*. Oxford: Oxford University Press.

Chua, Amy. 2011. *Battle Hymn of the Tiger Mother*. London: Bloomsbury.

Clark, Gregory. 2005. "The Condition of the Working Class in England, 1209–2004." *Journal of Political Economy* 113, 1307–1340.

———. 2007. *A Farewell to Alms*. Princeton, NJ: Princeton University Press.

———. 2014. *The Son Also Rises*. Princeton, NJ: Princeton University Press.

Coady, C. A. J. 1992. *Testimony*. Oxford: Oxford University Press.

Coates, Ta-Nehisi. 2014. "The Case for Reparations." *The Atlantic*, June 2014.

Cohen, G. A. 1978. *Karl Marx's Theory of History*. Princeton, NJ: Princeton University Press.

———. 1988. *History, Labor, and Freedom*. Oxford: Oxford University Press.

———. 1995. *Self-Ownership, Freedom, and Equality*. Cambridge: Cambridge University Press.

———. 2000. *If You're an Egalitarian, How Come You're So Rich?* Cambridge, MA: Harvard University Press.

———. 2008. *Rescuing Justice and Equality*. Cambridge, MA: Harvard University Press.

———. 2011. "On the Currency of Egalitarian Justice." In his *On the Currency of Egalitarian Justice and Other Essays in Political Philosophy*. Princeton, NJ: Princeton University Press.

Cohen, Joshua. 2010. "Philosophy, Social Science, Global Poverty." In *Thomas Pogge and His Critics*, ed. Alison Jaggar. Cambridge: Polity Press.

Coleman, Jules. 1992. *Risks and Wrongs*. Cambridge: Cambridge University Press.

Collier, Paul. 2007. *The Bottom Billion*. Oxford: Oxford University Press.

Comin, Diego, William Easterly, and Erick Gong. 2010. "Was the Wealth of Nations Determined in 1000 BC?" *American Economic Journal: Macroeconomics* 2, 65–97.

Corak, Miles. 2016. "Inequality from Generation to Generation: The United States in Comparison." IZA Discussion Paper No. 9929.

Cowen, Tyler. 2012. *An Economist Gets Lunch*. New York: Dutton.

———. 2014. "Capital Punishment." *Foreign Affairs*, May–June. Online.

Crisp, Roger. 2003. "Equality, Priority, and Compassion." *Ethics* 113, 745–763.

Cullity, Garrett. 2004. *The Moral Demands of Affluence*. Oxford: Oxford University Press.

d'Addio, Anna. 2007. "Intergenerational Transmission of Disadvantage: Mobility or Immobility across Generations?" OECD Social, Employment and Migration Working Papers 52. Paris: OECD.

Dahl, Gordon, and Lance Lochner. 2012. "The Impact of Family Income on Child Achievement: Evidence from the Earned Income Tax Credit." *American Economic Review* 102, 1927–1956.

Dancy, Jonathan. 1993. *Moral Reasons*. Oxford: Blackwell.

Davies, Nigel. 1987. *The Aztec Empire*. Norman: University of Oklahoma Press.

Davis, Robert. 2003. *Christian Slaves, Muslim Masters*. New York: Palgrave.

Dawson, John, and John Seater. 2013. "Federal Regulation and Aggregate Economic Growth." *Journal of Economic Growth* 18, 137–177.

De Greiff, Pablo. 2006. *The Handbook of Reparations*. Oxford: Oxford University Press.

De Las Casas, Bartolomé. 1992. *A Short Account of the Destruction of the Indies*. Ed. and trans. Nigel Griffin. London: Penguin.

DePaul, Michael, and William Ramsey. 1998. *Rethinking Intuition*. Lanham, MD: Rowman & Littlefield.

Diamond, Jared. 2011. *Collapse*. New York: Penguin.

Díaz del Castillo, Bernal. 2012. *The True History of the Conquest of New Spain*. Trans. Janet Burke and Ted Humphrey. Indianapolis: Hackett.

Diener, Ed. 2006. "Beyond the Hedonic Treadmill." *American Psychologist* 61, 305–314.

Diener, Ed, Richard Lucas, Ulrich Schimmack, and John Helliwell. 2009. *Well-Being for Public Policy*. Oxford: Oxford University Press.

Donadio, Rachel. 2012. "Sicily's Fiscal Problems Threaten to Swamp Italy." *New York Times*, July 22. Online.

Drelichman, Mauricio. 2005. "All That Glitters: Precious Metals, Rent Seeking and the Decline of Spain." *European Review of Economic History* 9, 313–336.

Drummond, Michael, Diana Brixner, Marthe Gold, et al. 2009. "Toward a Consensus on the QALY." *Value in Health* 12 sup. 1, S31–S35.

Dworkin, Ronald. 2000. "Equality of Welfare." In his *Sovereign Virtue*. Cambridge, MA: Harvard University Press.

———. 2002. *Sovereign Virtue*. Cambridge, MA: Harvard University Press.

Easterbrook, Gregg. 2004. *The Progress Paradox: How Life Gets Better While People Feel Worse*. New York: Random House.

Easterlin, William. 1974. "Does Economic Growth Improve the Human Lot?" In *Nations and Households in Economic Growth: Essays in Honor of Moses Abramovitz*, ed. Paul A. David and Melvin W. Reder. New York: Academic Press.

———. 1995. "Will Raising the Incomes of All Increase the Happiness of All?" *Journal of Economic Behavior and Organization* 27 (1), 35–48.

Easterlin, William, and Laura Angelescu. 2010. "The Happiness-Income Paradox Revisited." *PNAS* 107 (52), 22463–22468.

Easterly, William. 2002. *The Elusive Quest for Growth*. Cambridge, MA: MIT Press.

———. 2006. *The White Man's Burden*. New York: Penguin.

The Economist. 2013. "Curse of the Mummyji." December 21. Online.

Eldeib, Duaa. 2016. "Controversial Law Charges People with Murder for Death at Others' Hand." *Chicago Tribune*, February 20. Online.

Elster, Jon. 1985. *Making Sense of Marx*. Cambridge: Cambridge University Press.

Elster, Jon, and Ole-Jørgen Skog. 1999. *Getting Hooked: Rationality and Addiction*. Cambridge: Cambridge University Press.

Emerson, Ralph Waldo. 2000. *The Essential Writings of Ralph Waldo Emerson*. New York: Modern Library.

Epstein, Richard. 2011. *Design for Liberty*. Cambridge, MA: Harvard University Press.

Espenshade, Thomas, and Alexandria Radford. 2009. *No Longer Separate, Not Yet Equal*. Princeton, NJ: Princeton University Press.

Estlund, David. 2014. "Utopophobia." *Philosophy and Public Affairs* 42, 113–134.

Feinberg, Joel. 1978. "Euthanasia and the Inalienable Right to Life." *Philosophy and Public Affairs* 7, 93–123.

———. 1984. *Harm to Others*. Oxford: Oxford University Press.

Feldman, Richard. 2010. *What Is This Thing Called Happiness?* Oxford: Oxford University Press.

Feldstein, Richard. 1997. *Political Correctness: A Response from the Cultural Left*. Minneapolis: University of Minnesota Press.

Ferguson, Niall. 2008. *The Ascent of Money*. New York: Penguin.

———. 2011. *Civilization*. New York: Penguin.

Ferleger, Lou. 1990. *Agriculture and National Development*. Ames: Iowa State University Press.

Fish, Stanley. 1994. *There's No Such Thing as Free Speech*. New York: Oxford University Press.

Flanagan, Owen. 2007. *The Really Hard Problem: Meaning in a Material World*. Cambridge, MA: MIT Press.

Foster, Benjamin. 2005. *Before the Muses*. Bethesda, MD: CDL Press.

Foster, Richard, and Sarah Kaplan. 2001. *Creative Destruction*. New York: Doubleday.

Fouquet, Roger, and Stephen Broadberry. 2015. "Seven Centuries of European Economic Growth and Decline." *Journal of Economic Perspectives* 29, 227–244.

Frankfurt, Harry. 1988. "Equality as a Moral Ideal." In his *The Importance of What We Care About*. Cambridge University Press.

———. 1999. "On Caring." In his *Necessity, Volition and Love*. Cambridge: Cambridge University Press.

Frey, Bruno, and Alois Stutzer. 2002. *Happiness and Economics*. Princeton, NJ: Princeton University Press.

Friedman, David. 2000. *Law's Order*. Princeton, NJ: Princeton University Press.

Friedman, Marilyn, and Jan Narveson. 1995. *Political Correctness: For and Against*. London: Rowman & Littlefield.

Friedman, Milton, and Rose Friedman. 1980. *Free to Choose*. Orlando: Harcourt.

Fukuyama, Francis. 1992. *The End of History and the Last Man*. New York: Free Press.

Gaus, Gerald. 2010. "Coercion, Ownership and the Redistributive State: Justificatory Liberalism's Classical Tilt." In *Ownership and Justice*, ed. Ellen Paul, Fred Miller, and Jeffrey Paul. Cambridge: Cambridge University Press.

———. 2016. *The Tyranny of the Ideal*. Princeton, NJ: Princeton University Press.

Gauthier, David. 1986. *Morals by Agreement*. Oxford: Oxford University Press.

Gendler, Tamar. 2011. "On the Epistemic Costs of Implicit Bias." *Philosophical Studies* 156, 33–63.

George, Henry. 2008. *Progress and Poverty*. New York: Robert Schalkenbach Foundation.

Gibbard, Allan. 1976. "Natural Property Rights." *Nous* 10, 77–86.

———. 1985. "What's Morally Special about Free Exchange?" In *Ethics and Economics*, ed. Ellen Frankel Paul, Fred Miller, and Jeffrey Paul. Oxford: Basil Blackwell.

Gilbert, Daniel. 2006. *Stumbling on Happiness*. New York: Knopf.

Gladwell, Malcolm. 2008. *Outliers*. New York: Little Brown.

Goklany, Indur. 2007. *The Improving State of the World*. Washington, DC: Cato Institute.

Goldschlag, Nathan, and Alex Tabarrok. 2014. "Is Regulation to Blame for the Decline in American Entrepreneurship?" GMU Working Paper in Economics No. 15-11.

Guiso, Luigi, Paola Sapienza, and Luigi Zingales. 2006. "Does Culture Affect Economic Outcomes?" *Journal of Economic Perspectives* 20 (2), 23–48.

Hamermesh, David. 2011. *Beauty Pays*. Princeton, NJ: Princeton University Press.

Hampton, Jean. 2006. *The Intrinsic Worth of Persons*. Cambridge: Cambridge University Press.

Haskins, Ron, Julia Isaacs, and Isabel Sawhill. 2008. *Getting Ahead or Losing Ground: Economic Mobility in America*. Washington, DC: Brookings Institution Press.

Haskins, Ron, and Isabel Sawhill. 2009. *Creating an Opportunity Society*. Washington, DC: Brookings Institution Press.

Haybron, Daniel. 2008. *The Pursuit of Unhappiness*. Oxford: Oxford University Press.

Hayek, F. A. 1945. "The Use of Knowledge in Society." *American Economic Review* 35, 519–530.

———. 1960. *The Constitution of Liberty*. Chicago: University of Chicago Press.

———. 1988. *The Fatal Conceit*. Chicago: University of Chicago Press.

Heath, Joseph. 2009. *Economics without Illusions*. New York: Broadway Books.

———. 2014. *Morality, Competition and the Firm*. Oxford: Oxford University Press.

Heuman, Gad, and Trevor Burnard, eds. 2012. *The Routledge History of Slavery*. New York: Routledge.

Heywood, Linda, and John Thornton. 2007. *Central Africans, Atlantic Creoles, and the Foundation of the Americas, 1585–1660*. Cambridge: Cambridge University Press.

Hirsch, Arnold. 1983. *Making the Second Ghetto: Race and Housing in Chicago 1940–1960*. Chicago: Chicago University Press.

Hirschl, Thomas, and Mark Rank. 2015. "The Life Course Dynamics of Affluence." *PLoS One* DOI: 10.1371/journal.pone.0116370.

Hitchcock, Christopher, and Joshua Knobe. 2009. "Cause and Norm." *Journal of Philosophy* 106, 587–612.

Hochschild, Adam. 1999. *King Leopold's Ghost*. New York: Mariner Books.

Holmes, Stephen, and Cass Sunstein. 1999. *The Cost of Rights*. New York: Norton.

Honoré, Tony. 1961. "Ownership." In his *Making Law Bind*. Oxford: Oxford University Press, 1987.

Houston, David, and Lilliard Richardson. 2007. "Risk Compensation or Risk Reduction? Seatbelts, State Laws, and Traffic Fatalities." *Social Science Quarterly* 88, 913–936.

Huemer, Michael. 2013. *The Problem of Political Authority*. New York: Palgrave Macmillan.

Hume, David. 1978. *A Treatise of Human Nature*. Oxford: Oxford University Press.

Humphreys, Macartan, Jeffrey Sachs, and Joseph Stiglitz, eds. 2007. *Escaping the Resource Curse*. New York: Columbia University Press.

Hurley, Susan. 2003. *Justice, Luck, and Knowledge*. Cambridge, MA: Harvard University Press.

Jaggar, Alison, ed. 2010. *Thomas Pogge and His Critics* Cambridge: Polity Press.

Jaimovich, Nir, and Sergio Rebelo. 2017. "Nonlinear Effects of Taxation on Growth." *Journal of Political Economy* 125, 265–291.

James, William. 2000. *Pragmatism and Other Writings*. New York: Penguin.

Jansen, Marius. 2000. *The Making of Modern Japan*. Cambridge, MA: Harvard University Press.

Jaspers, Karl. 1953. *The Origin and Goal of History*. London: Routledge.

Johnson, Walter. 2013. *River of Dark Dreams*. Cambridge, MA: Harvard University Press.

Kagan, Shelly. 1991. *The Limits of Morality*. Oxford: Oxford University Press.

———. 1998. *Normative Ethics*. Boulder, CO: Westview Press.

Kahneman, Daniel, and David Schkade. 1998. "Does Living in California Make People Happy? A Focusing Illusion in Judgments of Life Satisfaction." *Psychological Science* 9, 340–346.

Kant, Immanuel. 1964. *Groundwork of the Metaphysic of Morals*. Trans. H. J. Paton. New York: Harper Torchbooks.

———. 1983. *Perpetual Peace and Other Essays*. Trans. Ted Humphrey. Indianapolis: Hackett Press.

Kelley, Harold. 1950. "The Warm-Cold Variable in First Impressions of Persons." *Journal of Personality* 18, 431–439.

Kenessey, Zoltan. 1987. "The Primary, Secondary, Tertiary and Quaternary Sectors of the Economy." *Review of Income and Wealth* 33, 359–385.

Kirzner, Israel. 1989. *Discovery, Capitalism, and Distributive Justice*. Oxford: Basil Blackwell.

Klein, Naomi. 2000. *No Logo*. New York: Picador.

———. 2007. *Shock Therapy*. New York: Picador.

Kreps, David. 2012. *Microeconomic Foundations*. Princeton, NJ: Princeton University Press.

Kuran, Timur. 1995. *Private Truths, Public Lies*. Cambridge, MA: Harvard University Press.

Kuttner, Robert. 1999. *Everything for Sale*. Chicago: University of Chicago Press.

Landes, David. 1999. *The Wealth and Poverty of Nations*. New York: Norton.

Larson, William. 2015. "New Estimates of the Value of Land of the United States." Bureau of Economic Analysis Working Paper.

Layard, Richard. 2005. *Happiness*. London: Penguin.

Lee, Yueh-Ting, et al. 1995. *Stereotype Accuracy: Toward Appreciating Group Differences*. Washington, DC: American Psychological Association.

Leslie, Sarah Jane, et al. 2015. "Expectations of Brilliance Underlie Gender Distributions across Academic Disciplines." *Science* 347 (6219), 262–265.

Levathes, Louise. 1994. *When China Ruled the Seas*. Oxford: Oxford University Press.

Lichtenberg, Judy. 2014. *Distant Strangers*. Cambridge: Cambridge University Press.

Lindert, Peter. 2004. *Growing Public*. Cambridge: Cambridge University Press.

Lipsey, R. G., and Kelvin Lancaster. 1956. "The General Theory of Second Best." *Review of Economic Studies* 24, 11–32.

Locke, John. 1979. *An Essay Concerning Human Understanding*. Oxford: Oxford University Press.

———. 1980. *Second Treatise of Government*. Indianapolis: Hackett.

Loftus, Elizabeth. 1996. *Eyewitness Testimony*. Cambridge, MA: Harvard University Press.

Lomasky, Loren. 1987. *Persons, Rights, and the Moral Community*. Oxford: Oxford University Press.

Loury, Glenn. 1994. "Self-Censorship in Public Discourse." *Rationality and Society* 6, 428–461.

Lucas, Richard. 2007. "Adaptation and the Set-Point Model of Subjective Well-Being." *Current Directions in Psychological Science* 16 (2), 75–79.

Lukianoff, Greg, and Jonathan Haidt. 2015. "The Coddling of the American Mind." *The Atlantic*, September. Online.

Machiavelli. 1994. *The Prince*. Indianapolis: Hackett.

Mack, Eric. 2006. "Non-absolute Rights and Libertarian Taxation." *Social Philosophy and Policy* 23, 109–141.

Mackie, John. 1974. *The Cement of the Universe*. Oxford: Oxford University Press.

———. 1980. *Hume's Moral Theory*. London: Routledge & Kegan Paul.

MacQuarrie, Kim. 2007. *The Last Days of the Incas*. New York: Simon & Schuster.

Maddison, Angus. 2007. *Contours of the World Economy, 1–2030 AD*. Oxford: Oxford University Press.

The Maddison Project. 2013. http://www.ggdc.net/maddison/maddison-project/home.htm.

Marx, Karl. 1976. *Capital*. Trans. Ben Fowkes. London: Penguin.

Marx, Karl, and Friedrich Engels. 1978. *Manifesto of the Communist Party*. In *The Marx Engels Reader*, ed. Robert Tucker. New York: Norton.

May, Larry, and Stacey Hoffman, eds. 1991. *Collective Responsibility: Five Decades of Debate in Theoretical and Applied Ethics*. Savage, MD: Rowman & Littlefield.

Mayer, Susan. 1997. *What Money Can't Buy*. Cambridge, MA: Harvard University Press.

McCloskey, Deirdre. 2006. *The Bourgeois Virtues*. Chicago: University of Chicago Press.

———. 2010. *Bourgeois Dignity*. Chicago: University of Chicago Press.

McDowell, John. 1978. "Are Moral Requirements Hypothetical Imperatives?" *Proceedings of the Aristotelian Society Supplementary Volumes* 52, 13–29.

McMahan, Jeff. 2005. "Preventing the Existence of People with Disabilities." In *Quality of Life and Human Difference*, ed. David Wasserman, Jerome Bickenbach, and Robert Wachbroit. Cambridge: Cambridge University Press.

———. 2009. *Killing in War*. Oxford: Oxford University Press.

Miller, Richard. 2010. *Globalizing Justice*. Oxford: Oxford University Press.

Mintz, Sidney. 1985. *Sweetness and Power*. New York: Penguin.

Mitchell, B. D., et al. 2012. "Living the Good Life? Mortality and Hospital Utilization Patterns in the Old Order Amish." *PLoS One* 7 (12): e51560.

Mokyr, Joel. 2009. *The Enlightened Economy*. New Haven: Yale University Press.

Moller, Dan. 2006. "Should We Let People Starve—for Now?" *Analysis* 66, 240–247.

————. 2007. "Love and Death." *Journal of Philosophy* 104, 301–316.

————. 2009. "Meta-reasoning and Practical Deliberation." *Philosophy and Phenomenological Research* 79, 653–670.

————. 2017. "Property and the Creation of Value." *Economics and Philosophy* 33, 1–23.

More, Thomas. 1992. *Utopia*. New York: Norton.

Morris, Christopher. 1984. "Existential Limits to the Rectification of Past Wrongs." *American Philosophical Quarterly* 21, 175–182.

————. 1998. *An Essay on the Modern State*. Cambridge: Cambridge University Press.

Morris, Craig, and Adriana von Hagen. 2011. *The Incas*. London: Thames & Hudson.

Morris, Ian. 2010. *Why the West Rules—for Now*. New York: Farrar, Straus and Giroux.

Moyo, Dambisa. 2009. *Dead Aid*. New York: Farrar, Straus and Giroux.

Mueller, Dennis. 2003. *Public Choice III*. Cambridge: Cambridge University Press.

Munzer, Stephen. 1990. *A Theory of Property*. Cambridge: Cambridge University Press.

Murphy, Liam. 1993. "The Moral Demands of Beneficence." *Philosophy and Public Affairs* 22, 267–292.

Murphy, Liam, and Thomas Nagel. 2002. *The Myth of Ownership*. Oxford: Oxford University Press.

Murray, Charles. 2012. *Coming Apart*. New York: Crown.

Nagel, Thomas. 1975. "Libertarianism without Foundations." *Yale Law Journal* 85, 136–149.

————. 2008. "Poverty and Food: Why Charity Is Not Enough." In *Global Justice*, ed. Thomas Pogge and Darrel Moellendorf. St. Paul: Paragon Press.

Narveson, Jan. 2001. *The Libertarian Idea*. Peterborough: Broadview Press.

Nelkin, Dana. 2005. "Freedom, Responsibility and the Challenge of Situationism." *Midwest Studies in Philosophy* 29, 181–206.

Newhouse, Joseph. 1996. *Free for All?* Cambridge, MA: Harvard University Press.

New York Times. 2013. "Pilots in Crash Were Confused about Control Systems, Experts Say." December 13. Online.

Nietzsche, Friedrich. 1989. *On the Genealogy of Morals and Ecce Homo*. Trans. Walter Kaufmann. New York: Vintage.

Nord, Erik, Norman Daniels, and Mark Hamlet. 2009. "QALYs: Some Challenges." *Value in Health* 12, sup. 1, S10–S15.

Nordhaus, William. 2013. *The Climate Casino*. New Haven: Yale University Press.

Nozick, Robert. 1974. *Anarchy, State, and Utopia*. New York: Basic Books.

Oakeshott, Michael. 1962. *Rationalism in Politics and Other Essays*. Indianapolis: Liberty Fund.

O'Brien, Patrick. 1982. "European Economic Development: The Contribution of the Periphery." *Economic History Review* 35, 1–18.

————. 1988. "The Costs and Benefits of British Imperialism 1846–1914." *Past and Present* 120, 163–200.

Offer, Avner. 1993. "The British Empire, 1870–1914: A Waste of Money?" *Economic History Review* 46, 215–238.

Officer, Lawrence, and Samuel Williamson. 2015. "Annual Wages in the United States, 1774–Present." MeasuringWorth, 2015. http://www.measuringworth.com/uswages/.

Ogletree, Charles. 2003. "Repairing the Past: New Efforts in the Reparations Debate in America." *Harvard Civil Rights–Civil Liberties Law Review* 38, 279–320.

Orszag, Peter. 2015. "To Fight Inequality, Tax Land." Bloomberg View, March 3.

Orwell, George. 1946. "Politics and the English Language." In his *Collection of Essays.* New York: Harcourt Brace.

Otsuka, Michael. 2003. *Libertarianism without Inequality.* Oxford: Oxford University Press.

Parfit, Derek. 1984. *Reasons and Persons.* Oxford: Oxford University Press.

———. 1997. "Equality and Priority." *Ratio* 10, 202–221.

Parthasarathi, Prasannan. 2011. *Why Europe Grew Rich and Asia Did Not.* Cambridge: Cambridge University Press.

Persico, Nicola, et al. 2004. "The Effect of Adolescent Experience on Labor Market Outcomes: The Case of Height." *Journal of Political Economy* 112, 1019–1053.

Piketty, Thomas. 2014. *Capital in the Twenty-First Century.* Cambridge, MA: Harvard University Press.

Plato. 1997. *The Complete Works.* Ed. John Cooper. Indianapolis: Hackett.

Plutarch. 2001. *Plutarch's Lives.* New York: Modern Library.

Pogge, Thomas. 2002. *World Poverty and Human Rights.* Cambridge: Polity Press.

———. 2007. "Severe Poverty as a Human Rights Violation." In *Freedom from Poverty as a Human Right,* ed. Thomas Pogge. New York: Oxford University Press.

———. 2010. *Politics as Usual.* Cambridge: Polity Press.

Pommeranz, Kenneth. 2001. *The Great Divergence.* Princeton, NJ: Princeton University Press.

Popper, Karl. 1962. *The Open Society and Its Enemies.* Vol. 1. Princeton, NJ: Princeton University Press.

Portmore, Douglas. 2011. *Commonsense Consequentialism.* Oxford: Oxford University Press.

Posner, Eric, and Adrian Vermeule. 2003. "Reparations for Slavery and Other Historical Injustices." *Columbia Law Review* 103, 689–747.

Proctor, Bernadette, Jessica Semega, and Melissa Kollar. 2016. "Income and Poverty in the United States: 2015." US Census Bureau, Current Population Reports.

Proudhon, Pierre-Joseph. 2011. *Property Is Theft!* Ed. Iain McKay. Oakland: AK Press.

Qian, Sima. 1995. *Records of the Grand Historian: Qin Dynasty.* New York: Columbia University Press.

Rawls, John. 1971. *A Theory of Justice.* Cambridge, MA: Harvard University Press.

———. 1999. *The Law of Peoples.* Cambridge, MA: Harvard University Press.

Raz, Joseph. 1999. "The Central Conflict: Morality and Self-Interest." In his *Engaging Reason.* Oxford: Oxford University Press, 2002.

Reinhart, Carmen, and Kenneth Rogoff. 2009. *This Time is Different.* Princeton, NJ: Princeton University Press.

Reitberger, Magnus. 2008. "Poverty, Negative Duties and the Global Institutional Order." *Politics, Philosophy and Economics* 7, 379–402.

Rey, George. 2006. "Does Anyone Really Believe in God?" In *The Experience of Philosophy,* 6th ed., ed. D. Kolak and R. Martin. Oxford: Oxford University Press.

Risse, Thomas. 2005. "How Does the Global Order Harm the Poor?" *Philosophy and Public Affairs* 33, 349–376.

Robinaugh, Donald, and Richard McNally. 2011. "Trauma Centrality and PTSD Symptom Severity in Adult Survivors of Childhood Sexual Abuse." *Journal of Traumatic Stress* 24, 483–486.

Rodrik, Dani. 2007. *One Economics, Many Recipes*. Princeton, NJ: Princeton University Press.

Roemer, John. 1988. *Free to Lose*. Cambridge, MA: Harvard University Press.

———. 1998. *Equality of Opportunity*. Cambridge, MA: Harvard University Press.

Rognlie, Matt. 2015. "Deciphering the Fall and Rise in the Net Capital Share." Brookings Papers on Economic Activity, Spring.

Rorty, Richard. 1998. *Achieving Our Country*. Cambridge, MA: Harvard University Press.

Roth, Martha. 1995. *Law Collections from Mesopotamia and Asia Minor*. Atlanta: Scholars Press.

Rothbard, Murray. 2000. *Egalitarianism as a Revolt against Nature*. Auburn: Ludwig von Mises Institute.

———. 2009. *Man, Economy, and State*. Auburn: Ludvig von Mises Institute.

Rousseau, Jean-Jacques. 1983. *Discourse on the Origin of Inequality*. In *On the Social Contract and Discourses*. Trans. Donald Cress. Indianapolis: Hackett.

Russell, Daniel. 2004. "Locke on Land and Labor." *Philosophical Studies* 117, 303–325.

Sachs, Jeffrey. 2006. *The End of Poverty*. New York: Penguin.

Sandel, Michael. 2012. *What Money Can't Buy*. New York: Farrar, Straus and Giroux.

Sander, Richard, and Stuart Taylor. 2012. *Mismatch*. New York: Basic Books.

Sanger-Katz, Margot. 2014. "Oregon Health Study: The Surprises in a Randomized Trial." *New York Times*, November 21. Online.

Satz, Deborah. 2010. *Why Some Things Should Not Be for Sale*. Oxford: Oxford University Press.

———. 2012. "Countering the Wrongs of the Past: The Role of Compensation." *Nomos* 51, 129–150.

Scanlon, Thomas. 1998. *What We Owe to Each Other*. Cambridge, MA: Harvard University Press.

Scheffler, Samuel. 1994. *The Rejection of Consequentialism*. Oxford: Oxford University Press.

———. 2001. *Boundaries and Allegiances*. Oxford: Oxford University Press.

———. 2003. "What Is Egalitarianism?" *Philosophy and Public Affairs* 31, 287–337.

Schmidtz, David, and Robert Goodin. 1998. *Social Welfare and Individual Responsibility*. Cambridge: Cambridge University Press.

Scitovsky, Tibor. 1992. *The Joyless Economy*. Oxford: Oxford University Press.

Selmrod, Joel, and Jon Bakija. 2009. *Taxing Ourselves*. Cambridge, MA: MIT Press.

Sen, Amartya. 1985. "The Moral Standing of the Market." In *Ethics and Economics*, ed. Ellen Frankel Paul, Fred Miller, and Jeffrey Paul. Oxford: Basil Blackwell.

———. 2009. *The Idea of Justice*. Cambridge, MA: Harvard University Press.

Sher, George. 2005. "Transgenerational Compensation." *Philosophy and Public Affairs* 33, 181–200.

Shi, Julie. 2016. "Income Responses to Health Insurance Subsidies: Evidence from Massachusetts." *American Journal of Health Economics* 2 (1), 96–124.

Shiffrin, Seana. 2007. "Lockean Arguments for Private Intellectual Property." In *New Essays in the Legal and Political Theory of Property*, ed. Stephen Munzer. Cambridge: Cambridge University Press.

Shue, Henry. 1996. *Basic Rights*. Princeton, NJ: Princeton University Press.

Sidgwick, Henry. 1966. *The Methods of Ethics*. New York: Dover.

Simmons, A. John. 1992. *The Lockean Theory of Rights*. Princeton, NJ: Princeton University Press.

———. 2001. *Justification and Legitimacy*. Cambridge: Cambridge University Press.

Singer, Peter. 1994. *Rethinking Life and Death*. New York: St. Martin's Griffin.

———. 2006. "Questions for Peter Singer." *New York Times*, December 24.

———. 2015. *The Most Good You Can Do*. New Haven: Yale University Press.

Slote, Michael. 1984. "Morality and Self-Other Asymmetry." *Journal of Philosophy* 81, 179–192.

Smith, Adam. 1994. *The Wealth of Nations*. New York: Random House.

Smith, Dylan, Ryan Sherriff, Laura Damschroder, and George Loewenstein. 2006. "Misremembering Colostomies?" *Health Psychology* 25, 688–695.

Solon, Gary. 2015. "What Do We Know So Far about Multigenerational Mobility?" NBER Working Paper No. 21053.

Sparks, Randy. 2014. *Where the Negroes Are Masters*. Cambridge, MA: Harvard University Press.

Sreenivasan, Gopal. 1995. *The Limits of Lockean Rights in Property*. Oxford: Oxford University Press.

Stanton, Elizabeth Cady. 1997. *The Selected Papers of Elizabeth Cady Stanton and Susan B. Anthony*. Ed. Ann D. Gordon. Vol. 4. New Brunswick, NJ: Rutgers University Press.

Stedman, John. 1988. *Narrative of a Five Years Expedition against the Revolted Negroes of Surinam*. Baltimore: Johns Hopkins.

Stevenson, Betsey, and Justin Wolfers. 2008. "Economic Growth and Subjective Well-being: Reassessing the Easterlin Paradox." NBER Working Papers No. 14282.

Sugarman, Stephen. 2003. "*Vincent v. Lake Erie Transportation Co.*: Liability for Harm Caused by Necessity." In *Torts Stories*, ed. Robert Rabin and Stephen Sugarman. New York: Foundation Press.

Sunstein, Cass. 2005. "Moral Heuristics." *Behavioral and Brain Sciences* 28, 531–573.

———. 2011. "Deliberating Groups versus Prediction Markets." In *Social Epistemology: Essential Readings*, ed. Alvin Goldman and Dennis Whitcomb. Oxford: Oxford University Press.

Swift, Jonathan. 1973. *The Writings of Jonathan Swift*. New York: Norton.

Temkin, Larry. 1993. *Inequality*. Oxford: Oxford University Press.

———. 2003. "Egalitarianism Defended." *Ethics* 113, 764–782.

———. 2012. *Rethinking the Good*. Oxford: Oxford University Press.

Thomas, Hugh. 1993. *Conquest: Cortés, Montezuma, and the Fall of Old Mexico*. New York: Simon & Schuster.

Thomson, Judith. 1990. *The Realm of Rights*. Cambridge, MA: Harvard University Press.

Thornton, John. 1992. *Africa and Africans in the Making of the Atlantic World, 1400–1800*. Cambridge: Cambridge University Press.

———. 1999. *Warfare in Atlantic Africa, 1500–1800*. London: Routledge.

Thoreau, Henry David. 1997. *Walden*. Boston: Beacon Press.

Thucydides. 1993. *On Justice, Power and Human Nature*. Trans. Paul Woodruff Indianapolis: Hackett.

Tomasi, John. 2012. *Free Market Fairness*. Princeton, NJ: Princeton University Press.

Trabandt, Mathias, and Harald Uhlig. 2009. "How Far Are We from the Slippery Slope? The Laffer Curve Revisited." NBER Working Paper No. 15343.

Turner, Michelle. 1999. "The Innocent Buyer of Art Looted during World War II." *Vanderbilt Journal of Transnational Law* 32, 1511–1532.

Ubel, Peter, George Loewenstein, Norbert Schwarz, and Dylan Smith. 2005. "Misimagining the Unimaginable: The Disability Paradox and Health Care Decision Making." *Health Psychology* 24, supplement: S57–S62.

Valentini, Laura. 2011. "On the Duty to Withhold Global Aid Now to Save More Lives in the Future." *Ethics and Global Politics* 4 (2), 125–134.

Vallentyne, Peter, and Hillel Steiner, eds. 2001. *Left Libertarianism and Its Critics: The Contemporary Debate*. New York: Palgrave.

van Parijs, Philippe. 1995. *Real Freedom for All*. Oxford: Oxford University Press.

Varian, Hal. 1975. "Distributive Justice, Welfare Economics, and the Theory of Fairness." *Philosophy and Public Affairs* 4, 223–247.

Volokh, Eugene. 2015. "UC Teaching Faculty Members Not to Criticize Race-Based Affirmative Action, Call America 'Melting Pot,' and More." *Washington Post*, June 16. Online.

Vosters, Kelly. 2016. "Is the Simple Law of Mobility Really a Law? Testing Clark's Hypothesis." UNC Charlotte Economics Working Paper No. 2016-003.

Waldfogel, Joel. 1993. "The Deadweight Loss of Christmas." *American Economic Review* 83, 1328–1336.

Waldron, Jeremy. 1988. *The Right to Private Property*. Oxford: Oxford University Press.

———. 1992. "Superseding Historical Injustice." *Ethics* 103, 4–28.

———. 2012. *The Harm in Hate Speech*. Cambridge, MA: Harvard University Press.

———. 2013. "'To Bestow Stability upon Possession': Hume's Alternative to Locke." In *Philosophical Foundations of Property Law*, ed. J. Penner and H. Smith. Oxford: Oxford University Press.

Wallace, R. Jay. 2004. "The Rightness of Acts and the Goodness of Lives." In *Reason and Value*, ed. R. Jay Wallace Philip Pettit, Samuel Scheffler, and Michael Smith. Oxford: Oxford University Press.

Walzer, Michael. 1977. *Just and Unjust Wars*. New York: Basic Books.

———. 1983. *Spheres of Justice*. New York: Basic Books.

Watkins, James. 1908. *King Cotton*. New York: James Watkins and Sons.

Weimann, Joachim, Andreas Knabe and Ronnie Schöb. 2015. *Measuring Happiness*. Cambridge, MA: MIT Press.

Die Welt. 1995. "Keiner hat etwas gemerkt." January 12. Online.

Wenar, Leif. 2008. "Property Rights and the Resource Curse." *Philosophy and Public Affairs* 36, 2–32.

Wessely, Simon. 2005. "Victimhood and Resilience." *New England Journal of Medicine* 353, 548–550.

Wilde, Gerald. 1998. "Risk Homeostasis Theory: An Overview." *Injury Prevention* 4, 89–91.

Williams, Eric. 1944. *Capitalism and Slavery*. Chapel Hill: UNC Press.

Wilson, John. 1995. *The Myth of Political Correctness*. Durham, NC: Duke University Press.

Wong, Edward. 2013. "A Chinese Virtue Is Now the Law." *New York Times*, July 2. Online.

Wright, Erik, Andrew Levine, and Elliott Sober. 1992. *Reconstructing Marxism*. London: Verso.

■ ACKNOWLEDGMENTS

I am grateful for permission to incorporate material from the following articles:

"Property and the Creation of Value," *Economics and Philosophy* 33 (2017), 1–23.
"Dilemmas of Political Correctness," *Journal of Practical Ethics* 4 (2016), 1–22.
"Justice and the Wealth of Nations," *Public Affairs Quarterly* 28 (2014), 95–114.
"The Epistemology of Popularity and Incentives," *Thought* 2 (2013), 148–156.
"Wealth, Disability and Happiness," *Philosophy & Public Affairs* 39 (2011), 177–206.

INDEX

Tables and figures are indicated by an italic *t* and *f* following the page number